Creole

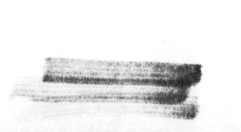

Creole

THE HISTORY AND LEGACY OF LOUISIANA'S FREE PEOPLE OF COLOR

EDITED BY

SYBIL KEIN

LOUISIANA STATE UNIVERSITY PRESS

BATON ROUGE

03   05   07   09   08   06   04   02
4   5

Designer: Rebecca Lloyd Lemna
Typeface: Janson Text
Typesetter: Coghill Composition Co.
Printer and binder: Thomson-Shore, Inc.

LIBRARY OF CONGRESS CATALOGING-IN-PUBLICATION DATA:

Creole : the history and legacy of Louisiana's free people of color /
edited by Sybil Kein.
    p. cm.
Includes bibliographical references and index.
    ISBN 0-8071-2532-6 (alk. paper)—ISBN 0-8071-2601-2 (pbk. : alk. paper)
    1. Creoles—Louisiana—History.   2. Creoles—Louisiana—Social condition.   3. Free
Afro-americans—Louisiana—History.   4. Free Afro-Americans—Louisiana—Social
conditions.   5. Louisiana—History.   6. Louisiana—Race relations.   7. Creoles in
literature.   8. Louisiana—In literature.   I. Kein, Sybil.
    F380.C87   C7   2000
    976.3004'44—dc21   00-008449

This book is dedicated to the memory of my cousin, Ulysses S. Ricard Jr. (December 1, 1950–October 7, 1993). The essay he was writing for this text would have been a great contribution to the canon of American culture. Ulysses was a pioneer in Creole studies. He was a linguist, historian, educator, scholar, printer, poet, and genealogist. He grew up in the 7th Ward, the section of New Orleans that gave the world many famous Creoles, such as Jelly Roll Morton and Homer Plessy. Rick, as he was known to his friends, attended Corpus Christi Elementary School, St. Augustine High School, and Lake Forest University, the latter on a four-year scholarship. He graduated magna cum laude with a bachelor's degree in philology, and went on to study French at the Institute of Paris and Spanish at the Institute de Cultural Hispanica, Madrid. An ardent advocate of Creole culture, language, and history, Rick held a teaching position at a college in rural Louisiana, and designed and taught that school's first course in Louisiana Acadian and Creole French. He also authored one of the first textbooks for such a course—*Lagniappe: A Louisiana French Reader* (1978).

Rick spent most of his professional life collecting data for a dictionary of Louisiana Creole that he was compiling. He delivered papers on Creole culture and history at various professional meetings around the country, and was prominently involved in international projects aimed at disseminating information on Louisiana Creoles and building cultural exchanges between that group and Creoles in other countries. For many years Rick worked with the Smithsonian Folklife Program and the New Orleans Jazz and Heritage Festivals as spokesperson and exhibitor of Louisiana Acadian and Creole Folklife. Li té un vrai Créole.

Contents

Illustrations

Acknowledgments

I wish to thank the many people who contributed to this project in various ways. First of all, I am grateful to Mary L. Morton, professor emerita at Nicholls State University, for her hours of labor and devotion at the beginning of this project. I would also like to thank Greg Osborn, Brenda Square, Rebecca Hankins, and my dear cousin Ulysses Ricard Jr., to whom this book is dedicated. The many hours I spent at the Amistad Research Center in New Orleans were guided and aided by archivists and staff employed there from 1992 to 1996. When Rick was archivist himself, he not only helped me locate hard-to-find materials but also shared with me documents from his private collection. In addition to aiding my research, Brenda, Rebecca, and Greg—as well as Wayne Coleman and Alvery Rodney—made me feel as though they were genuinely interested in the book.

I want to thank several experts who gave graciously of their time to talk to me. To Florence Borders, archivist at Southern University in New Orleans and truly a walking library of Louisiana history, many thanks. I also spent hours with Mr. Charles B. Roussève, now deceased, author of an indispensable book on the history of African-Americans in Louisiana. Published in 1937, his text is still a major source for historians. I will always treasure the time I spent with him. Thanks, too, to Mrs. Ora Lewis Martin, who years ago thought enough of my work to publish my very first volume. Conversations with her were both enlightening and encouraging.

I am also grateful to Louisiana historian Mary White for furnishing me with valuable leads on obscure Creole material and for her invaluable help in tracking down information on my father's people, the Creole Kindlers and Moores. I always look forward to sharing her wisdom and her figs.

Many thanks to Lester Sullivan, archivist at Xavier University, for his gracious help to me in locating some of the beautiful photographs used in this text.

Merci beaucoup to Michel Fabre, former director of the Université de la Sorbonne Nouvelle, for lending his expertise to this project. Through the years both Professor Fabre and his wife, Professor Genevieve Fabre, have given me support and help in the various projects that I have undertaken on Creole culture. Furthermore, I am thankful to them for generating the international conferences which proved valuable to so many of us involved in research on the Creoles.

I thank Professor Elizabeth Brown-Guillory of the University of Houston and Professor Anthony Barthelemy of the University of Miami, both of whom came to my rescue at the eleventh hour and offered advice and encouragement. And I have enormous gratitude for all of the contributing scholars, whose patience with the process and belief in the project made it possible. Special thanks to my niece, Lisa C. Moore, editor and publisher of RedBone Press, who took time from her important first publication, *does your mama know?* to help with the editing.

It has been wonderful working with Sylvia Frank, acquisitions editor of LSU Press. Her patience and help made all the difference in the project's final stages. Much gratitude to editors Gerry Anders and Sara Anderson.

Finally, I give undying gratitude to my spiritual great-aunt, Alice Ruth Moore, who has been at my side to ensure that this endeavor would be completed.

Introduction

When examining the history of the Louisiana French, one may wonder why the Louisiana Creoles have been marginalized by scholars, and why no extensive study of the group has been done before now. One reason may well be the seemingly infinite number of possible definitions of *Creole*. The *Harvard Encyclopedia of American Ethnic Groups* explains that the word "refers to people, culture, to food, and music, and to language. Originally from the Portuguese *crioulo*, the word for a slave brought up in the owner's household, which in turn probably derived from the Latin *creare* (create), it became *criollo* in Spanish and *créole* in French."[1] This encyclopedia's definition of Creole as it refers to Louisiana is worth noting in its entirety:

> Louisianians of French and Spanish descent began referring to themselves as Creoles following the Louisiana Purchase (1803) in order to distinguish themselves from the Anglo-Americans who started to move into Louisiana at this time. The indigenous whites adopted the term, insisting, most unhistorically, that it be applied exclusively to them. The life of this dying group is depicted in George Washington Cable's *Old Creole Days* (1879) and in some of the works of Lafcadio Hearn.
>
> In the United States, in the 20th century, Creole most often refers to the Louisiana Creoles of color. Ranging in appearance from mulattos to northern European whites, the Creoles of color constitute a Caribbean phenomenon in the United States. The product of miscegenation in a seigneurial society, they achieved elite status in Louisiana, and in the early 19th century some were slaveholders. Many, educated in France, were patrons of the opera and of literary societies. A description of their lives is provided by Alice Dunbar-Nelson in the *Alice Dunbar*

1. Stephan Thernstrom, ed., *Harvard Encyclopedia of American Ethnic Groups* (Cambridge, Mass.: Belknap Press of Harvard University, 1980), 247.

Nelson Reader (1979) and Rodolphe Lucien Desdunes's *Nos hommes et notre histoire* (1911; English translation, 1978). Francis J. Woods tells the life story of one extended family in *Marginality and Identity: A Colored Creole Family Through Ten Generations* (1972).

Louisiana Creoles of color thus constitute a self-conscious group, who are perceived in their locale as different and separate. They live in New Orleans and in a number of other bayou towns. Historically they have been endogamous, and until late in the 19th century spoke mostly French. Perhaps the best-known Creole of color is the jazz musician Jelly Roll Morton, whose own social status must have been marginal in Creole society. Overwhelmingly Catholic, the New Orleans Creoles usually attend parochial schools; Xavier University is closely associated with them. Their ethnicity is exceedingly difficult to maintain outside the New Orleans area. Over time, a great many have passed into white groups in other parts of the country, and others have become integrated as blacks. This latter choice is not based wholly on appearance, for many Creoles who choose to identify as Afro-Americans are white in appearance.[2]

In *White by Definition*, Virginia Domínguez discusses the idea of social status defined by the terms of identity used in Louisiana as well as in the United States as a whole. This is, of course, a crucial issue in any examination of Creoles, and her concluding comments should be considered when formulating a definition of Louisiana Creole:

> The long history of slavery in the United States and of white ownership of African slaves left in Louisiana, as in other parts of the United States, a traditional association of whites with upper status and of blacks with lower status. To white Creoles today the mere suggestion of possible African ancestry invokes a lowering of social and economic status for the people in question. To colored or black Creoles, on the other hand, the claim of at least a partial European ancestry accords the group in question a status (or an expectation of status) higher than that accorded to "pure" blacks. Moreover, to colored or black Creoles the association with early European settlers in Louisiana signals a tie to the state's "old families" and, by extension, higher status. Thus to identify someone as Creole is to invoke in the course of a particular conversation historically linked connotations of social and economic status. But this is not to say just that "ethnic" identities have status connotations; it is to say that

2. Ibid.

New Orleanians' perception of status, of how things used to be and how in their opinion they ought to be, is often the major criterion by which individuals are identified as Creole. What many of us normally assume to be likely *connotations* of membership in a particular group are, in the case of southern Louisiana, often, if not always, the crucial variables that individual New Orleanians manipulate in making themselves members of a group, or in identifying others as members of a group. Status, then, is frequently more of a determining factor on group membership than genealogical ancestry.[3]

Gwendolyn Midlo Hall, in her book *Africans in Colonial Louisiana*, gives a historical sketch of the various meanings of the term *Creole*, and offers a current definition of the word: "a person of non-American ancestry, whether African or European, who was born in the Americas."[4] This inclusive definition is as it should be; Creoles are the New World's people, and, given the known historical data, the term should not exclude anyone based on color, caste, or pigmentation. While the present study employs the common twentieth-century usage of *Creole*, cited by the *Harvard Encyclopedia* as referring to Creoles of color, this usage is not meant to imply any exclusivity, but merely to indicate those people in Louisiana who chose to so self-identify and to accept the status and/or marginalization that accrues with identifying themselves as Creole.

Mixed like the people, Louisiana Creole culture is examined here in light of its African, French, and Spanish as well as its Caribbean components. Recognizing the macaronic reality of the culture, Hall explains, "*Creole* has come to mean the language and the folk culture that was native to the southern part of Louisiana where African, French, and Spanish influence was most deeply rooted historically and culturally." Interestingly, the recent scholarship of Hall and others supports the belief that Louisiana Creole culture is a major source of the African roots of American culture, as Creole heritage is seen to be firmly based on African and black slave culture. These Africans and black slaves generated the Creole language, the Creole folklore, and the roots of jazz and other indigenous Creole music. It is also true that Creoles are a great part of Louisiana's

3. Virginia R. Domínguez, *White by Definition: Social Classification in Creole Louisiana* (New Brunswick, N.J.: Rutgers University Press, 1986), 263.

4. Gwendolyn Midlo Hall, *Africans in Colonial Louisiana: The Development of Afro-Creole Culture in the Eighteenth Century* (Baton Rouge: Louisiana State University Press, 1995), 157.

Francophone culture, although they have been marginalized with respect to other Francophones.[5]

The Louisiana Creole culture presently has the support of various Creole groups both in Louisiana and in other states. Each year, there are Creole festivals at which thousands gather in Louisiana, Texas, and California. Two internationally distributed monthly publications are dedicated to Creole life and lifestyles. *Bayou Talk*, the older of the two, is published by Louis Metoyer, a descendant of Marie Thérèse, the founder of the historic Melrose Plantation in Natchitoches Parish, Louisiana. Its motto is "Keep the Culture Alive." The other periodical is *Creole Culture Magazine*, published by Ruth Foote of Lafayette, Louisiana (publication suspended in 1997). Both reach wide audiences. In addition, many Creoles celebrate their heritage by wearing T-shirts and/or jewelry which proudly proclaim their identity. There are Creole flags, Creole pins, and Creole prayers. In 1996, a compact disc was produced, *Creole Ballads & Zydeco*, which featured never-before-recorded Creole folk songs. Besides the various zydeco recordings that contain songs in Creole, two exclusively Creole CDs appeared in 1997: *Creole Blues*, a collection of old jazz songs, and *Creole Man*, a popular disc whose songs are in Creole.

Several organizations attest to the vibrancy of Creole culture and keep busy preserving it. One such group is the St. Augustine Historical Society of Natchitoches, which maintains a Web site and promotes Creole culture through its annual festival held each January. This society has recently generated the necessary support for the opening of a Creole Cultural Center on the campus of the University of Northwestern Louisiana in Natchitoches. Lafayette is home to two organizations dedicated to the promotion and preservation of Creole heritage: C.R.E.O.L.E. Inc. and the Creole Preservation Society of America. Based in California are the International French Creole Cultural Society and the Creole Association of America, among others. This Creole nationalism may be compared to the concept of *Créolité*, or Haitian Creole nationalism, as presented by Bernabé, Chamoiseau, and Confiant in their excellent study, *Eloge de la Créolité*. While not as uniformly defined as that of the West Indies, a *Créolité* is indeed identifiable in the United States. At this

5. Ibid.

writing, a controversy is still very much alive over the demarcation of this cultural group.

Written from a variety of angles, the essays in the present collection make possible a clearer image of Louisiana Creoles, their history, and their culture, with the intent of diminishing the impact of past and present stereotypes that cloud the path to understanding this important segment of Americana. The need for such a study is evidenced by the paucity of pertinent material over the centuries during which these people have existed in the United States. Usually ignored or negatively stereotyped, these unique Americans have lived and prospered since the late 1600s, yet very little has been written about them. The need for scholarship on Creoles became particularly apparent at the historic 1992 Paris conference, "African-Americans and Europe." Most of the prominent African American writers and scholars were gathered there, along with most of the prominent scholars who study African American culture and literature. There were three sessions on the Louisiana Creoles, and the presentations and heated debates pointed up the need for a collection such as this one. This book is in great part the result of networking by some of the scholars who participated in that Paris conference, notably Michel Fabre of the Sorbonne's *Centre d'Etudes Afro-américaines de la Sorbonne Nouvelle.*

The essays were selected in an effort to give the reader an in-depth examination of the Louisiana Creole culture by presenting multidisciplinary approaches to various topics. The first section of the book concentrates on the early history of the Louisiana Creoles. Alice Moore Dunbar-Nelson establishes her perspective by examining the development of the caste system and the history of terms applied to people of color. Offering her own definition, "The true Creole is like the famous gumbo of the state, a little bit of everything, making a whole, delightfully flavored, quite distinctive, and wholly unique," she adroitly adds, "From 1724 to the present time [1916], frequent discussions as to the proper name by which to designate this very important portion of the population of Louisiana waged more or less acrimoniously." Dunbar-Nelson takes a broad view of the history of the Creoles along with the history of the state of Louisiana up to her time of writing. She details the Code Noir of 1724 and the early reasons for the animosity based on color, including laws drawn from the belief in white supremacy. She points out the continuing race mixing and shows how, despite laws designed to limit them, free people of color did flourish.[6]

Violet Bryan's essay, "Marcus Christian's Treatment of *Les Gens de Couleur Libre*," focuses on the eighteenth chapter of Christian's unpublished "Black History of Louisiana" and his notes labeled "Genealogy." Bryan notes the highlights of Christian's research on free people of color, lawsuits in colonial times, and manumission of slaves, and comments on his list of nineteenth-century writings regarding the quadroon balls. Bryan points out that Christian's interest in *les gens* was an important part of the larger picture he attempted to draw—that of the history of all blacks in Louisiana.

Joan Martin's piece on the history of the quadroon balls considers the legal designation given to Creole women who were engaged in the form of concubinage known as "plaçage." They were referred to as "quarteronne," yet another appellation which came to be accepted by the population at that time. Martin gives an account of the fabled tradition of the balls, demystifying them in light of recent scholarship.

Lester Sullivan examines nineteenth-century Creole composers of classical and popular music who were expatriates in Europe, principally France. He details the background and accomplishments of such figures as Edmond Dédé and Sidney and Lucien Lambert, all expatriates, and discusses the lives of Victor-Eugène Macarty, Samuel Snaër, and Basile Barès, who traveled to France but spent most of their time in New Orleans. Rounding out his topic, Sullivan also treats non-Creole black New Orleans musicians, and includes a useful appendix listing the titles and sources of the sheet music composed by these musicians.

In "The Yankee Hugging the Creole: Reading Dion Boucicault's *The Octoroon*," Jennifer DeVere Brody looks at the historical Creole image as seen in performances of this popular nineteenth-century stage drama. She examines issues of racial classification as well as of gender. The free woman of color (specifically, the octoroon), represented by the main character Zoe, is seen as the Other, and the machinations of white males who work to secure their control of the status quo under the sys-

---

6. Alice Dunbar-Nelson, "People of Color in Louisiana," *Journal of Negro History* 2 (1917): 367.

tem of slavery, particularly in regard to the concept of "family values," are brought to light.

In my own essay, "The Use of Louisiana Creole in Southern Litera-ture," I study the tradition of using the Creole language in literature. From the labeling of the language as "baby talk" to the outright charac-terization of it as a negative minstrel-show stereotype, I discuss its por-trayal by southern writers, many of whom associated it with the poor and the ignorant of rural Louisiana. It was not until such native Creole schol-ars as Ulysses Ricard Jr. took steps in the twentieth century to maintain and preserve the language that it was elevated to its rightful place as a useful and even poetic tongue.

The essays in Part II seek to establish the many-faceted legacy of Creole culture that developed despite the Creoles' exclusion from the main-stream. The first three pieces trace the Creoles' participation in nine-teenth-century life in both Louisiana and France. In "Marie Laveau: The Voodoo Queen Repossessed," Barbara Rosendale Duggal points out that this Creole healer of nineteenth-century New Orleans and standard-bearer of the Creole Afro-Caribbean religion has been seen only through biases of Western religion, race, class, and culture, as the Creole lan-guage, too, was once only seen through Western biases. As a central fig-ure in the nineteenth-century Creole community, Marie Laveau was labeled as a "witch," a whore, and even by some writers a procurer of fancy girls for white men.[7] The truth is, however, that to say she was a great help to her community whose members had little or no resources to turn to for healing of physical or emotional illness is perhaps the least compliment that can be paid to her life. Duggal recounts the known facts of that life and details the development of stereotypes about Laveau based on sexist accounts of her supposed activities. In thus refuting previ-ous white male writers, Duggal gives back to Marie Laveau her role as leader of the African-based religion known as Voodoo.

Michel Fabre, former director of the Sorbonne's program in Afro-American Studies, has written widely on African American artists' experi-ences in France. In "New Orleans Creole Expatriates in France: Ro-mance and Reality," he discusses two nineteenth-century Creole

7. See Al Rose, *Storyville, New Orleans; Being an Authentic, Illustrated Account of the Notorious Red-Light District* (University: University of Alabama Press, 1974), 54.

writers—an inventor and a musician—and their lives as men who considered France their second home. Fabre's work reveals the need of these talented men to find recognition and acceptance of their art in France when such was not possible in Louisiana. As a group, the expatriates were displaced geniuses who sought to find receptive audiences and support for their art. Some did find in France the educational opportunities and rewards unavailable to them in the United States, although others did not achieve the degree of success they expected. Fabre goes on to investigate four free men of color of the nineteenth century: engineer Norbert Rillieux, poet Camille Thierry, dramatist Victor Séjour, and composer Edmond Dédé. Detailing their struggles with family and professional matters, Fabre recounts the private life and accomplishments of each.

If Fabre's artists had difficulty finding a place for themselves in France, Mary Gehman's middle-class free men of color who stayed in New Orleans did find a niche for their businesses in the nineteenth-century Crescent City and its environs. In "Visible Means of Support: Businesses, Professions, and Trades of Free People of Color," Gehman traces this commerce to its beginnings in the 1700s. Some slaves brought skills with them, and both freed slaves and free people of color acquired skills early. These skills, coupled with the drive to succeed, helped the free people of color to find their places in a society where, despite racism and caste problems, many succeeded and acquired wealth. Gehman details the lives and business ventures of men and women who were pioneers in retail cloth making, tobacco shops, shoemaking, leatherworking, architecture, importing, real estate investing, mortuaries, and other businesses. Before the Civil War, some also participated in the plantation system, owning large estates and slaves, and in the retail selling of food at the various markets.

In the next two essays, the Afro-Caribbean connection to the Creole culture is explored through an examination of the food and the language. Two facts support the connection of the two categories: Dunbar-Nelson's comparison of the Creole people to the popular Creole food dish, gumbo, and numerous early writers' referral to the Creole language, which developed out of a mixture of other languages, as a "gombo dialect." In the nineteenth and early twentieth centuries, Creole was the first language of many people. Well into the twentieth century, most Creoles knew some Creole, although it was not their first language. It was spoken in rural towns as well as in the city of New Orleans, and it was commonly heard in conversations between master and slave.

Linguist Fehintola Mosadomi, in "The Origin of Louisiana Creole," examines the origin of the grammar of the Louisiana Creole language and demonstrates how the language has been seen in the past through the racial biases of others. The discussion clarifies the process by which the definitions of terms affect personal identity through the branding of a people as inferior; negative stereotypes of Creoles were built around early linguistic attitudes on the part of certain scholars. Mosadomi considers three theories of the derivation of Louisiana Creole and the problems involved in searching for the origins of this language. She concludes by asserting that Louisiana Creole is a dying language and urging a revival of it through in-depth study.

In my own second essay, "Louisiana Creole Food Culture: Afro-Caribbean Links," I echo the idea of mixture and inclusiveness, applying it to Creole foods that are traced to their possible origins and connected to strikingly similar dishes along the slave trade route from West Africa to the West Indies and South America, and on to Louisiana. I examine recipes whose composition is accounted for by the use of certain ingredients which were only found in a particular place. For example, since coconut is plentiful in the West Indies, then that is used as a main ingredient in the candies made there. In Louisiana, the abundance of pecan trees results in those nuts' becoming the main ingredient for that area's Creole candies. The West African and Caribbean origin of many of the Louisiana Creole foods is clear, both in the ingredients used and in the methods of cooking, making for many connections between the diets of Afro-Caribbean people and the Louisiana Creoles. It comes as no surprise that Creole food is popular the world over, owing to the legacy it bears from no less than four continents.

In Anthony Barthelemy's "Light, Bright, Damn *Near* White: Race, the Politics of Genealogy, and the Strange Case of Susie Guillory," the problem of racism based on skin color as a major tenet of American society is examined. Illustrating how that tenet controls and manipulates people's lives and psyches, Barthelemy discusses the case of Susie Guillory, who in the early 1980s sued the state of Louisiana to be defined as "white." Through his investigation of other lawsuits of similar ilk, Barthelemy shows how such racism effectively changes legal situations and skirts the law in order to maintain the racial status quo. He explains that race "embraces culture, and racism denies other cultures validity. Efforts to classify phenotypes reflect efforts to justify cultural domination." He goes on to cite the examples of groups such as the Catholic and Protestant Celts and the Serbs and Croats who have killed in the name of group purity, and to spotlight the dangers of ruling groups forcing certain people into "outsider" status and then using racist notions to keep them dominated. Barthelemy's inquiry constitutes a warning regarding racist practices in the state of Louisiana as well as elsewhere in the United States.

One of the issues of Creoles' being forced into the role of Other is the question of "passing." Arthé Anthony explains that the concept of racial passing "is used in cultural studies as a metaphor for masking the real—and most often marginalized—self." In effect, many Creoles felt it necessary to trade their identities for that of the dominant Other in order to survive economically. Based on an analysis of thirty oral history interviews of Creoles who lived in New Orleans in the early nineteenth century, Anthony's essay sheds light on the myth of Creoles who are often accused of "wanting to be white." For the most part, the degree of economic success in the segregated South depended on being able to work as other than black. In New Orleans, the depth of racist segregation was reflected in the dominant culture's preference for "light-colored" workers even for the most menial jobs. This preference became so widespread that Creoles who were light enough to pass as white did so in order to make a living, which in turn sometimes led to those Creoles who did get such jobs being despised and displaced by family, friends, and community. Anthony examines the history of the so-called privilege of this "third class" of people, including the various levels of segregated life and their effect on the economic status of these Creoles of color. It is evident from the various interviews that these people did struggle against the segregation laws, but felt they had to either share the burden of passing or immigrate to other states where work was available without the problems of this variety of racism.

If the writers and poets of the nineteenth-century Reconstruction period in New Orleans had been able to realize their dream of a new American nation based on ideals gleaned from their Creole world view born of their mixed heritage and political yearnings, then the Susie Guillorys of the twentieth century might not have had a problem with state laws regarding race. Influenced by the romanticism of their prede-

cessors, the Creole writers of *Les Cenelles* were men who wrote poems
and editorials aimed at infusing into the reconstruction of the nation a
Creole vision of America. When faced with the black-white racial division, they chose to side with the black freedmen in their struggle for freedom and equality. In Caroline Senter's "Creole Poets on the Verge of a
Nation," we see a strikingly bold political stance taken at a time of racial
and economic upheaval in Louisiana. Despite the imposition of Catholic
and Protestant American views, these Creoles of color attempted to
bring into the "new country" a feeling of brotherhood and sense of
equality which was garnered by their affinity with the ideas of the French
revolutionaries. The vehicle for their voices was the Creole bilingual
newspaper, the *Tribune*, published between 1865 and 1867. Senter says of
the poetry, "The *Tribune* poems invoked the dream of the Reconstruction to remind, inspire, and shame readers. The poet's vision would af-
firm or condemn the actual events reported in the surrounding news
columns." She stresses that these writings sided politically with the ideas
of justice and equality for everyone, and with the condemnation of the
evils of slavery. With the imposition of American negative racial values
into the Reconstruction process, freedom was not yet won for the freedmen or for the Creoles, but, as Senter explains, "The *Tribune* poets deter-
minedly sought to bridge the Creole past to the imagined American
future."

In Mary Morton's "Creole Culture in the Poetry of Sybil Kein," we
are once again reminded of Dunbar-Nelson's definition of the Creoles.
Morton finds that the poet speaks of the mixed heritage of Creoles and
shows the complexity of their lives and their legacy. She discovers the
often intimate histories of individual voices through characters who reflect twentieth-century Creoleness, especially that of women. Often, the
personalities created by the poet reflect the harshness and debilitating
circumstances of life as the Other and the displacement from community
owing to a lack of well-defined and accepted self-identities. According to
Morton, Kein uses the particular language of the community about
which she writes. Kein's work catches the Creoles in their daily lives as
well as in the distinctly Creole rites of passage. Morton sees the poet as
using components of the Creole experience in order to remember the
past and give voice to the individual spirit. Kein's work has images of
houses, for instance, and Morton explains, "The poetry of Kein uses the

metaphor not only of the house for the heart, but both the house and the heart as havens for memories that shape each character's destiny."

As a group, these essays—many of which were written by descendants of the Louisiana Creoles—offer the reader a wide view of the history and legacy of this unique group of Americans. The collection is an important study that touches the nerve center of race and color problems persisting in the nation as a new millennium dawns. Moreover, it may well provide insights that will serve as the seeds of alternative action in attempted solutions to these problems of race and color.

Sybil Kein
New Orleans

I

HISTORY

1

People of Color in Louisiana

ALICE MOORE DUNBAR-NELSON

PART I

The possible title of a discussion of the Negro in Louisiana presents difficulties, for there is no such word as Negro permissible in speaking of this State. The history of the State is filled with attempts to define, sometimes at the point of the sword, oftenest in civil or criminal courts, the meaning of the word Negro. By common consent, it came to mean in Louisiana, prior to 1865, slave, and after the war, those whose complexions were noticeably dark. As Grace King so delightfully puts it, "The pure-blooded African was never called colored, but always Negro." The *gens de couleur*, colored people, were always a class apart, separated from and superior to the Negroes, ennobled were it only by one drop of white blood in their veins. The caste seems to have existed from the first introduction of slaves. To the whites, all Africans who were not of pure blood were *gens de couleur*. Among themselves, however, there were jealous and fiercely guarded distinctions: "griffes, briqués, mulattoes, quadroons,

Editor's note: Although this is an early-twentieth-century essay, Alice Dunbar-Nelson's history seems to me to be a rich source that warrants inclusion in the present collection. It is also interesting to note that at the time the essay was written, Dunbar-Nelson was forbidden by law to use the libraries and archives in Louisiana because of her race. I would like to take this opportunity to thank Lester Sullivan and Irwin Lachoff of Xavier University Archives for their help in locating the full names of Dunbar-Nelson's references.—S. K.

octoroons, each term meaning one degree's further transfiguration toward the Caucasian standard of physical perfection."[1]

Negro slavery in Louisiana seems to have been early influenced by the policy of the Spanish colonies. De las Casas, an apostle to the Indians, exclaimed against the slavery of the Indians and finding his efforts of no avail proposed to Charles V in 1517 the slavery of the Africans as a substitute.[2] The Spaniards refused at first to import slaves from Africa, but later agreed to the proposition and employed other nations to traffic in them.[3] Louisiana learned from the Spanish colonies her lessons of this traffic, took over certain parts of the slave regulations and imported bondmen from the Spanish West Indies. Others brought thither were Congo, Banbara, Yaloff, and Mandingo slaves.[4]

People of color were introduced into Louisiana early in the eighteenth century. In 1708, according to the historian, Gayarré, the little colony of Louisiana, at the point on the Gulf of Mexico now known as Biloxi, in the present State of Mississippi, had been in existence nine years. In 1708, the population of the colony did not exceed 279 persons. The land about this region is particularly sterile, and the colonists were little disposed to undertake the laborious task of tilling the soil. Indian slavery was attempted but found unprofitable and exceedingly precarious. So Bienville, lacking the sympathy of De las Casas for the Indians, wrote his government to obtain the authorization of exchanging Negroes for Indians with the French West Indian islands. "We shall give," he said, "three Indians for two Negroes. The Indians, when in the islands, will not be able to run away, the country being unknown to them, and the Negroes will not dare to become fugitives in Louisiana, because the Indians would kill them."[5]

Bienville's suggestion seems not to have met with a very favorable reception. Yet, in 1712, the King of France granted to Anthony Crozat the exclusive privilege for fifteen years of trading in all that immense territory which, with its defined limits, France claimed as Louisiana. Among other privileges granted Crozat were those of sending, once a year, a ship

1. Grace King, *New Orleans, the Place and the People,* 333.

2. Luis de las Casas, "Historia General," *Louisiana History,* XX, 320.

3. Antonio de Herrera, Tordesillas, "Historia General," *Louisiana History,* XIX, 146.

4. B. F. French, *Historical Collections of Louisiana,* Part V, 119 et seq.

5. Charles Gayarré, *History of Louisiana,* 4th edition, I, 242, 254.

to Africa for Negroes.[6] When the first came, is not known, but in 1713 twenty of these Negro slaves from Africa are recorded in the census of the little colony on the Mississippi.[7]

In 1717 John Law flashed meteor-wise across the world with his huge scheme to finance France out of difficulty with his Mississippi Bubble. Among other considerations mentioned in the charter for twenty-five years, which he obtained from the gullible French government, was the stipulation that before the expiration of the charter, he must transport to Louisiana six thousand white persons, and three thousand Negroes, not to be brought from another French colony. These slaves, so said the charter, were to be sold to those inhabitants who had been two years in the colony for one half cash and the balance on one year's credit. The new inhabitants had one or two years' credit granted them.[8] In the first year, the Law Company transported from Africa one thousand slaves, in 1720 five hundred, the same number the next March, and by 1721 the pages of legal enactments in the West Indies were being ransacked for precedents in dealing with this strange population. But of all these slaves who came to the colony by June, 1721, but six hundred remained. Many had died, some had been exported. In 1722, therefore, the Mississippi Company was under constraint to pass an edict prohibiting the inhabitants of Louisiana from selling their slaves for transportation out of the colony, to the Spaniards, or to any other foreign nation under the penalty of the fine of a thousand livres and the confiscation of the Negroes.[9]

But already the curse of slavery had begun to show its effects. The new colony was not immoral; it may best be described as unmoral. Indolence on the part of the masters was physical, mental and moral. The slave population began to lighten in color, and increase out of all proportion due to the importation and natural breeding among themselves. La Harpe comments in 1724 upon the astonishing diminution of the white population and the astounding increase of the colored population.[10] Something was undoubtedly wrong, according to the Caucasian stan-

6. French, *Historical Collections of Louisiana*, Part III, 42.
7. Gayarré, *History of Louisiana*, I, 102.
8. Gayarré, *History of Louisiana*, I, 242, 254.
9. Ibid., I, 366.
10. Ibid., 365–6.

dard, and it has remained wrong to our own day.[11] The person of color was now, in Louisiana, a part of its social system, a creature to be legislated for and against, a person lending his dark shade to temper the inartistic complexion of his white master. Now he began to make history, and just as the trail of his color persisted in the complexion of Louisiana, so the trail of his personal influence continued in the history of the colony, the territory and the State.

Bienville, the man of far-reaching vision, saw the danger menacing the colony, and before his recall and disgrace before the French court, he published, in 1724, the famous Black Code.[12] This code followed the order of that of the West Indies but contains some provisions to meet local needs. The legal status of the slave was that of movable property of his master. Children born of Negro parents followed the condition of their mother. Slaves were forbidden to carry weapons. Slaves of different masters could not assemble in crowds by day or night. They were not permitted to sell "commodities, provisions, or produce" without permission from their masters, and had no property which did not belong to their masters. Neither free-born blacks nor slaves were allowed to receive gifts from whites. They could not exercise such public functions as arbitrator or expert, could not be partners to civil or criminal suits, could not give testimony except in default of white people, and could never testify against their masters. If a slave struck his master or one of the family so as to produce a bruise or shedding blood in the face, he had to be put to death. Any runaway slave who continued to be so from the day his master "denounced" him suffered the penalty of having his ears cut off and being branded on his shoulder with a fleur-de-lis. For a second offence the penalty was to hamstring the fugitive and brand him on the other shoulder. For the third such offence he suffered death. Freed or free-born Negroes who gave refuge to fugitive slaves had to pay 30 livres for each day of retention and other free persons 10 livres a day. If the freed or free-born Negroes were not able to pay the fine, they could be reduced to the condition of slaves and sold as such.

The slaves were socially ostracized. Marriage of whites with slaves

11. In 1900 a writer in *Pearson's Magazine* in discussing race mixture in early Louisiana made some startling comments as to the results of the miscegenation of these stocks during the colonial period.

12. Code Noir, 1724.

was forbidden, as was also the concubinage of whites and manumitted or free-born blacks with slaves. The consent of the parents of a slave to his marriage was not required. That of the master was sufficient, but a slave could not be forced to marry against his will.

There were, however, somewhat favorable provisions which made this code seem a little less rigorous. The slaves had to be well fed and the masters could not force them to provide for themselves by working for their own account certain days of the week, and slaves could give information against their owners, if not properly fed or clothed. Disabled slaves had to be sent to the hospital. Husbands, wives, and their children under the age of puberty could not be seized and sold separately when belonging to the same master. The code forbade the application of the rack to slaves, under any pretext, on private authority, or mutilation of a limb, under penalty of confiscation of the slave and criminal prosecution of the master. The master was allowed, however, to have his slave put in irons and whipped with rods or ropes. The code commanded officers or justices to prosecute masters and overseers who should kill or mutilate slaves, and to punish the murder according to the atrocity of the circumstance.

Other provisions were still more favorable. The slaves had to be instructed in the Catholic religion. Slaves appointed by their master as tutors to their children were set free. Moreover, manumitted slaves enjoyed the same rights, privileges and immunities that were enjoyed by those born free. "It is our pleasure," reads the document, "that their merit in having acquired their freedom shall produce in their favor, not only with regard to their persons, but also to their property, the same effects that our other subjects derive from the happy circumstance of their having been born free."[13]

From the first appearance of the *gens de couleur* in the colony of Louisiana dates the class, the *gens de couleur libre*. The record of the legal tangles that resulted from the attempts to define this race in Louisiana is most interesting. Up to 1671, all Creoles, Mulattoes, free Negroes, etc., paid a capitation tax. In February 12 of that year, M. de Baas, Governor-General of Martinique, issued an order exempting the Creoles. Those Mulattoes who were also designated as Creoles claimed the same exemption and resisted paying the tax. M. Patoulet, Intendant, rendered a deci-

13. Code Noir.

sion in 1683 and said: "The Mulattoes and free Negroes claimed to be exempt from the capitation tax: I have made them pay without difficulty. I decide that those Mulattoes born in vice should not receive the exemption, and that for the free Negro, the master could give him freedom but could not give him the exemption that attaches to the whites originally from France."[14] The next year, the Mulattoes refused to pay, and the successor of Minister Patoulet, M. Michel Begou, asked for a law to compel them.[15] In 1696, an agreement was reached exempting the Mulattoes and Creoles, leaving only the free black subject to the tax.[16] But in 1712, a M. Robert, in a decision on a subject, again included the Mulattoes, without, however, mentioning the Creoles, so that only the free Negroes and Mulattoes paid.[17] Thus they were held as a class apart. A free Negro woman, Magdelaine Debern, further contested the matter, and in 1724, in the colony of Louisiana, won a decision exempting free Negroes and Mulattoes, and again placing them on the same footing with the Creole. The Creoles had a decided advantage, however, because through the favor of those in authority, there was always a disposition to exalt them.[18]

It is in the definition of the word Creole that another great difficulty arises. The native white Louisianian will tell you that a Creole is a white man, whose ancestors contain some French or Spanish blood in their veins. But he will be disputed by others, who will gravely tell you that Creoles are to be found only in the lower Delta lands of the state, that there are no Creoles north of New Orleans; and will raise their hands in horror at the idea of being confused with the "Cajuns," the descendants of those Nova Scotians whom Longfellow immortalized in *Evangeline.* Sifting down the mass of conflicting definitions, it appears that to a Caucasian, a Creole is a native of the lower parishes of Louisiana, in whose veins some traces of Spanish, West Indian or French blood runs.[19] The

14. Auguste Lebeau, *De la condition des gens de couleur libres sous l'ancien régime*, 49.

15. Ibid., 49.

16. Ibid., 50.

17. Ibid., 51.

18. In the treaty of 1803 between the newly acquired territory of Louisiana and the government of the United States, they and all mixed bloods were granted full citizenship.

19. Most writers of our day adhere to this definition. See King, *New Orleans, the Place and the People,* and Gayarré, *History of Louisiana.*

Caucasian will shudder with horror at the idea of including a person of color in the definition, and the person of color will retort with his definition that a Creole is a native of Louisiana, in whose blood runs mixed strains of everything un-American, with the African strain slightly apparent. The true Creole is like the famous gumbo of the state, a little bit of everything, making a whole, delightfully flavored, quite distinctive, and wholly unique.

From 1724 to the present time, frequent discussions as to the proper name by which to designate this very important portion of the population of Louisiana were waged more or less acrimoniously.[20] It was this Creole element who in 1763 obtained a decision from Louis XV that all mixed bloods who could claim descent from an Indian ancestor in addition to a white outranked those mixed bloods who had only white and African ancestors.[21] In Jamaica, in 1733, there was passed a law that every person who could show that he was three degrees removed from a Negro ancestor should be regarded as belonging to the white race, and could sit as a member of the Jamaica Assembly.[22] In Barbados, any person who had a white ancestor could vote. These laws were quoted in Louisiana and influenced legislation there.[23]

20. Lebeau, *De la condition des gens de couleur libres sous l'ancien régime*, passim.
21. Ibid., 60.
22. Laws of Jamaica.
23. Litigation on the subject of the definition of the free person of color reached its climax in the year of our Lord, 1909, when Judge Frank D. Chretien defined the word Negro as differentiated from person of color as used in Louisiana. The case, as it was argued in court, was briefly thus. It was charged that one Treadway, a white man, was living in illegal relations with an octoroon, Josephine Lightell. The district attorney claimed that any one having a trace of African blood in his veins, however slight, should be classed as a Negro. Counsel for the defense had taken the position that Josephine Lightell had so little Negro blood in her veins that she could not be classed as one. Judge Chretien held in his ruling that local opinion, custom, and sentiment had previously agreed in holding that the black, and not the white, blood settled the ethnological status of each person and that an octoroon, no less than a quadroon and a mulatto, had been considered a Negro. But he held that if the Caucasian wished to be considered the superior race, and that if his blood be considered the superior element in the infusion, then the Caucasian and not the Negro blood must determine the status of a person. The case went to the Supreme Court of Louisiana on an appeal from the decision of Judge Chretien, who held that a mulatto is not a Negro in legal parlance. The Supreme Court, in a decision handed down April 25, 1910, sustained the view of

Gov. Perier succeeded Bienville as Governor of Louisiana. His task was not a light one; the colony staggered under "terror of attack from the Indians, sudden alarms, false hopes, anxious suspense, militia levies, colonial paper, instead of good money, industrial stagnation, the care of homeless refugees, and the worst of all, the restiveness of the slaves." Many of the slaves had been taken in war, and were fierce and implacable. Some were of that fiercest of African tribes, the Banbaras. A friendliness, born of common hatred and despair, began to show itself between the colored people and the fierce Choctaw Indians surrounding the colony, when Gov. Perier planned a master-stroke of diplomacy. Just above New Orleans lived a small tribe of Indians, the Chouchas, who, not particularly harmful in themselves, had succeeded in inspiring the nervous inhabitants of the city with abject fear. Perier armed a band of slaves in 1729 and sent them to the Chouchas with instructions to exterminate the tribe. They did their work with an ease and dispatch that should have been a warning to their white masters. In reporting the success of his plan Perier said: "The Negroes executed their mission with as much promptitude as secrecy. This lesson taught them by our Negroes, kept in check all the nations higher up the river."[24] Thus, by one stroke the wily Governor had intimidated the tribes of Indians, allayed the nervous fears of New Orleans, and effected a state of hostility between the Indians and the Africans, who were beginning to be entirely too friendly with each other. Then Perier used the slaves to make the entrenchments about the city. Thus we have the first instance of the arming of the Negro in Louisiana for the defense of the colony. On the 15th of January, 1730, Gov. Perier sent a boat containing twenty white men and six Africans to carry ammunition to the Illinois settlement up the Mississippi river whence tales of massacre and cruelty by the Indians filtered down.[25]

The arming of the slaves in defense of the whites gave impetus to the struggle for their own freedom. In the massacre of the French by the Natchez, at the village of that name, over three hundred women and slaves were kept as prisoners, and in January of the same year which witnessed the massacre of the Chouchas, the French surprised the Natchez

---

Judge Chretien. This decision was an interpretation of an act of 1908 which set forth a definition of the word Negro. See *State vs. Treadway*, 126 Louisiana, 300.

24. Gayarré, *History of Louisiana*, I, 444, 448.

25. Ibid., 365, 442, 454.

Indians with the intention of recovering their women and slaves, and avenging the death of their comrades. Some of the Africans who had been promised their freedom if they allied themselves with the Natchez Indians, fought against their erstwhile masters, others were loyal, and helped the French. The battle became an issue, as it were, between the slaves. Over one hundred of them were recovered from the Indians.[26]

The first tribute we have paid to the black man as a soldier in Louisiana was paid by Gov. Perier in this war in his dispatch to the French government. "Fifteen negroes," he wrote, "in whose hands we had put weapons, performed prodigies of valor. If the blacks did not cost so much, and if their labors were not so necessary to the colony, it would be better to turn them into soldiers, and to dismiss those we have, who are so bad and so cowardly that they seem to have been manufactured purposely for this colony."[27]

But the tiger had tasted blood. Perier's cruel logic was reactionary. Since he had used blacks to murder Indians in order to make bad blood between the races, the Indians retaliated by using blacks to murder white men. In August of that same fateful year, the Chickasaws, who had given asylum to the despoiled Natchez in order to curb the encroachments of the white men, stirred the black slaves to revolt. We have noted before the prevalence of the Banbara Negroes in the colony. It was they who planned the rebellion. Their plan was, after having butchered the whites, to establish a Banbara colony, keeping as slaves for themselves all blacks not of their nation. The conspiracy was discovered by the hints of a woman in the revolt before it had time to ripen, and the head of the revolt, a powerful black named Samba with eight of his confederates was broken on the wheel, and the woman hanged.[28]

Gov. Perier's administration did not lack interest. The next year, in 1731, we find him still struggling with his old enemies, the Natchez. His dispatches mention that a crew under one De Coulanges, with Indians and free blacks had been massacred by the Indians. One dispatch has the greatest interest for us, because of the expression "free blacks"[29] used. Here is one of the great mysteries of the person of color in Louisiana.

26. Ibid., 448.
27. Ibid., 435.
28. Ibid., 440.
29. Ibid., 444.

Whence the free black? We are told explicitly that up to this time all Negroes imported into Louisiana were slaves from Africa, for the West Indian migration did not occur until a half century later. This dispatch from Gov. Perier recalls articles in the Black Code of 1724, where explicit directions are given for the disposition of the children of free blacks. In the regulations of police under the governorship of the Marquis of Vaudreuil, 1750, there is an article regulating the attitude of free Negroes and Negresses toward slaves. Here is the very beginning of that aristocracy of freedom so fiercely and jealously guarded until this day, a free person of color being set as far above his slave fellows as the white man sets himself above the person of color. Three explanations for this aristocracy seem highly probable: Some slaves might have been freed by their masters because of valor on the battlefield, others by buying their freedom in terms of money, and not a few slave women by their owners because of their personal attractions. It makes little difference in this story which of the three or whether all of the three were contributors to the rise of this new class. It existed as early as 1724, twelve years after the first recorded slave importation. It was in 1766 that some Acadians, complaining of their treatment to the Governor Ulloa, represented that Negroes were freemen while they were slaves.

Bienville returned to the colony as its governor in 1733, after an absence of eight years, and it is recorded that in 1735, when he reviewed his troops near Mobile while making preparations for an Indian war, he found that his army from New Orleans consisted of five hundred and forty-four white men, excluding the officers, and forty-five Negroes commanded by free blacks.[30] Here we note free black officers of Negro troops in 1735. If not actually the first regular Negro troops to appear in what is now the United States, they were certainly the first to be commanded by Negro officers.

The engagement with the Choctaw Indians was not altogether successful for the French. Disaster succeeded disaster, and the day closed with the French army deeply humiliated, and making a retreat as dignified as possible under the circumstances. A number of the French officers, as Gayarré tells us, stood under the shade of a gigantic oak discussing the defeat, and with them Simon, a free black, the commander

30. Dumont de Montigny, *Mémoires Historiques sur la Louisiane*, 225, 226.

of the troop of Negroes. He was deeply vexed because his troops had not stood fire, and expressed himself with so much freedom and disgust, that the French officers kept bantering him without mercy at the timidity of his soldiers, soothing their own wounded pride by laughing at his mortification. Stung to the heart, Simon finally exclaimed wrathfully, "A Negro is as brave as anybody and I will show it to you." Seizing a rope which was dangling from one of the tents, he rushed headlong toward one of the horses which were quietly slaking their thirst under the protection of the Indian muskets. To reach a white mare, to jump on her back with the agility of a tiger, and to twist around her head and mouth the rope with which to control her, was the affair of an instant. But that instant was enough for the apparently sleeping Indian village to show itself awake, and to flash forth in a hail of bullets. Away dashed Simon toward the Indian village, and back to the French camp where he arrived safe amid the cheering acclamations of the troops, and without having received a wound from the shots of the enemy.[31] This feat silenced at

31. Another interesting story is related to Dumont, a historian of Louisiana, who published a work in 1753. The colony was then under the administration of Gov. Kerlerec, whose opinion of colonial courage was not very high. The colony was without an executioner, and no white man could be found who would be willing to accept the office. It was decided finally by the council to force it upon a Negro blacksmith belonging to the Company of the Indies, named Jeannot, renowned for his nerve and strength. He was summoned and told that he was to be appointed executioner and made a free man at the same time. The stalwart fellow started back in anguish and horror, "What! cut off the heads of people who have never done me any harm?" He prayed, he wept, but saw at last that there was no escape from the inflexible will of his masters. "Very well," he said, rising from his knees, "wait a moment." He ran to his cabin, seized a hatchet with his left hand, laid his right hand on a block of wood and cut it off. Returning, without a word he exhibited the bloody stump to the gentlemen of the council. With one cry, it is said, they sprang to his relief, and his freedom was given him. Dumont, *Mémoires Historiques sur la Louisiane*, 244, 246.

The story is also told by Grace King of one slave, an excellent cook, who had once served a French governor. When, in one of her periodic transitions from one government to another, Louisiana became the property of Spain, the "Cruel" O'Reilly was made governor of the colony. He was execrated as were all things sent by Spain or pertaining to Spanish rule. However, having heard of the fame of the Negro cook, he sent for him. "You belong now," said he, "to the king of Spain, and until you are sold, I shall take you into my service." "Do not dare it," answered

once the jests of the French officers, of which Simon thought himself the victim.[32]

The beginning of the Revolutionary war in 1776 found Louisiana a Spanish province and the natives of the colony beginning to tolerate and even to like their erstwhile hated Spanish masters. Don Bernardo de Gálvez was governor of the colony. His administration has a peculiar interest to us, because it was during his rule that the Court of Madrid, fully alive to the policy of extending the agriculture of Louisiana, issued a decree permitting the introduction of Negroes into Louisiana by French vessels, from whatever ports they might come.[33] This was the beginning of the rapid migration from the West Indian islands.

While Andrew Jackson was still a child, Louisiana had a deliverer from the British in the person of this brave Gov. Gálvez. The strategical importance of the Mississippi River and of New Orleans was at once apparent to the British commanders, and Louisiana, being neutral territory, offered a most fascinating field of operation. Gálvez, in July 1777, had secured declaration of neutrality from the 25,000 or more Creeks, Choctaws and Chickasaws, but even this did not seem to satisfy the combatants. New Orleans was at the mercy of first the American troops and then the British. The mediation of Spain between France and England having been rejected in the courts of Europe, Spain decided to join France in the struggle against Great Britain. So on May 8, 1779, Spain formally declared war against Great Britain, and on July 8 authorized all Spanish subjects in America to take their share in all hostilities against the English. No news could be more welcome to the dashing young Gálvez, to whom a policy of neutrality was decidedly distasteful. He decided to forestall the attack on New Orleans, which he had learned was to be made by the British, by attacking first, and on August 26 gathered his little army together. From New Orleans, as Gayarré tells, were 170 veteran soldiers, 330 recruits, 20 carabiniers, 60 militiamen, and 80 free blacks and mulattoes. On the way up the river, they were reinforced by 600 men from the coast of "every condition and color," besides 160 Indians.[34]

On the march, the colored men and Indians were ordered to keep

---

the slave, "you killed my master, and I would poison you." O'Reilly dismissed him unpunished. Gayarré, *History of Louisiana*, II, 344.

32. Gayarré, *History of Louisiana*, I, 480.

33. Ibid., III, 108.

34. Ibid.

ahead of the main body of troops, at a distance of about three quarters of a mile, and closely to reconnoitre the woods. In capturing the two forts of Baton Rouge and Natchez, which were held by the British, Gálvez found a considerable number of Negro slaves who had been armed by the British. Many of these he set free. In his dispatch to his government at Madrid, Gálvez reports that the companies of free blacks and mulattoes, who had been employed in all the false attacks, and who, as scouts and skirmishers, had proved exceedingly useful, behaved on all occasions with as much valor and generosity as the white soldiers.[35] But not alone were the exploits of Gálvez's little army celebrated in history. Poetry added her laurel wreath to its crown. Julien Poydras de Lalande, known to all Louisianians as Poydras, celebrated the victory in a poem, "The God of the Mississippi," wherein the brave deeds of the army, white and colored, are hailed in French verse, lame and halting, it may be in places, but impartial in its tribute.

The close of the Revolutionary war found the colony partially paralyzed as to industry. During the Spanish domination the indigo industry declined, tobacco was difficult to raise, and the production of cotton was not then profitable. Sugar raising was the only other industry to which they could turn. In 1751 the Jesuit fathers had received their first seed, or rather layers, from Santo Domingo and from that time sugar-cane had been grown with more or less success. But it was a strictly local industry. The Louisianians were poor sugar-makers. The stuff was badly granulated and very moist, and when in 1765 an effort was made to export some of the sugar to France, it was so wet that half of the cargo leaked out of the ship before it could make port. It was just at this psychological moment, in 1791 to 1794, when the planters of the lower Delta saw ruin staring them in the face, that there came to the rescue of the colony a man of color, one of the refugees from Santo Domingo, where the blacks had risen in 1791. From the failure of this abortive attempt to emulate the spirit of the white man, refugees flew in every direction, and Louisiana welcomed them, if not exactly with open arms, at least with more indifference than other colonies. And these black refugees were her saviors. For they had been prosperous sugar-makers, and the efforts to make marketable sugar in Louisiana, which had ceased for nearly twenty-five years, were revived. Two Spaniards, Mendez and Solis, erected on the

35. Ibid., 126–32.

outskirts of New Orleans, the one a distillery, the other a battery of sugar-kettles, and manufactured rum and syrup. Still, the efforts were not entirely successful, until Etienne de Boré appeared. Face to face with ruin because of the failure of the indigo crop, he staked his all on the granulation of sugar. He enlisted the services of these successful Santo Dominicans, and went to work. In all American history there can be fewer scenes more dramatic than the one described by careful historians of Louisiana, the day when the final test was made and there was passed around the electrical word, "It granulates!"[36]

That year de Boré marketed $12,000 worth of super or sugar. The agriculture of the Delta was revolutionized; seven years afterwards New Orleans marketed 2,000,000 gallons of rum, 250,000 gallons of molasses, and 5,000,000 pounds of sugar. It was the beginning of the commercial importance of one of the most progressive cities in the country. Imagination refuses to picture what would have been the case but for the refugees from San Domingo.

But the same revolution which gave to Louisiana its prestige to the commercial world, almost starved the province to death. In the year 1791, the trade, which had flourished briskly between Santo Domingo and New Orleans, was closed because of the uprising, and but for Philadelphia, famine would have decimated the city. One thousand barrels of flour were sent in haste to the starving city by the good Quakers of Philadelphia. The members of the Cabildo, the local council, prohibited the introduction of people of color from Santo Domingo, fearing the dangerous ideas of the brotherhood of man. But it was too late. The news of the success of the slaves in Santo Domingo, and the success of the French Revolution, says Gayarré, had penetrated into the most remote cabins in Louisiana, and in April, 1795, on the plantation of the same Poydras who had sung the glory of the army of Gálvez, a conspiracy was formed for a general uprising of the slaves throughout the parish of Pointe Coupée. The leaders were three white men. The conspiracy failed because one of the leaders was incensed at his advice not being heeded and through his wife the authorities were notified. A struggle ensued, and the conspiracy was strangled in its infancy by the trial and execution of the slaves most concerned in the insurrection. The three white men were exiled from the

36. Ibid., 348.

colony.[37] This finally ended the importation of slaves from the West Indies.

PART II

Louisiana was transferred to Spain but was not long to be secure in the possession of that country. France again claimed her in 1800, and Napoleon, busy with his English war and realizing the dangers of a province so open to British attack as was this bounded by the Mississippi and the Gulf of Mexico, readily listened to the proposition of the United States. Twenty days after the French tri-color waved in place of the Spanish flag in the old Place d'Armes, the American stars and stripes proclaimed the land American territory. The Creoles, French though they were in spirit, in partisanship, in sympathy, could not but breathe a sigh of relief, for Napoleon had dangerous ideas concerning the freedom of slaves, and already had spoken sharply about the people of color in the province.[38] Were the terrors of San Domingo to be reenacted on the banks of the Mississippi? The United States answered with a decided negative.

Men of color, however, were to be important factors in the maintenance of order in the province.[39] Laussat, the Colonial Prefect of France, placed in charge of Louisiana in 1803, tells how the old Spanish Governor Salcedo, in his anxiety to keep the province loyal to Spain, had summoned all the military officers of the militia to come to his lodgings and declare whether they intended to remain in the service of the king of Spain. "The Marquis," writes Laussat to his friend Decrès, "went so far

37. Ibid., 354.
38. J. Holland Rose, *Life of Napoleon I*, 333–6.
39. As to the ability of a man of color to rise in this territory, the life of one man, recorded by the Pennsylvania Abolition Society, will furnish a good example. James Derham was originally a slave in Philadelphia, sold by his master to a physician, who employed him in the shop as an assistant in the preparation of drugs. During the war between England and America, he was sold by this physician to a surgeon, and by that surgeon to Dr. Robert Dove of New Orleans. Here he learned French and Spanish so as to speak both with ease. In 1788, he was received into the English church, when he was twenty-one and became, says the report, "one of the most distinguished physicians in New Orleans." "I conversed with him on medicine," says Dr. Rush, "and found him very learned. I thought I could give him information on the treatment of diseases, but I learned more from him than he could expect from me." *The Columbian Gazette*, II, 742–3.

as to exact a declaration in the affirmative from two companies of men of color in New Orleans, which were composed of all the mechanics whom that city possessed. Two of these mulattoes complained to me of having been detained twenty-four hours in prison to force them to utter the fatal yea which was desired of them."[40]

Within the next six years New Orleans doubled in population and that population was far from white. Those refugees from San Domingo who had escaped to Cuba were now forced by the hostilities between France and Spain again to become exiles. Within sixty days between May and July in one year alone, 1809, thirty-four vessels from Cuba set ashore in the streets of New Orleans nearly 5,800 persons, 4,000 of these being free colored and blacks.[41] Later others came from Cuba, Guadeloupe and neighboring islands until they amounted to 10,000. The first American governor of Louisiana certainly had no easy task before him. Into the disorganized and undisciplined city, enervated by frequent changes and corruption of government, torn by dissensions, uncertain whether its allegiance was to Spain or to France, reflecting the spirit of upheaval and uncertainty which made Europe one huge brawl—into this cosmopolitan city swarmed ten thousand white, yellow and black West Indian islanders, some with means, most of them destitute, all of them desperate. Americans, English, Spanish, French—all cried aloud. Claiborne begged the consuls of Havana and Santiago de Cuba to stop the movement; the laws forbidding the importation of slaves were more rigidly enforced; and free people of color were ordered point blank to leave the city.[42] Where they were to go, however, no one seemed to care, and as the free people of color had no intention of going, the question was not discussed. For some reason the enforcement of the law was not insisted upon. When a meagre attempt was made, it proved unsuccessful, and the complexion of Louisiana was definitely settled for many years to come.[43]

The administration of Governor Claiborne from 1803 to 1816 was one long wrestle, not only with the most superhuman task of adjusting a practically foreign country to American ideals of government but of wrestling with the color problem. Slowly and insidiously it had come to

40. Gayarré, III, 595.
41. Ibid., IV, 218.
42. Ibid., 219.
43. Ibid.

dominate every other problem. The people of color had helped to settle the territory, had helped to make it commercially important, had helped to save it from the Indians and from the English, and they seemed likely to become the most important factors in its history.

The Louisianians were greatly mortified at the enforcement by Claiborne of the law against the importation of slaves. They were undecided whether to blame Claiborne for enforcing the law or to blame Philadelphia for harboring the first Abolition Society which met in 1804 and promulgated doctrines as dangerous as those of Napoleon regarding human slavery. Slaves were daily smuggled into the territory by way of Barataria Bay, the lakes, and all the innumerable outlets to Spanish possessions.[44] Claiborne was alternately accused of conniving at this smuggling and abused for trying to suppress it. Jean and Pierre Lafitte, infamous in history for their feats of smuggling and piracy, made capital of the slave trade, and but for their stalwart Africans would have been captured and hung long before Louisiana had suffered from their depredations and the bad reputation which they gave her. The Lafittes appealed to the romantic temperament of the French, and the fact that the American governor, Claiborne, had set a price upon their heads was almost sufficient in itself to secure them immunity from the Creoles.[45]

"Americans," says Grace King, "were despised and ridiculed." Men, women and children of color, free and slave, united to insult the American Negro—or "Mericain Coquin," as they called him. The French and the Spaniards, moreover, united in using the people of color to further

44. Ibid., 229.
45. Grace King tells a pretty story of the saving of Jean Lafitte's life. On the very day that a price was set upon his head by Gov. Claiborne he was invited to be the guest at a plantation, and almost at the same instant there arrived unexpectedly Mrs. Claiborne, the wife of the governor. The hostess, with quick presence of mind, introduced the gentleman to the wife of the governor as Monsieur Clement, and then hurriedly went out of the room, leaving her guests together. She called Henriette, her confidential servant, and looking her straight in the eyes, said: "Henriette, Gov. Claiborne has set a price upon Monsieur Lafitte's head. Anyone who takes him prisoner and carries him to the governor will receive five hundred dollars reward, and M. Lafitte's head will be cut off. Send all the other servants away; set the table yourself, and wait on us yourself. Remember to call M. Lafitte, M. Clement—and be careful before Mme. Claiborne." The colored woman responded with perfect tact and discretion. See King, *New Orleans, the Place and the People*, 204.

their own interests, or to annoy the new American government while the intrigues of Spain and France weakened the feeble territory. It was difficult to know how to treat this almost alien people. Governor Claiborne found the militia in the territory entirely inadequate for the purposes of protection, should Spain make an attempt to wrest the land back from the United States. In one of his anxious despatches to headquarters he says plaintively: "With respect to the Mulatto Corps in this city, I am indeed at a loss to know what policy is best to pursue."[46] The corps, old and honorable, as it was, had been ignored by the previous Legislative Council, and was now disaffected. The neglect had "soured them considerably with the American government."[47]

Claiborne, however, determined to procure a census of free people of color in the city. He estimated that there were five hundred capable of bearing arms, and added that he would do all in his power to conciliate them, and secure a return of their allegiance to the American government. One Stephen, a free black man, had appeared before Claiborne and declared on oath that the people of color were being tampered with by the Spanish government.[48] This caused the governor to redouble his energies toward conciliating the doubtful militia. Louisiana bordered on the Spanish territory, Texas, and a constant desertion of people of color to this foreign land continued, Spain doing all in her power to make the flight of these free men and slaves interesting. Colored men were furnished the Spanish cockades, and dances were given in their honor when they escaped over the border. The disaffected adherents of Aaron Burr on the border-land of Texas kept up the underhand warfare against the government, through these people of color. Perhaps it was as a means of protection that a much restricted Louisiana was admitted as a State in 1812.

Writers describing the New Orleans of this period agree in presenting a picture of a continental city, most picturesque, most un-American, and as varied in color as a street of Cairo. There they saw French, Spaniards, English, Bohemians, Negroes, mulattoes; varied clothes, picturesque white dresses of the fairer women, brilliant cottons of the darker

46. Gayarré, IV, 127.
47. Ibid.
48. Ibid., 131.

ones. The streets, banquettes, we should say, were bright with color, the nights filled with song and laughter. Through the scene, the people of color add the spice of color; in the life, they add the zest of romance.[49]

Such was the situation in the city of New Orleans. The condition of the free people of color in Louisiana as a whole, however, and the form of slavery which existed in that state are somewhat difficult to determine because of the conflicting statements of observers who did not distinguish between the conditions obtaining in the metropolis and those obtaining in the parishes. All seem to agree, however, that on account of the extensive miscegenation so common in the French colonies there had been produced in that state various classes of mixed breeds enjoying degrees of freedom in conformity with their proximity or separation from the white race. Paul Alliot said in his reflection on Louisiana in 1803: "The population of that city counting the people of all colors is only twelve thousand souls. Mulattoes and Negroes are openly protected by the Government. He who was to strike one of those persons, even though he had run away from him, would be severely punished. Also twenty whites could be counted in the prisons of New Orleans against one man of color. The wives and daughters of the latter are much sought after by the white men, and white women at times esteem well-built men of color."[50] Elsewhere the same writer, in speaking of the white men, said that few among them married, choosing rather to live with their slaves or with women of color.[51]

A generation later the situation was apparently the same despite the reactionary forces which seemed likely to change the social order. While on a tour through this country in 1818 Evans saw much in New Orleans to interest him. "Here," said he, "may be seen in the same crowds, Quadroons, mulattoes, Samboes, Mustizos, Indians, and Negroes; and there are other commixtures which are not yet classified. As to the Negroes, I may add that whilst in this place I saw one who was perfectly white. This peculiarity, however, is rarely witnessed in this country."[52] Thereafter

49. King, *New Orleans, the Place and the People.*

50. Paul Alliot's Reflections in James Alexander Robertson's *Louisiana Under the Rule of Spain*, I, 67.

51. Ibid., 103, 111.

52. Estwick Evans, *A Pedestrian's Tour*, etc.; Reuben Gold Thwaites (not author), *Early Western Travels*, VIII, 336.

the tendency seemed to be not to check promiscuous miscegenation but to debase the offspring resulting therefrom.[53]

In the midst of this confusing commixture of population and unstable society of mixed breeds of three nations the second war between England and the United States came like a thunderbolt to upset the already seething administration of Claiborne. As of old, Louisiana was the strategical point upon which both powers had their eyes. It was the intention of England to weaken the United States by capturing Louisiana and handing it over in its entirety to the Spanish government waiting greedily over the border of Texas. On the same day that Gov. Claiborne sent the communication to the Secretary of War containing this astounding piece of information which he had obtained from authentic sources, he wrote to General Jackson, the despised "red Indian" of the aristocratic Louisianians. He had reason, he said in this letter, to doubt the loyalty of many men in the state, because of their known adherence to foreign nations, but he hopefully adds, "Among the militia of New Orleans there is a battalion of chosen men of color, organized under a special act of Legislature, of which I inclose a copy for your perusal."

Under the Spanish Government the men of color of New Orleans were always relied upon in time of difficulties, and on several occasions

53. Harriet Martineau painted in 1837 a picture of this society, showing how the depravity of the settlers had worked out. "The Quadroon girls of New Orleans," said she, "are brought up by their mothers to be what they have been, mistresses of white gentlemen. The boys are some of them sent to France; some placed on land in the back of the State; and some are sold in the slave market. They marry women of a somewhat darker color than their own; the women of their color objecting to them. '*Ils sont si dégoûtants!*' The girls are highly educated, externally, and are, probably, as beautiful and accomplished a set of women as can be found. Every young man early selects one and establishes her in one of those pretty and peculiar houses, whole rows of which may be seen in the Ramparts. The connexion now and then lasts for life; usually for several years. In the latter case, when the time comes for the gentleman to take a wife, the dreadful news reaches his Quadroon partner, either by letter entitling her to call the house and furniture her own, or by the newspaper which announces his marriage. The Quadroon ladies are rarely or never known to form a second connexion. Many commit suicide, more die heartbroken. Some men continue the connexion after marriage. Every Quadroon woman believes that her partner will prove an exception to the rule of desertion. Every white lady believes that her husband has been an exception to the rule of seduction." See Harriet Martineau, *Society in America*, II, 326–7; see also Nuttall's Journal in Thwaites, *Early Western Travels*, XIII, 309–10.

evinced in the field the greatest firmness and courage.[54] "With these gentlemen, Colonel Fortier and Major Lacoste, and the officers attached to companies," Claiborne continued, "I had an interview on yesterday, and assured them that, in the hour of peril, I should rely on their valor and fidelity to the United States. In return, they expressed their devotion to the country and their readiness to serve it."[55] Claiborne then ordered the taking of a census of the men of color in the city capable of bearing arms, and found that they numbered nearly eight hundred. In his appeal to General Jackson, Claiborne said, "These men, Sir, for the most part, sustain good characters. Many of them have extensive connections and much property to defend, and all seem attached to arms. The mode of acting toward them at the present crisis, is an inquiry of importance. If we give them not our confidence, the enemy will be encouraged to intrigue and corrupt them."[56] General Jackson took the cue from Governor Claiborne and enlisted the services of the battalion of men of color, addressing them in stirring and thrilling words. There were not wanting objections to this address. Its publication was delayed a few days to give him time to reconsider the matter, since advisers of Gov. Claiborne thought it a little too free with its suggestions of perfect equality between the companies. But the well-known temper of General Jackson precluded the possibility of any retraction, and the address came down in history as he originally drafted it.[57]

54. Gayarré, *History of Louisiana*, IV, 335.

55. Ibid., 336.

56. Ibid.

57. He said: "Through a mistaken policy you have heretofore been deprived of participation in the glorious struggle for national rights in which our country is engaged. This no longer exists.

"As sons of freedom, you are now called upon to defend our most inestimable blessing. As Americans, your country looks with confidence to her adopted children for a valorous support as a faithful return for the advantages enjoyed under her mild and equitable government. As fathers, husbands and brothers, you are summoned to rally round the standard of the eagle to defend all which is dear in existence.

"Your country, although calling for your exertions, does not wish you to engage in her cause without amply remunerating you for the services rendered. Your intelligent minds are not to be led away by false representations. Your love of honor would cause you to despise the man who would attempt to deceive you. In the sincerity of a soldier and the language of truth I address you.

"To every noble-hearted, generous freeman—men of color, volunteering to

The American soldiers on the field aggregated 3,000, among whom were 430 colored. The first battalion of men of color was commanded by Major Lacoste, a wealthy white planter. In reviewing the troops, Gen. Jackson was so well pleased with Major Lacoste's battalion, that he deemed it prudent to levy a new battalion of the same description. Jean Baptiste Savary, a colored man who had fled from Santo Domingo during the struggle there, undertook, therefore, to form a battalion of his countrymen. Savary obtained the rank of captain, and was remarkably successful.[58] The new battalion was put under the command of Major Jean Daquin, also a native of Santo Domingo. Whether or not Major Daquin was a white man as Gayarré tells us, or a quadroon as other writers assert, is a disputed question.[59]

But not only was this regiment of free men of color to have all the honor of the struggle. The colored men were enlisted in more ways than one. Slaves were used in throwing up the famous entrenchments. The idea of a fortification of cotton bales, which we are told practically saved the city, was that of a colored man, a slave from Africa, who had seen the same thing done in his native country. It was the cotton breastworks that nonplussed the British. Colored men, free and slave, were used to recon-

---

serve during the present contest with Great Britain and no longer, there will be paid the same bounty in money and lands now received by the white soldiers of the United States, viz.: $124 in money and 160 acres of land. The non-commissioned officers and privates will also be entitled to the same monthly pay and daily ration and clothes, furnished to any American soldier.

"On enrolling yourselves in companies, the Major-General commanding will select officers from your government from your white citizens. Your non-commissioned officers will be appointed from among yourselves.

"Due regard will be paid to the feelings of freemen and soldiers. You will not, by being associated with white men in the same corps, be exposed to improper comparisons, or unjust sarcasm. As a distinct, independent battalion or regiment, pursuing the path of glory, you will undivided, receive the applause and gratitude of your country men.

"To assure you of the sincerity of my intentions and my anxiety to engage your invaluable services to our country, I have communicated my wishes to the Governor of Louisiana, who is fully informed as to the manner of enrollment, and will give you every necessary information on the subject of this address." See Williams, *History of the Negro Race*, II, 25, 26.

58. Gayarré, *History of Louisiana*, IV, 406.

59. He was probably regarded as a quadroon who had been accepted by the white race. See Gayarré, *History of Louisiana*, IV, 406.

noitre, and the pirate Lafitte, true to his word, to come to the aid of Louisiana should she ever need assistance, brought in with his Baratarians a mixed horde of desperate fighters, white and black.

On the British side was a company composed of colored men, and historians like to tell of their cowardice compared with the colored men of the American side.[60] Evidently a scarlet coat does not well fit a colored skin. To the eternal credit of the State troops composed of the men of color, not one act of desertion or cowardice is recorded against them. There was a most lamentable exhibition of panic on the right bank of the river by the American troops, but the battalion of the men of color was not there. They were always in the front of the attack.[61]

In the celebration of the victory which followed in the great public square, the Place d'Armes, now Jackson Square, where a statue of the commander rears itself in the center, the colored troops came in for their share of glory.[62] The train which brought in the four hundred wounded prisoners was met by the colored women, the famous nurses of New Orleans, who have in every war from the Revolutionary until the Spanish-American held the reputation of being some of the best nurses in the world.

The men of color were apparently not content with winning the victory; they must furnish material for dissension for many days afterwards. When the British army withdrew from Louisiana on January 27, 1815, they carried away with them 199 slaves, whom they had acquired by the very easy method of taking them willy-nilly. The matter of having these bondmen restored to their original owners, of convincing the British that

60. Ibid., 451.
61. Ibid., 427 et passim.
62. For years after the Civil War, one of the most picturesque figures in New Orleans was Jordan B. Noble, who at the time of the Battle of New Orleans was a slim youth. It was his tireless beating of the drum which led to battle the American forces on the nights of December 23 and January 8. He lived to be an old man, and appeared on several occasions at the St. Charles theatre, where a great audience turned out to do him honor and give an ovation when he beat the drum again as he had on those memorable nights. The *Delta* records a benefit given him at the theatre in 1854. In 1851 *The New Orleans Picayune* in commenting on the celebration of the victory of New Orleans notes the presence in the line of parade of 90 colored veterans. "And who did more than they to save the city?" it asks in the midst of a highly eulogistic review of the battle. King, *New Orleans, the Place and the People*, 256; and Grace King's letter to A. O. Stafford in 1904.

the Americans did not see the joke of the abduction caused one of the most acrimonious discussions in the history of the State. The treaty between the two countries, England and America, was distorted by both sides to read anything they wished. The English took a high stand of altruism, of a desire to free the oppressed; the Louisianians took as high a stand of wishing to grow old with their own slaves. It was an amusing incident which the slaves watched with interest. In the end the colored men were restored, and the interpretation of the treaty ceased.[63]

Following the War of 1812 the free people of color occupied a peculiar position in Louisiana, especially in New Orleans. There were distinct grades of society. The caste system was almost as strong as that of India. Free people of color from other states poured into Louisiana in a steady stream. It was a haven of refuge. Those were indeed halcyon times both for the Creole and the American, who found in the rapidly growing city a commercial El Dorado. For the people of color it was indeed a time of growth and acquisition of wealth. Three famous streets in New Orleans bear testimony to the importance of the colored people in the life of the city. Congo Square, one of the great open squares in the old Creole quarter, was named for the slaves who used to congregate in its limits and dance the weird dances to the tunes of blood-stirring minor strains. Those who know the weird leit-motif of Coleridge-Taylor's Bamboula dance have heard the tune of the Congo dance, which every child in New Orleans could sing. Gottschalk's Danse des Nègres is almost forgotten by this generation but in it he recorded the music of the West Indians. Camp Street, to-day one of the principal business streets in the city, was so called because it ran back of the old Camp de Negroes.[64] Julia Street, which runs along the front of the so-called New Basin, a canal of great commercial importance, connecting, as it does, the city with Lake Pontchartrain, and consequently, the greater gulf trade, was named for one Julia, a free woman of color, who owned land along the banks.[65] What Julia's cognomen was, where she came from, and whence she obtained the valuable property are hidden in the silent grave in which time encloses mere mortals. Somewhere in the records of the city it is recorded that one Julia, a F.W.C. (free woman of color), owned this land.

63. Gayarré, *History of Louisiana*, IV, 517–31.

64. Alcée Fortier, *Louisiana*, II, 231.

65. George Washington Cable, *The Creoles*, 211; Grace King, *New Orleans, the Place and the People*, 260.

The minor distinctions of complexion and race so fiercely adhered to by the Creoles of the old regime were at their height at this time. The glory and shame of the city were her quadroons and octoroons, apparently constituting two aristocratic circles of society,[66] the one as elegant as the other, the complexions the same, the men the same, the women different in race, but not in color, nor in dress, nor in jewels. Writers on fire with the romance of this continental city love to speak of the splendors of the French Opera House, the first place in the country where grand opera was heard, and tell of the tiers of beautiful women with their jewels and airs and graces. Above the orchestra circle were four tiers, the first filled with a second array of beautiful women, attired like those of the first, with no apparent difference; yet these were the octoroons and quadroons, whose beauty and wealth were all the passports needed. The third was for the hoi polloi of the white race, and the fourth for the people of color whose color was more evident. It was a veritable sandwich of races.

With the slaves, especially those outside of New Orleans, the situation was different. The cruelty of the slave owners in the State was proverbial. To be "sent down the Mississippi" became a by-word of horror, a bogie with which slave-holders all over the South threatened their incorrigible slaves. The slave markets, the tortures of the old plantations, even those in the city, which Cable has immortalized, help to fill the pages of romance, which must be cruel as well as beautiful.

The reaction against the Negro was then well on its way in Louisiana and evidences of it soon appeared in New Orleans where their condition for some time yet differed much from that of the blacks in the parishes. Moved by the fear of a rising class of mixed breeds resulting from miscegenation, the whites endeavored to diminish their power by restraining the free people of color from exercising influence over the slaves, who were becoming insurrectionary as in the case of those of the parish of St. John the Baptist in 1811. The State had in 1807 and 1808 made additional provisions for the regulation of the coming of free Negroes into Louisiana, but when there came reports of the risings of the blacks in various places in the Seaboard States, and of David Walker's appeal to Negroes to take up arms against their masters, it was deemed wise to prohibit the immigration of free persons into that Commonwealth.[67] In 1830

66. Martineau, *Society in America*, 326 et passim.
67. Edward Channing, *The Jeffersonian System*, 84.

it was provided that whoever should write, print, publish or distribute anything having the tendency to produce discontent among the slaves, should on conviction thereof be imprisoned at hard labor for life or suffer death at the discretion of the court. It was further provided that whoever used any language or became instrumental in bringing into the State any paper, book or pamphlet inducing discontent should suffer practically the same penalty. Any person who should teach or permit or cause to be taught, any slave to read or write should be imprisoned not less than one month nor more than twelve.[68]

Under the revised Black Code of Louisiana special care was taken to prevent free Negroes from coming in contact with bondsmen. Free persons of color were restricted from obtaining licenses to sell spiritous liquors, because of the fear that intoxicants distributed by this class might excite the Negroes to revolt. The law providing that there should be at least one white person to every thirty slaves on a plantation was re-enacted so as to strengthen the measure, the police system for the control of Negroes was reorganized to make it more effective, and slaves although unable to own property were further restricted in buying and selling. Those taken by masters beyond the limits of the State were on their return to be treated as free Negroes. But it was later provided on the occasion of the institution of proceedings for freedom by a slave who had been carried to the Northwest Territory[69] that "no slave shall be entitled to his or her freedom under the pretense that he or she has been, with or without the consent of his or her owner, in a country where slavery does not exist or in any of the States where slavery is prohibited."[70]

After that the condition of the Negroes in Louisiana was decidedly pitiable, although in certain parts of the State, as observed by Bishop Polk,[71] Timothy Flint,[72] and Frederic Law Olmsted[73] at various times, there were some striking exceptions to this rule. About this time Captain Marryat made some interesting remarks concerning this situation. "In the Western States," said he, "comprehending Louisiana, Arkansas, Mis-

68. For a general sketch see Henry Adams Bullard and Thomas Curry's *A Digest of the Statutes of the State of Louisiana*, 65 et seq.

69. Jacob Pratt Dunn, *Indiana*, 234.

70. See *The Revised Statutes of Louisiana*, 1852, 524 et seq.

71. James Ford Rhodes, *History of the United States*, III, 331.

72. Timothy Flint, *Recollections of the Last Ten Years*, 345.

73. Frederic Law Olmsted, *The Cotton Kingdom*, II, 213.

sissippi, Georgia, and Alabama, the Negroes are, with the exception, perhaps, of the latter States, in a worse condition than they were in the West
India Islands. This may be easily imagined," continued he, "when the
character of the white people who inhabit the larger portion of these
States is considered—a class of people, the majority of whom are without
feelings of honor, reckless in their habits, intemperate, unprincipled, and
lawless, many of them having fled from the Eastern States, as fraudulent
bankrupts, swindlers or committers of other crimes, which have sub-
jected them to the penitentiaries, miscreants, defying the climate, so that
they can defy the laws. Still this representation of the character of the
people, inhabiting these States, must from the chaotic state of society in
America be received with many exceptions. In the city of New Orleans,
for instance, and in Natchez and its vicinity, and also among the planters,
there are many honorable exceptions. I have said the majority: for we
must look to the mass—the exceptions do prove the rule. It is evident
that slaves under such masters can have but little chance of good treatment, and stories are told of them at which humanity shudders."[74]

The free people of color, however, kept on amassing wealth and edu-
cating their children as ever in spite of opposition, for it is difficult to
enforce laws against a race when you cannot find that race. Being well-
to-do they could maintain their own institutions of learning, and had access to parochial schools. Some of them, like their white neighbors, sent
their sons to France and their daughters to the convents to continue their
education beyond the first communion. The first free school ever opened
for colored children in the United States was the "Ecole Des Orphelins
Indigents," a School for Indigent Orphans opened in 1840. Mme.
Couvent, a free woman of color, died, leaving a fund in trust for the establishment and maintenance of this institution. It has been in continuous operation ever since. Later, it was aided by Aristide Mary, a well-to-
do Creole of color, who left $5,000 for its support, and by Thomy Lafon,
also a colored Creole, one of the noted benefactors of the city. Until
now, the instruction is in both English and French, and many children,
not orphans, are willing to pay a fee to obtain there the thorough education obtainable.[75]

In 1859 John F. Cook, afterwards of Washington, D.C., went to

74. Captain Frederick Marryat, *Diary in America*, 67–68.
75. Rodolphe Lucien Desdunes, *Nos Hommes et Notre Histoire*, 32.

New Orleans from St. Louis, Missouri, and organized a school for free children of color. This was just at the time when discontent among Southern States was rife, when there was much war-talk, and secession was imminent. Mr. Cook had violated two laws, he was an immigrant, and he opened a school for children of persons of color. He continued as a successful instructor for one year, at the expiration of which he was forced to leave, being warned by one John Parsons, a barber, who had been told by his white friends that Mr. Cook was to be arrested and detained.[76]

Mr. Trotter, in his "Music and Some Musical People," gives unwittingly a picture of the free people of color of this epoch in fortune and education. He quotes the *New Orleans Picayune* in its testimony to their superior taste for and appreciation of the drama, particularly Shakespeare, and their sympathetic recognition of the excellence of classical music. Grace King aptly says "even the old slaves, the most enthusiastic of theatre-goers, felt themselves authorized to laugh any modern theatrical pretension to scorn."[77] Trotter records a number of families whose musical talent has become world-wide. The Lambert family, one of whom was decorated by the King of Portugal, became a professor in Paris, and composer of the famous Si J'Etais Roi, L'Africaine, and La Somnambula.[78] In this same field Basile Barès also achieved unusual fame.

Natives of New Orleans remember now how some years ago Edmond Dédé came from Paris, whence he had been sent in 1857 by an appreciative townspeople to complete his musical education. He became director of the orchestra of L'Alcazar in Bordeaux, and a great friend of Gounod. When he returned to New Orleans after an absence of forty-six years to play for his native city once more, he was old, but not worn, nor bent, the fire of youth still flashed in his eye, and leaped along the bow of his violin.[79] One may mention a long list of famous musicians of color of the State, but our picture must be filled in rather with the broad sweep of the mass, not of the individual.

Across the cloudless sky of this era of unexampled commercial, artis-

76. This fact is based on the statements of the persons concerned.
77. King, *New Orleans, the Place and the People,* 272.
78. James Monroe Trotter, *Music, and Some Musical People,* 339–340.
79. Ibid., 340–341; Desdunes, *Nos Hommes et Notre Histoire,* 117–118.

tic and social sphere[80] the war cloud crept with ominous grimness. It burst and drenched the State with blood. Louisiana made ready to stand with the South. On the 23rd of November, 1861, there had been a grand review of the Confederate troops stationed in New Orleans. An associated press despatch announced that the line was seven miles long. The feature of the review, however, was one regiment composed of fourteen hundred free colored men. The state militia was reorganized entirely for whites but Governor Moore ordered the men of color into the army. Another grand review followed the next spring. The *New Orleans Picayune* made the following comment. "We must also pay a deserved compliment to the companies of free colored men, all very well drilled and comfortably uniformed. Most of these companies, quite unaided by the administration, have supplied themselves with arms without regard to cost or trouble."[81] On the same day, one of these colored companies was presented with a flag, and every evidence of public approbation was manifested.

These men of color in New Orleans were the only organized body of Negro soldiery on the Confederate side during the Civil War. They were accepted as part of the State militia forming three regiments and two batteries of artillery. In the report of the Select Commission on the New Orleans Riots, Charles W. Gibbons testified that when the war broke out, the Confederacy called on all free people to do something for the seceding States, and if they did not a committee was appointed to look after them, to rob, kill, and despoil their property. Gibbons himself was advised by a policeman to enlist on the Confederate side or be

80. The most definite picture, and the best possible of the state of the persons of color in Louisiana, is to be found in Parton's *Butler in New Orleans.* History will never agree about Gen. Butler. He is alternately execrated by the South, sneered at by the North, written down by his contemporary officers, and canonized by the abolitionists. If he did nothing else worthy of record, at least he gave the splendid militia composed of the free men of color a chance to prove their loyalty to the union by entering the Civil War as fighters.

We are indebted to him for the pictures he draws of the slave population of Louisiana; of the wealth and beauty of the free men and women of color. Their population was 18,647. "The best blood of the South flows in the veins of these free people of color," he writes, "and a great deal of it, for the darkest of some of them were about the complexion of Daniel Webster." Parton, *General Butler in New Orleans,* 517.

81. *New Orleans Picayune,* Feb. 9, 1862.

lynched. This accounts for the seeming disloyalty of these free men of color.[82] The first victories of the South made their leaders overconfident thereafter and the colored troops were dismissed.

When Unionists finally got control of New Orleans they found it a city of problems. Wherever there was a Union fort, slaves, the famous "contrabands of war," made their appearance, and in a few months General Butler, then in command, found himself face to face with one of the most serious situations ever known in the history of a State. Obviously, the only thing to do was to free all of the slaves, but with Gen. Hunter's experience in South Carolina to warn him, and with Lincoln's caution, Butler was forced to fight the problem alone. He did the best he could under the circumstances with this mass of black and helpless humanity. The whipping posts were abolished; the star cars—early Jim Crow street cars—were done away with. Those slaves who had been treated with extreme cruelty by their masters were emancipated, and by enforcing the laws of England and France, which provided that no citizen of either country should own slaves, many more were freed. But the problem increased, the camps filled with runaway slaves, the feeling grew more intense, and the situation more desperate every day. Gen. Butler asked repeatedly for aid and re-enforcement from the North. Vicksburg was growing stronger, Port Hudson above the city became a menace with its increasing Confederate batteries, and Mobile and a dozen camps near the city made the condition alarming. No help coming from the North, General Butler turned to the free men of color in the city for aid, and as usual, they responded gallantly to his appeal.

The free people of color in Louisiana then furnished the first colored contingent of the Federal Army, just as they had furnished the first colored contingent of the Confederate Army.[83] The army records likewise show that Louisiana furnished more colored troops for the war than any other State. By the 27th of September, 1862, a full regiment of free men of color entered the service of the government, many of them being taken over from the State militia. It was in the beginning called the First Regiment of the Louisiana Native Guards. In June, 1863, its designation was changed to the First Regiment Corps D'Afrique, and later to the

82. Report of the Select Committee on the New Orleans Riots, 126.
83. John Rose Ficklen, *Reconstruction in Louisiana*, 121.

73rd Regiment U.S.C. Infantry.[84] In October, 1862, another regiment of heavy artillery was organized. About the same time a fourth regiment of men of color answered the call. Gen. Butler was succeeded in Louisiana by General Banks, who was so pleased with the appearance and drill of the colored regiments, that he issued an order for the organization of more in 1863, contemplating 18 regiments, comprising infantry, artillery, and cavalry. These were entirely officered by colored men, at first, but, as Col. Lewis tersely puts it, after the battle of Port Hudson,[85] a

84. From Ex-Lieutenant Governor Antoine we have a statement as to how the troops were organized at Baton Rouge. Of the gallant officers of this first regiment, one man lives to tell of its glories. This was Col. James Lewis, who was in command for four months at Port Hudson.

85. The battle of Port Hudson, like the battle of New Orleans, is almost too well known to be told of. It takes its place naturally in history with desperate fights, reminding one somewhat of the battles of Balaklava. It was early in the morning of May 27, 1863, that the engagement began. The colored men in line numbered 1,080. When the order for assault was given they charged the fort, which belched forth its flame and shot and shell. The slaughter was horrible, but the line never wavered. Into the mill of death the colored troops hurled themselves. The colors were shot through and almost severed from the staff; the color-sergeant, Anselmas Planciancois, was killed, and two corporals struggled for the honor of bearing the flag from his dying hands. One of them was killed.

The bravest hero of the day was Capt. André Caillioux, whose name all Louisianians remember with a thrill of pride. He was a freeman of West Indian extraction, and fond of boasting of his blackness. With superb heroism and splendid magnetism he led his men time and again into the very "jaws of death" in the assault, and fell at the front in one last heroic effort within fifty yards of the fort.

> "Still forward and charge for the guns," said Caillioux,
> And his shattered sword-arm was the guidon they knew;
> But a fire rakes the flanks and a fire rakes the van,
> He is down with the ranks that go down as one man.

A correspondent of the *New York Times* gave a most glowing account of the battle. "During the time the troops rallied, they were ordered to make *six distinct charges*, losing 37 killed, 155 wounded, and sixteen missing. . . . The deeds of heroism performed by these colored men were such as the proudest white men might emulate. . . . I could fill your columns with startling tales of their heroism. Although repulsed in an attempt which, situated as things were, was almost impossible, these regiments, though badly cut up, are still on hand, and burning with a passion ten times hotter from their fierce baptism of blood." See Williams, *History of the Negro Race*, II, 321.

"steeple-chase was made by the white men to take our places."[86] These troops thereafter acquitted themselves with great honor in this battle and also at that of Milliken's Bend.

The Emancipation Proclamation of January, 1863, was a most complicated matter in Louisiana, for the reason that out of the forty-eight parishes in the State, thirteen were under federal control, and consequently the slaves there were left in their original state. Many of the masters even in those parishes where the slaves were declared emancipated sent their most valuable slaves to Alabama and Texas, some of them themselves fleeing with them. In parishes far removed from Union headquarters, news of the Emancipation Proclamation did not reach the slaves until long after it had been issued. Even then, in many cases, the proclamation had to be read at the point of sword, federal soldiers compelling the slave owners to tell their chattels the news.[87]

From the time of the accession of General Banks to 1876, the history of Louisiana becomes a turmoil of struggle, centering around the brother in black.[88] It is no longer romance; it is grim war, and the colored man is

---

The battle of Milliken's Bend will always rank as one of the hardest fought engagements in the Civil War. It was an important point on the river, because it commanded Vicksburg, and in General Grant's scheme to effect the reduction of that city, it was necessary to control this point. That engagement was on June 6, 1863, and continued from three in the morning until twelve noon. Never did men fight with greater courage against such odds at the point of bayonet than did these colored troops. The appalling list of casualties shows how they stood the test. Of the officers in the colored forces, seven were killed, nine wounded, three missing. Of the enlisted men, 123 killed, 182 wounded, 113 missing. In commenting on this battle, Schouler, in his history of the United States, speaks of the great bravery shown by the troops, and points out there was a sudden change of opinion in the South about enlisting colored troops on the side of the Confederacy. "Many of the clear-sighted leaders of this section proposed seriously to follow the Northern President's example—and arm Negro slaves as soldiers." He adds: "That strange conclusion, had it ever been reached, would perhaps have reunited North and South eventually in sentiment—by demonstrating at length the whole fallacy upon which the social difference of sections had so long rested. For as a Confederate writer expressed it, 'if the Negro was fit to be a soldier, he was not fit to be a slave.'" Schouler, *History of the U.S.*, VI, 407; and Williams, *History of the Negro Race*, II, 326–8.

86. Colonel Lewis' statement.
87. Based on the statements of slaves.
88. Rhodes, *History of the U.S.*, VII, 104 et seq.; Schouler, *History of the U.S.*, VI, 245 et seq.

the subject of the struggle, not the cause of it. Political parties in 1862 were many and various. The Free State party was in favor of abolishing slavery, but wanted representation based altogether on the white population. This was opposed by the Union Democrat party, which repudiated secession, but wished slavery continued or rather revived, believing that emancipation was only a war measure, and that after cessation of hostilities, slavery could be reestablished. But the plans of both parties fell to the ground.[89] The colored man became more and more of a political factor from day to day.

Cognomens here too proved to be another difficulty. Louisiana had two classes of colored men, freedmen and free men, a delicate, but carefully guarded distinction, the latter distinctly more aristocratic. In 1863, the free men of color held a meeting and appealed to Governor Shepley for permission to register and vote. In the address to him, they reviewed their services to the United States from the time of General Jackson through the Civil War, and stated that they were then paying taxes on over $9,000,000. Several petitions of this sort failed to move General Banks,[90] for he thought it unfeasible to draw the line between free men of color and the recently emancipated Negroes.

The war of Reconstruction in Louisiana was fairly well launched in the Constitutional Convention of 1864. The issue on which this body divided was what treatment should be accorded the freedmen. The two parties had much difficulty in reaching an agreement.[91] P. M. Tourne was sent to Washington to see President Lincoln. He had already suggested the ratification of the Emancipation Proclamation and the education of the colored youth.[92] In a letter congratulating the recently elected Governor Hahn on his election as the "first free-state governor of Louisiana" in 1864, Lincoln suggested suffrage for the more intelligent Negroes, and those who had served the country in the capacity of soldiers. This letter of Lincoln's, says Blaine, was the first proposition from any authen-

89. Ficklen, *Reconstruction in Louisiana*, 47 et seq.

90. Ibid., 64, 65.

91. In the meanwhile, Confederates had set up a capital at Shreveport, and their governor recommended Negro conscripts in the Confederate army. His reasoning was acute and clear: He said, "The Negro must play an important part in the war. He caused the fight, and he must have his portion of the burden to bear." See Ficklen, *Reconstruction in Louisiana*, 63.

92. Ibid.

tic source to endow the Negro with the right of suffrage.[93] In his last public utterance on April 11, 1865, Lincoln again touched the subject of suffrage in Louisiana, repeating that he held it better to extend to the more intelligent colored men the elective franchise, giving the recently emancipated a prize to work for in obtaining property and education.[94] The Convention tried in vain to declare what constituted a Negro, giving it up in disgust. It did abolish slavery in general; granted suffrage to those whites who were loyal to the government; and to colored men according to educational and property qualifications. In 1865, the Thirteenth Amendment was ratified and the body adjourned.

The culmination of the fight between the Democrat and the Radical was in the struggle over the adoption of the Fourteenth Amendment in July, 1866. An attempt was made to re-open the Constitutional Convention of 1864.[95] The delegates, who favored the reopening of the convention, formed in the streets of New Orleans, and proceeded to march to the famous Mechanics' Hall, the scene of almost every political riot in the history of the city. The paraders became involved in a brawl with the white spectators; the police were called in; and the colored members of the convention and their white sympathizers fled to the hall where they attempted to barricade themselves. A general fight ensued, and over two hundred were killed.[96] The effect of this riot was electrical, not only in Louisiana but in the North, where it was construed as a deliberate massacre, and an uprising against the United States Government by the unreconstructed Louisianians.[97]

Efforts were made to bring about changes satisfactory to all. In 1867, Sheridan, in charge of the department of Louisiana, dismissed the board of aldermen of New Orleans, on the ground that they impeded the work of reconstruction and kept the government of the city in a disorganized

93. James Gillespie Blaine, *Twenty Years of Congress*, II, 39, 40.

94. Lincoln, Address of, April 11, 1865.

95. 39 Cong. House of Representatives, No. 16.

96. Ficklen, *Reconstruction in Louisiana*, 146–79.

97. Not all Southern sympathizers saw menace in granting the Negro political privileges. Seeing it inevitable, General Beauregard wrote in 1867, "If the suffrage of the Negro is properly handled and directed, we shall defeat our adversaries with their own weapons. The Negro is Southern born. With education and property qualifications, he can be made to take in interest in the affairs of the South, and in its prosperity. He will side with the whites." Letter of Gen. Beauregard.

condition. He appointed a new board of aldermen, some of whom were men of color, and in the next month this council appointed four assistant recorders, three of whom were colored, and two colored city physicians. In this month, September, 1867, the first legal voting of the colored man under the United States Government was recorded, that being their voting for delegates to the Constitutional Convention of 1868.[98]

This body proved to be an assemblage of ardent fighters for the rights of the factions they represented. Pinckney Benton Stewart Pinchback proposed the adoption of the Civil Rights Bill, and the abolition of separate schools. In the convention was proposed the most stringent of all suffrage laws which would practically disfranchise many whites. Mr. Pinchback voted against this. He saved the day for the Republican party by opposing Wickliffe and other demagogues who wished to use the vote of the colored man by promising a majority of the offices to Negroes. Pinchback maintained that offices should be awarded with reference not to race, but to education and general ability.[99] In this he was fiercely opposed by many who were anxious for office, but not for the good of the State.[100]

Louisiana did not long delay in returning to the Union. On the same day on which she voted for the constitution which restored her to the Union, H. C. Warmoth was elected governor, and Oscar J. Dunn, a colored man, Lieutenant-Governor. Pinchback was then a State senator.[101]

98. With the year 1868 one of the most picturesque and splendid figures in the history of the state springs fully into the light. Pinckney Benton Stewart Pinchback had already made himself known by his efforts to recruit soldiers for the Louisiana Native Guards; by his stringent demands for the rights of the colored man on all occasions. He was the dashing young Lochinvar of the political struggle. He had made his first move in 1867 by organizing the Fourth Ward Republican Club, and had been appointed Inspector of Customs by Collector of Port Kellogg. In the Constitution of 1868 he took his definite role of a fighter to be feared, respected and followed—and for many a year afterwards, the history of Louisiana is written around his name. William J. Simmons, *Men of Mark*, 672.

99. Accounts of this appeared in the *Tribune*, the best, and almost the only influential organ of the Republican party in the state, the editor of which was Dr. Roudanez, a well-to-do man of color. It was not a financial success, though a powerful factor in the political arena. Dr. Roudanez said that he spent over $35,000 on the paper in the effort to keep up an honest organ. It was suspended in April, 1868, but was revived later.

100. Journal of the Convention, 124, 192, 205 et passim.

101. Simmons, *Men of Mark*, 678.

When the State legislature met in New Orleans in 1868, more than half of the members were colored men. Dunn was President of the Senate, and the temporary chairman of the lower house was R. H. Isabelle, a colored man. The first act of the new legislature was to ratify the Fourteenth Amendment.[102]

And then ensued another halcyon period for the colored man in Louisiana, a period about which the average historian has little but sneers. Government in Louisiana by the colored man was different from that in other Southern States. There the average man who was interested in politics had wealth and generations of education and culture back of him. He was actuated by sincerest patriotism, and while the more ignorant of the recently emancipated were too evidently under the control of the unscrupulous carpet-bagger, there were not wanting more conservative men to restrain them.

The period following the meeting of the State legislature in 1868 was a stirring one. The Louisiana free people of color had a larger share in their government than that class had in any other Southern State. Among their representatives were Lieut.-Governor Oscar J. Dunn, State Treasurer Antoine Dubuclet, State Superintendent of Education Wm. G. Brown, Division Superintendent of Education Gen. T. Morris Chester, a Pennsylvanian by birth, congressmen William Nash and J. Willis Menard, the first colored representative elected, although he was not seated. Col. Lewis became Sergeant of the Metropolitan Police, following his service as Collector of the Port. Upon the death of Dunn, C. C. Antoine, who had served his country as a captain in the famous Seventh Louisiana, and then in the State Senate, succeeded him. Antoine was Lieutenant-Governor for eight years, first under Governor Kellogg, and then re-elected to serve under Governor Packard.

But the most thrilling part of the whole period centers about the person of that redoubtable fighter, Pinchback. He was nominated for Governor, and to save his party accepted a compromise on the Kellogg ticket. In 1872 he ran the great railroad race with Governor Warmoth, being Lieutenant-Governor and Acting Governor in the absence of the Governor from the State. His object was to reach the capital and sign two acts of the legislature, which involved the control of the State and possibly the national government.[103] It was a desperate undertaking, and the story

102. Journal of the Senate, 1868, 21.
103. Pinchback's own statement.

of the race, as told by Governor Pinchback himself, reads like a romance. By a clever trick and the courage to stay up and fight in the senate all night, he saved the senate to the Republicans and perpetuated their rule four years longer in Louisiana than it would have continued.[104]

By the impeachment of Governor Warmoth in December, 1872, he became Acting Governor of the State until Jan., 1873, when the term expired and the Kellogg government was inaugurated, with C. C. Antoine, Lieutenant-Governor. That period when Pinchback was Governor of Louisiana was the stormiest ever witnessed in any state in the Union; but he was equal to the emergency. Then followed his long three years' fight for the seat in the United States Senate, with the defeat after the hard struggle.

The campaign of 1874 was inaugurated. The White Camelias, a league formed of Southern white men, determined to end the existing government, stood armed and ready. The Governor was garrisoned at the Custom-house, a huge citadel, and the fight was on between the White League and the Metropolitan Police. It was characteristic of this community that the fight should take place on Sunday. The struggle lasted all day, September 14, 1874, and by evening the citizens were in command of the situation. President Grant ordered troops to the place; the insurgents were ordered to disperse in five days, and the Governor resumed his office. But it was the end of the government by the men of color and their allies in the State. President Hayes, in order to conciliate his constituents in the South, withdrew federal support, and the downfall was complete.[105]

The history of the Reconstruction and the merits and demerits of the men who figured in that awful drama belong to the present generation. The unstable Reconstruction regime was overthrown in 1874 and the whites, eliminating the freedmen and free people of color from the government, established what they are pleased to call "home rule." The Negroes, who had served the State, however, deserved well of their constituents. It should be said to the credit of these black men that upon an investigation of the Treasurer's office which had for years been held by Antoine Dubuclet, a man of color, the committee of which Chief Justice Edward D. White of the United States Supreme Court was then chair-

104. Based on the statements of the persons participating in these affairs.
105. Rhodes, *History of the U.S.*, VII, 287.

man, made a report practically exonerating him. Although making some criticisms as to irregularities and minor illegalities, the committee had to report that "the Treasurer certainly by a comparison deserves commendation for having accounted for all moneys coming into his hands, being in this particular a remarkable exception." A minority report signed by C. W. Keeting and T. T. Allain[106] thoroughly exonerated him. The expected impeachment proceedings which were to follow this investigation did not materialize.[107]

106. Mr. T. T. Allain is now living in Chicago. He has much to say in praise of the efficient, honest and courageous men of color who administered the affairs of Louisiana during this period. Mr. Allain himself was a State Senator.

107. The report consisted of answers to the following questions:

1. What was the condition of the accounts of the Treasurer connected with the verification of the entries of such accounts as well as ascertaining by such verification whether the receipts had been correctly entered and disbursed, and the cash properly and legally applied.

2. What mode of settlement had been established by the Treasurer in receiving revenue turned in by tax collectors.

3. What discrimination, if any, had been exercised in the payment of warrants.

The report in part was:

"Beyond these matters your committee find the books of the Treasury to have been kept in an orderly manner; the disbursements have been regularly entered, and the cash presently all accounted for up to the first of January, 1877, to which period this report alone extends. These vouchers and orders are all on hand and the warrants for each payment are properly canceled. . . .

"These figures do not of necessity import proof absolute and conclusive of any undue favoritism, although by circumstances and legitimate inference they point to that conclusion. Warrants being negotiable it has been impossible to ascertain who held those outstanding, and therefore impossible to fix a proper proportion of payment, but the fact that the multitude of payments made to the same person, while other warrant holders were forced to wait, and the intimacy existing between themselves or their employees and the Treasurer are, undeniably, circumstances which, unexplained, justify at least a suspicion that these parties have enjoyed facilities, preferences and privileges at the Treasury over the general public, to which they were not entitled.

"It is true that these figures are explained by statements that the proportion paid the respective persons mentioned were only in proportion to the amount which the warrants held by them bore to the whole amount of outstanding warrants, but this explanation in itself merits notice and explanation, because of the fact that the persons named were the holders of such a large amount of warrants imply some inducement on their part to invest in them, more especially as by avocation the majority of them were not brokers but employees in the Custom-House. Some of

More about the people of color in Louisiana might be written. It is a theme too large to be treated save by a master hand. It is interwoven with the poetry, the romance, the glamour, the commercial prosperity, the financial ruin, the rise and fall of the State. It is hung about with garlands, like the garlands of the cemeteries on All Saints Day; it may be celebrated in song, or jeered at in charivaris. Some day, the proper historian will tell the story. There is no State in the Union, hardly any spot of like size on the globe, where the man of color has lived so intensely, made so much progress, been of such historical importance and yet about whom so comparatively little is known. His history is like the Mardi Gras of the city of New Orleans, beautiful and mysterious and wonderful, but with a serious thought underlying it all. May it be better known to the world some day.

---

them have testified that all the warrants they held were paid. Another has refused to disclose for whom he collected. A third was a relative of a personal employee of the Treasurer. One has been shown to be a constant frequenter of his office, and must have been an intimate of the Treasurer's from the fact that he appears to have been the payee of a check for $75,000 illegally drawn, as mentioned before. They point, at least, to the necessity of such legislation as may be adequate to prevent even possible suspicion of favoritism in the future. Under the provisions of the acts of the General Assembly, passed at the session of 1877, the danger of favoritism has been very much safeguarded and needs supplementing in only minor particulars.

"The Treasurer certainly by comparison deserves commendation for having accounted for all moneys coming into his hands, being in this particular a remarkable exception. EDWARD D. WHITE, JAMES D. HULL, SAM H. BUCK." Report of Joint Committee to Investigate the Treasurer's Office, State of Louisiana, to the General Assembly, 1877, 7–12, Majority Report.

2

Marcus Christian's Treatment of *Les Gens de Couleur Libre*

Violet Harrington Bryan

In 1936 Lyle Saxon asked Marcus Christian (1900–1976), reporter for the *Louisiana Weekly* (a black New Orleans newspaper in existence from 1925 to the present), poet, and owner of a small dry-cleaning business, to participate in "a Negro unit" of the Federal Writers' Project. The unit would be housed at Dillard University and would "collect Negro material for a history of the Negro in Louisiana."[1] Christian accepted the offer.

When Saxon met Christian, the latter was poetry and contributing editor for the *Weekly* and had published poems in that paper as well as two other New Orleans papers (the *Daily States* and the *Item-Tribune*) and such national journals as *Phylon*, the *Crisis*, *Opportunity*, the *New York Herald-Tribune*, the *Pittsburgh Courier*, and the *Baltimore Afro-American*.

---

1. "Biographical Material," The Marcus B. Christian Collection, The Archives and Manuscripts Department of the Earl K. Long Library of the University of New Orleans. All of the unpublished manuscripts, source material, correspondence, and creative writing of Marcus Christian are found in this collection. For further information, see Violet Harrington Bryan, *The Myth of New Orleans in Literature: Dialogues of Face and Gender* (Knoxville: University of Tennessee Press, 1993).

Mel Washburn, *Item-Tribune* columnist, had labeled him "the poet laureate of New Orleans Negroes."[2]

Christian was born in Mechanicsville (now Houma), Louisiana, where his father and grandfather had both been teachers. As he noted on the book jacket of his poem *High Ground* (1958), his father "taught all his children the art of writing poetry" and read poetry to them in original French. "One of the earliest remembrances I have of my father," wrote Christian, "is of being perched upon one knee and my little twin-sister on the other, while he read French poetry to us amid screams of childish laughter."[3] His father died when he was thirteen, and Christian went to work in cane fields for fifty to seventy-five cents a day; he later got a job as a yard boy and general handyman in the town nearby, where he received five dollars a month and board. At seventeen (in 1920) Christian took a train to New Orleans, where he proceeded to develop a cleaning business and a printing press, which were both housed in his shotgun home. He continued his education in night school.

During the WPA years and later, Christian edited a book of poetry, *From the Deep South* (1937), and contributed to *The Negro Caravan*, edited by Sterling Brown (1941), and *The Poetry of the Negro*, edited by Arna Bontemps (1949). He wrote the long poems *In Memoriam—Franklin Delano Roosevelt* (1945) and *Common People's Manifesto of World War II* (1948), the history *Negro Soldiers in the Battle of New Orleans* (1955), the collection of poetry *High Ground* (1958), the long Whitmanesque poem *I Am New Orleans* (1968), and the history *Negro Ironworkers in Louisiana, 1718– 1900* (1972). When he died on March 21, 1976, he left numerous unpublished poems (1,175 in the Marcus Christian Collection, University of New Orleans) and pieces of fiction and nonfiction as well as voluminous notes and diaries.[4]

The Dillard unit of the Louisiana Writers' Project included many of the region's major African American intellectuals of the 1930s, 1940s, and 1950s. Lawrence D. Reddick, professor of history at Dillard Univer-

2. "Biographical Material," Marcus B. Christian Collection. See also Joseph Logsdon, "Marcus Bruce Christian," in *A Dictionary of Louisiana Biography*, ed. Glenn R. Conrad (New Orleans: Louisiana Historical Association, 1988), 1:1778–9.

3. "Biographical Material," Marcus B. Christian Collection.

4. Ibid.

sity, became the first director of the project, but was soon succeeded by Christian. The original members of the group were Reddick, director, Christian, Clarence A. Laws, Octave Lilly Jr., Eugene B. Willman, Alice Ward-Smith, and James La Fourche. Under Christian's directorship the membership changed; added to Lilly and Reddick, who remained members, were Horace Mann Bond, Elizabeth Catlett, St. Clair Drake, Arna Bontemps, Rudolphe Moses, and Benjamin Quarles. Margaret Walker passed through and met Langston Hughes in New Orleans before taking a job with the Chicago Federal Writers' Project. In addition to Reddick, Frank Yerby and Randolph Edmonds were also professors at Dillard during the years of the WPA. In fact, Christian was certain that the core of Yerby's novel *The Foxes of Harrow* (1946) was from his own notes for a plantation novel.[5] The project group compiled "A Black History of Louisiana" between 1936 and 1943, but the manuscript was never completely edited and published in book form; today it is a part of the Marcus Christian Collection in the archives of the University of New Orleans.

Most of the original research that Christian and the other members of the Dillard unit collected remained unpublished except in the case of other writers' use of it as source material, acknowledged or unacknowledged. The group made use of local archives, university and public libraries, the Louisiana State Museum, and newspapers (including the Creole newspapers published during Reconstruction). They also referred to histories of Louisiana, particularly those by Gayarré, Martin, Grace King, and Lyle Saxon, and studies of blacks and race in the United States.[6]

In "A Black History of Louisiana," Christian was primarily interested in the history of African Americans in New Orleans and surrounding parishes. As in all of his historical works, the focus was on origins; Christian felt that to understand black Louisianians, it was of paramount importance to know something of the African background of the slaves

5. Diary, Notes, Business Cards, Box 1, September 1, 1948, Marcus B. Christian Collection. See my *Myths of New Orleans in Literature* for a discussion of Christian's ideas about practices of exclusion by the Federal Writers' Project leadership.

6. The historians consulted were François St. Xavier Martin, *History of Louisiana* (1827; Gretna, La.: Pelican, 1975), Charles Gayarré, *History of Louisiana*, 4 volumes (1854–66), Grace King, *New Orleans: The Place and the People* (1892), and Lyle Saxon, *Lafitte the Pirate* (New York: Century, 1930).

brought to the area. Thus the first chapters refer frequently to African traditions in religion, art, trades, and occupations such as blacksmithing, gold artificing, wood-carving, and other skilled crafts. In order to paint a clearer picture of slavery than had been created by most popular historians, Christian also researched the insurrections and attempted insurrections that slaves in Louisiana planned and carried out in the eighteenth and nineteenth centuries.

Christian's discussion of free people of color is an important part of his overall study of blacks in Louisiana, which included both slave and free and people of all colors and religions. In the introduction to "A Black History," he writes:

> This work is mainly interested in a recital of facts gleaned from available sources and poses no questions and offers no arguments. It is enough to say that Louisiana has produced such inventors as the Rillieux brothers, the most famous being Norbert Rillieux, who invented the vacuum pan and thereby revolutionized the sugar-making industry. It is possible to say that Louisiana almost pioneered in the matter of Negro religious education and that the first anthology of American Negro poetry was published in this State. . . . A free colored class . . . gave to the world such a musician as Edmond Dédé, sculptors and stone engravers such as the Warburg brothers, and such a dramatist as Victor Séjour.[7]

Christian's research on the free people of color *(les gens de couleur libre)* has been collected under several divisions of his work. Most prominent is probably chapter 18 of "A Black History," which he titled "The Free Colored Class of Louisiana"; also in that historical manuscript are chapter 9, "The Creole Dialect," chapter 10, "Folklore of French- and English-Speaking Negroes of Louisiana," chapter 11, "Voodooism and Mumbo-Jumbo," chapter 22, "Negro Periodicals, Literature and Art in Louisiana," chapter 23, "Negro Painters, Sculptors, Architects and Craftsmen," chapter 24, "The Negro and the Theater," and chapter 42, "Carnival Groups and Social, Aid, and Pleasure Clubs." Christian also did research labeled "Genealogy," which he considered "a study of the

7. Manuscript for "A Black History of Louisiana," Boxes 35 and 36, Literary and Historical Manuscripts. Rillieux, Dédé, and Séjour are treated in detail in Michel Fabre's essay in the present volume, while Mary Gehman sketches the career of the Warburg brothers.

amalgamation which has already taken place between the races" since colonial days, citing a select number of Creole families as examples, and of
"certain factors which may discourage or encourage it in the future."[8] In
other studies he examined "Artists and Art Forms" and some well-known
Creole families and persons, such as the Metoyers and Marie Laveau.
The present paper will focus primarily on Christian's research findings
and narrative collected in chapter 18 of "A Black History of Louisiana"
and in "Genealogy."

In chapter 18, "The Free Colored Class of Louisiana," Christian treats
the history of free people of color in the Louisiana colony from its founding to the years immediately preceding the Civil War. According to
Christian's research, less than five years after Antoine Crozat relin-
quished his 1712 charter to the crown in 1717 and the Company of the
West had formed, there were free Negroes in Louisiana. As evidence of
the presence of free people of color, Christian notes a court case of September 13, 1722, which was one of several omitted from earlier records
but listed in the *Louisiana Historical Quarterly*. The case resulted in "Conviction and Sentence of Flogging and Incarceration during six years of a
free negro, Lacroze, for theft committed in the Company's stores."[9]

   Other early legal proceedings, of which Christian discovered records
in the Louisiana State Museum, were the suit of Raphael Bernard, a free
Negro, against Paulin Cadot, a white man, in 1724, and the case of Jean
Mingo (from the Carolinas), who purchased his wife "on the instalment
[*sic*] plan." Mingo was one of many free Negroes who bought women
slaves that they married and later manumitted.[10]

   Grants of freedom were also gained by male slaves due to military
duty, for example, in the Natchez revolt and massacre of 1729. The conflicts between the French settlers of the Natchez settlement of the Louisiana colony, which ended in the massacre of about half of the settlers,
had been the result of a conspiracy between the Natchez and African
slaves. Some of the Africans, however, were loyal to the French and

   8. "Genealogy," Boxes 13 and 14, "Preface," Box 14, Literary and Historical
Manuscripts.
   9. Chapter 18, "The Free Colored Class of Louisiana," in "Black History of
Louisiana," 2; *Louisiana Historical Quarterly* 7 (1924): 678.
   10. "Free Colored Class of Louisiana," 2–3.

fought with the French and the Choctaw who recaptured the settlement in 1730. Christian notes the story of Diocou, or Tiocou, who won his freedom through fighting against the Natchez on the side of the French and then worked for his wife's freedom by serving at Charity Hospital for seven years.[11]

Trades or skills learned by African slaves enhanced their value and also gave them a chance to make extra pay, sometimes enough to buy their freedom. Ex-slaves who purchased their freedom and who knew trades often taught those trades to their children. In the early days of the colony, the manumissions of slaves accounted for "a considerable portion" of the free people of color. For example, Marie and Jorge, a Negro couple, were manumitted by Bienville, "the Father of New Orleans." "For a slave to buy his freedom during the Spanish administration of Louisiana (1766–1803) seems to have been a very simple affair— provided he had the price of purchase," notes Christian. Under Spanish rule, there was a more tolerant view of race in Louisiana. "When there was only a sixth of Negro or Indian blood in the veins of a colonist, he was granted the title of white: *que se tenga por blanco.*" White Louisianians even accused Don Antonio de Ulloa, the first Spanish governor of Louisiana, of favoring Creoles of color over whites. Christian refers to Charles Gayarré's discussion of the Louisiana Superior Council's expulsion of Ulloa in 1766 after a very brief tenure in office. The council noted that Ulloa had forbidden slaves to be whipped in New Orleans, had condoned the marriage of a white man and a black woman, and had threatened the subjects of France (specifically, the Acadians) with slavery, "whilst negroes were raised by degrees to the dignity of freemen."[12]

Christian claims that by 1788 there were 1,701 free people of color in New Orleans. According to Kimberly S. Hanger, however, the population of free persons of color in New Orleans was given as 820 in the 1788 Census, along with 2,131 slaves and 2,370 whites. In that year Governor Miró tried to lessen the popularity of the free people of color in several ways. He enforced the requirement that free women of color wear

11. For a brief but detailed summary of the Natchez revolt, see Gwendolyn Midlo Hall, *Africans in Colonial Louisiana: The Development of Afro-Creole Culture in the Eighteenth Century* (Baton Rouge: Louisiana State University Press, 1995), 100–6.

12. "Free Colored Class of Louisiana," 4, 5; "Genealogy," 144; Charles Gayarré, *History of Louisiana*, 3rd ed. (New Orleans, 1885), 2: 219–20, 222.

a *tignon* and forbade them to wear any plumes or jewelry in their hair.
They were also forbidden to go out at night without a lantern or to meet
in assemblages at night. He decreed that there would be severe punishment accorded to any free person of color living in "concubinage." According to Lyle Saxon in *Lafitte the Pirate*, Miró's actions were probably
instigated by the white women of the community who had grown jealous
of these "daughters of joy."[13]

Governor Miró's edict was probably in force only in New Orleans,
notes Christian, for there had been a marriage ceremony performed at
Natchez between a quadroon woman and a white man—Mary Glass and
John Glass—who later lived in Pointe Coupée. This marriage was made
public when Mary Glass was arrested and executed for the murder of
Maria Emeline, a white girl of fifteen, who had been her indentured servant. Christian estimated that the court case took place around 1762.[14]

The practice of interracial sexual relationships and marriage in New Orleans accounted also for the growth of the class of free people of color.
Christian addressed the dilemma and prevalence of interracial relationships at various times throughout his historical manuscripts and even in
his poetry. For example, two of the divisions under which he grouped his
poems for a proposed volume were "For Colored Girls Only" and "For
White Girls Only." In discussing the interracial relationships of early
Louisiana, Christian explained: "According to testimony introduced in
several court cases of miscegenation between white men and free colored
and slave women, a few of these interracial unions had the sanction of
the Catholic clergy. Even in instances where sanction was not sought for
such unions, some masters assumed full responsibility for their free colored children and legitimated them, thus making them eligible for inheritances where there were no forced heirs. The free colored population
steadily increased in numbers, wealth, and influence because of these 'unequal marriages.' "[15]

The leaving of property to the free children, who were often the

13. Kimberly S. Hanger, "Avenues to Freedom Open to New Orleans' Black
Population, 1769–1779," *Louisiana History* 31 (1990): 239; Saxon, *Lafitte the
Pirate*, 56.

14. "Genealogy," 150–1. Christian credits this information to the *Louisiana
Historical Quarterly* 2 (4): 589, but I did not find the case recorded in that issue.

15. "Free Colored Class of Louisiana," 8.

products of these unions, by their white fathers was a tradition that one can observe in court records. This type of inheritance often raised difficulties, as was evidently true in the case of Eugène and Augustin Macarty. When Eugène Macarty died, he left property worth $12,000. The free colored woman he had lived with from 1796 (forty-nine years) was a descendant of one of the most distinguished white families in Louisiana—the Marigny de Mandevilles. This "Mrs. Macarty" also made a significant amount of money in her dry-goods business. Her estate was worth $155,000 in 1848. The Macartys had five children, three boys and two girls. White relatives tried later to disinherit the woman, but the judge decided in her favor. In the subsequent case of Augustin Macarty, his love affairs were in "such a chaotic state" that there were several heirs of different free colored mothers.[16]

Virginia Meacham Gould has pointed out that many free women of color, like Mrs. Macarty, became heirs at their white partners' deaths and obtained significant property. She mentions the case of Louison Chastang, whose cohabitant for thirty years, Jean Chastang of Mobile, left her and the ten children of their union all of his real estate and dwellings on one side of the Mobile River, a lot in Mobile, four slaves, and other provisions. According to Gould, "Louison Chastang was only one of the many propertied, influential free women of color in the Gulf ports who found at least a part of their identities through their white cohabitants and/or white fathers and their other ties to the white community."[17]

Sometimes the romantic relationships between slave women and white masters led to their manumission and that of their children. Christian notes the court cases *Mari v. Acart, Lopez's Heirs v. Mary Berge, Heirs of Grubb v. Henderson,* and *Adams v. Routh.* Of course, the decision to manumit or not depended on the personality and financial situation of the slaveholder involved.

In some cases, the romantic relationships led to marriage. "During the entire period between the founding of the Louisiana Territory, and the beginning of the Civil War, there was occasional marriage between

16. *Macarty et al. v. Mandeville,* 3; *Louisiana Annals* (March 1848): 239–45; "Free Colored Class of Louisiana," 10.

17. Virginia Meacham Gould, " 'A Chaos of Iniquity and Discord': Slave and Free Women of Color in the Spanish Ports of New Orleans, Mobile, and Pensacola," in *The Devil's Lane: Sex and Race in the Early South,* ed. Catherine Clinton and Michele Gillespie (New York: Oxford University Press, 1997), 243.

persons of color and whites, and there was also much marriage by whites, free persons of color, and Negroes, with the Indians, according to their tribal customs of marriage." According to Christian, white persons who married persons of color were sometimes aware of their spouses' racial makeup, and sometimes they were not. But court records assure us that many such marriages occurred. "It was probably difficult in many communities, where there were many Indians, to adhere to any straight line of demarcation in free persons of color, Indians, mustees, and mulattoes."[18]

Many of the foreign travelers who came to New Orleans during the period wrote about such practices between these racial groups, especially the fascinating tradition of the quadroon balls. Christian refers to the comments of Bernard, Duke of Saxe-Weimar Eisenbach, Harriet Martineau, and G. W. Featherstonbaugh. Saxe-Weimar described the quadroons as "almost entirely white." Too proud to mix with the free Negro and slave elements and unable to marry white men legally, "the only course left to them was to become 'friends . . . of the white men.' " Harriet Martineau remarked that quadroons were selected by white men and established in "one of the pretty houses in the Ramparts." And according to Featherstonbaugh,

> The quadroon balls are places to which these young creatures are taken as soon as they have reached womanhood, and there they show their accomplishments in dancing and conversation to the white men, who alone frequent these places. When one of them attracts the attention of an admirer, and he is desirous of forming a liaison with her, he makes a bargain with the mother, agrees to pay her a sum of money, perhaps 2000 dollars, or some sum in proportion to her merits, as a fund upon which she may retire when the liaison terminates. She is now "*une placée.*"[19]

18. "Genealogy," 172a. Christian refers to Reuter, *The Mulatto in the United States*, 39, and also lists the following recorded court cases of intermarriage: *Succession of Minvielle*, La. Ann. 342 (May 1860): 15; *Domec v. Barjac, ex. and Cora Lallande*, La. Ann. 1: 342; *Dupre v. Boulard's Execution*, La. Ann. 10: 411; and *Succession of Mingo*, La. Reports, 143: 143; and *Southern Reporter*, 78: 565. *Mustee* was a term used to designate a biracial person of white (particularly Spanish) and Native American parentage. See "Free Colored Class of Louisiana," 7.

19. "Free Colored Class of Louisiana," 14–7. Christian quotes from Frederic Law Olmsted, *A Journey in the Seaboard Slave States* (New York: Dix and Edwards, 1856), Harriet Martineau, *Society in America* (Paris: A&W Galignani, 1837), and

Christian himself seems to have been just as intrigued with the balls, which were held by the quadroon mothers, as most contemporary observers. He marks the 1790s as the beginning of the balls, and explains that at that time, "the *placer* arrangements reached the status of *quasi-legal marriage*. The women of mixed-blood did not work, but their white 'protectors' kept them from labor, and gave them slaves to do their work for them."[20]

Two balls were often in operation at the same time— a quadroon ball and a white Creole ball. In the early days the quadroon balls were held at the Theatre St. Philippe, and the mothers of the girls would sit around the walls of the theater. The price of admission was higher than admission to the white Creole balls, says Christian. The young quadroon ladies were always under the eyes of their mothers; gracefully dressed, they conducted themselves with propriety and modesty. In Christian's words:

> After cautionings and advice to the free colored girl from her older female connections, the romance proceeded to ripen into a state of intimacy. Whether his payment of money to the parent were done in the manner of a marriage settlement by the white man, or whether it was merely a minor sum of money by which he gained the respect of the mother who guarded the inner sanctum of his lady's heart, is not known, although many writers speak of it as having been a specific contract. . . . Wishing to be near his love, he either casually moved into her home under the pretext of renting a room, or else, he moved her into a home of their own and proceeded to rear a family and live the life of a married man. It is more probable that he remained in the girl's home as a 'roomer' until the girl's relatives became sure of his affections, and then they went housekeeping for themselves.[21]

The phenomenon of Creole mothers encouraging their daughters to accept relationships with white men who would care for them financially, have relations with them, and then perhaps leave them in order to marry white women was a mystery Christian tried to decipher.

The Globe, on the corner of St. Peter and St. Claude Streets, the Washington, and the Louisiana ballrooms were homes of the quadroon balls, with each devoting one night a week to the masquerade affairs.

G. W. Featherstonbaugh, *Excursion Through the Slave States* (New York: Harper and Brothers, 1841).

20. "Genealogy," 148.

21. Ibid., 164–5.

Each had a restaurant, a bar, and a policeman. In Christian's day, the place most noted for its quadroon balls had become a convent of the Sisters of the Holy Family at 717 Orleans Street.[22]

The era of the quadroon balls is generally considered to be between 1780 and the 1850s. Christian notes that most of the city ordinances aimed at limiting the balls were passed between 1812 and 1857. Nevertheless, traditions such as the quadroon balls and interracial sexual relationships continued to have their effect on how the caste or status of free men and women of color was determined in Louisiana society. For example, when the state legislature in 1806 enacted a law prohibiting free men of color from entering the territory, the same was not true of free women of color. As a result of such gender distinctions, "According to the tax records of the Eighth District of 1858, the free women of color owned nearly twice as much property values as did the free men of color."[23]

Christian's interest in the wealth and culture of the free people of color led him to do much research into the kinds of trades and professions they held, especially during the heyday of their activity. He notes that following the Battle of New Orleans during the War of 1812, the free colored class reached its most powerful period as a distinct class. According to the U.S. Census, there were 16,710 free persons of color in Louisiana in 1830. By 1840, that number had increased to 25,502. "Never again in the years prior to the Civil War did the free people of color reach such numbers."[24]

The free people of color became so powerful that in 1833 the Citizens Bank of New Orleans passed a resolution forbidding free men of color to hold stock thereafter in the corporation. White directors later sought to oust the free people of color who owned stock in the bank, and two free men of color, Boisdoré and Goulé, brought action against them in the Supreme Court of Louisiana and were sustained in their action (*Boisdoré and Goulé [free persons of color] v. Bank*). In 1836 in New Orleans, 855 free persons of color owned property assessed at $2,462,470 as well as 620 slaves. In 1860, the group's property was worth between

22. "Free Colored Class of Louisiana," 17; "Genealogy," 18.
23. "Genealogy," 169, 152.
24. "Free Colored Class of Louisiana," 20.

$13,000,000 and $15,000,000. Free colored planters owned property in land and slaves worth between $25,000 and $150,000.[25]

The New Orleans City Directory of 1860, when there were 10,000 free persons of color in the city, lists the many tradesmen, mechanics, and professionals in the free colored class. The occupations most often noted were barber, bricklayer, mason, carpenter, cigar maker, drayman, rooming-house owner, plasterer, painter, shoemaker, seamstress, tailor, blacksmith, cooper, cook, and butcher. Among the places of business listed were the tailoring establishment of the Dumas brothers on Chartres Street; the retail shoes and undertaking establishment of Pierre Casenave on Toulouse Street; the blacksmith shop of Charles Moore on Ursulines; the butcher shop of Charles and Louis Porée on Felicity; the carpentry shops of Paul Porée on Gravier and L. D. Doliol on Hospital; the grocery of Marie Doliol on Urquhart; and the cigar maker's shop of F. C. Boissiere on Marais.[26]

Nevertheless, as American influence in the city of New Orleans grew and the wealth of free people of color increased, the state legislature passed a number of laws designed to curb their prosperity, and hostility mounted toward them. In the legislature's inaugural session, in 1806–1807, free men of color were prohibited from entering the territory from other states (Act of June 7, 1806). Christian comments, "This drastic law against the free people of the city was passed because of the fear which followed the overthrow of white rule in San Domingo." Other prohibitions included Section 13 of the marriage laws of that first session, which decreed: "Free persons and slaves are incapable of contracting marriage together." Slaves and Indians were permitted to give testimony against free negroes, mulattoes, or mustees. Free persons of color were not permitted to insult or strike white people or presume themselves equal to

25. Ibid., 22–24. On the wealth of free people of color, Christian consulted—among others—Alfred Holt Stone, "The Negro in the South," in *The South in the Building of the Nation*, vol. 10 (Richmond, Va.: Southern Historical Publication Society, 1909).

26. "Genealogy," 89–100. Later in the present volume, Lester Sullivan points out that Christian—who, along with the rest of the WPA writers, was often fed wrong information—misidentified mixed Creole Eugène Macarty *fils* (a son of Macarty *père* and Eulalie de Mandeville) as the accomplished musician and composer Victor-Eugène Macarty.

them. In 1806 free people of color could still hold white indentured servants, or "Redemptioners," but on March 20, 1818, the legislature enacted a law declaring that thereafter only free white persons could make contracts with white Redemptioners in return for their passage to America.[27]

Around 1825 there began to be increasing abolitionist sentiment, which fueled the persecution of the free colored population. "The planters regarded such persons with hatred and distrust, as they were direct refutations that the Negro could not survive out of slavery. They were also considered bad examples to the slaves who longed for freedom." But, as Christian also noted: "It was curious that persons of color should have been the main ones to suffer most at this period since they had but little share in creating the anti-slavery feeling. This was especially true of the free colored owners of slaves who, with the abolition of slavery, would suffer as much as the dominant whites. The majority of them, through blood relationship and property interests, were a part of the dominant white group."[28]

The most stringent laws against the free persons of color were probably those enacted in 1830, as a result of increasing fears in southern states of slave insurrections. On March 16, 1830 the legislature passed "An Act to Prevent Free Persons of Color from Entering into the State and for Other Purposes." Free persons of color were no longer permitted to enter the state, and if they had entered after 1825, they were ordered to leave within sixty days. Those who had entered between 1812 and 1825 were not expelled, but had to register their names with the judge of their parish. These laws were modified in 1831, when expulsion was reserved for undesirable free persons of color. On March 16, 1830, the legislature made it a criminal offense to publish, write, or print anything that might produce discontent within the colored population. A conviction for this offense brought life imprisonment or capital punishment.[29]

There was a sharp decline in free persons of color in Louisiana during these years. Referring to the book *Negro Population 1790–1915*, Christian notes that the number of free people of color in the state dropped from 25,502 to 17,462 between 1840 and 1850. He adds, "De-

27. "Free Colored Class of Louisiana," 33.
28. Ibid., 36–7.
29. Ibid., 37–8.

spite the fact that the free people of color were able to cite excellent examples of public service, proscriptions against them increased. In 1859, the Louisiana Legislature passed a law directing 'free persons of African descent to choose their own masters and become slaves for life.' "[30]

The story of free people of color in Louisiana is a dramatic one of increasing population, accomplishments, and prosperity, and then of drastic decline, especially in terms of population and wealth, owing to the accumulation of legislative acts based on the fears of the white population. The greatest fear was probably that of slave insurrection (later abolition), and the help that a well-educated and financially able free Negro class could offer to the enslaved. Marcus Christian's abiding interest in the history and culture of black Louisiana predated and postdated the writing of his "Black History of Louisiana" during the WPA movement of the 1930s. He attempted to complete the manuscript with a Rosenwald Fund in the 1940s and get it published but was not able to do so. Nevertheless, he continued to research, take notes, and write. His interest in the free people of color was a part of his overall interest in the contributions of African Americans to Louisiana's culture and history.

Christian's documentation shows that the history of free people of color began virtually at the beginning of the Louisiana colony in 1718. And as the colony grew, the population of free people of color also grew, due to intermarriage, interracial sexual relations, and manumission, particularly to military duty, and self-purchase and the purchase of spouses. The skills that Africans acquired or brought to Louisiana from Africa as gold artificers, wood-carvers, blacksmiths, carpenters, and other trades provided them with the extra money that they needed to purchase their freedom. His research shows the kinds of lawsuits that involved free people of color in terms of financial transactions, inheritances, and marriages.

With the approach of the Civil War in the late 1850s, restrictions on free people of color increased tremendously and many of them left

---

30. Ibid., 41. Christian refers to the book *Negro Population 1790–1915*, 57. See also Martin, *The History of Louisiana*, 456. As Martin notes: " 'Quaint and curious' reading, in the light of these after years, is the act of the legislature of 1859, permitting 'free persons of African descent to choose their own masters and become slaves for life.' " In point of fact the law did *permit*, not *direct*, free persons of color to take this action.

Louisiana for less oppressive regions, where some of them "passed" for white and others continued their culture in new settings. During Reconstruction free people of color fought gallant political battles, making use of Creole newspapers—such as the *Tribune*, *L'Union*, the *Crusader*, the *New Orleans Republican*, and the *Daily Crusader*—and political organizations, such as the *Comité des Citoyens*, in an attempt to maintain their civil rights. However, "between 1888 and 1895, the last of the state's Negro office-holders were discontinued in office. . . . White secret organizations for the political control of the South, such as the Knights of the White Camellia, the Ku Klux Klan, the White Liners, the Night Riders, and others, spread wide wholesale terror and anxiety."[31]

Christian ends his discussion of the free people of color in Louisiana as a separate class with the account of Reconstruction, although the history of the wide span of "Black Louisiana" continues.

31. "Genealogy," 135. See the file "The Creoles of Louisiana during Reconstruction: Mixed-Bloods in Local and State Politics," as well as Rodolphe Desdunes, *Nos hommes et notre histoire* (Montreal: Arbour et Dupont, 1911), published later as *Our People and Our History*, trans. Sister Dorothea McCants (Baton Rouge: Louisiana State University Press, 1973).

3

Plaçage and the Louisiana *Gens de Couleur Libre*

How Race and Sex Defined the Lifestyles of Free Women of Color

Joan M. Martin

Sexual relations among European settlers, African slaves, and native Americans during the period of French rule in Louisiana (1718–1768) resulted in the creation of a third race of people neither white nor black and neither slave nor completely free. These are the *gens de couleur libre*, or free people of color. The history of this group, and that of their women in particular, is both flamboyant and controversial.

Stories about the grace, charm, and legendary beauty of these women—identified collectively in the popular imagination as "quadroons"—abound. For centuries the term *quadroon* (meaning one-quarter Negro blood) has been nearly synonymous with "seductress." This idea is based primarily on the fact that the very existence of the quadroons is bound up with the notion of illicit sex and forbidden love. Whether the sex was consensual, forced, or something in between, its end results were the same: the establishment of a new race of people with ties to both blacks and whites, itself more privileged than the one but less esteemed than the other.

One cannot discuss the free people of color or the quadroons without simultaneously considering *plaçage*, the system that brought them into being. *Plaçage* was the practice that existed in Louisiana (and other

French and Spanish slaveholding territories) whereby women of color—
the option of legal marriage denied them—entered into long-standing,
formalized relationships with white European men. This practice was so
common that laws were written in an effort to prevent it. The laws had
no impact, nor did the futile public indignation. The controversy began
with the inception of *plaçage* in the colony, and rages even today. The
present essay will consider to what degree the sexual relations were
forced, why the women in some cases willingly chose to live with white
men over their own kind, and why those who were members of this elite
group (male and female) seemed to be granted privileges nearly always
denied their darker brothers.

For expediency's sake, the term "quadroon" will be used interchangeably with "free people of color," and/or "Creoles of color," but
these terms must first be clarified. Because the people were mixed, they
came in a range of colors. They were identified as mulattos, mestizos,
quadroons, octoroons, and other terms, all of which were used by the
colonists to define the varying degrees of Negro blood in the nonwhite
population. It would be erroneous, though, to assume that all the *gens de
couleur libre* were quadroons or even fair-skinned, although many were;
there were many who were dark as well. Gwendolyn Midlo Hall's findings show that most of the free Negroes in the French colonial period
were African-born. They were probably members of the African people
known as the Wolof, called Senegal in Louisiana, and they, she argues,
are the persons chiefly responsible for formulating and transmitting Louisiana culture because they were the first women to arrive in the colony.
She claims that these dark-skinned, elegant Senegalese women "largely
reared the first generation of Louisiana Creoles of all statuses and racial
designations." In fact, according to Donald Everett, a mulatto-led free
colored society was not immediately established in New Orleans, but "as
miscegenation increased, mulattos gradually assumed a more dominant
role . . . and the degree of white blood in one's veins became an increasingly important factor." It also created a permanent and nearly impene-
trable barrier that lasts to this day in the relationship between Louisiana's
mixed-race and dark-skinned blacks.

The term "Creole" has also generated its share of confusion and
controversy, but most scholars agree that historically the term was used
to describe *all* people native to Louisiana. Historian James Dormon explains:

The precise definition of the term "Creole" has been the source of un-
ending controversy in Louisiana studies. My own working definition
. . . holds the realities of historical usage; i.e., "creole" meant simply
"native to Louisiana" during the period between circa 1720 and the
outbreak of the Civil War. As such, blacks (both slave and free) as well
as free persons of color and indeed white Europeans were all designated
"Creoles" if they were born in Louisiana, or if they descended from
those who were born there (Tregle [1982]; but see also Domínguez
[1986] and DeVille [1989]). After the Civil War, white Europeans
claimed the term as exclusive of all except "pure" white Louisiana inhabitants of European descent, but Creoles of color maintained the
designation (and the distinction) as the term signifying basic group
identity for themselves as well.[1]

The beginnings of the schism between the blacks and the free people of
color are directly traceable to the parentage of the mixed-race individuals. In the majority of the relationships, the parties involved were European males and African or Indian females, who very often were the
property of the men who seduced them. Research shows that most enslaved Indians were women, and the Indian women from the villages and
female Indian slaves were said to be "quickly absorbed into the Franco-
African communities through concubinage and intermarriage." In fact,
when Spanish governor Alejandro O'Reilly outlawed Indian slavery in
1769, the owners simply reclassified them as blacks and kept them enslaved. When children resulted from the European/African or Indian
unions, they were classified as slaves, because under the French Code
Noir, children assumed the status of their mothers. Very often, though,
the white father freed both his mixed-race children and his concubine.
He did this by granting them freedom if he owned them or by buying

1. Gwendolyn Midlo Hall, "African Women in French and Spanish Louisiana:
Origins, Roles, Family, Work, Treatment," in *The Devil's Lane: Sex and Race in the
Early South*, ed. Catherine Clinton and Michele Gillespie (New York: Oxford University Press, 1997), 249; Donald E. Everett, "Free Persons of Color in Colonial
Louisiana," *Louisiana History* 7 (1966): 33; James H. Dormon, "Louisiana's 'Creoles of Color': Ethnicity, Marginality, and Identity," *Social Science Quarterly* 73
(1992), 616. A quadroon had one-quarter Negro blood; an octoroon (the offspring
of a white and a quadroon), one-eighth Negro blood; a mulatto, one white and one
Negro parent; a mestizo, mixed European and Indian ancestry or a general mixed-
race background.

their freedom if they belonged to someone else. The parties were legally free following manumission, and were therefore different from African slaves, but they were not accorded legal or social equality with whites. They, together with whites and slaves, made up the three-tiered racial classification system upon which Louisiana society was built.[2]

According to Virginia R. Domínguez, this system was dependent on two criteria of differentiation: being legally free or not, and having African blood or not. For the children born of these unions and their mothers, manumission occurred because the European fathers did not wish to see their children or their children's mothers live as slaves. Their subsequent racial classification was, therefore, determined de facto by ancestry. Though Domínguez shows only six individuals designated as free persons of color in New Orleans in 1732, all were identified as *mulâtre(sse)*, a label indicating racially mixed parentage. This practice of manumitting mixed-race slave children and their mothers set the stage for a range of privileges based on both skin color and European ancestry. Together with other factors, this privileged status given to free mulattos or mixed-race individuals made alliances between African women and European men both attractive and inevitable.[3]

Dormon argues that although pinpointing the precise timing of the ethnogenesis of the free people (or Creoles) of color is impossible, it almost certainly occurred in the last decades of the eighteenth century. Conditions in New Orleans, including the makeup of its population, actually set the stage for *plaçage* and the free-colored class it engendered. In 1728 there were a few high officials and their wives in the territory from France, but the majority of the men were trappers, soldiers, miners, slaves, and adventurers. White women were not only few in number, but

2. Hall, "African Women," 248, 250; Kimberly S. Hanger, *A Medley of Cultures: Louisiana History at the Cabildo* (New Orleans: Louisiana Museum Foundation, 1996), 26; Virginia Meacham Gould, " 'A Chaos of Iniquity and Discord': Slave and Free Women of Color in the Spanish Ports of New Orleans, Mobile, and Pensacola," in *The Devil's Lane*, ed. Clinton and Gillespie, 234. See also Virginia R. Domínguez, *White by Definition: Social Classification in Creole Louisiana* (New Brunswick, N.J.: Rutgers University Press, 1986), 23; Everett, "Free Persons of Color," 22; and Kimberly S. Hanger, *Bounded Lives, Bounded Places: Free Black Society in Colonial New Orleans, 1769–1803* (Durham, N.C.: Duke University Press, 1997), 11.
3. Domínguez, *White by Definition*, 24.

also were frequently former inmates of asylums and houses of correction in France who had been brought to the frontier territory by force; they were typically described by many of the men as "ugly, ignorant, irascible, and promiscuous." According to George Washington Cable, it is this situation that is the genesis of the proud Creoles of Louisiana. The other white women who are said to have been available to European men are the famed "casket girls." Reputed to be from middle-class families and chosen for their "skill in housewifely duties" and "excellence of character," they are reported to have reached New Orleans in 1728, with others arriving in intervals, until 1751. If myth is correct, they must have been extremely fertile since "practically every [white] native family of Louisiana is able to trace its descent in an unbroken line from one of the *filles à la cassette*." Recent scholarship, however, casts serious doubt on the existence of the casket girls, since there are no historical documents to support the alleged shipments, and since the Ursuline nuns in New Orleans, who "according to popular myth received, housed, and guarded the *filles de cassette* until they were found husbands, deny having had anything to do with such girls."[4]

Regardless of whether the casket girls existed or not, there is evidence to show that race mixing was common for many reasons. For one thing, white men chose their mulatto paramours quite intentionally, and not just because white women were few in number. The precedent for this had been established nearly two hundred years before when French planters from St. Domingue took the finest slave women for their mistresses. Many of those women were described as being handsome, with silky black hair and straight features. By carefully selecting the women with whom they mated, the French (and, to a lesser degree, the Spanish) produced in St. Domingue women of exotic beauty who have been described as resembling the high-born Hindus of India. According to pop-

4. Dormon, "Louisiana's 'Creoles of Color'," 616; David C. Rankin, *The Forgotten People: Free People of Color in New Orleans, 1850–1870* (Ann Arbor: Xerox University Microfilms, 1976), 85; quoted in Charles B. Rousseve, *The Negro in Louisiana: Aspects of His History and His Literature* (New Orleans: Xavier University Press, 1937), 22; Herbert Asbury, *The French Quarter: An Informal History of the New Orleans Underworld* (Garden City, N.J.: Garden City Press, 1938), 12–3; Mary Gehman, *Women and New Orleans: A History* (New Orleans: Margaret Media, 1988), 2.

ular historian Eleanor Early, the women were known as *"Les Sirènes,"* and they, along with their children, were brought to Louisiana by the planters when the latter fled St. Domingue during the slave uprisings. Furthermore, race mixing had begun in Louisiana long before the arrival of the refugees from St. Domingue, because some of the first slave women were made pregnant on the voyage over from Africa.[5]

The mixture of European, African, and eventually Indian blood combined in New Orleans to create women described as being so hauntingly beautiful that in response to pressure from angry white females, Governor Miró enacted on June 2, 1786, his infamous *"tignon* law," which made "excessive attention to dress" by women of "pure or mixed African blood" a criminal offense. The women were told, among other things, that they had to refrain from wearing the fine clothes and jewelry they owned, they could not wear feathers or jewels in their hair, and, finally, they had to cover their hair with kerchiefs. Miró, like other European colonial officials, believed that one's dress was a visible manifestation of social standing or status, and his ban was an attempt to prevent the women from dressing beyond what he felt was their proper station in life. According to Virginia Gould, what Miró hoped to do with his sumptuary law was to force the free women of color to symbolically reestablish their ties to slavery by wearing the kerchief, the garment traditionally worn by slave women to signify their status as workers. This ruling of course ignored both the economic and legal status of the free women and completely disavowed their blood ties to the white community. Miró, Gould says, was convinced that debasing the women of color this way was the only thing to do to control women "who had become too light skinned or who dressed too elegantly, or who, in reality competed too freely with white women for status and thus threatened the social order." Despite these and other laws, colonial European men, as would have been any other men, were drawn to the women for their sheer beauty and elegance, and in many cases simply preferred women of color over whites.[6]

The major cause, however, of white male/black female relationships in the colony was the gender imbalance, which cut across racial and class

5. Eleanor Early, *New Orleans Holiday* (New York: Rinehart, 1947), 188.
6. Roussève, *The Negro in Louisiana*, 26; Gould, "Chaos of Iniquity and Discord," 237.

lines. In her exciting research on the role of free women of color in Spanish New Orleans, historian Kimberly Hanger describes the conditions in the territory as essentially guaranteeing long-term sexual arrangements between white European men and free black and slave women. First, she notes that New Orleans was often ravaged by disease and death due to its semitropical climate and its terrain, which suffered notoriously from mosquito infestation. Diseases such as smallpox, influenza, yellow fever, and malaria were common, and often decimated the population. Children were the most vulnerable to disease, while women tended to die in childbirth. Men's lives were shortened through warfare. Hanger's most compelling evidence supporting the inevitability of interracial sex between free women of color and European settlers comes in the form of startling demographic statistics:

> The median age at death for white males was 30.6 years and white females 18.1 years; the figures for free blacks were even more dismal, although reversed by sex, with a median age at death for free black males of 8.1 years and for free black females 30.3 years. Interracial unions and the offspring they produced resulted at least partly from these demographic circumstances, as well as from a shortage of white women and an abundance of libre [free blacks] and slave women. White male New Orleanians outnumbered white women (with a sex ratio of 175 males per 100 females in 1777, 162 males in 1791, and 115 in 1805) and free black females outnumbered free black males about two to one.[7]

Considering these statistics, those who would disparage the free woman of color for her decision to engage the affections and support of a white male choose to ignore the basic numerical fact that she had no other choice. In addition to the scarcity of free black men for her to marry, she lived with the fact that she was considered a woman without honor or morals solely because of her skin color. In Hanger's words, "Libre women had to tread carefully and artfully within a patriarchal society that valued males more than females but that did not afford them the paternal protection due the weaker sex because they ostensibly did not possess honor and virtue—attributes accorded only to whites." These women were thus trapped between the biases of race-based slavery

7. Kimberly S. Hanger, "Coping in a Complex World: Free Black Women in Colonial New Orleans," in *The Devil's Lane*, ed. Clinton and Gillespie, 220.

and ancient European cultural beliefs. In *White by Definition*, Domínguez states that in 1768 when the Spanish took control of Louisiana, they brought with them their "legacy of medieval concerns" about purity of blood. Because the *gens de couleur libre* had black blood as well as white, they were considered "contaminated" and therefore to be avoided by those of "pure" or white blood. This was designed to discourage white males from elite families from allying their fortunes with women of color. Domínguez further quotes Civil Code 1808 (page 24, article 8) as follows: "Free persons and slaves are incapable of contracting marriage together; the celebration of such marriages is forbidden, and the marriage is void; it is the same with respect to the marriages contracted by free white persons with free people of color." Free women of color, then, by law could not marry slaves and they could not marry free white men. And free *men* of color of marriageable age were virtually unavailable. The free woman had to accept the fact that with her choice of a mate taken out of her hands, she was at the mercy of any man, white or black, who chose to do her harm. Her decision to use the *plaçage* system to save herself and her progeny was not only pragmatic, but, in a sense, ingenious.[8]

In her book of essays on "womanist ethics," Katie G. Canon offers an intriguing commentary on the moral and ethical nature of the choices with which the free women of color found themselves as they tried to find a mate under extraordinarily challenging circumstances. She argues, "The real-lived texture of Black life requires moral agency that may run contrary to the ethical boundaries of mainline [religion]. . . . Blacks may use action guides that have never been considered within the scope of traditional codes of faithful living. Racism, gender discrimination, and economic exploitation, as inherited, age-long complexes, require the Black community to create and cultivate values and virtues in their own terms so that they prevail against the odds with moral integrity."[9]

Canon eloquently states what should be evident, and that is that considering the scope of the obstacles they must face daily, persons who are victims of extreme oppression cannot embrace the normal moral and ethical codes of a society as though their lives and choices were framed by the same paradigms as those of persons whose freedom has never been

8. Ibid., 219; Domínguez, *White by Definition*, 24–5.
9. Katie Geneva Canon, *Katie's Canon: Womanism and the Soul of the Black Community* (New York: Continuum, 1995), 58.

questioned. They must adapt their behavior to the situations in which they find themselves and then do what their sense of humanity and decency tells them to do. When *plaçage* is viewed within this framework, the actions of the free woman of color can be deemed not only as moral and ethical, but also as courageous. They didn't choose to live in concubinage; what they chose was to survive.

In large part as a consequence of *plaçage*, many of the *gens de couleur libre* over time acquired wealth, "owning large plantations with numerous slaves, and equaling in education, refinement, and culture the best of their white fellow-citizens. In New Orleans a class of rich families of color became known as the *'cordon bleus.'* " It is their class that gave rise to the illustrious *Bal de Cordon Bleu*. Designed to facilitate their survival as a race, the *Bal de Cordon Bleu* was an elegant affair similar to a debutante ball. It was at these balls that the proud quadroons and other Creoles of color were reduced to presenting their daughters to wealthy European men for the purpose of finding them a life partner. The affairs took place under tightly controlled circumstances with every modicum of decorum observed.[10]

Popular belief holds that the first of these affairs originated at the end of the eighteenth century, while Louisiana was controlled by Spain. They are said to have lasted "for nearly a hundred years, degenerating after the War Between the States into shabby, ill-mannered affairs with no resemblance to their ancient elegance and decorum." Most critics have failed to make a distinction between the *Bal de Cordon Bleu* given by the aristocratic *gens de couleur libre* and the later public and semi-private affairs popularly known as the quadroon balls. They were two different events with very different purposes. In his *Southern Travels: Journal of John H. B. Latrobe, 1834*, the author gives an interesting account of his visit to a quadroon ball. The one-dollar entrance fee, for example, admitted him to the ballroom, which he describes as brilliant and beautiful. He comments that it was "erected for the quadroons . . . the light mulattos of this country—who prohibited by custom and law from many of the enjoyments of the whites pass their life in a prostitution." Moreover, he goes on to explain, "I was informed that this ball, by no means exhibited the handsomest, and *genteelest* of the quadroons. In the first place it was

10. Roussève, *The Negro in Louisiana*, 27.

the opening Ball to which it was not fashionable for them to come—and again it was more promiscuous than those balls which they have and where a ticket is not a matter of purchase but of favor. These last are called the Society Balls—and *the best quadroon society* is to be found at them."[11]

The "Society Ball" to which Latrobe refers is the *Bal de Cordon Bleu*, which was always known by this name among the Creoles. It was sponsored by the *Société Cordon Bleu*, an organization of wealthy quadroon matrons who used the balls as mechanism for securing for their daughters *plaçage* arrangements with well-born white Creole men. Each mother's aim was to engage an unmarried Creole gentleman as "Protector" for her daughter. This practice elicited its share of critics who have suggested that the quadroon mothers "bartered their girls into concubinage, and sold them like slaves." Yet black historian Carter G. Woodson reminds us that laws in the South were written to protect white women, while black women, slave or free, "were legally unprotected and left a prey to every man in the master class." Females of color had reason to fear white women as well, since any one of them could have a woman of color flogged for almost any reason. Threats of retaliation by Creole husbands usually kept their jealous wives in check. Therefore the colored Creole mothers' efforts to obtain arrangements with white men in no sense compromised their daughters' honor. The fact is that women of this elite class "were as tenderly and carefully brought up as any white girl, and until they secured a 'protector' they were just as virtuous." Because marital prospects with free men of color were so dim, the Creole mothers devised this elaborate method to ensure their daughters' future. Virginia Gould states that based on Spanish census records of 1788, the sex ratio for the free colored population was 677+, which means that there were 677 free women of color for every 100 free men of color. The by-invitation-only ball, then, was a means of ensuring that the young daughters of these well-to-do Creole families would not face life alone. In order to make sure that *plaçage* worked as it was intended, only wealthy men were invited to attend the *Bal de Cordon Bleu*. The entrance fee was

11. Early, *New Orleans Holiday*, 194; John H. Latrobe, *Southern Travels: Journal of John H. B. Latrobe, 1834*, ed. with an introduction by Samuel Wilson, Jr. (New Orleans: Historic New Orleans Collection, 1973), 77. Elsewhere in the present volume, Violet Harrington Bryan discusses the tradition of the quadroon balls in detail.

set high enough to guarantee the quality of the clientele, and every propriety was observed. Eleanor Early describes one setting as follows:

> The patrons for each ball sat on a dais carpeted in crimson beneath a
> winged fan called a punka, that was suspended from the ceiling, and
> kept in motion by a slave child who pulled at the string that descended
> from the wings. Around the room sat the rest of the chaperones, all in
> evening gowns, and fanning themselves with palmetto fans. Every girl's
> mother [or guardian] was there and stayed until the end. . . . Girls from
> plantations, in town for the social season, were placed under the strict
> surveillance of a friend of the family. Until a 'protector' was found for
> them, free girls of color were as discreet as nuns.[12]

At the ball, formal presentations were made, compliments ex-
changed, and the dancing commenced. Once a man found a girl who attracted him, he danced with her. If the girl found him equally attractive,
she sent him to her mother or guardian. If for some reason she did not
like him, she tactfully declined any further dances, and relied on her
chaperone to prevent her any embarrassment. Once agreement was
reached, the girl was spoken of as *placée*. This gave her a status similar to
an honorable betrothal and secured her future. Custom dictated that the
man buy a small house on or near *rue de Rampart* and present it to her.
Until the house was finished, he never saw the young woman without her
chaperone. It was also understood that he would care for her completely
during their life together, provide totally for any children they might
have, and present her with a proper settlement in the event of their separation. Some of the relationships terminated when the man married; others lasted for life. Seldom did any of them end in scandal. The fact that
financial considerations were involved in the *plaçage* arrangement should
certainly not be cause to view it in a negative light. White girls of compa-
rable social status nearly always made *mariages de convenance*, and a dowry
was always a part of their arrangements. Early claims that white women
usually had less choice in picking a husband than Creoles of color had in

12. Early, *New Orleans Holiday*, 194, 198–9; quoted in Sister Audrey Marie De-
tiege, *Henriette Delille, Free Woman of Color: Foundress of the Sisters of the Holy Family*
(New Orleans: privately printed by the Sisters of the Holy Family, n.d.), 30; Mel
Leavitt, *A Short History of New Orleans* (San Francisco: Lexikos, 1982), 93, 193;
Gould, "Chaos of Iniquity and Discord," 239.

choosing a lover. The *plaçage* arrangements were referred to as *mariages de la main gauche*, "left-handed marriages," by the people of color.[13]

It was because of these left-handed marriages that many women of color became extremely wealthy. Property was frequently willed equally to legitimate and illegitimate heirs. Sometimes bitter fights ensued, and most often the mixed-blood heirs won in court. An executor was usually necessary in order to protect the interests of a man's colored wife and children. Yet despite legal disputes, "these colored concubines or common-law wives, because of their associations with white men, were placed . . . in the position of being the richest and most powerful of the Negro group." Sons and daughters of such unions were most often educated in France, and if the young men returned to live in Louisiana, they were usually given a parcel of land which they developed, allowing them to earn a quite comfortable living. Unfortunately, however, in 1832 American lawmakers declared the old French laws no longer binding. New restrictions were passed to protect white heirs from what was termed "too great fondness of the natural parents of mulatto children."

Children of the *plaçage* unions were known as "natural" children because they were given legal recognition by their fathers in contradistinction to "bastard" children whose fathers were unknown. Because of this acknowledgment, white fathers were enabled by law to leave their estates or a portion thereof to their mixed-race children. This type of support was greatly encouraged by the church. A quasi-acceptance of the *plaçage* arrangements continued into the American occupation of Louisiana. In the Fauborg Tremé area in New Orleans, for example, many of these *plaçage* liaisons formed the man's only home. He lived monogamously with his *placée* and produced natural children who were his heirs and automatically free. During the decade between 1830 and 1840, the free colored class had reached such a level of culture, wealth, and influence that they attracted the notice of all persons traveling to New Orleans.[14]

13. Early, *New Orleans Holiday*, 200.

14. Marcus Christian, "Manuscript 19," Unpublished Manuscripts, Correspondence, and Poetry, Marcus B. Christian Collection, Archives and Manuscripts Department, Earl K. Long Library, University of New Orleans; quoted in J. A. Rogers, *Sex and Race: A History of White, Negro, and Indian Miscegenation in the Two Americas* (St. Petersburg, Fla.: Helga M. Rogers, 1984), 2:183; Detiege, *Henriette*

There were some obvious drawbacks to the institution of *plaçage*. For one thing, because it was not a legal marriage, the woman involved always lived with the fact that she lacked the social and legal protection inherent in marriage. In addition, the knowledge that the man could leave the relationship at any time had to have been stressful for her, even though he had to provide for her and her children's future if he did so. Finally, because her ties to the man's family were cut off by law and social practice, both the young woman and her children were denied the familial closeness of the paternal relations.

In a larger view, the system created a third race of people in Louisiana. Their unique position between master and slave, together with the fact that they could find a home with neither, caused them to become a separatist, self-focusing community. The group was bound by ties of language, birth, culture, religion, and wealth. This and the favored treatment they received from whites created a gap between them and non-Creole blacks which lasts to this day. Finally, they lost a number of their population who disappeared into the white race seeking opportunities only whites could claim.

On the positive side, *plaçage* created a class of free people of color which was well-educated, cultured, wealthy, and powerful. Though the majority were not members of the elite class, they were highly skilled people who made tremendous contributions both in their own community and in some cases to the world community. Many were distinguished poets, artists, musicians, sculptors, novelists, statesmen, valiant soldiers, humanitarians, and excellent family people. Though not true of all of them, a number of this free colored class with money used it to buy slaves which many eventually freed. Kimberly Hanger states that free blacks "frequently bought, sold, and inherited property—personal, slave, and real. . . . [They] primarily owned slaves to help them in their trades and work in the cities and fields. . . . In addition, free blacks could afford to purchase their slave relatives and free them with few constraints." So just

---

Delille, 7; Roulhac Toledano and Mary Louise Christovich, *New Orleans Architecture*, vol. 6, *Faubourg Tremé and the Bayou Road* (Gretna, La.: Pelican, 1980), 91; Christian, "Manuscript 26," 26. According to the Louisiana Code (in effect until 1832) legitimate children could not be disinherited under any but the most extreme circumstances, such as striking a parent or failing to ransom a parent held on the high seas.

as many white fathers freed their mixed-race children, many free Creoles bought and freed their slave relatives.[15]

A final word in defense of the quadroon or free colored *placée:* one author wrote, "Like other women of history whose race was held in bondage, the Negro mother through miscegenation was able to obtain educational advantages and economic security for her colored sons and daughters in an oppressed, hostile environment where most of the members of her race were held in bondage."[16] That she survived is remarkable; that she prevailed is laudatory.

15. Kimberly S. Hanger, "Avenues to Freedom Open to New Orleans' Black Population, 1769–1779," *Louisiana History* 31 (Summer 1990), 241–2.
16. Detiege, *Henriette Delille*, 9–10.

4

Composers of Color of Nineteenth-Century New Orleans

The History Behind the Music

Lester Sullivan

Perhaps the least noted of the many kinds of music that New Orleans has produced is its nineteenth-century popular sheet music. Essentially genteel entertainment music on the European model, it is now sometimes called "concert" music, but a person was as likely to encounter this music at the theater as at the concert hall. Likewise, the term "salon" music does not always apply, because some of it was dance music, frequently heard in the ballroom. The genteel sheet music repertoire in New Orleans in the 1800s consisted almost entirely of dances for piano, piano scores of marches with occasional instrumental indications, and songs with piano accompaniment. The emphasis was on dance. To call the music "classical," as is now sometimes done, is misleading because it suggests a separation between popular and art music that was certainly less evident then than now. Nevertheless, in this repertoire, unlike in minstrelsy, Negro spirituals, or even Louisiana's own Creole slave songs, European models remain preeminent.

The least-known category within this relatively unknown repertoire is the music composed by people of color, of which quite a bit survives. Between 1848 and the end of the century, people of African descent wrote at least fifty pieces of music of this sort that found their way into print through a then-thriving local sheet-music industry. By the 1920s this industry was virtually dead. The purpose of the present essay is to survey all such black music imprints in New Orleans. A few of the city's composers of color became expatriates in their search for wider opportunity; the essay also attempts to treat that subject. Most New Orleans composers of color were French-speaking free people, and nearly all of the previous research has focused on them. This study, however, discusses an American (that is to say, English-speaking), free black composer, and offers new evidence that a second composer was a slave. The study also uncovered a piece by a woman, another phenomenon treated for the first time.

Today, nearly a century after most of these black composers penned their last notes, relatively little is known about them. The present survey draws on three sources: the pioneering efforts of such authors as Trotter (1878), Desdunes (1911), Cuney-Hare (1936), and Christian (1982); new leads from recent research by scholars in New Orleans black history, most of whom are not working directly on music; and a fresh look at local and other archival holdings. What emerges is clearer biographical data about the handful of black composers who managed to get their music published.[1]

Composers of color in antebellum New Orleans found themselves in a unique situation. Notwithstanding its crucial role in commerce in the slavocracy, the city had one of the largest free black populations in the country, North or South, and by far the wealthiest. This free black population, like the white population, was divided by language, religion, and

---

1. James Monroe Trotter, *Music and Some Highly Musical People* (Boston: Lee & Shepard, 1878); Rodolphe Lucien Desdunes, *Nos hommes et notre histoire* (Montreal: Arbour et Dupont, 1911); Maude Cuney-Hare, *Negro Musicians and Their Music* (Washington, D.C.: Associated Publishers, 1936); Marcus B. Christian, Marcus B. Christian Collection, Archives and Special Collections, Earl K. Long Library, University of New Orleans. Many archivists, civil servants, and historians have contributed information for this paper, but special thanks are due Lawrence Gushee, whose work on the transition from this music to jazz was presented at the Southern Historical Association convention in New Orleans, and Sonya McCarthy, great-granddaughter of one of the nineteenth-century New Orleans black composers treated in this paper.

custom into two groups, Creole and American. The depth of the division may be measured by the fact that between 1836 and 1852 the city was separated into three almost autonomous municipalities: the French Quarter, or the original city, where Creoles predominated; the American city upriver from Canal Street; and the Creole suburbs downriver from Esplanade Avenue, which then were receiving a big influx of European immigrants.[2]

The word *Creole* has its origins in the Portuguese slave trade. It has been used in Louisiana since the Spanish colonial period to identify native-born Louisianians descended from the original French-speaking, Roman Catholic population. Apparently the oldest Louisiana manuscript to use *Creole* is a document that dates from 1782 and applies the term to a slave. Not much later in the manuscript record the word is applied to free blacks, whites, even to things, such as food. In other words, a Creole was a Louisiana-born descendant of colonial ancestors regardless of whether the ancestors were African, European, or both. Qualifying the word makes its use more precise. "Creole of color," "white Creole," and "Creole slave" are all terms with foundation in Louisiana history.[3]

Creoles of color still made up the majority of free people of color in mid-nineteenth-century New Orleans. This remained true despite much migration to Haiti, Mexico, and other places in response to competition from European immigrants, repressive legislation against free blacks, and other economic and social change. English-speaking, Protestant free blacks, themselves driven from the old southeastern states by legislation, did not begin to move to New Orleans in large numbers until the Louisiana Purchase of 1803. Free Creoles of color were more numerous, prosperous, and powerful than American free blacks. Most free Creoles of color were of the artisan class. Others were wholesale grocers, real-estate speculators, and financiers. Many owned slaves themselves, sometimes

2. Leonard P. Curry, *The Free Black in Urban America, 1800–1850: The Shadow of the Dream* (Chicago: University of Chicago Press, 1981), 244–5, 267–71.

3. Lester Sullivan, "A Note on the Word 'Creole,' " in *Guide to ARC Light: A Series of Multi-image Shows about Afro-Americans, Other Ethnic Groups, and Race Relations History* (New Orleans: Amistad Research Center, 1984), 19–25. In the present volume, most of the essays similarly address the origin of the term and then designate their particular usage; all agree with the explanation here of the multiple associations of *Creole* and the consequent employment of the more descriptive terms such as *Creoles of color*.

for the purpose of preventing enslaved relatives and friends from falling into the hands of others, sometimes for profit. Many more Creoles of color owned slaves than did their American free black counterparts, and New Orleans free blacks owned more slaves than any other blacks in the nation.[4]

The two oldest books to discuss New Orleans black composers are considered to be primary sources: *Music and Some Highly Musical People*, by Mississippi-born and midwestern-educated James Monroe Trotter (1878), and *Nos hommes et notre histoire*, by the Creole of color Rodolphe Lucien Desdunes (1911). Trotter's work is not only a monument of black-music research but also the first American music history of any kind to transcend New England or to cover sacred and secular music together. More in the nature of a memoir than a history, *Nos hommes et notre histoire* is rather casual about where it gets its information. Neither book contains source documentation, and the notes that have been added to the published English translation of Desdunes are unreliable. There are two unpublished translations: an anonymous one held at the Amistad Research Center at Tulane University and another by Marcus Christian, held in his papers at the University of New Orleans.[5]

Trotter and Desdunes have been quoted repeatedly, and often misquoted, by subsequent writers, but two later scholars have each contributed some new detail about one or two of the New Orleans composers of color. The first, Marcus Christian, served as the final director of the Negro Division of the Federal Writers' Project under the Works Progress Administration in the 1930s and 1940s. He was able, before his death in 1976, to write some entries about nineteenth-century New Orleans musicians for the *Dictionary of American Negro Biography*, including an especially useful one about Basile Barès. His other truly original contribution, the important information he culled from the Negro Division's research about Thomas J. Martin, remains unpublished in his personal papers. The other scholar to contribute to knowledge about one of these

---

4. Curry, *The Free Black*, 271; Carter G. Woodson, *Free Negro Owners of Slaves in the United States in 1830, Together with Absentee Ownership of Slaves in the United States in 1830* (Washington, D.C.: Associated Publishers, 1924), 9–15, 52.

5. Robert Stevenson, "America's First Black Music Historian," *Journal of the American Musicological Society* 26 (1973): 384–5; Rodolphe Lucien Desdunes, *Our People and Our History*, trans. Sister Dorothea McCants (Baton Rouge: Louisiana State University Press, 1973).

composers was Maude Cuney-Hare. Her book *Negro Musicians and Their Music* (1936) recalls her encounters with one of the expatriate New Orleanians who had become one of the most successful of all nineteenth-century black composers born in the United States, Edmond Dédé.[6]

EDMOND DÉDÉ

Dédé was born in New Orleans on November 20, 1827. According to Cuney-Hare, the composer's parents were free Creoles of color who had immigrated to the Crescent City around 1809 from the West Indies. His father became *chef de musique* of a local militia unit and was the boy's first professor. Dédé's first instrument, as befitted the son of a bandmaster, was the clarinet, but he soon developed into a violin prodigy, studying that instrument under both a white and a black teacher. Ludovico Gabici, the white teacher, was an Italian-born composer and theater-orchestra conductor who was also among the early New Orleans publishers of music. Free Creole of color Constantin Debergue was young Dédé's other teacher, and is identified by Trotter as a conductor of the local Philharmonic Society, founded by free Creoles of color sometime in the late antebellum period. This was the first nontheatrical orchestra in the city and even included some whites among its hundred instrumentalists.[7]

Dédé also studied counterpoint and harmony under teachers of both races. One was Eugène Prévost, French-born winner of the 1831 Prix de Rome and conductor of the orchestras at the Théâtre d'Orléans and, later, the local French Opera. The other, Charles Richard Lambert, was a New York–born free black musician, music teacher, and conductor of the Philharmonic Society. He was somehow related through his first

6. Marilyn S. Hessler, "Marcus Christian: The Man and His Collection," *Louisiana History* 28 (1987), 39–43; Marcus Christian, "Basile Barès," in *Dictionary of American Negro Biography* (New York: W. W. Norton, 1982), 28–9; Stevenson, "America's First Black Music Historian," 386–7. Elsewhere in the present volume, Violet Harrington Bryan discusses Christian's work on the free persons of color.

7. Cuney-Hare, *Negro Musicians*, 237; *L'Artiste de Bordeaux* 3, series 2 (30): 1186–7; *New Orleans Tribune*, April 2, 1865; Marcus Christian, "Edmond Dédé," in *Dictionary of American Negro Biography*, 168; Trotter, *Music and Some Highly Musical People*, 350–2; Henry A. Kmen, *Music in New Orleans: The Formative Years, 1791–1841* (Baton Rouge: Louisiana State University Press, 1966), 234; Robert C. Reinders, *End of an Era: New Orleans, 1850–1860* (New Orleans: Pelican, 1964), 188.

marriage to Joseph Bazanac, a free Creole of color who was a popular teacher not only of music but also of French and English.[8]

In 1848 Dédé moved to Mexico, as did many other New Orleans free Creoles of color after the Mexican War, probably in reaction to changes in their city's race relations. There he met virtuoso pianist Henri Herz, who was on an extended concert tour of the Americas. Illness eventually drove Dédé back to New Orleans in 1851. The next year, his mélodie "Mon pauvre coeur" appeared. It is the oldest piece of sheet music by a New Orleans Creole of color. Like most antebellum imprints of music by local blacks, it was probably published by the white proprietors of the leading local music stores. Dédé supplemented his income from music with what today would be characterized as his day job. Christian says that he was a cigar maker, as were a number of local musicians. According to Trotter, by 1857 he had saved enough money to book passage to Europe. Desdunes explains that, through the intervention of friends, Dédé was admitted to the Paris Conservatoire, which is compatible with later evidence that identifies as his teachers Jacques-François Fromental Halévy and Jean-Delphin Alard, both of whom belonged to the Conservatoire. About 1860 Dédé went to Bordeaux, where he first worked as conductor of the orchestra at the prestigious old Grand Théâtre. New Orleans and Bordeaux were once closely related, and trade and other connections were still strong between the two at the time. Quite a few Louisiana Creoles of color, including musicians and *littérateurs*, had settled in Bordeaux in the 1850s and 1860s in order to escape first the growing sentiment at home against free blacks and later the Civil War and its aftermath. Photographs of Dédé clearly show his African ancestry to be more obvious than that of many Creoles of color of New Orleans, where racial mixing was a way of life. When, in 1864, he married a Frenchwoman, Sylvie Leflat, and the marriage was announced in black-interest newspapers in

8. Julia Truitt Bishop, "Musical History of Louisiana," *New Orleans Times-Democrat*, October 31, 1909; Trotter, *Music and Some Highly Musical People*, 347–52; Louis Panzeri, *Louisiana Composers* (New Orleans: Dinstuhl, 1972), 60; Succession of Charles Richard Lambert, 1862–1878, Orleans Parish Second District Court, docket no. 20,494, Louisiana Division, New Orleans Public Library. See also the *New Orleans City Directory* (1846), 353; *New Orleans City Directory* (1853), 153; and *L'Artiste*.

both New Orleans and New York, much was made of his appearance. He and Sylvie later had a son, Eugène Arcade, who also became a composer.[9]

French sheet music by Dédé held by the Bibliothèque Nationale in Paris has been surveyed by the Center for Black Music Research in its *Updated Music List: Six Composers of Nineteenth-Century New Orleans* (1987), which is a revision of the list compiled by Lucius Wyatt in the spring 1987 *BMR Newsletter*. It shows that all of Dédé's music from 1865 to 1881 was published in Bordeaux.[10] All of the earliest pieces are songs, including "Le serment de l'Arabe," which Trotter reproduced, and "Quasimodo," which was performed by black musicians in New Orleans on May 10, 1865, and which is available in microform in the Louisiana Collection at Tulane University.[11]

After leaving the Grand Théâtre, except brief stints in Algiers and Marseilles and his last years in Paris, Dédé spent his career in Bordeaux as a theater orchestra conductor, where the light music of the *café-concert* held sway. During his Bordeaux period, he wrote ballets, *ballets-divertissements*, operettas, *opéra-comiques*, overtures, and over 250 dances and songs. Among the overtures is *Le Palmier*, which was performed by black New Orleanians on August 22, 1865, making it one of the few of Dédé's orchestral pieces ever played in the United States. In addition to writing all of this theatrical music, much of which may survive in Bordeaux and ought to be located, Dédé produced at least six string quartets and an unpublished cantata, *Battez aux champs* (1865), which was deposited at the Bibliothèque and may have been submitted as a contest piece. This variety and volume of output contrasts sharply with the production of the New Orleans black composers who remained at home.[12]

By the mid-1880s Dédé had a Paris publisher and a membership in

9. *L'Artiste*; Christian, "Edmond Dédé," 168; Trotter, *Music and Some Highly Musical People*, 340; Desdunes, *Nos hommes*, 117; *New Orleans Tribune*, September 6 and 8, 1864; *National Anti-Slavery Standard*, May 11, 1865. None of the local archival repositories holds the original of "Mon pauvre coeur," but the Amistad Research Center possesses a facsimile.

10. A comparison of facsimiles of the Bibliothèque Nationale catalog cards, generously provided by the Center, and the *Updated Music List* (1987) discloses some misreadings of "1855" for "1865."

11. *New Orleans Tribune*, May 10, 11, 1865.

12. Ibid., August 15–23, 1865; Music Catalog Cards, Bibliothèque Nationale, Paris; *L'Artiste*.

the French Society of Authors, Composers, and Editors of Music. By
1894 he was a full member of the Society of Dramatic Authors and Composers in Paris. His only piece now available on a commercial recording
dates from this period: *Mephisto masqué: Polka fantastique* for orchestra
(1889) is included on *Turn of the Century Cornet Favorites*, with Gerard
Schwarz on cornet and euphonium and the Columbia Chamber Ensemble conducted by Gunther Schuller (1977). The orchestration on the recording, by Schuller, substitutes the euphonium for an ophicleide and
eliminates the parts for four mirlitons, or French kazoos.[13]

Dédé returned to New Orleans only once, in 1893, when he was in
his mid-sixties.[14] His Paris publisher had just released his new comic
vocal duet, the latest piece now held by the Paris Bibliothèque. He was
on his way home to visit relatives when, during a rough crossing, the ship
on which he was traveling was disabled. In the confusion, his Cremona
violin was lost. The passengers were taken aboard a Texas steamer to
Galveston, where Cuney-Hare's parents were among those who entertained Dédé during the two-month layover. For several months after arriving in New Orleans, Dédé gave many concerts, even garnering some
attention from *L'Abeille*, the last major French-language organ of white
Creole New Orleans. He was assisted at these concerts by local black
musicians and, once, by the music critic of *L'Abeille*. The fare consisted
mostly of pieces for violin with piano accompaniment, including a paraphrase on *Rigoletto* by his old teacher Delphin Alard. He introduced two
new songs. The first, "Si j'etais lui" ("Should I Be He"), was published

13. *L'Artiste;* Arthur R. LaBrew, "Edmond Dédé (dit Charentos), 1827–1901,"
Afro-American Music Review 1 (1984): 75–8; calling card of Edmond Dédé [ca.
1893], Historical Source Material, Box 5, Marcus Christian Collection, Earl K.
Long Library, University of New Orleans.

14. LaBrew, "Edmond Dédé," 76, claims that Dédé returned to New Orleans
in 1865. He bases this on a report in New York that "at one of Mrs. Louise de
Mortie's musical soirees in New Orleans, in favor of the Orphan's Home, Mr. Edmond Dede took part" (*National Anti-Slavery Standard*, August 12, 1865). The re-
mainder of the article, however, is identical to one in the English-language edition
of the *New Orleans Tribune* of May 11, 1865, which reports on the same concert
and makes no mention of Dédé's presence. In fact, none of the 1865 articles in the
Tribune that make reference to Dédé or his music mentions his presence in the city,
and it is highly unlikely that this local newspaper would have failed to do so. Something appears to have been garbled in the news as it was reported in New York
many months later.

locally by A. E. Blackmar and is reproduced in slightly incomplete form by Arthur LaBrew, who received a copy from late Creole slave-song authority Camille Nickerson. (Her father, William J. Nickerson [1851–1927], played with Dédé on one of his New Orleans programs.) Dédé regarded the other song, "Patriotisme," as his farewell to home. In it, as paraphrased by Cuney-Hare—who gives the words but not the music—the composer laments his destiny to live far away because of "implacable prejudice" at home. Neither song has been located in any New Orleans repository.[15]

Grateful for receiving honorary membership in the Société des Jeunes-Amis, a leading social group composed mostly of Creoles of color of free antebellum background, but weary of the inconveniences and indignities of Jim Crow, Dédé returned to France in 1894. He died in Paris in 1901. It is unclear whether or not he completed his magnum opus, the opera *Le sultan d'Ispahan*, which may have been inspired by his stay in Algeria.[16]

THE LAMBERT FAMILY

In many ways surpassing Dédé among black Orleanians who had musical careers abroad were the half-brothers Lucien and Sidney Lambert. Their

15. *Updated Music List: Six Composers of Nineteenth-Century New Orleans* (Chicago: Center for Black Music Research, Columbia College, Chicago, 1987); Desdunes, *Nos hommes*, 117; LaBrew, "Edmond Dédé," 84–5; Vaughn Glasgow, Al Rose, and Diana Rose, "Played with Immense Success: Smithsonian Institution Traveling Exhibit" (Office of Special Projects, Louisiana State Museum, New Orleans), 434; Cuney-Hare, *Negro Musicians*, 237–8. W. J. Nickerson wrote at least two published pieces before 1901. His teaching career provides historians with a link between the genteel nineteenth-century tradition and jazz, through his most famous pupil, Jelly Roll Morton.

16. Charles B. Roussève, *The Negro in Louisiana: Aspects of His History and His Literature* (New Orleans: Xavier University, 1937), 151–2; Edmond Dédé, Letter to S. Perrault, New Orleans [1894], Joseph Logsdon Collection, accession no. 117–1, Archives and Special Collections, Earl K. Long Library, University of New Orleans. Some writers maintain that when Dédé died, *Le sultan d'Ispahan* was left incomplete. LaBrew, "Edmond Dédé," 81, however, finds an announcement for an upcoming performance at the Bordeaux Grand Théâtre in 1886. If "Le serment de l'Arabe" is indeed an aria from this opera, as a recent author says without citing any evidence (Lucius R. Wyatt, "Composers Corner: Six Composers of Nineteenth-Century New Orleans," *Black Music Research Newsletter* 9 (1987): 8, then the

father, Dédé's early teacher Richard Lambert, was their first teacher. Lucien was born about 1828 or 1829. His mother appears to have been a Louisiana free Creole of color who was somehow related to Joseph Bazanac. Sidney was born about 1838. His mother was Charles Richard's second wife Coralie Suzanne Ory, also a Louisiana free Creole of color. Charles Richard died in 1862, while he and Sidney were in Port-au-Prince, Haiti. The court appointed Bazanac undertutor of the minor children. He died about the time the succession was finally completed, in 1878.[17]

The careers of the Lambert brothers extended far beyond their hometown. Like the white Creole Louis Moreau Gottschalk, they did not remain long in New Orleans. Both grew up playing piano in the pit at the Théâtre d'Orléans. Lucien, some ten years older than Sidney, was a contemporary of Gottschalk, and according to Desdunes the two enjoyed a friendly artistic rivalry as aspiring virtuoso pianists and composers. This could have been as early as the late 1830s and early 1840s, when the two were still preteens and before Gottschalk left for Europe in 1842. When he returned to New Orleans for a few months in 1853, Lucien already may have gone to Paris, where, in 1854, his presence is reported in *L'Illustration*. Also in 1854, his earliest piece held by the Bibliothèque, "L'angélus au monastère: Prière" for piano, was published.[18]

From the start, Lucien Lambert was more successful than Dédé in securing publication in Paris. Then, in 1858, just outside the city, his son Lucien-Leon-Guillaume was born and became a successful composer himself. Even in their own day, father and son were confused for one another. The recent Center for Black Music Research *Updated Music List* combines compositions by both among the entries under "Lucien Lambert." The sheet-music catalog cards of the Bibliothèque show at least

---

opera must have been fairly long in preparation, because the song is included in Trotter, *Music and Some Highly Musical People*, Appendix, 53–9.

17. Trotter, *Music and Some Highly Musical People*, 338; Seventh Census of the United States (1850), New Orleans, Third Municipality, Ward 1. See also Succession of Charles Richard Lambert.

18. Desdunes, *Nos hommes*, 114; Louis Moreau Gottschalk, *Notes of a Pianist*, ed. Jeanne Behrend (New York: Knopf, 1964), xv; John Smith Kendall, "The Friend of Chopin, and Some Other New Orleans Musical Celebrities," *Louisiana Historical Quarterly* 31 (1948): 867; *Updated Music List*; *New Orleans Daily Crusader*, March 22, 1890; Glasgow, Rose, and Rose, "Played with Immense Success," 427.

forty pieces by the father, twenty-eight under the full name "Charles-Lucien," dating from 1857 to 1890, and twelve others under "Lucien" alone, dating from 1854 to 1862—all Paris publications and most of them dances. The father is also called Charles-Lucien in *Die Musik in Geschichte und Gegenwart*. All but three of the pieces recorded by the Bibliothèque as by Charles-Lucien are also included in a list of music by Lucien Lambert *père* compiled by Lawrence Gushee. This unpublished list is based on publisher's catalogs and other bibliographic works and includes references to at least a dozen other French imprints not found at the Bibliothèque as well as a few German and other imprints.[19]

Charles-Lucien Lambert moved his family to Brazil sometime in the 1860s. He had become so identified with French musical life that at least one Brazilian music historian has misidentified him as a *"famoso pianista francês."* In Rio de Janeiro, he opened a piano and music store and taught music, eventually becoming a member of the Brazilian National Institute of Music. Then in 1869, Gottschalk arrived in Rio for a series of spectacular appearances, fated to be his last. Lucien *fils*, then not yet a teenager, and his father both performed in at least one of Gottschalk's monster concerts, in which thirty-one pianists played simultaneously.[20]

Lambert *père* became a good friend of the family of the young Ernesto Nazareth (1863–1934) and that great Brazilian composer's first professional teacher. Now that Nazareth's piano music is enjoying a revival on recordings, it has become increasingly evident that he may have gained from Lambert not only his love for Chopin but also an inclination toward the *style pianola*, which, coupled with Gottschalk's pioneering use of American color in his compositions, suggests a line of influence from Lambert *père* and Gottschalk to Nazareth and thence to Heitor Villa-Lobos and even Darius Milhaud. Lambert's own compositional efforts in Rio await better documentation, but Gushee has already found references to at least three Brazilian imprints of pieces previously published

19. Baptista Siqueira, *Ernesto Nazareth na musica Brasileira* (Rio de Janeiro: Universidade Federal, 1967); Guy Ferchault, "Lucien Leon Guillaume Lambert," in *Die Musik in Geschichte und Gegenwart*, ed. Friedrich Blume (1960), 8, col. 124; Lawrence Gushee, unpublished list of compositions by Lucien Lambert, n.d., held by the author.
20. Trotter, *Music and Some Highly Musical People*, 338; Siqueira, *Ernesto Nazareth*; Francisco Curt Lange, "Vida y muerte de Louis Moreau Gottschalk en Rio de Janeiro (1869), II parte," *Revista de Estudios Musicales* 2 (1951), 316–7.

in Paris in 1859 and 1861 and four other pieces published in Brazil and not duplicated among the French imprints at the Bibliothèque. Lambert died in Rio in 1896.[21]

Lucien Lambert *fils* was taught first by his father and then, in France, by Theodore Dubois and Jules Massenet. The young Lambert's *Prométhée enchainé* won the Concours Rossini in 1885. The Bibliothèque holds at least nine pieces listed as by Lucien-Léon-Guillame Lambert and included in the *Updated Music List*. These show a much wider range in forms, performing forces, and length than his father's music, including several stage works from 1892 to 1911 and two pieces written in Porto, Portugal, and still in manuscript: the 1912 *Cloches de Porto* for piano and orchestra and a 1924 "Prelude, Fugue, and Postlude" for piano. Two works by Lambert *fils* not explicitly labeled with his full name are 1898 publications by A. Noël in Paris: a vocal arrangement of Gottschalk's piano *Berceuse*, Op. 47 (RO 27), and an orchestral *Esquisses Créoles* on Gottschalk themes in an arrangement for piano four-hands.[22] *Die Musik in Geschichte und Gegenwart* lists many more works by Lambert *fils*, including a ballet, symphonic poems, a piano concerto, a work for organ and orchestra, and a *Requiem*.[23]

Like Lucien Lambert *fils* in the latter part of his life, Sidney Lambert had a career in Portugal, serving as a pianist in the royal court. Sometime in the mid-1870s he was decorated by the King, Dom Pedro, for a new piano method. He later taught in Paris, where the Bibliothèque now holds thirty-two of his pieces dating from 1866 to 1899. This sampling shows Sidney to have been somewhat less original than his brother, with about one-quarter of the pieces being arrangements. One of these again gives evidence of the Lambert family connection to Gottschalk: *Célèbre tarantelle* [sic] (1890) is a two-piano arrangement of Gottschalk's *Grande*

21. Marilyn Cooley, Mozart de Araujo, and Beth Greenburg, jacket notes, *Tangos, Waltzes, Polkas of Ernesto Nazareth* (ProArte PAD-144, 1983); Siqueira, *Ernesto Nazareth*.

22. The vocal arrangement has French lyrics and is different from that of the "Berceuse" for male voice (RO 28) listed in the Gottschalk *Centennial Catalogue* as an arrangement of RO 27, presumably composed by Gottschalk himself, with English and Italian lyrics, and first published in 1863. Robert Offergeld, *The Centennial Catalogue of the Published and Unpublished Compositions of Louis Moreau Gottschalk* (New York: Stereo Review, 1970), 16.

23. Ferchault, "Lucien Leon," cols. 124–5.

tarantelle for piano and orchestra (1868, RO 259)—not to be confused with the arrangement listed in the *Centennial Catalogue*, which is by Nicolas Ruiz Espadero (RO 260). Sidney seems to have been the only Lambert to have published a piece in New Orleans. His arrangement of "Mon étoile," a waltz by F. A. Rente, first published in Paris, was copyrighted in 1879 as "Stella (Mon étoile)" by Philip Werlein in New Orleans. Sidney Lambert died in Paris sometime in the first decade of the twentieth century.[24]

VICTOR-EUGÈNE MACARTY, SAMUEL SNAËR, AND BASILE BARÈS

The remaining nineteenth-century New Orleans composers of color had, for the most part, local careers. Victor-Eugène Macarty (also variously McCarty, McCarthy, and Macarthy) produced perhaps the fewest published pieces of the entire group—only two items—but he stands out as a frequent performer and organizer among local musicians of color and as a significant figure in Reconstruction politics and civil rights. Among the earliest of the composers, he was born a free Creole of color in New Orleans sometime between 1817 and 1823. (Most researchers claim more definite dates, but without producing any documentation.) Macarty's parentage also remains unclear. Christian incorrectly identifies as the composer the mixed Creole Eugène Macarty who was the son of the wealthy free woman of color Eulalie Macarty. That Eugène Macarty, however, died in 1866 (though Christian's sources at the time prompted him to give the date as 1845), at least fifteen years before Victor-Eugène.[25]

Victor-Eugène Macarty's first music teacher was a local white man, Jules Nores, with whom he studied piano. According to Trotter, Macarty was admitted to the Imperial Conservatoire in Paris about 1840, even though by then he was over the official maximum age for admission. The

24. Trotter, *Music and Some Highly Musical People*, 339; Offergeld, *Centennial Catalogue*, 30; Music Catalog Cards; Marcus Christian, "Lucien and Sidney Lambert," n.d., Marcus B. Christian Collection, Literary and Historical Manuscripts, box 12, Archives and Special Collections, Earl K. Long Library, University of New Orleans.

25. Succession of Eugène Macarty, f.m.c. 1866, Orleans Parish Second District Court, docket no. 27,100, Louisiana Division, New Orleans Public Library.

French-born Pierre Soulé, a prominent attorney in antebellum Louisiana who later served as United States ambassador to Spain, intervened with the French ambassador to the United States to effect an exception to the rule. At the Conservatoire, Macarty studied voice, harmony, and composition. Sometime before 1845, he began playing in New Orleans for various social functions. The only surviving pieces by Macarty are two brief polkas, and only one of them is an original composition. These appeared locally together in 1854, and, like almost all of the antebellum publications of sheet music by people of color in New Orleans, they were copyrighted by the composer and apparently self-published. The description of Macarty on the cover as "Pianist of the fashionable Soirées of New Orleans" clearly reads as an advertisement by someone trying to earn a living through his music, not as one of the amateur musicians Trotter describes as "pursuing their studies, not with a pecuniary view (being in easy circumstances)."[26]

Little else is known about Macarty's activities until after the Civil War, when he began to organize concerts aimed principally at audiences of Creoles of color. His leading cohorts in this work were two men of markedly different background, Samuel Snaër and Basile Barès. François-Michel-Samuel Snaër was born a free Creole of color in New Orleans between 1832 and 1834. His family was of mixed African, French, and German ancestry and had emigrated from St. Domingue, first to Cuba and then to New Orleans, arriving there no later than 1818. The father, François Snaër, was a wholesale grocer with real property worth over $20,000 in 1850. According to unpublished research by Wayne Everard, Snaër's mother, Anne Emerine Beluche Snaër, was a purported daughter of the Caribbean pirate René Beluche. Almost all that is known about Samuel Snaër's antebellum musical activity is that his first song, "Sous sa fenêtre," was written when he was eighteen, about 1851.[27]

26. Trotter, *Music and Some Highly Musical People*, 334, 343; *New Orleans Tribune*, June 18, 1865.

27. Desdunes, *Nos hommes*, 115; Trotter, *Music and Some Highly Musical People*, 341–2; Seventh Census of the United States (1850), New Orleans, First Municipality, 205, Dwelling 1119, Family 1627; U.S. House of Representatives, *Report of the Select Committee on the New Orleans Riots* (Washington, D.C.: Government Printing Office, 1867), 17; Death certificate of François Snaër [grandfather], May 5, 1838, Orleans Parish Recorder of Births, Marriages, and Deaths, Death Register, vol. 6, colored vol., Louisiana Division, New Orleans Public Library, 244; Marriage Con-

Basile Jean Barès's origins long have been hidden, perhaps even intentionally at one time, for Barès was unique among New Orleans composers of color. The first clue to just how unusual he was appeared in Christian's note in the Dictionary of American Negro Biography, which suggests a connection between Barès, a piano virtuoso who grew up working in a Royal Street piano and music emporium, and the French-born proprietor of the store, Adolphe Périer. Christian observes that the black-owned newspaper the *New Orleans Tribune* often refers to the young pianist in the mid-1860s as Basile "Perrier." A search of the 1860 succession of Adolphe Périer's estate, which has been virtually hidden for years in a nonarchival setting not ordinarily open for research use, was located in the course of this study but did not yield the expected evidence that Barès was Périer's free, mixed son. Instead, it revealed no Périer children, mixed or otherwise, and only one heir, his French-born wife. Périer's widow inherited the estate valued in excess of $30,000, including dozens of pianos of every description, but mostly Pleyels; real estate; and six slaves. Intriguingly, the first and most valuable slave listed is a sixteen-year-old mulatto boy worth $1,000 named Basile.[28]

How is it possible to know whether the slave Basile is the musician Basile Jean Barès? Actually, the facts in at least six manuscript sources dating from 1845 to 1902 all point in the same direction. The inventory of Périer's estate says that the slave Basile was born in Périer's possession in about late 1844 or early 1845 and that Basile's mother was Périer's slave, Augustine. Basile Jean Barès's marriage certificate lists his mother as Augustine Celestine. It lists his age as thirty-two, indicating birth in about late 1844 or early 1845, and lists his father as Jean Barès. The rec-

---

tract of Jean Baptiste Snaër and Louise Josephine Utrosse Pelissier, 1827, Notarial Acts of Louis T. Caire, September 17, Orleans Parish Notarial Archives, Civil Courts Building, New Orleans; Certificate of Apprenticeship of Jean Baptiste Snaër, October 19, 1818, New Orleans Mayor's Office Indenture Book no. 3, Louisiana Division, New Orleans Public Library, 82; J. Richard Schenkel, Robert Sauder, and Edward R. Chatelain, *Archaeology of the Jazz Complex and Beauregard (Congo) Square, Louis Armstrong Park, New Orleans, Louisiana* (New Orleans: University of New Orleans, 1980), 71.

28. Desdunes, *Nos hommes*, 119; Christian, "Basile Barès," in *Dictionary of American Negro Biography*, 28; Succession of Adolphe Périer, 1860, Orleans Parish Second District Court, docket no. 17,370, transferred to Civil District Court, docket no. 88,478, Orleans Parish Civil Court Records, Howard and Baronne Storage Center, New Orleans.

ords seem to indicate but one possible father, that is, the only Jean Barès listed in ship arrivals and city directories in New Orleans at the time. He was a French carpenter who immigrated to the city in 1838 and became a grocer. This is corroborated by Basile Barès's death certificate, which lists his father as having been "born in France." It gives the musician's age as fifty-seven years and eight months, indicating birth in January 1845. The 1880 United States manuscript census also indicates the same approximate birth date for the son and the same nationality for the father. Additional evidence linking father and son comes in Basile's first pieces to reach print after the Civil War, which date from 1866 and all but one of which give the composer's name as "Basile J. Bares." The discovery of an antebellum record originating from St. Mary's Roman Catholic Church in the French Quarter brought the evidence full circle. There, in the chapel of the archbishops of New Orleans, the one-month-old slave Jean was baptized on February 9, 1845, exactly one month to the day after January 9, 1845, which is the birth date "Bazile Jean Barès" himself provides and the widow Périer confirms on his 1871 passport application for travel to Europe. The baptismal record identifies the slave Jean as the son of the slave Augustine and, like his mother, as the property of Adolphe Périer. No father and godmother are listed. The godfather is a white man named "Jean."[29]

The deduction that Basile Barès began as a former slave means that the 1860 New Orleans sheet-music imprint "Grande polka des Chasseurs à Pied de la Louisiane" for piano is indeed a rare thing in American musical history. The composer of this piece is given simply as "Basile,"

29. Succession of Adolphe Périer; Marriage Certificate of Basile Jean Barès and Leontine Araiza, October 27, 1877, Orleans Parish Recorder of Births, Marriages, and Deaths, Register vol. 6, Louisiana Division, New Orleans Public Library, 428; passenger lists of vessels arriving at New Orleans, 1820–1902, microcopy no. 259, National Archives, Washington, D.C.; New Orleans City Directory (1846), 61; ibid. (1849), 15; ibid. (1850), 7; ibid. (1851), 9; Death Certificate of Basile Barès, September 4, 1902, Orleans Parish Recorder of Births, Marriages, and Deaths, Death Register, vol. 128, Louisiana Division, New Orleans Public Library, 227; Eighth Census of the United States (1880), New Orleans, Ward 7, Enumeration District no. 45; passport application 11,551, May 10, 1871, Records of the Department of State, RG 59, Passport Division, 1795–1905, entry 700, National Archives, Washington, D.C.; Baptism of the slave Jean, February 9, 1845, Baptism Book no. 2, 1844–1867, unnumbered p. 10, Act 58, St. Mary's Catholic Church, New Orleans, Archdiocesan Archives, Ursuline Convent, New Orleans.

without a last name, but the piece traditionally has been attributed to Basile Barès. It is not a particularly remarkable work musically, save for a few chromatic bits and some interesting passage work at the extremes of the keyboard, but it certainly would have been quite an accomplishment for a sixteen-year-old. What now makes this sheet music so unusual is that it appears to be the work of a slave published while he was still a slave. Furthermore, contrary to all laws at the time, the copyright appears to have been assigned to the slave. This was no doubt inadvertent on the part of the registrar at the New Orleans federal district court, but the implication of the lack of a last name for the copyright holder, "Basile," seems evident.

In addition to the strong documentary evidence that Basile J. Barès was a slave, there are strong internal musical similarities between the 1860 "Grande polka des Chasseurs" by "Basile" and the first five pieces of sheet music by Basile J. Barès, which appeared in 1866. All six pieces are in flat keys, and a theoretical analysis based on unpublished research by Ruth Rendleman reveals that the left-hand patterns are strikingly similar, showing a tendency to go from the root to an inversion of the chord and to use octaves rather than single notes on the strong beat. Harmonically, although there is greater chromaticism in the later pieces, all six employ the chromatically diminished seventh chord as a favorite device. The highly sectional nature of the music, coupled with a uniform tempo within each piece, may be characteristic of other contemporary dance music, but the "feel" of the music for the performer is distinctive and uniform throughout the six pieces, with single-note melodies drawn comfortably from notes next to each other on the keyboard to form melodies consisting of five-finger patterns. All six also display a fondness for octave melodies. In short, musical evidence alone points compellingly to the conclusion that the Basile of the "Grande polka des Chasseurs" and Basile J. Barès are one and the same.[30]

References to a musician named Basile appear as late as April 6, 1865, three days before the end of the Civil War, when the *New Orleans Tribune* reported on a concert by several musicians, including (Victor-) Eugène Macarty and a "Mr. Bazile" ("M. Bazile" in the French-language edition of April 8). Throughout its remaining coverage of the 1865 concert season by Creoles of color, the newspaper refers to a pianist who

---

30. Ruth Rendleman, unpublished manuscript, 1987, held by the author.

seems to be the same musician as "Mr. Bazile" and is performing with Macarty and Snaër as "Basile Périer." What Basile appears to have done, of course, is to have briefly used for a stage name the last name Périer, with which he had been associated publicly for his entire life up to that time. The paper's reference to "Basile Perrier" in the review of May 11 as "the self-made artist in all the strength of that expression" may even be an oblique Victorian allusion to the young musician's emergence from slavery and progress toward his eventual status as one of the most popular pianists and composers of dance music of postbellum New Orleans. More than a decade later, Trotter, himself a former slave, uses almost the same phrase, "self-made man," to describe Basile Barès.[31]

Although some of Barès's earlier pieces contain a few parts that probably reflect a lack of familiarity with some aspects of orthodox notation, he definitely was not self-made in the sense of being entirely self-taught. He studied piano under Dédé's old hometown teacher Eugène Prévost and harmony and composition under C. A. Predigam. He may also have gained further training in Paris. After the war, the widow Périer kept the music store, and Basile kept his old job. He traveled several times to Paris on business for the Périer firm, a fact confirmed by photographs of the pianist taken in Paris and held by Xavier University in New Orleans. Trotter writes about what seems to have been the first such trip, in 1867, during which Barès played for four months at the Paris International Exposition. His continued close association with his former owner, however, did not prompt him to keep the stage name Périer for long or to use it for any publications, and it disappears from the newspaper record after 1865, to be replaced by Barès.[32]

The 1865 concert season by Creole-of-color musicians is the only one documented sufficiently to allow for fruitful study. An examination of the programs reported in the *Tribune* reveals some interesting specifics with

    31. *New Orleans Tribune*, May 10–11, June 14, July 2, 8, 11, 18–19, August 12, 23, October 4, 27, 1865; Bishop, "Musical History of Louisiana"; Trotter, *Music and Some Highly Musical People*, 341.

    32. Trotter, *Music and Some Highly Musical People;* "War Between the States Sheet Music," n.d., case 5, M-R, Manuscripts Department, Howard-Tilton Memorial Library, Tulane University, New Orleans; Desdunes, *Nos hommes,* 119; Basile Jean Barès Collection, Archives and Special Collections for Black Studies, Xavier University of New Orleans.

regard to opportunity for blacks in the immediate postwar period and the musical tastes of the organizers. The newspaper is also the most reliable source for information about unpublished pieces, particularly repertoire other than the usual dances and songs favored by local printers.

The temporary changes in the relative status of whites and blacks in New Orleans wrought by federal occupation were dramatized in concerts that functioned as benefit performances for groups favoring black male suffrage and for such charitable institutions as the Third District Freedmen's Orphan Asylum, located in a prominent Confederate's Esplanade Avenue home, which had been seized by the Union. The Orphanage— where, ironically, one of these affairs took place—had been the mansion of Victor-Eugène Macarty's old benefactor, Pierre Soulé. Most of the concerts, however, were held for profit in the Théâtre d'Orléans, the stage of which was opened for the first time to people of color. This access was limited nevertheless to the off-season from May to October, when the weather generally was hot, tropical disease was prevalent, and many of those who could afford to leave were absent from town. These evenings usually were billed as "spectacle-concerts" and included everything from recitations, sketches, and entire plays to operatic overtures by Auber and Meyerbeer and French *vaudevilles* and *chansonnettes comiques*. The last was a specialty of Macarty's, who had a good baritone voice. He functioned as organizer and performer in many capacities: vocal, instrumental, and theatrical, most everything but compositional. Basile Barès's participation was almost entirely at the piano, although he was pressed into performing a small part in a play by Alexandre Dumas *père*. Barès performed not only his own works such as *"Fusées musicales"* and "Magic Bells," which may have been dance pieces that survive as publications under other names, but also *fantaisies* on themes from *Robert le diable* and *L'Africaine*. The latter two soon disappeared without a trace, probably because there was no local sheet music market for them.[33]

Samuel Snaër's principal job was to conduct the orchestra. Among his compositional contributions to programs were an orchestral polka, an overture, and an entire evening consisting mostly of his own music and for his benefit, including three songs published by Grunewald in 1865 and 1866. Among these was "Rapelle-toi: Romance pour voix de tenor

33. Desdunes, *Nos hommes*, 115; *New Orleans Tribune*, May 10–11, July 1–2, 8–9, 11, 13, 15–16, 18, September 5, October 4, November 1, 1865.

[and piano]," with words by Alfred de Musset. It may be compared with
Gottschalk's *romanza* of the same title and set to the same poem (RO
219), which may be found in an undated manuscript in the Americana
Collection of the Lincoln Center Library and Museum of the Performing Arts in New York. The August 22 concert also featured unpublished
works that have not been located, an *Allegro for Grand Orchestra*, the solo
song "Le vampire," and the vocal duet "Dormez donc, mes chères
amours." Among Snaër's unpublished pieces that were performed at that
time, only one, the "Chant Bachique," a drinking song for male chorus,
is currently available for research use, in the form of a facsimile at the
Amistad Research Center. A second unpublished work is also available in
facsimile only, the "Magdalena valse" for piano. The original manuscripts of these works are reported to be part of the private collection of
the late E. Lorenz Borenstein; the Snaër music in the collection is mostly
liturgical, including at least two masses, one bearing orchestral indications and one that may be the same *Mass for Three Voices* from which
Trotter reproduces a "Gloria" and an "Agnus Dei." This music stems
from the composer's long-term job as organist at St. Mary's. Trotter
mentions other, mostly later, unpublished works, including a song "Le
Bohémien," a vocal trio titled "Le chant de canotiers," the *Graziella
Overture*, and many dances. Not much more about Snaër was discovered
in the course of the present study, except that he became involved in several court cases against his mother-in-law and that one member of his
family was a state representative and another the first black attorney in
the state. Snaër died about 1896.[34]

Much more information is available about the careers of Macarty
and Barès in the years following the 1865 concert season by Creoles of
color. The lives of the two developed in different directions. Macarty for
the most part moved away from music, turning his talent for elocution
toward politics. At a time when the majority of voters were illiterate—

---

34. Offergeld, *Centennial Catalogue*, 27; Trotter, *Music and Some Highly Musical
People*, 342, 350, Appendix, 127–52; *New Orleans Tribune*, May 28, June 1, 14, 17–
18, July 23, August 8, 12–13, 15–20, 22–23, 1865; Desdunes, *Nos hommes*, 116; *New
Orleans Daily Southern Star*, February 24, 1866; Charles Vincent, *Black Legislators
in Louisiana during Reconstruction* (Baton Rouge: Louisiana State University Press,
1976), 147, 227, 235; Wayne Everard, unpublished genealogical research on the
Snaër family, n.d., Louisiana Division, New Orleans Public Library; Glasgow,
Rose, and Rose, "Played with Immense Success," 440.

including the former slaves, who held the majority of votes following the disenfranchisement of Confederates—Macarty's effectiveness as a public speaker in French was most helpful to the Republican Party cause in southern Louisiana. As a result, he won a term in the state house of representatives, from 1870 to 1872. Perhaps his single most important contribution, however, combined politics and civil rights with his love for music; in 1869 he brought the first suit against segregated seating in the New Orleans French Opera House (*Eugène Victor Macarty v. E. Calabresi*). Even though the case, which was tried in federal district court, seems never to have been resolved, other such suits against the Opera followed several years later in local courts. Macarty died in 1881.[35]

Barès also became involved in the issue of segregation at the French Opera when, in 1875, he served as accompanist at a concert in Economy Hall for the benefit of some foreign opera singers stranded in the city. Throughout its history the Opera had had serious financial problems that left it open to the vagaries of shifting race relations. At once eager to keep the patronage of people of color and anxious about losing the larger support of color-conscious white Creoles, the Opera management bounced back and forth throughout Reconstruction between strict and lax enforcement of rules requiring separate seating of the races. When, in the 1874–75 season, the management tried to restore strict enforcement, Creoles of color staged a boycott that many of them believed precipitated the financial shortfall that caused the Opera to fail to pay its singers at the end of the season. The benefit for the foreign singers, at which Barès performed with other local musicians and the singers, played to great success before a large black audience, permitting the singers to return to France and dramatizing mixed Creole resistance to segregation.[36]

While Macarty was becoming involved in politics, the much younger Barès was in his early twenties and still at the beginning of his musical career. In the next two decades he developed an enviable public following, even by the testimony of such a staunch white supremacist as local

35. Vincent, *Black Legislators*, 118, 230; *New Orleans Daily Picayune*, November 3, 1872; *Eugène-Victor Macarty v. E. Calabresi and Paul Alhaiza*, 1869, U.S. District Court for the Eastern District of Louisiana, New Orleans, docket no. 9,301, RG 21, National Archives, Regional Archives and Records Center, Fort Worth, Texas.

36. Death certificate of Victor Eugène McCarthy, June 25, 1881, Orleans Parish Recorder of Births, Marriages, and Deaths, Death Register, vol. 79, p. 7, Louisiana Division, New Orleans Public Library.

turn-of-the-century *littérateur* Grace King. He became especially prominent in playing for white Carnival balls, for which purpose he led a string band. Between 1869 and the late 1880s he secured the publication of at least nineteen of his dances for piano, including several associated with Carnival. One of these, the "Mardi Gras Reminiscences Waltz" (1884), has not been located in any local archives or library. Most of Barès's music copyrighted in the 1870s was published by Louis Grunewald, in whose music store Barès worked for a large part of that decade. In 1880 he went to work at the store of Junius Hart, who also published some of the pianist's works, including "Elodia: Polka Mazurka," the only other known piece that has not been located. Between the end of the 1880s, when he was still in his early forties, and his death in 1902, no further works by Barès seem to have been published. It may never be possible to determine whether this standstill was owing to the absence of further composition, increasing Jim Crowism, or changing tastes leading toward ragtime and Tin Pan Alley.[37]

LAURENT DUBUCLET

A Creole of color who was less well known than Snaër, Macarty, or Barès wrote most of the late nineteenth-century publications identified in local repositories. He was Laurent—or Lawrence—Dubuclet, born in New Orleans on October 4, 1866, a grandson of Reconstruction state treasurer Antoine Dubuclet. His uncles George and Eugène were both musicians. A pianist and saxophonist, Laurent Dubuclet was taught by Giovanni Luciani. Dubuclet became an early member of the New Orleans affiliate of the American Federation of Musicians, an ostensibly all-white local organization, raising the possibility that, in this setting, he was passing for white. He died in Chicago on November 25, 1909.[38]

37. *New Orleans Weekly Louisianian*, March 13, 20, May 15, 1875; Grace King, *New Orleans, the Place and the People* (New York: Macmillan, 1896), 338; *New Orleans Bee*, July 25, 1880; Junius Hart, *Descriptive Catalogue of Sheet Music* (New Orleans: Junius Hart, 1888), 29; Glasgow, Rose, and Rose, "Played with Immense Success," 338.

38. *New Orleans Daily Picayune*, September 5, 1902; *New Orleans Republican*, January 17, 1873; Succession of Paul Luciani, August 31, 1869, Inventory, Notarial Acts of Charles Martinez, no. 50, Orleans Parish Notarial Archives, Civil Courts Building, New Orleans.

THOMAS J. MARTIN AND FRANCES GOTAY

Two black composers who were not Louisiana Creoles but who were also active in New Orleans in the nineteenth century were Thomas J. Martin and Frances Gotay, whose careers marked, respectively, the beginning and the end of the period under consideration. At least eight pieces of sheet music by one or more persons named Thomas J. Martin were published in New Orleans between 1854 and 1860. Two earlier pieces by a Thomas J. Martin, "Genl. Persifor F. Smith the Hero of Contreras' March" and "The Creole Waltz," were copyrighted by F. D. Benteen in Baltimore in 1848. After their initial publication in Baltimore, they were republished in New Orleans and several other places. There is a direct connection, however, between "Persifor Smith's March" and one of the original New Orleans publications, "Free Mason's Grand March," which was copyrighted in 1854. The composer of "Free Mason's Grand March" is identified on the first page of music as "Thomas J. Martin, the author of Percifor F. Smith's March [and] Had I Never Known Thee." The latter work, which was so popular that it went through at least ten editions, is identified in 1860 by the *New Orleans Daily Crescent* as by the free black Thomas J. Martin, "the author of the once popular song, 'Had I never, never known thee.' He once composed a piece of music which he dedicated to the New Orleans Crescent; and has composed numerous other pieces of music." The reference to this dedication no doubt is a misunderstanding of the cover of "Free Mason's Grand March," which was part of a series called *The Crescent, a Collection of the Most Beautiful Pieces.* Therefore, despite the fact that the name Thomas J. Martin was a common one, at least three of the ten New Orleans imprints listed under that name—"Percifor Smith's March," "Free Mason's Grand March," and "Had I Never Known Thee"—all seem clearly to be by the same black composer.[39]

How the local press came to identify the black Thomas J. Martin is part of the story that broke on June 25, 1860, when Martin was arrested for allegedly threatening to burn down the house of Ann Severs, a retired white actress. According to these accounts, Martin had been responding to her threats that she would expose his three-year affair with her white

39. Musician's Mutual Protective Union, Local No. 174, American Federation of Musicians, *Constitution, By-laws, and Price List* (New Orleans: Musician's Mutual Protective Union, 1903), 44–5.

daughter, Fanny Thayer, which relationship had produced a child. Within a few days, the press was awash with claims about nearly thirty well-to-do, northern-born white women with whom he had been intimate in New Orleans. He was described as a guitarist and "a well-informed, Northern-educated" man of refined manners who had come to know these women as his piano students. Within three days of the first news, about two thousand whites, mostly curious spectators, gathered in Lafayette Square, the principal public place in the American part of town, to hear demands that Martin be lynched and all free blacks driven out. When a group of mostly boys broke off, however, and walked to Parish Prison (where the musician was being held) the police scared them off with a few warning shots. Eventually, Martin's bail was reduced, but he did not immediately come out of prison. The press speculated that he would wait until he could leave town quietly. Apparently this is what he did, because the First District Court records, which are complete for this period, contain no reference to a trial for over two years after the incident.[40]

Little is known about what happened to Martin after he left New Orleans. "General Sigel's Grand March," which first appeared in 1862, is identified on the cover as by "T. J. Martin, author of 'Percifer Smith's March.'" The catalog of Junius Hart published in New Orleans in 1888 lists three songs variously described as by Thomas J. Martin, T. J. Martin, or simply Martin; "Gate City March" by Martin (which became a rather famous piece); and, in an unnumbered addendum, guitar arrangements of "Freemason's Grand March" and "General Sigel's Grand March."[41]

Frances Gotay, the only woman identified among black composers in New Orleans, was born in Puerto Rico on May 21, 1865, and arrived in the city in 1883. She was still a teenager when she joined the Sisters of the Holy Family, one of the few orders of Roman Catholic nuns of African ancestry in North America. As Sister Marie Seraphine, she was ad-

40. *New Orleans Daily Crescent*, June 25–27, July 13–14, 1860; *New Orleans Bee*, June 25, 29, July 12–14, 1860; *New Orleans Courier*, June 26, 29, July 13, 1860; *New Orleans Daily True Delta*, June 26, 28–29, July 12, 1860; *New Orleans Daily Delta*, June 28–29, 1860.
41. Hart, *Descriptive Catalogue*.

mitted to a local Roman Catholic music school that was not ordinarily open to people of color; there she mastered many instruments, including strings, reeds, brass, percussion, and harp. She was in charge of musical instruction in schools of the order for nearly half a century and produced quite a lot of music in manuscript, which inadvertently was dispersed or discarded when the sisters left their convent on the former site of the Orleans Ballroom in the French Quarter in the 1960s. All that remains is one published piece, "La Puertorriqueña: Reverie" for piano. Gotay frequently performed with the St. Louis Cathedral Choir and, in later life, became a friend of Camille Nickerson. She died on September 11, 1932.[42]

What conclusions and further questions may be drawn from this study? For one thing, it confirms the primacy of French-speaking persons among local black composers in the nineteenth century. It also reveals the range of music written by nineteenth-century Orleanians of color to be narrow, embracing the entertainment qualities in demand by local sheet music publishers and the buying public, especially those who played the piano. This range, however, is no narrower than that written by other racial groups in the same place at the same time. Without a doubt, expatriate musicians enjoyed wider scope for their creativity, but how much of this was a function of different race relations abroad as opposed to different demands from publishers and the public in such metropolitan centers as Paris and Rio remains to be determined. How did growing tendencies toward racial segregation at home, which became more pronounced after the Civil War, affect the local environment in which music was made? How did white Creoles and American whites differ from the foreign-born French residents in the city in relating to musicians of color? Compared with the white Gottschalk, why did New Orleans black composers make so little use of local color? These and more questions about those who made the music and about the music itself remain to be answered. Nevertheless, the present study has attempted to correct inaccuracies and ambiguities in previous reports on

42. Sister Mary Frances Borgia Hart, *Violets in the King's Garden: A History of the Sisters of the Holy Family of New Orleans* (n.p., 1976), 87; Sister Mary Boniface Adams, Letter to the author, August 12, 1987; Sister Mary Boniface Adams, interview by author, August 24, 1987.

the lives of nineteenth-century black composers in New Orleans. By making use of local archival holdings, this study has uncovered new biographical information about some of the composers, but foreign repositories have yet to be exploited fully for their resources about the expatriates. The local holdings of the relevant local sheet music imprints also invite further analysis.

APPENDIX

Nineteenth-Century New Orleans Imprints and Music in Manuscript by Composers of Color in Local Repositories

Abbreviations

ARC: Amistad Research Center, Tulane University, Louisiana Music Collection

HNOC: Historic New Orleans Collection, Library, Sheet Music Collection

LSM: Louisiana State Museum, Old United States Mint, Louisiana Historical Center, Sheet Music Collection

LU: Loyola University, Department of Archives and Special Collections, Bound Sheet Music

NOPL: New Orleans Public Library, Main Branch, Louisiana Division, Early Sheet Music Collection

TU-J: Tulane University, Howard-Tilton Memorial Library, William Ransom Hogan Jazz Archive

TU-L: Tulane University, Robert Merrick Jones Hall, William Ransom Hogan Jazz Archive, Sheet Music Collection

TU-M: Tulane University, Robert Merrick Jones Hall, Special Collections, Blackmar Collection

UNO-A: University of New Orleans, Earl K. Long Library, Archives and Special Collections, Marcus Bruce Christian Papers

UNO-L: University of New Orleans, Earl K. Long Library, Louisiana Collection, Sheet Music Collection

XU: Xavier University of New Orleans, Library, Archives and Special Collections for Black Studies, Basile Jean Barès Collection

Basile Jean Barès

Grande polka des Chasseurs à Pied de la Louisiane [for piano]. © 1860 Basile. N.p. Dedication: Capitaine Tne. Hy. St. Paul de la 1re Compagnie. 3 pp. (Cover:

"En vente chez les Marchands de Musique." Music: "La casquette.") [The composer is listed only as "Basile," with no last name. The piece has always been attributed to Basile Barès.] LSM, TU-L.

La belle Créole: Quadrille des Lanciers Américain pour le piano. © March 20, 1866 A. élie. Pub. A. élie. Dedication: Mon Ami Eugène Macarthy. 4 pp. [Cover: "Basile J. Barès."] HNOC, TU-L, TU-M, UNO-L.

La coquette: Grande polka de salon pour le piano. © March 20, 1866 A. Elie. Pub. A. Elie. Dedication: Mme. Louise Hunt. 5 pp. TU-L.

La séduisante: Grande valse brillante [for piano]. © 1866 A. E. Blackmar. Pub. A. E. Blackmar. 10 pp. [Cover: "Basile J. Barès."] LU, TU-L, XU.

Les folies du Carnaval: Valse brillante [for piano]. © 1866 A. E. Blackmar. Pub. A. E. Blackmar. 8 pp. [Cover: "Basile J. Barès."] HNOC, TU-L, TU-M, UNO-A, XU.

La course: Galop brillante [for piano]. © 1866 A. E. Blackmar. Pub. A. E. Blackmar. 4 pp. (P.1: "Basile J. Barès.") HNOC, LSM, UNO-A.

La capricieuse: Valse de salon pour le piano, Op. 7. © 1869 A. E. Blackmar. Pub. A. E. Blackmar. Dedication: Melle. Theresa Labranche. 7 pp. HNOC, TU-L, TU-M, UNO-A.

Basile's Galop pour piano, Op. 9. © 1869 A. E. Blackmar. Pub. A. E. Blackmar. 5 pp. TU-M, UNO-A.

La Créole: Souvenir de la Louisiane, marche pour piano, Op. 10. © 1869 A. E. Blackmar. Pub. A. E. Blackmar. 7 pp. TU-L, TU-M.

Delphine: Grande Valse brillante [for piano], Op. 11. © 1870 Louis Grunewald. Pub. Louis Grunewald. Dedication: Melle. Delphine Dolhonde. 7 pp. TU-L, HNOC.

———. Reprinted as Exhibition Waltz, dedicated to the Cotton Exposition, 1884. TU-L, UNO-A.

———. Reprinted as Exhibition Waltz, dedicated to the Cotton Exposition, 1884–1885. (Cover: "10th Edition.") HNOC.

Temple of Music: Polka Mazurka [for piano]. © 1871 A. E. Blackmar. Pub. A. E. Blackmar. Dedication: Mme. M. J. Tassin. 5 pp. TU-L.

Minuit: Valse de salon composée pour piano, Op. 19. © 1873 Henri Wehrmann. Dedication: Louis Barbey. 5 pp. Pub. A. E. Blackmar, HNOC; Pub. Louis Grunewald, LSM; N.p. TU-J (Uncatalogued Maxwell Transfer, Accession No. 52), TU-L.

Merry Fifty *Lanciers* [for piano], Op. 21. © 1873 Henri Wehrmann. Pub. Philip Werlein. Dedication: The Merry Fifty Club. 5 pp. LSM, UNO-A.

Les cent gardes: Valse [for piano], Op. 22. © 1874 Henri Wehrmann. Pub. Louis

Grunewald. Dedication: Les Cent Gardes of New Orleans. 6 pp. LSM, TU-L.

Les variétés du Carnaval [for piano], Op. 23. © 1875 Louis Grunewald. Pub. Louis Grunewald. Dedication: His Royal Majesty Rex, King of Carnival. 5 pp. (Music: "L'invitation valse," "L'étoile polka," "Le prisonnier valse," "L'alternate mazurka," "La rosace valse," "Coda.") HNOC, TU-L, UNO-A.

Galop de Carnaval [for piano], Op. 24. © 1875 Louis Grunewald. Pub. Louis Grunewald. Dedication: My Friend L. E. Koniuszeski of St. Louis, Mo. 3 pp. TU-L.

Les violettes: Valse [for piano], Op. 25. © 1876 Louis Grunewald. Pub. Louis Grunewald. Dedication: Melle. Marie Heyob. 6 pp. TU-J (Uncatalogued Al Rose Collection, Accession No. 152), UNO-A. [See also Baron (1980) for a reproduction.]

The Wedding: Heel and Toe Polka [arrangement for piano], Op. 26. © 1880 Junius Hart. Pub. Louis Grunewald. Dedication: Miss Céleste Stauffer. 3 pp. (Cover: "Op. 25.") HNOC, NOPL, TU-L.

Mamie: Waltz pour le piano, Op. 27. © 1880 Junius Hart. Pub. Junius Hart. Dedication: John Davis. 7 pp. HNOC, LSM, TU-L, TU-M, UNO-A, XU.

Regina: Valse pour le piano, Op. 29. © 1881 Louis Grunewald. Pub. Louis Grunewald. Dedication: Melle. R. Gènois. 6 pp. TU-J (Uncatalogued Blackmar Collection, Accession No. 59). TU-L, UNO-A, XU.

La Créole: Polka mazurka [for piano]. © 1884 A. E. Blackmar. N.p. 5 pp. (Cover: Advertisement for "Mardi Gras Reminiscences Waltz, Basile Barès.") TU-M.

La Louisianaise: Valse brillante [for piano]. © 1884 A. E. Blackmar. N.p. 5 pp. (Cover: Advertisement for "Mardi Gras Reminiscences Waltz, Basile Barès.") LSM, TU-L, UNO-A.

Los Campanillas [for piano]. N.d. Unpublished manuscript. 1 p. XU.

Edmond Dédé

Mon pauvre coeur: Melodie [for voice and piano]. No ©. N.p. (1852). Dedication: Mlle. Fne. B. 2 pp. (Cover: Words by "C. Sentmanat," printer "B. Simon," lithographer "L. Pessou.") ARC (facsimile from a now-dispersed private collection of Louis Panzeri).

Laurent [Lawrence] Dubuclet

Bettina Waltz [for piano]. © 1886 Lawrence Dubuclet. N.p. Dedication: My Professor Signor Giovani Luciani. 5 pp. TU-L.

Les yeux doux (Sweet Eyes) [for piano], Op. 2. © 1886 Lawrence Dubuclet. N.p. Dedication: Mon Ami C. Laizer. 7 pp. HNOC, TU-L.

World's Fair March [for piano], Op. 7. © 1893 Lawrence Dubuclet. N.p. 3 pp. TU-L.

The Belle of the Carnival: March Two Step [for piano]. © 1897 Louis Grunewald. Pub. Louis Grunewald. 3 pp. HNOC, TU-L.

National Defense March, Dedicated to the American Nation [for piano]. © 1899 Lawrence Dubuclet. Pub. Lawrence Dubuclet. 3 pp. HNOC.

Frances Gotay (Sister Marie Seraphine)

La Puertorriqueña: Reverie [for piano]. © 1896 Sister Marie Seraphine. Pub. Junius Hart. Dedication: "In memory of the late Rev. Mother Magdalene of the Sisters of the Holy Family." 4 pp. UNO.

Victor-Eugène Macarty

L'alzea: Polka mazurka, souvenir de Charles VI [arrangement for piano]. © 1854 Eugene Macarty. N.p. Dedication: Mlle. A. Boudousquie. 2 pp. (Cover: "Pianist of the fashionable Soirées of New Orleans," "Sold at the principal Music Stores," Published with "La caprifolia" as Fleurs de salon: 2 Favorite Polkas.) TU-L, UNO-A.

La caprifolia: Polka de salon [for piano]. © 1854 Eugene Macarty. N.p. Dedication: Mlle. Delphine Forstall. 2 pp. (Additional information as above.)

Thomas J. Martin

Genl. Persifor F. Smith the Hero of Contreras' March [for piano]. © 1848 F. D. Benteen (Baltimore). Pub. F. D. Benteen (Baltimore) & William T. Mayo (New Orleans). 3 pp. (Music: "Tromboni," "Salutation, Trumpets," "Cannon," "Cornet à piston.") LSM, TU-J (Catalogued); Miller & Beacham (Baltimore) edition, TU-L, UNO-A; A. Blackmar & Bro. (Augusta, Ga.) edition, TU-M.

The Creole Waltz, composed and arranged for the piano forte. © 1848 F. D. Benteen (Baltimore). Pub. F. D. Benteen (Baltimore) & William T. Mayo (New Orleans). 2 pp. LSM, TU-L; Miller & Beacham (Baltimore) edition, UNO-A.

The Golden Bird of Hope [for voice and piano]. © 1850 William T. Mayo. N.p. Dedication: Little Nannie Nye Mayo. 2 pp. (Cover: "T. J. Martin.") TU-L.

Free Mason's Grand March, Dedicated to That Ancient Brotherhood [for piano]. © 1854. T. J. Martin. Pub. P. P. Werlein. 3 pp. (Cover: "The Crescent, a

Collection of the Most Beautiful Pieces"; p. 1: "Thomas J. Martin, author of Persifor F. Smith's March, Had I Never Known Thee.") HNOC, NOPL, TU-L, TU-M, UNO-A.

The Wife's Polka [for piano]. © 1855 T. J. Martin. Pub. Philip P. Werlein. Dedication: Mrs. Julia Whann. 2 pp. (p.1: "Thomas J. Martin.") NOPL, TU-L.

The Self-Composer: The Problem by Benedick Roefs arranged and harmonized [for piano]. © 1857 T. J. Martin. N.p. 8 pp. (Front cover: "Thomas J. Martin" and "To Be Sold at all Music Stores"; back cover: Advertisement for "Philip P. Werlein, pub.") TU-L.

Had I Never Known Thee: Song Composed and Arranged for [voice and] the Piano Forte. © 1858 P. P. Werlein. Pub. Louis Grunewald. 3 pp. (Cover: "10th Edition"; music: "4me Edition.") LSM, TU-L.

The Song of Returning Spring [for voice and piano]. © 1859 P. P. Werlein. Pub. P. P. Werlein. 3 pp. (p. 1: "T. J. Martin"; music: "Guitar.") TU-L.

Ah! It Was a Dream [for voice and piano]. © 1860 P. P. Werlein. Pub. P. P. Werlein. Dedication: Miss Maria L. Low. 3 pp. HNOC, TU-L.

Oratorial Grand March to the Memory of Henry Clay [for piano]. © 1860 F. Hartel. Pub. F. Hartel. 4 pp. (Music: "Tromboni," "Drum and Fife," "Corni.") HNOC, LSM.

François-Michel-Samuel Snaër

Rapelle-toi: Romance pour voix de tenor [and piano]. © 1865 Louis Grunewald. Pub. Louis Grunewald. 3 pp. (Cover: "Words by A[lfred]. de Musset." Published with "Le chant du déporté" as *Deux nouveautés*.) TU-L.

Le chant de déporté: Melodie pour voix de baryton [and piano]. © 1865 Louis Grunewald. Pub. Louis Grunewald. 3 pp. (Cover: Words by "A. Garreau." Joint publication as above.) TU-L.

Sous sa fenêtre (Come to Me, Love) [for voice and piano]. © 1866 Louis Grunewald. Pub. Louis Grunewald. 3 pp. (Music: Words by "L. P[lacide]. Canonge.") TU-L.

5

The Yankee Hugging the Creole

Reading Dion Boucicault's *The Octoroon*

Jennifer DeVere Brody

> The very name octoroon was an emotion. What word
> could better hide a plot, a privy conspiracy of seduction
> and anarchy?[1]

> Zoe, Zoe, witching and beautiful Zoe,
> Thy charms unto my fancy seem,
> a radiant impossible dream!
> —*The Creole*[2]

Zoe Peyton, the central character in Dion Boucicault's play, *The Octoroon; or, Life in Louisiana*, which opened in New York in 1859, is the supposedly freed "natural" daughter of a Judge Peyton, original owner of
Terrebonne, the Louisiana plantation where the story takes place. In this
melodrama the heroic lovers, Zoe and the judge's prodigal nephew,
George, are thwarted in their quest for romantic love by the evil machinations of a monied overseer named Jacob M'Closky. M'Closky covets
Zoe and Terrebonne and contrives a way to buy both; in the last act,

1. Townsend Walsh, *The Career of Dion Boucicault* (New York: Dunlop Books,
1915), 64.
2. A drama by Reece and Farnie with music by Offenbach. The play was performed in London at the Holbern Theatre in September of 1877.

however, the "good" overseer Scudder, a "Yankee and Photographic Operator," provides a snapshot as evidence that M'Closky has murdered a young slave, thus hastening the play's denouement.[3]

We are told in Act I that Zoe has "the education of a lady"—which in her case means her wild black roots have been trained and thoroughly tamed so that she is virtually a white gentlewoman. The purely passionate Zoe, the tragic heroine of the melodrama, is reared by the judge's white widow but is actually the product of his illicit adulterous affair with a quadroon slave.[4] Long-standing American antimiscegenation laws made marriage between blacks and whites impossible, although they did not expressly forbid mere sexual relations between them. The exogamous arrangements represented in Boucicault's play were a normal part of the peculiar institution, and at times were perhaps its very raison d'être. Such forms of amalgamation were seen as one of "the customs of Louisiana," where in mid-nineteenth-century New Orleans, adultery with octoroon fancy girls was an indicator (if not a requirement) of gentlemanly status. Such illegal couplings undergird the belief that the octoroon's story was inherently dramatic since it was ipso facto concerned with illicit desire, seduction, and anarchy.[5]

3. Myron Matlaw, ed., *Nineteenth Century American Plays* (New York: Applause Theater Books, 1985), 97–150; hereafter referred to by page numbers in parentheses. An exception to the more common reading of the play is Harley Erdman's essay, "Caught in the Eye of the Eternal: Justice, Race, and the Camera, from *The Octoroon* to Rodney King," *Theater Journal* 45 (1993): 333–48. This interesting article discusses Boucicault's novel use of the camera and photographic evidence. He concludes his discussion of visual technology with a discussion of the 1992 videotaped beating of Rodney King by the Los Angeles Police Department.

4. Zoe, as a hybrid herself, seems to implicitly understand Wahnotee, the "redskin" who speaks a "mash up of Indian, French, and Mexican." She also wholeheartedly endorses Wahnotee's love for a young slave boy; indeed, it is she who exclaims that the Indian is "a gentle, honest, creature . . . [who] loves the boy with the tenderness of a woman." Here, noble savages recognize one another as belonging to a class apart from the unnamed chorus of "little niggers, black trash or varmin [who] steal bananas . . . dem tings, dem darkies" (135). Indeed, all of the named characters, with the exception of Wahnotee, who are not white are described as "octoroon, quadroon, or yellow."

5. Boucicault's dramatic narrative of the octoroon contrasts with the lived realities of actual men and women of this description. For example, many poor white men established monogamous "common law" marriages with women of African descent. So too, there were many slave owners who became involved with such

Boucicault describes the origins and import of the octoroon's story:

The word Octoroon signifies "one-eighth blood" or the child of a Quadroon by a white. The Octoroons have no apparent trace of the negro
in their appearance but still are subject to the legal disabilities which
attach them to the condition of blacks. The plot of this drama was suggested to the author by the following incident, which occurred in Louisiana and came under his notice during his residence in that State. The
laws of Louisiana forbid the marriage of a white man with any woman
having the smallest trace of black blood in her veins. The Quadroon
and Octoroon girls, proud of their white blood, revolt from union with
the blacks and are unable to form marriages with the white. They are
thus driven into an equivocal position and form a section of New Orleans society, resembling the demi-monde of Paris. A young and
wealthy planter of Louisiana fell deeply and sincerely in love with a
Quadroon girl of great beauty and purity. The lovers found their union
opposed by the law; but love knows no obstacles. The young man, in
the presence of two friends, who served as witnesses, opened a vein in
his arm and introduced into it a few drops of his mistress's blood; thus
he was able to make oath that he had black blood in his veins, and being
attested the marriage was performed. The great interest now so broadly
felt in American affairs induces the author to present "The Octoroon"
as the only American drama which has hitherto attempted to portray
American homes, American scenery, and manners without either exaggeration or prejudice. The author has been informed of the strong ob-
jection to the scenes in this drama representing the slave sale at which
Zoe is sold and to avoid her fate commits suicide. It has been stated that
such circumstances are wholly improbable. In reply to these remarks he
begs to quote from Slave history the following episode: a young lady
named Miss Winchester, the daughter of a wealthy planter in Kent had
been educated in Boston where she was received in the best circles of
society and universally admired for her great beauty and accomplishments. The news of her father's sudden death recalled her to Kentucky.
Examination into the affairs of the deceased revealed the fact that Miss
Winchester was the natural child of the planter by a quadroon slave; she
was inventoried in chattels of the estate, and sold; the next day her body
was found floating in the Ohio.[6]

---

women and never married or had relations with other women, black or white.
Some of these men went on to provide in their wills for the children of such
unions. Indeed, most of the free mulattoes and octoroons (or to use my neologism,
mulattaroons) were resourceful, self-sufficient, independent-minded women.

6. Dion Boucicault, unpublished note, 1861, Theatre Museum, London.

Like Harriet Beecher Stowe in her *Key to Uncle Tom's Cabin* (1854), Boucicault justifies his script by quoting an episode from slave history. The passage is also notable for its explanation of the "equivocal position" of the white-appearing octoroons, as resulting from the pride in their white blood. The octoroons' valued whiteness means they logically must "revolt from union with the black." Thus the real problem is that these desirable (because white-appearing) young women are prevented from forming marriages with white men. This aspect of Boucicault's drama signals a shift toward a marked concern with "white slaves." The term *white slave* refers not only to enslaved light-hued octoroons such as Zoe, but also, and more importantly, to any white-appearing (both mixed-race and actually white) women who were mistreated. The octoroon is decidedly a feminine creature. Indeed, as Phillip Harper argues, "the mulatto figure's tragic quality derives from (and thus indicates) her fundamental femininity, which itself contributes greatly to her economical connotation of illicit sexuality—always . . . the mulatto's primary referent." The horror of slavery was therefore increasingly emblematized by the degradation suffered by "white" women.[7]

There is no doubt that Zoe is a lady, yet because she is one-eighth black she is seen as being luxurious. She is the supreme object of desire. "Niggers get fresh at the sight of her," the overseer M'Closky "shivers to think of her," and George is captivated instantly. Zoe becomes the common denominator between these disparate men, but only the southern hero George—a perfect specimen of the aristocratic planter class—is deemed worthy of Zoe's love. In this way, Boucicault may have played to southern sentimental ethnocentrism that worked to smooth over the raw economics of slavery.

The New Orleans fancy-girl auctions serve as the most blatant reminder that the nation's formation is inextricably bound up with (dark) female subjects. As Joseph Roach explains, the auctions which took place in the Rotunda at New Orleans' famous St. Louis Hotel were staged as

---

7. Philip Brian Harper, *Are We Not Men? Masculine Anxiety and the Problem of African-American Identity* (New York: Oxford University Press, 1996), 108. Among the most prolific and popular nineteenth-century dramatists, Boucicault produced works well known by theater historians in both the United States and Britain. His plays were frequently performed through the early decades of this century. See the introduction to the play in Matlaw, ed., *Nineteenth-Century American Plays*, 97–9.

"competitions between men, the auctions seethe[d] with the potential for homosocial violence. As theatrical spectacle, [the auctions] materialize the most intense of symbolic transactions in circum-Atlantic culture; money transforms flesh into property; property transforms flesh into money; flesh transforms money into property." The first scene of the play allows and even elicits potential buyers in the form of the audiences who have paid money to see the white actress Agnes Robertson perform the part of Zoe and to look at her body. Moreover, we must remember that the audiences no doubt attempted to scrutinize her body for signs of her buried "black" life. As dramatic strategy, the signs of Zoe's blackness are staged in such a way that unlike in a film, where the camera could zoom in for a close-up of the blue tinge of the actress's fingernails, the audience must imagine how her "deviant" difference might be written upon her body.[8]

Zoe's status changes several times during the play, beginning with Act I, wherein she believes herself to be free but then learns she is a slave. The mixed-race heroine undergoes various transformations in which her contradictory body is pushed and pulled among its multiple significations. Zoe is free, then slave, then free again—the last time permanently in death. She "falls" in status, her major fall (the transformation from free woman to slave) being ironically represented at the play's climax by a scene in which Zoe stands on top of a table, elevated above both the fleshmongers who bid on her body and the other black characters in the play. This staged inversion of the dominant codes demonstrates how value is inscribed in Zoe's body. She is in fact more valuable (as were the fancy girls) when the blackness of her body is showcased in this manner. "The body of the white-appearing Octoroon . . . offers itself as the crucible in which a strange alchemy of cultural surrogation takes place. In the defining event of commercial exchange, from flesh to property, the object of desire mutates and transforms itself, from African to Woman."[9]

When the hero, George Peyton, declares his love to "African-

8. Joseph Roach, *Cities of the Dead: Theories of Circum-Atlantic Culture* (New York: Columbia University Press, 1996), 101.
9. Gayle Rubin, "The Traffic in Women: Notes on the Political Economy of Sex," in *Towards an Anthropology of Women*, ed. R. R. Reiter (New York: Monthly Review Press, 1975), 179–80; Roach, *Cities of the Dead*, 179.

derived" Zoe (and not to the white woman Dora Sunnyside), he says that
"love knows no prejudice" (119) and offers to marry Zoe despite the fact
that she is illegitimate.[10] George has just returned home from being educated in Europe. No doubt his European education, if it were true to
gentlemanly form, included trips to brothels, as was de rigueur for those
taking the grand tour. Indeed, George's sojourn in Paris—the land of the
sexually adventurous French—was meant to be an initiation into a man's
world. We learn that "all the girls were in love with him in Paris," and
he even admits that he has been in love two hundred and forty-nine
times. Scudder alludes to this fact when he comments upon George's ad-
miration of Zoe's beauty, by saying he guesses George "didn't leave anything female in Europe that can lift an eyelash beside that girl, or who is
more beautiful and polished in manners" (104). True to the description,
Zoe proves herself to be a lady not only in appearance but also in fact
when she does the honorable thing and informs George of her maternal
heritage.

   In a dramatic moment, Zoe declares herself "an unclean thing, forbidden by the laws" (120), and asks for George's "pity." George, who is
ignorant of the American antimiscegenation legislation, is mortified to
learn that the object of his desire cannot be recognized as his legal wife.
Zoe points out the "bluish tinge under her nails and around her eyes as
evidence of her Black" maternal roots and states that "the dark fatal mark
. . . is the ineffaceable curse of Cain" (120).[11] Her solution to this dilemma is, eventually, to commit suicide. Here Zoe's person calls into
question the disjunction between literal and figurative blackness, underscoring the extent to which race must be understood as "performative."
The law that labels Zoe literally black, possessing black blood, is under-

   10. Interestingly, Peyton's phrase is used as a slogan by the contemporary
Cross-Colors clothing company, owned by black youth in Los Angeles. The company's self-styled moniker reads: "Clothing without Prejudice: Post Hip-Hop Academic Hardware for the Next Generation."
   11. A similar confession occurs in a climactic moment in Bram Stoker's *Dracula*
(1897) when the newly hybridized heroine, Mina, is branded with a red scar by Dr.
Van Helsing. At this moment when conflicting Christian and vampire signs meet
on Mina's body, the vampirized woman wails, "Unclean! Unclean! Even the Al-
mighty shuns my polluted flesh! I must bear this mark of shame upon my forehead
until Judgment Day!" (chapter 22). Like Zoe, Mina's wretched condition does not
preclude her from marrying a pure, upstanding middle-class man. Moreover, Cain
has been seen as the first "amalgamationist."

cut by its plainly figurative use. In appearance, manner, and form she is not "black"; her blackness must be written upon her. It is her belabored confession that "delivers" her blackness. The ontological assurance of what blackness "is" is never guaranteed in the play. Indeed, it is the purpose of the octoroon to pose (as) the problem of racial discernment. Her paradoxical social placement is clear from the beginning of the play, but it is continually—and with increasing overtness—confirmed during performance. The inevitable drive toward Zoe's degradation (and increased gradation) is heightened by the presumption in the first act that she is free. In Act II, she learns that, in fact, she is enslaved. These massive contradictions that underwrite the play work to delegitimate certain societal values. The oppositions of slave/free and white/black are disrupted when figures like Zoe enter the dominant nationalistic familial structures. Read as disrupting forces, they must be destroyed.

In Boucicault's original version of the play, performed in New York in 1859, Scudder's discovery comes too late to save Zoe from suicide; in another version, presented in London a year later, Zoe lives, and in the final tableau, George sweeps her up in his arms. In the English version Zoe thus ends up in the arms of her lover, an American man (merely of English descent) with whom it is declared she will "solemnize a lawful union in another (unspecified) land." In the American version, Zoe reacts to her fate in a Juliet-like fashion, by drinking poison. This action relieves her from becoming a slave and the property of the vile M'Closky and is presented as the noble choice since she lost her opportunity to become the wife and property of the aristocratic George. She opts to go to the "free" land so often celebrated in Negro spirituals, and will be thus purified in death. Zoe's ingestion of the poison is an attempt to solidify her body formally, to make her taint more permanent. If she has been poisoned with the blood of her African-American mother, then she replicates this original sin for George. At the very end of the play, however, the script says that she turns "white"—again following the typical trajectory of the octoroon.

The difference between the two versions of Zoe's fate points to the divergent politics of race in the two nations. Only English audiences, removed from the direct divisions of racial conflict, could radically rewrite the octoroon's narrative. As Boucicault reported in one of the 1861 London playbills: "Mr. B. begs to acknowledge the hourly receipt of so many letters entreating that the termination of the Octoroon should be modified and the slave heroine saved from an unhappy end. He cannot resist the kind feeling expressed throughout this correspondence nor refuse compliance with the request so easily granted. A new last act of the drama composed by the public and edited by the author will be represented on Monday night."[12]

In the original version of the play, Zoe enacts her understanding of cultural binaries and her low-Other position vis-à-vis such boundaries. Furthermore, she decides to maintain and not transgress such boundaries. In the English version, however, she allows George to follow his heart even at the expense of breaking the law. That true love triumphs is the stock-in-trade of melodrama; but even here, the implied blissful future of the lovers is not guaranteed. Their reconsolidation is also undercut by the fact that in all versions of the drama, Agnes Robertson, a white woman and Boucicault's wife, played the part of Zoe, ensuring that an "actual" interracial kiss did not occur—only an apparent (or a white-parented) white woman can portray purity properly as a property only of "whites." I put "whites" in quotation marks because as we are beginning to see, the definition of this term was not fixed.

Boucicault's decision to cast his wife in the lead role of the octoroon resonates with Robertson's repertoire. Before being cast as the octoroon, she had a reputation for playing breeches roles with great panache (her daughter would go on to originate the breeches role of *Peter Pan*), as well as multiple parts in single dramas. Known for the acumen with which she performed multiple parts in single dramas, Robertson seemed to be the perfect figure to dramatize the destabilized body of Zoe. In this regard she epitomized Victorian actresses who used disguises to change themselves and to emphasize the fact that women's bodies, like viscous material, are malleable and cannot be contained. So too, more than her impersonation, her performances remind us of Becky Sharp's acting the part of the perfect innocent ingenue though her roots were dirty, dark,

12. The "happy ending" was written in 1861 in response to British audiences, who were disappointed with Zoe's tragic death in the 1859 version. For the text of this new version, see *The Selected Plays of Dion Boucicault*, ed. Andrew Parkin (Washington, D.C.: Catholic University Press, 1987, pp. 184–90. For a fuller account of the politics of the different productions, see Peter Thompson's introduction to the *Plays of Dion Boucicault*, ed. Peter Thompson (Cambridge, England: Cambridge University Press, 1984), 9.

and dangerous. Such representations may be said to be both represented and erased in performances by Agnes Robertson. Although "tawny" stage makeup was manufactured in the 1800s, it is unlikely that Robertson would have "blacked up" for her performances. Indeed, that was the beauty of these roles; they required only the skills of melodramatic femininity. In an edition of the drama printed for Dicks' Standard Plays, the cover shows Zoe with M'Closky and Scudder. Interestingly, Zoe wears a white dress and has a white face and long straight black hair, whereas her white male companions are drawn with dark faces and clothes. (See the illustrations section of this volume.)

Again we come to see how white and black as morally coded terms signified in melodrama could be misapplied to racially white or black figures. This problem of mismatching signifiers and signified was examined in legal discourse. In America, the courts were one authoritative cultural arena that attempted to define "whiteness" and "blackness." In her analysis of the genre of legal miscegenation discourse, Eva Saks reveals how "courts, looking for external objective referents for blood (brown skin) were also implicitly attempting to forge a way of representing race that was referential, to invent mimetic terms that referred to something beyond figures of speech. But the ironic result of this double search—for referents and for *referentiality*—was that courts often found only other legal texts, prior to legal inscriptions" (emphasis hers). In short, race must always be understood to be a performance rather than a stable under-lying characteristic.[13]

Technically, the octoroon is not obliged to perform in concert with the law that both denies and creates her—but in fact she plays out over and over this specifically gendered tragic role that marks her as an obliging octoroon. The exemplary instance occurs in Boucicault's drama when Zoe decries her "tainted" maternal lineage by stating "I am an unclean thing forbidden by the laws!" Because the octoroon's origins almost always are obscured, audiences must succumb to the pleasure of reading an "open secret" and connecting the lines of descent torn asunder under the aegis of miscegenation law. A harsher view of this situation is expressed in the unpublished play "Cora, the Octoroon Slave of Louisiana" (1861), when a character named Marbee exclaims, "paternal love is a wealth a slave ought not possess." For by possessing legitimizing pa-

13. Eva Saks, "Representing Miscegenation Law," *Raritan* 8 (fall 1998): 61.

ternal love, the slave can shift from being property to having property. As we saw earlier, the "wealth" of the benevolent white father could uplift his daughter. The bestowal of property is a gift of paternal love to the daughter. Indeed, most nineteenth-century Anglo-American narratives present her as the twice-owned property of a white patriarch.[14]

The aptly named Amanda America Dickson (1849–1893) was one such "woman of color and daughter of privilege," born in pre–Civil War Georgia. Her birth was the result of a planter's rape of a female slave belonging to his mother, an incident narrated by a recent biographer: "One day in the middle of February 1849, [wealthy, white] David Dickson rode across his fallow fields . . . he spotted a young female slave playing. . . . Deliberately, he rode up beside the slave child and reached down and swung her up behind him on his saddle. . . . The slave's childhood ended as Amanda America Dickson's life began, on that day when her father raped her mother." Both despite and because of her historic entrance into the world, Amanda's fate, which might have been disastrous, turned fortunate because her father was kind and doting. She grew up "in her white father's household, inside the boundary of his family, as his daughter, and went on to marry a white Civil War veteran and have children of her own. She inherited her father's enormous estate . . . [and] died amid luxury and comfort." Consideration of her personal identity reveals that "her class solidarity with her father, that is, her socialization as his daughter, and her gender role as lady," complicated her racial demarcation.[15]

Similarly, the scientist Nott believed that "when a Negro man married a white woman, the offspring partook more largely of the Negro type than when the reverse [between white male and black female] con-

14. In contrast, male mulattoes appear in antagonistic relationships with their "white" fathers and in conjunction as well as in sympathy with their African "mothers." For example, I am thinking of Frederick Douglass' *Narrative of the Life of Frederick Douglass* (1845), James Weldon Johnson's *The Autobiography of an Ex-Colored Man* (1912), and Langston Hughes' play *Mulatto* (1935). Of course, narratives of male mulattoes who are the sons of black fathers, arguably a more recent phenomenon, portray this problematic trait differently. The manuscript of the "Cora" play is housed in the Theatre Collection at the British Museum.

15. Kent Anderson Leslie, *Woman of Color, Daughter of Privilege: Amanda America Dickson, 1849–1893* (Athens: University of Georgia Press, 1995), 1–2.

nection had effect." The dark daughter can be cast as the closest comfort to the white father. Her story provides the occasion for speculation about his own difference, identity, and desire. Because white men controlled miscegenation, they were the ones who made black women and women black. In many fictional accounts, the closeness between the white father and the black daughter was expressed as having an incestuous character. One nineteenth-century theorist even claimed that: "Hybridism is heinous. Impurity of races is against the law of nature. Mulattoes are monsters. The law of nature is the law of God. The same law which forbids consanguineous amalgamation forbids ethnical amalgamation. Both are incestuous. Amalgamation is incest."[16]

An example of this illicit relationship between father and daughter is hinted at in *The Octoroon*. The dialogue in the drama makes continual references to young Peyton's striking similarity to his dead uncle, the judge, who is Zoe's father, making Peyton her cousin. This similarity provides evidence of the "incest" that is read as being coterminous with "miscegenation" and other forms of illicit amalgamation.

Some nineteenth-century thinkers elided the differences between incest, miscegenation, and adultery, placing all three phenomena in the common category of the illegitimate or culturally anomalous. These confused and confusing categories are consistently juxtaposed with a pure and proper category, namely, the nuclear family epitomized by white Christian marriage. If the proper family is the building block of a strong nation, then incest, miscegenation, and hybridity threaten the family (of man) and by extension, the nation (of proper gentlemen). The precarious sexual nature of women who are not wives and mothers, like Zoe, threatens and complicates the pure and proper perpetuation of this national family. Victorian conventions (predominantly promoted by middle-class men) about female sexual transgression impose borders by systematically classifying and differentiating between pure women and passionate women and between licit and illicit sex. *The Octoroon* represents this ideology, being continually concerned with the maintenance and produc-

16. Hortense Spillers, "The Permanent Obliquity: In the Time of Fathers and Daughters," in *Changing Our Own Words*, ed. Cheryl Wall (New Brunswick, N.J.: Rutgers University Press, 1989); Henry Hughes, quoted in John Mencke, *Mulattoes and Race Mixture: Images, 1865–1918* (Ann Arbor: UMI Research Press, 1976), 18.

tion of civilized subjects; ultimately the drama allows the Christian characters to prevail.[17]

In the words of Scudder, "Natur' has said that where the white man sets his foot the red man and the black man shall up sticks and stan 'round." (They will salute him and make him the center.) "Now, what do we pay for that possession? In cash? No—in kind—that is, in protection . . . in gentleness [gentlemanliness?] and in all them goods that show the critturs the difference between the Christian and the Savage. Now what have you done to show 'em the distinction?" (147). This sermon of sorts to the Western white men who are seen to be behaving like savages affirms the divide between the two groups at the same time that it reveals one can become the other—that the tame and the wild are only *relative* positions, in both senses of that word. Here again, good characters are seen as white while bad characters are seen as "black."

Boucicault's drama provides us with a parable called "the Yankee hugging the Creole" (Act I) which is told by Scudder, the northern overseer who is "here somewhere interferin' " (and is indeed the voice of God-fearing, Christian "right reason" in the text), to M'Closky. The parable presents a model of northern white appropriation: "D'ye see that tree? It's a live oak, and is a native here; beside it grows a creeper; year after year that creeper twines its long arms round . . . the tree—sucking the earth dry all about its roots—living on its life—over-running its branches until at last the live oak withers and dies out. Do you know what the niggers call that sight? They call it the Yankee hugging the Creole."

Not only is this a metaphor for miscegenation; it also comments on the idea of nation formation in the form of appropriative violence—what has been described as the rape of the land under colonialism. Scudder's tale, told from the "native" perspective, casts the Yankee as the vampiric, parasitic substance that creeps and kills (Creole) life. The Yankee sees to it that the native dies out. Here, "forgetting, like miscegenation, [proves to be] an opportunistic tactic of whiteness." The patriarchal bias of some forms of miscegenation does privilege whiteness. "Bred (retrospectively) to be pure, the national-family tree is miscegenated at its roots." This

17. The term *miscegenation* is the title of an anonymously published tract that appeared in the United States in 1864. The subtitle, "A Theory of the Blending of Races: White Men and Negroes," provided the definition of the term. See Joel Williamson, *New People: Miscegenation and Mulattoes in the United States* (New York: Free Press, 1980), 8.

means that the production of whiteness depends upon miscegenation and is therefore not "pure." It too is "divided." As Hillis Miller explains, "The uncanny antithetical relation exists not only between pairs of words in the system, host and parasite, . . . but within each word itself. . . . Each word in itself becomes divided by the strange logic of the 'para' [hyphen/hybrid] membrane which divides inside from outside and yet joins them in a hymeneal bond, or which allows an osmotic mixing, making the stranger friend, the distant near, the *Umheimlich heimlich*, . . . without for all its closeness and similarity, ceasing to be strange, distant, dissimilar."[18]

The references here signify in another way because the Yankee himself was already a Creole according to the definition of the term. A "Creole" is one born in the Americas whose parents, of whatever race, were born in Europe. But one could also become a Creole by staying in the colonies long enough. The slippage between race and national origin, of living at home and abroad made purity impossible. The Yankee is only a Yankee because he has remembered to forget that he was a Creole. The category "whiteness" is an identity to be performed, preserved, restored, retained, contained, and "achieved" through repetition. Anxiety about the destruction of one's whiteness as legacy is expressed through references to the figure of the blackened woman.

Miller defines the most dangerous parasite as "the virus, the uneasy border between life and death, . . . that does not eat but only reproduces." Moreover, "the genetic pattern of the virus is so coded that it can enter a host cell and violently reprogram all the genetic material in that cell, turning the cell into a little factory for manufacturing copies of itself,

18. Roach, *Cities of the Dead*, 10; Russ Castronovo, *Fathering the Nation: American Genealogies of Slavery and Freedom* (Berkeley: University of California Press, 1995), 9–10; Hillis Miller, "The Critic As Host," in *Deconstruction and Criticism*, ed. Jeoffrey Hartmann (New York: Continuum Press, 1990), 221. It is interesting to note that Miller goes on to say: " 'Parisitical'—the word suggests the image of the obvious or univocal reading as the mighty oak, rooted in solid ground, endangered by the insidious twining around it of deconstructive ivy. That ivy is somehow feminine, secondary, defective, or dependent. It is a clinging vine, able to live in no other way but by drawing the life sap of its host, cutting off its light and air. I think of Hardy's 'The Ivy-Wife' or the end of Thackeray's 'Vanity Fair': 'God bless you, honest William!—Farewell, dear Amelia—Grow green again, tender little parasite, round the rugged old oak to which you cling!' " This quotation uncannily resembles the above scene from Boucicault's play.

so destroying it." This is the process of vampirism practiced not only by the infecting black figures, but from another perspective, by the white figures as well. Indeed, this is the ideology of whiteness, when without an unmarked body of its own appropriates, needs, and wants to co-opt technology to reproduce itself, all the while denying the utility of the native power for the fulfillment of such a project.[19]

This concept of absorption—the ultimate assimilation—problematizes notions of "whiteness" and purity by alluding to the fundamental hybridity of nations. The re-membering of the artificial construction of historical "development" dismembers the "naturalized" teleological notion of the progress and unity deployed in most narratives of national history. Thus does "nation-time" work by a future-anterior logic of identity that claims "we will be what we have been." Such false homologies connect the past, unknown origins that once selected can be revised and endlessly (if not effortlessly) performed in the present.

Zoe ultimately serves to reinforce the Establishment. The play performs the otherwise hidden and private artificial construction of national identity that is naturalized as unmediated inheritance. For example, in Boucicault's English version, Zoe's suicide frees George from entering a tainted affair. The elimination or sublimation of the disturbing dark lady results in the reconsolidation of discrete and dominant forms. In other words, "Value . . . inevitably remembers itself by dismembering the Other."[20]

It was believed that good women are pure and good men have passion (for work, class, and nation).[21] The dominant code of the era presumed that good women passively existed in the world, as does Mrs. Peyton, while good men actively asserted themselves in the world, as does Judge Peyton. At midcentury, however, the status quo of Victorian

19. Miller, "Critic As Host," 222.

20. Lindon Barrett, "In the Dark: Issues of Value, Evaluation and Authority in Twentieth Century Critical Discourse" (Ph.D. dissertation, University of Pennsylvania, 1991), 86.

21. White middle-class women marked or ironically displayed their racial, class, gender, and national identities by remaining on the pedestal built for them by patriarchal ideology and by following the injunction to "suffer and be still." See Martha Vicinus, ed., *Suffer and Be Still: Women in the Victorian Period* (Bloomington: University of Indiana Press, 1972).

ideology, which the hybrid woman like Zoe both embodied and challenged, required that there be strict divisions not only between the sexes, but within "the sex," as well as between sexual acts and between races. This movement that links the *stain* or *taint* of "blackness" to the formerly "white" woman is represented by some vernacular sayings:

> When a woman falls from purity there is no return for her—as well one may attempt to wash the stain from the sullied snow. Men sin and are forgiven; but the memory of a woman's guilt cannot be removed on earth.
>
> To wash a negro, to attempt an impossible task.[22]

Such women are controlled through the assertion that both the prostitute and the mulatta, should they live, will prove to be barren. In this sense, they are stereotypical hybrids who are incapable of proper or substantial reproduction. Indeed, in nineteenth-century England, France, and America, prostitution, slavery, and miscegenation were among the great social evils. These evils are inextricably connected with the replication of the nation that would maintain union in disturbing times. The sex instinct simultaneously is conflated with and divorced from the fraught issue of race preservation. This is another great paradox in which the figure of the mulattaroon woman plays a key role. She was seen on the one hand as a preserver of the patriarchal family—an outlet for the father who would not contest his legitimate reproduction—and on the other as a threat to the "legitimate" family because she was a source of potential confusion of illicit and licit. If the "suppression of natural similarities . . . [could continue to be] expressed as natural" differences, if the incestuous miscegenation that produced the octoroon could be forgotten and erased, then proper reproduction would flourish. If Zoe could be classed as outside of and different from the true white family, if her whiteness could be suppressed or expressed as pure blackness, then order would be maintained.[23]

Zoe, like the fancy-girl characters whom she resembles, challenged

22. William Starbuck, *A Woman against the World* (1864), quoted in Richard Cox, ed., *Sexuality and Victorian Literature* (Knoxville: University of Tennessee Press, 1984), 69; *Oxford English Dictionary*.

23. Thomas Laqueur, *Making Sex: The Body from the Greeks to Freud* (Cambridge, Mass.: Harvard University Press, 1990), 205. This work provides interesting and important background to historical theories of sex/gender differentiation.

the idea that women were to be defined solely in relation to the patriarchal family, as wife, daughter, mother, if they were to remain in their proper separate sphere of the home. Therefore she disrupts distinctions between oppositional cultural categories. We can see how "beyond the sphere of domesticity, the sexual . . . effects synonymity with the illicit, the wild, the mysterious, without permutation. One of its signs is the mulatta, who has no personhood, but locates in the flesh a site of cultural and political maneuver."[24] Reading the fallen mulattaroon as "still-life" in the double sense of this term shows how (mostly male) authors like Boucicault both feared and maintained some control over such representations of blackened femininity. The mulatta's shifting cultural placement is symptomatic of her ambiguous character. She occupies a central space that is perpetually being erased or effaced in an effort to stabilize (reify) the tenuous, permeable boundaries between white and black, high and low, male and female, pure and impure. Thus, scholars of American culture are obliged to study the octoroon not only because she is one of the most important American inventions but also because her performance has yet to be played out.[25]

24. Spillers, "Permanent Obliquity," 183.
25. Here I refer to the fact that a mixed-race female character named Zoe is at the center of the San Francisco Mime Troupe's anti–Proposition 209 performance, "Escape to Cyberia." So too, in her 1997 presidential address to the American Studies Association, Mary Helen Washington hailed the album by Lisa Love entitled *Octoroon* as an exemplar of American culture at the end of the century.

6

The Use of Louisiana Creole in Southern Literature

Sybil Kein

> Gae, gae soulangae,
> bailé chemin-là.
> M'a dit li, oui,
> m'a dit li,
> cowan li connais parlé
> ti cowan li connais parlé.
> —*from a Creole lullaby*

> Gae, gae soulangae,
> Sweep the road.
> I tell her, yes,
> I tell her,
> The turtle knows how to talk,
> The little turtle knows how to talk.

These words from a Creole lullaby allude to the origin of that language and its roots in African culture. For purposes of this essay, the Creole language is best understood as a language that was developed in Louisiana by Africans, black slaves, and free people of color during the state's early colonial period. In *Africans in Colonial Louisiana*, Gwendolyn Midlo Hall explains, "It has been established, through linguistic as well as historical evidence, that Louisiana Creole was created in Louisiana and was not derived from Haitian or other West Indian varieties of French-based Creoles. Ingrid Neumann-Holzschuh, a German creolist, has recently argued, from linguistic evidence, that Louisiana Creole developed independently of the Creoles of the French West Indies. Neumann-Holzschuh's interpretation coincides with the historical facts. We have seen that the slaves brought to Louisiana during the formative period of the language came directly from Africa, not from the French West Indies." Indeed, there seems to be little doubt that this Creole language is indigenous to Louisiana. As Hall describes, "The . . . Louisiana Creole is overwhelmingly French in origin, but its grammatical structure is largely African." This description also points to the fact that Creoles and Creole speakers are a part of the Louisiana Francophone culture.[1]

Professor Vincent Bakpetu Thompson, in *The Making of the African Diaspora in the Americas, 1441–1900*, attributes the development of the Creole languages to the mulatto middlemen who were the progeny of one African parent and a European. These mulatto middlemen, who participated in the slave trade as translators, were numerous; Thompson says that in the seventeenth century or earlier they "spanned the entire Guinea Coast and became factors to be reckoned with." This evidence accords with Hall's conclusion that "Louisiana Creole evidently developed from a Portuguese-based pidgin that had been relexified with the French vocabulary in Senegal. This pidgin was spoken by a number of African slaves brought to Louisiana between 1719 and 1731. The first generation of creole slaves adopted the language as its mother tongue, expanding and nativizing its vocabulary, including Indian terms for local fruits and plants."[2]

The present essay will examine the use of the Louisiana Creole language in literature about the South. It will examine lyrics of some of the Creole slave songs and then move to the earliest use of the language by writers of the nineteenth and twentieth centuries. Presented here are selected examples of the available materials containing samples of Creole.

---

1. Gwendolyn Midlo Hall, *Africans in Colonial Louisiana: The Development of Afro-Creole Culture in the Eighteenth Century* (Baton Rouge: Louisiana State University Press, 1992), 188, 190.

2. Vincent Bakpetu Thompson, *The Making of the African Diaspora in the Americas 1441–1900* (New York: Longmans, 1987), 95; Hall, *Africans in Colonial Louisiana*, 192.

The totality of written work includes many romantic popular novels set in Louisiana which show scant use of Creole and which are excluded for the sake of brevity.

The earliest known sample of written Creole is by Louisiana's first historian, Le Page du Pratz. According to Hall, "du Pratz published several sentences in Louisiana Creole. Although he published his work . . . in book form in 1758, he lived in Louisiana between 1718 and 1734. These quotations, therefore, had to date from before 1734 and are some of the earliest documented examples of any creole language. One sentence quoted from Samba Bambara was '*M. le Page li diable li sabai tout*' ('Mr. Le Page is a devil who knows everything')." Another early source of written Creole is Jean Jacques Rousseau's *Dissertation sur la musique moderne* (1742). Rousseau uses the words of a Creole folk song, "Lisette Quittes la Plaine," as an example for his system of notation. He called it "Chanson nègre" but did not say where he found this song. Dena J. Epstein offers a comparison of Rousseau's one stanza to Tinker's nineteenth-century Louisiana notation of the same song: "The one stanza of text given in the facsimile of his [Rousseau's] manuscript, while closer to classical French, was substantially the same as that given in the 1811 version, where it was called 'Chanson Créole' and included five stanzas of eight lines each." Both the du Pratz and the Rousseau examples suggest a very early date for the use of Creole languages, either the 1700s or perhaps even the late 1600s.[3]

An examination of the Creole folk songs of Louisiana, which with few exceptions were created by slaves, offers insight into the development of the Louisiana Creole culture. A distinction may be drawn between those Creole slaves whose songs were purely secular and those who created the perhaps more widely known spirituals. In French Louisiana, in addition to the segment of the African American folk culture that produced the spirituals there developed another segment that emphasized the feelings of the individual self and undisguised reactions to immediate needs dictated by actual surroundings and actual events. While the makers of the spirituals used the Christian religion as a vehicle for emotional outlet

3. Hall, *Africans in Colonial Louisiana*, 191–2; Dena J. Epstein, *Sinful Tunes and Spirituals: Black Folk Music to the Civil War* (Urbana: University of Illinois Press, 1977), 94.

even when songs were employed as signals for escape routes, these other Creole slave songs, though just as lyrical, are highly individualized, stripped of disguise, sensual, and determinately worldly.

"It was said that the 'colored Creoles' of Louisiana who fought in the Battle of New Orleans had their own special war song, *En Avan' Grenadie* . . . which they sang along with *La Marseillaise* and other songs." Gottschalk, the New Orleans Creole pianist and composer, "made use of part of the *En Avan'* melody in one of his piano pieces." The extant verse in Creole is thus:

> En avant, grénadiers!
> ça qui mouri, n'a pas ration.
> En avant grénadiers!
> ça qui mouri, tant pis pou yé!

> Forward, Grenadiers!
> Those who die, no ration.
> Forward, Grenadiers!
> Those who die, all the worst for them!

The attitude expressed in this song may be seen as indicative of the juxtaposition of the Spanish "Que Sera" perspective and the West African religious view of man's ability to change his fate by manipulation of the lesser gods. In other words, if you must die and can do nothing about it, *tant pis*.[4]

Judging by their content, many other Creole songs likely predate this march song. One might well agree with Marcus Christian that "Those English-speaking slaves who learned Creole, and those coming from French Colonial provinces, began improvising songs upon their arrival at the auction-block in New Orleans." Christian cites a satirical song about a famous lawyer, a M. Etienne Mazureau, whom the slaves must have observed while he was employed to write legal confirmation of slave sales:

> Michie Mazureau
> Ki dan so bireau,

---

4. Epstein, *Sinful Tunes*, 94; Eileen Southern, *The Music of Black Americans: A History* (New York: W. W. Norton, 1971), 76; Nina Monroe, *Bayou Ballads* (New York: G. Schirmer, 1921), vi, 30. The translations of Creole included here are the author's unless otherwise noted.

Li semble crapo
Ki dan baille dolo.

Mr. Mazureau
Who in his office,
He looks like a frog,
In a bucket of water.

Further, some of the slaves and free men of color who composed these songs had contact with various ethnic groups before coming to Louisiana, and a certain amount of cultural borrowing took place. This borrowing, which is evident with regard to both form and content, is combined with the obvious rhythmical influence from Africa. A study has yet to be done to place these songs in precise historical order according to the content of the verses.[5]

The earliest notation of one of these Creole songs is found in *Le Villageois*, a bilingual weekly published at Marksville, Louisiana, between March 30, 1844, and April 23, 1859. *Chant du Vie Boscugo* appeared in the January 6, 1858, edition. In *Textes anciens en créole louisianais*, Ingrid Neumann-Holzschuh confirms: "A notre connaissance, cette chanson represente un des plus anciens textes publiés en créole louisianais. Il fut reproduit dans la collection de COLEMAN (1885: 158–60) avec de legères modifications orthographiques. D'après CABLE (1886: 12), 'il s'agit d'une des chansons les plus populaires de l'époque.' " According to the song, a M. Preval (who Christian says is a free man of color) gave a ball in his barn for both blacks and whites who came there to dance the Calinda and the Bamboula. He did not have a permit to hold such an affair, however, and was imprisoned and fined $100. In the sixteen stanzas, we are told how some slaves stole their masters' and mistresses' clothes to attend this ball, how the jailer reacted to the arrest of M. Preval, and how the guests enjoyed themselves. In the end, M. Preval has learned a lesson:

Li payé cent piasse
Li courri la chasse,
Li dit c'est fini
Ya pli bal sans permi.

5. Marcus Christian, "Black History of Louisiana," chapter 9, Marcus B. Christian Collection, Earl K. Long Library, University of New Orleans, 8–9.

He paid one hundred dollars
He was dismissed,
He said that is the end
No more ball without permit.[6]

The Creole songs, then, were developed by Creole slaves in the eighteenth century and continued to be created during the nineteenth. This
body of music is not be confused with Zydeco or LaLa, the dance music
of the country part of Louisiana, which was influenced by blues and rock
and roll, although a few tunes overlap the categories. The melody of the
Creole songs dominates the rhythm pattern. There are no blues or spirituals per se, although some of the songs have the feeling of the blues in
theme and a blues-like form of AAAB, as in the example below. There is
literally one religious song, "Marie Madeline," but no outpouring of
songs about God, faith, or church. The songwriters seem to have retained and emphasized, instead, the African sense of using song for purposes of satire or praise. They also created songs to memorialize
remarkable events or people and to accompany activities such as religious
rituals and hunting. The largest portion of the Creole songs is concerned
with love and courtship, including one between a female slave and her
master. This is a love duet in which she is clearly in control of the situation. The title is "Z'Amours Marianne."

Marianne:
    Si l'amour vous si fort, Michie-là,
    Si l'amour vous si fort, Michie-là,
    Si l'amour vous si fort,
    Faut plein d'argent dans poche!
Michie:
    Toutes mes cannes sont brûlées, Marianne,
    Toutes mes cannes sont brûlées, Marianne,
    Toutes mes cannes sont brûlées,
    Ma récolte est flambée!

6. Reginald Hamel, *La Louisiane (Créole) 1762–1900* (Montreal: La librarie des
Presses de l'université, 1977), 620; Ingrid Neumann Holzschuh, *Textes anciens en
créole Louisianais* (Hamburg: Buske, 1987), 93. For a good analysis of the structure
of Creole songs, see Mary Wilson, *Traditional Louisiana French Folk Music: An Ar-
gument for Its Preservation and Utilization as a State Cultural Heritage* (Ann Arbor:
University Microfilms International, 1978).

Marianne:
  Si cannes à vous brûlées, Michie-là,
  Si cannes à vous brûlées, Michie-là,
  Si cannes à vous brûlées,
  L'amour à vous flambé!

Marianne:
  If your love is strong, Sir,
  If your love is strong, Sir,
  If your love is strong,
  You must have money in your pocket!
Sir:
  All my canes are burnt, Marianne,
  All my canes are burnt, Marianne,
  All my canes are burnt,
  My harvest is gone to flames!
Marianne:
  If your canes are burnt, Sir,
  If your canes are burnt, Sir,
  If your canes are burnt,
  Your love has gone to flames!

This song, also titled "Dialogue d'Amour," was called a "Calinda, a dance that was linked to songs of derision and which ended the evening's gaiety at Place Congo." Besides the no-money-no-love theme, there is the blatant sexual comparison of the plantation owner's sugar cane to his sex organ. At this writing, "Z'Amours Marianne" is the only song of its kind that has yet been found, although some others have similar double meanings. There are also many lullabies, including the haunting "Gae, Soulangae," which alludes to the practice of Voodoo. Reminding its listeners, "You know the calabas knows how to sing" (the calabas, a medicine gourd, was used in African Voodoo as a spirit medium) and "the turtle knows how to talk" (animals also were used as mediums), it ends with a warning: "Tichou [or Wildcat] knows how to strangle!"[7]

Characteristic of the melodies of the Creole slave songs is the rhyth-

7. Holzschuh, 95; Monroe, *Bayou Ballads*, 26–9; Maude Cuney-Hare, *Six Creole Folk Songs* (New York: Carl Fischer, 1921), 21. "Marie Madeline," as sung by Inez Catalon, is included on *Zodico, Louisiana Creole Music* (Rounder Records, 1979).

mical "scotch snap" at the beginning of a song and the use of syncopated rhythm throughout, although some songs, notably "Soulangae," have a very smooth melody line. "Misu' Banjo" is a good example of the use of the snap. Also found in many of the songs is the initiation of the melody on the second beat of the measure instead of the first beat. This emphasis on the second beat was carried over into the development of early jazz, and is a hallmark of that music. The second-beat start can be heard today in the singing and playing styles of some of the older musicians who play the early jazz in New Orleans. They will "hesitate" for one beat before starting a song, even though that song may have been written to start on the first beat. Sweet Emma Barrett, an early jazz musician, was noted for this style of singing. Another attribute of the Creole tunes is their simplicity. "True to the usual character of folk music, the Creole songs are very simple in melodic and harmonic character." To elaborate, "Afro-American Creole folk musicians were able to structure most of the syncopated and complex rhythmic patterns into two-four, three-four, and six-eight meters." The harmony is not unlike those found in France or Spain, or the Caribbean. These close harmonies, however, are not as important as the melody line, which is set in major keys, minor keys being the exception and not the rule.[8]

Some of the Creole songs have found a niche in the Louisiana popular culture. A call and response tune, "Eh, Là-Bas," which is based on "Vous Conné Tit la Maison Denis," was sung by Creole men dressed as women and playing small guitars on Mardi Gras as late as the 1940s. "Eh, Là-Bas," and "Yé Tout Mandé pour Toi" or "They All Asked for You," are still very popular in the state; the latter was recorded by Dave Bartholemew in the early 1950s and again by the Meters in the 1970s. The chants of the Mardi Gras Black Indians also use the Creole language, although they have been diluted over the years by American black speech. A good example of the Black Indians' Creole is in the chant or prayer that opens their Mardi Gras observance. They sing "Madi cu defio, en dans dey," which is a corruption of the old Creole song, "M'allé couri dans déser," used in connection with Voodoo rituals and associated with the Calinda dance.[9]

8. Hare, *Six Creole Folk Songs*, 21; Wilson, *Traditional Louisiana French Folk Music*, 55; Camille Lucie Nickerson, "Africo-Creole Music in Louisiana" (master's thesis, Oberlin Conservatory of Music, 1932), 33.

9. Wilson, *Traditional Louisiana French Folk Music*, 59; Mrs. Augustine Moore, interview by author, 1980.

The categories of Creole songs vary according to the authors classifying them, such as Cable, Whitfield, Kreible, and Hearn. One category that is mentioned by all is that of dance tunes, music and words associated with Place Congo in New Orleans. The present site of Armstrong Park, once called "Circus Square" or "Congo Plains," was where slaves would assemble on Sunday afternoons to dance. The "Bamboula" and the "Calinda," both mentioned in some of the Creole songs, were popular dances, as were the "counjai," the "juba," the "carabine," and the "pilé chactas." "Many slaves of gentle surroundings essayed the more sophisticated forms of European dance, in imitation of their masters and mistresses." The chorus, "Dansé Calinda, boudoum, boudoum!" has been added to some of the songs, indicating that they were used to accompany dancing at the Place Congo. There are approximately eighty extant Creole songs, most of which have survived with musical notation intact. White folklorists have collected the songs in their work, and in the present century a few of these songs have had international exposure, owing in large part to the work of Creole musician Camille Nickerson. Nickerson's 1932 master's thesis at Oberlin Conservatory—"Africo-Creole Music in Louisiana"—is a standard source in the field. She toured extensively, not only performing these songs but also collecting many of them on field trips to the parishes of Louisiana.[10]

The Creole songs represent a forceful and creative use of the language by Creole slaves and former slaves. Creole historian Charles B. Rousseève claims that most of the free men of color who were writers of any sort during the early nineteenth century wrote Creole songs, but only one song connected with these writers is extant. Unlike his contemporaries, who used the language only sporadically, this composer, Joe Beaumont, concentrated his creative efforts on writing songs exclusively in Creole. Beaumont's song "Toucoutou" was used by Edward L. Tinker as the base for his 1928 novel, *Toucoutou*. Although he was

a quadroon, Joe Beaumont was not in sympathy with the custom of "passing" that was fairly common among the members of his class. The song, "Toucoutou," was a result of a court suit instituted to determine the legal status of a free colored family claiming that its members were of unmixed Caucasian descent. It was shortly before the Civil War and the suit was the outcome of a street brawl between two children of well-known free colored families. One child called the other a Negro, there-

10. Christian, "Black History of Louisiana," chapters 6, 14.

upon the family of the second child feeling itself slandered, brought suit
for damages, but lost the suit and was relegated to the free colored class,
rather than the white group to which they had formerly laid claim.[11]

"Toucoutou" became quite popular and survived with the people for
generations after the lawsuit. It contains many verses and is a satirical
song in the manner of many African and other Creole songs.

Refrain:
Ah! Toucoutou, yé conin vous,
Vous cé t'in Morico.
N'a pas savon qui tacé blanc
Pou blanchi vous lapo.

Ah! Toucoutou, They know you,
You are a Blackamore.
There is no soap so white
That it can bleach your skin.

The satirical slap of this song was—as Beaumont wrote in the last
verse—a lesson to others who may have had similar notions as Toucoutou.

Mo pré fini mo ti chanson
Pasque m'anvie dormi;
Mé mo pensé que la leson
Longtemps li va servi.

I'm almost finished my little song
Because I want to sleep;
But I think that the lesson
Will serve for a long time to come.[12]

Although a significant number of Creole songs have been lost, other lessons, proverbs, animal tales, and fables round out the body of Louisiana
Creole folklore created using the Creole language. Folktales and songs
composed by the Afro-French people of Louisiana were written down in
Creole by white men, some of whom seemed very familiar with the lan-

11. Ibid., chapters 5, 14; Charles B. Roussève, interview by author, 1988.
12. Christian, "Black History of Louisiana," chapters 9, 16.

guage. Seven Afro-French fables in Creole and many songs and verses were published in *Le Meschacébé* in St. John the Baptist Parish in Louisiana between 1858 and 1877. Neumann-Holzschuh cites six satirical letters to the editor written in Creole in 1867. They reflect the political climate of the post–Civil War era and "les textes refletent en partie la chasse aux voix des Noires ainsi que la reaction des anciens esclaves vis-à-vis de leurs nouveaux droits." The spellings used in these letters make for difficult reading even for one familiar with the language. The intent is clearly to make fun of the newly freed Blacks. These few lines may serve as example:

> Li pélé moun tou sort non, *Stinkin, Stilin, Lezi* Niga: cé ça ki soké mouen pli. Vou koné dan tan Rebel yé té di kom ça nég cé nég, grifé cé grifé, milat cé milat; a s'tere nou zot cé tou zens koulair, mem ça ki noua kom soudière, yé gainen pou pélé li ein zens koulair. Mo pa tandé Merikien boucou mé mo koné Niga cé pa ein parol pou di ein *Gemman* koulair.
>
> He called me all kinds of names, Stinking, Stealing, Lazy Nigger: It is that which provoked me more. You know in Rebel times they said that nigger is a nigger, griffe is a griffe, mulatto is a mulatto; now all of us are people of color, even one who is black as soot, they have to call him a person of color. I don't hear American much but I know Nigger is not a word to say to a *gentleman* of color.[13]

Another weekly, which appeared in New Orleans between 1873 and 1877, was similarly vicious in its attack on Afro-French people. The editors of *Le Carillon* aimed their invectives mainly at the Creole politician Caius César Antoine, who became lieutenant governor of Louisiana and president of the state legislature during Reconstruction. One verse of the dialect pieces published about Antoine compares him to a monkey.

Macaque là té sal Negue ein fois;
Le meillier que tou blancs asteur,
Pasque c'est li qui fait nou' les lois,
C'est li qui fait nou' Gouverneur.

13. Edward Larocque Tinker, *Toucoutou* (New York: Dodd, Mead, 1928), 280; Edward Larocque Tinker, "Gombo: The Creole Dialect of Louisiana Together with a Bibliography" (Worcester, Mass.: Reprinted from the April proceedings of the American Antiquarian Society, 1936), 45; Holzschuh, *Textes anciens*, 98.

That monkey once was a dirty nigger;
He's better than all the whites now,
Because it is he who makes us the laws,
It is he who is our governor.

Tinker sums up the effect in this manner: "Nowhere else can be found as vivid a picture of the acrimonious rancor engendered by Negro rule as in the numberless 'poems,' letters and parodies, in the dialect, which appeared in the 'Carillon' during this period. Their popularity established among white writers quite a vogue for the Gombo, which continued even after the bitterness of Reconstruction had abated." One such white writer was a poet-priest, the abbé Rouquette, who used the language in a ballad-type verse, which was later set to music by W. T. Francis as the song "Zozo Mokéur." Rouquette also wrote a series of verses in Creole in which he attacked the popular writer, George Washington Cable. Published in 1880, in a pamphlet called "Critical Dialogue between Aboo and Caboo," the verses compare Cable to a goat and accuse him of dancing with Marie Laveau, the Voodoo Queen, marrying a mulâtress and having children who looked like zombies. Rouquette, who was motivated by his displeasure over Cable's treatment of Creoles in the novel *The Grandissimes,* died insane a few years after this publication.[14]

The satirical use of the language and the first bits of Afro-French folklore appeared in Louisiana at about the same time, the second half of the nineteenth century. Also at this time, however, there appeared a use of the language that seems a departure from the typical, in that it lends a certain human dignity to the people portrayed. In 1881, the white Dr. Alfred Mercier published a novel in French about life on a Louisiana plantation owned by Creoles. Although Mercier was not against slavery, *L'Habitation Saint-Ybars; ou Maîtres et Esclaves en Louisiana* suggests that its author did not view the Creole language as evidence of the debasement of its users but rather as a normal dialectical collection of current idioms. In the beginning of the novel, a young Frenchman approaches a "negress" and addresses her as "Madame." She answers him in Creole and then, seeing that he does not understand her, answers him again in French. Having a black character respond in French shows at least a touch of sympathy for the humanity of that character. At points through-

14. Holzschuh, *Textes anciens,* 105; Tinker, "Gombo," 26.

out the novel, other slaves also speak French as well as Creole. In some instances, the white characters speak French and the slaves answer them in Creole, and the Creole song "Lissett To Kité la Plaine," is employed as a lullaby sung by La Folle, an aged slave. Such usages mark a definite departure from the debasing mockery of the language seen in the weekly papers of the day.[15]

The use of the language in the folktales, although charming and of great historical importance, is nevertheless in keeping with the widespread belief in the childlike quality of the Creole slaves. This noble-savage idea, as promoted in the publications of these folktales, promoted racist thought by reconfirming the notion that Creoles of color were inferior to whites. Alcée Fortier, professor of Romance languages at Tulane University, published ten Afro-French fables, some proverbs, and the words to several songs in his *Bits of Louisiana Folklore* in 1888. In 1895, he published fifteen animal fables, twelve fairy tales, and an appendix in English of fourteen other stories. In the introduction to this second work, *Louisiana Folktales*, Fortier writes, "The Louisiana folk-tales were brought over to this country by Europeans and Africans, and it is interesting to note what changes have been made in some well known tales by a race rude and ignorant, but not devoid of imagination and poetical feeling." Fortier's attitude toward Afro-French people is typical of southerners of his day. Of the language, he says, "It is curious to see how the ignorant African slave transformed his master's language into speech concise and simple, and at the same time soft and musical."[16]

Other contemporary collections of folklore include Lafcadio Hearn's 1885 *Gombo Zhebes*, a dictionary of Creole proverbs from Louisiana, Martinique, Haiti, Mauritius, Trinidad, and Guyana. Included in the collection, which is available in English as well as French, are fifty-one Louisiana proverbs, a good example of which is "Tout macaque trouvé so piti joli," or "Every monkey thinks its young one pretty." Another subgenre is animal tales, wherein African heroes and villains are often merged into English tales, as in a collection by Joel Chandler Harris.

15. Tinker, "Gombo," 27–8; Albert Mercier, *L'Habitation Saint-Ybars ou Maitres et Esclaves en Louisiana* (Nouvelle-Orléans: Imprimérie Franco-Américaine, 1881), 7–8, 126. The variations in the song title here and later in the essay reflect various authors' preferences.

16. Alcée Fortier, ed., *Louisiana Folktales* (Boston: Houghton, Mifflin, 1895), ix, x.

Compair Lapin is the clever rabbit hero, and Compair Bouki, the villain wolf. Of particular interest is "Piti Bonhomme Godron," the "Tar Baby" story in Fortier's appendix. There is an explicit connection between "Piti Bonhomme Godron" and the English version of "Tar Baby," which George Reinecke of the University of New Orleans has explored in a modern-day article. The folktales have also been set down by Jules Choppin, who published several in *Comptes-Rendus de L'Athénée Louisianais* between 1896 and 1902, and Lafayette Jarreau, who surveyed others in a 1931 Louisiana State University thesis, "Creole Folklore of Pointe Coupée Parish."[17]

Thus far, what has been found of the language in written form has been recorded by whites; but what of the Creole authors of the nineteenth century? It seems the *gens de couleur* writers chose to publish almost exclusively in French. Specifics are available in the words of Creole historian Charles Rousseve:

> With the appearance at New Orleans in 1843 of *L'Album Littéraire, Journal des Jeunes Gens, Amateurs de la Littérature* came the first recorded effort at literary publication by Louisiana free people of color. *L'Album Littéraire* was a little French review, originally appearing monthly, and later fortnightly, presenting poems, stories, fables, and articles both signed and anonymous. Through these writings their authors sought to arouse in young readers a stronger determination to stand firm against the oncoming tide of increasing discrimination, . . . to which free Negroes were being subjected. Associated with various contributions are the names of Joanni Questy, Armand Lanusse, Camille Thierry, Mirtil-Ferdinand Liotau, and Michel Saint-Pierre.

Rousseve also lists five early writers, Hippolyte Castra, who wrote "La Campagne de 1814–15," a five-stanza poem extolling "the valor of the men of color on that occasion"; Joseph Colastin Rousseau, who wrote prose and verse; Michel Seligny, who published prose and verse in various French newspapers; Lucien Mansion, who penned verses and essays; and Joe Beaumont, whose Creole songs have already been mentioned.[18]

17. Lafcadio Hearn, *Gombo Zhebes* (New York: Will H. Coleman, 1885), 36. See Reinecke's article, "The African 'Tar Baby' Tale: Its Survival in Creole Louisiana," *Urban Resources* 4 (1967).

18. Charles B. Rousseve, *The Negro in Louisiana: Aspects of His History and His Literature* (New Orleans: Xavier University Press, 1937), 63, 65.

In 1845, Armand Lanusse published *Les Cenelles*, a volume of the works of seventeen Creole poets writing in French. Though often ignored by modern anthologists, this book marks the first collection of poetry by Afro-Americans. One of those free men of color, Camille Thierry, later published a book of poetry in Paris in 1874, titled *Les Vagabondes*. It is here that we find one poem written in the Creole language, "Regrets d'une Vielle Mulâtress." All of the other works by Creole writers are in French. One reason for this seems to be the particular class/caste system of slave, free colored, and white that developed in Louisiana, but perhaps more important is the debasement of the language itself and its social connection with the stereotypes based on plantation life. Language is an integral part of one's identity, and the Creole language suffered from the same racist derision and oppression as did the people who invented and used it. It is no surprise, then, that the Creoles of color in antebellum times chose French as their medium of expression.

Language can also be a divisive tool. In this case, it tended to separate the schooled from the unschooled, the intellectual from the peasant, the free from the slave, the rich from the poor. Connected historically to the lowest class in Louisiana, the Creole language became an emblem of inauspicious roots. This was especially true after the Civil War and Reconstruction. Creole became further suppressed after *Plessy* v. *Ferguson* in 1896, which legally dismantled the free colored class. The term *Creole* was subsequently claimed by whites to apply exclusively to a class of people who were pure, white, and unblemished by a dash of the tar brush. Some of the same white writers who had collected the Creole folk material spearheaded the publication of numerous articles, statements, speeches, book inserts, and the like to claim the new definition of Creole as exclusively Caucasian. According to Virginia Domínguez, "Charles Gayarré . . . and Alcée Fortier . . . led the outspoken though desperate defense of the Creole. As bright as these men clearly were, they still became engulfed in the reclassification process intent on salvaging white Creole status. Their speeches consequently read more like sympathetic eulogies than historical analyses." George Washington Cable was one writer who instigated much of the wrath of these newly defined Creoles. With his penchant for the Creole language, his careful research, his attention to the slave songs, and his novels, especially *The Grandissimes*, he exposed their preoccupation with covering up bloodlines and in particular their blood connection with the free people of color and slaves.

"There was a veritable explosion of defenses of Creole ancestry. The more novelist George Washington Cable engaged his characters in family feuds over inheritance, embroiled them in sexual unions with blacks and mulattoes, and made them seem particularly defensive about their presumably pure Caucasian ancestry, the more vociferously the white Creoles responded, insisting on purity of white ancestry as a requirement for identification as Creole."[19]

This New England–educated native son stands alone among writers of his day in giving realistic treatment to the social climate in Louisiana. His black characters are humanely etched, and he uses the language as a leveling tool, by having aristocrats as well as quadroons and slaves speak Creole. In *The Grandissimes* and also in the short story "Old Creole Days," it is the common language of the characters. In "Madame Delphine," the title character explicitly tackles the issue:

> "Why Madame Delphine—"
>   "Oh, Père Jerome! I wan' see you so bad, so bad! Mo oulé dit quichose—I godd some' to tell you." The two languages might be more successful than one, she seemed to think. "We had better go back to my parlor," said the priest *in their native tongue*. (Emphasis added.)

In *The Grandissimes*, Agricola Fusilier and Honoré Grandissime, both members of the ruling class, speak to each other in Creole, a language Cable likewise gives to the Creole, the black, the quadroon, the plantation mistress, and the street merchant. He also uses eight of the Creole songs in this novel and demonstrates the characters' preference for the language. French phrases are scarce, and most are simply one- or two-word local-color additions such as "par example" or "Impertinente" and, rarely, single sentences such as "On dit . . . que ses eaux ont la propriété de contribuer même à multiplier l'espèce humaine." In her foreword to a collection of Cable's stories, *Old Creole Days*, Shirley Ann Grau says he was "one of the first American writers to portray the Negro as a human being, subject to feelings of hate, love, shame." She defines Creole as "a person of French and Spanish ancestry, who may or may not have colored blood." This, she says, is the way Cable uses the word. In "Madame

19. Virginia R. Domínguez, *White by Definition: Social Classification in Creole Louisiana* (New Brunswick, N.J.: Rutgers University Press, 1986), 142–3.

Delphine," set in the 1820s, a story of a retired quadroon woman and her daughter, Cable portrays the Creoles' language as an intrinsic part of their character. Madame Delphine and her daughter Olive use it as a matter of course, and the narrator explains, "She spoke in the patois most natural to her, and which her daughter had easily learned." The language becomes part of his description of them, particularly when he utilizes Creole sentences to emphasize a strongly emotional response or comment. "Dieu sait, ma chère, mo pas conné!" the unsettled Madame Delphine exclaims in response to a question from her daughter. Later, when excited, she stops Père Jerome: "Mo courri ci, mo courri-là, mo pas capable li trouvé." Cable thus makes skillful use of Creole to portray the Creole people as human with human emotions.[20]

One of Cable's contemporaries, Lafcadio Hearn, also used Creole in some of his writings. Hearn published three editorials on the language in the *New Orleans Times-Democrat* in 1886, the words of a Creole song in the *New Orleans Item* in 1880, and a collection of proverbs from six Creole languages in 1885, the previously mentioned *Gombo Zhebes.* He also refers to the Creole in several of his other works, notably *Occidental Gleanings* (1925), *American Miscellany* (1924), and *Creole Sketches* (1924). In Hearn's short story "Chita," the central character is a Creole child who is rescued from a hurricane. When it is discovered that she does not speak English, Spanish, Italian, or German, the captain of the rescuing ship tells one of his men, Laroussel, "You're the only Creole in this crowd, talk gumbo to her." Laroussel speaks to the girl in Creole and she responds. The dialogue is tender, and there seems to be no intent on Hearn's part to use the language negatively. One may surmise from what follows, however, that although the language is fine for use by young children, its appropriateness holds only up to a point: "the little ones were indulged in the habit of talking the patois; . . . after a certain age their mispronunciation would be made fun of in order to accustom them to abandon the idiom of the slave-nurses, and to speak only French."[21]

20. George Washington Cable, *Old Creole Days* (reprint, New York: New American Library of World Literature, 1961), viii, 47, 53, 57, 65; George Washington Cable, *The Grandissimes* (reprint, Athens: University of Georgia Press, 1988), 2, 10, 12, 57, 71, 82, 92, 132, 142.

21. Lafcadio Hearn, "Chita," in *Selected Writings of Lafcadio Hearn* (New York: Citadel Press, 1949), 166, 167.

Another prose writer of the time, Kate Chopin, used the language in two of her short stories. Her 1897 collection *A Night in Acadie* includes a story about a Creole character, César François Xavier, whose nicknames are "Neg," "Chicot" (stump), and "Maringouin" (mosquito). The title of the story is "Neg Creole," but the language use is slight. The character is described as "black, lean, lame, and shriveled." Further, "He wore a head-kerchief, and whatever rags the fishermen and their wives chose to bestow upon him. Throughout one whole winter he wore a woman's discarded jacket with puffed sleeves." Is this not the black-clown oddity that Thomas "Daddy" Rice made famous in the minstrel shows in the same century? Moreover, Chopin seems to be following the popular pattern of adding "neg" or Negro to Creole to make a distinction between white Creoles (like herself) and "les negs." Her collection *Bayou Folk* (1894) makes use of more of the language and also includes a verse from the Creole song "Lisette to quitté la plaine." In one of the *Bayou Folk* stories, "La Belle Zoraide,"

> a lovely mulatto girl is raised at her mistress's side. She has never performed more difficult labor than sewing, and she even has a black servant. Her mistress wishes Zoraide to make a "good" marriage with a mulatto, but Zoraide loves a man as black as ebony. When Zoraide's mistress shows fury, the slave girl answers: "since I am not white, let me have from out of my own race the one whom my heart has chosen." But her lover is sent away. Zoraide's one remaining happiness is the child she bears, but when that child is born, she is deceived into thinking it dead. The cost of all these foolish attempts to impose intraracial color prejudices [is] the girl's sanity. Zoraide lives to be an old woman, always clasping a "senseless bundle of rags shaped like an infant in swaddling clothes." Even when her real child is returned to her, Zoraide will not recognize her and holds instead her "bundle of joy." . . . This story is particularly ironic because the racial prejudice which destroys the lovely mulatto girl is not her own but her mistress's and it is not the white woman's hatred for the girl, but rather her love that destroys Zoraide.

"La Belle Zoraide" is told by a black character, Old Manna Loulou, who speaks Creole (it is she who sings the Creole song) and who is telling this as a bedtime story to her mistress, Madame Delisle. In "La Belle Zoraide" as in "Neg Creole," it is the speaker of Creole who is debased, rather than the language itself. Chopin shows Manna Loulou as she "bathed her mistress's pretty white feet and kissed them lovingly, one, then the other." Though the language is praised as "the soft Creole patois, whose music and charms no English words can convey," the servant who speaks it is reduced to the stereotypical deferential underling. At the end of the story the dialogue between Manna Loulou and her mistress is in Creole:

"Vou pré droumi, m'a zelle titite?"
"Non, pa pré droumi; mo y apre zongler. Ah, la pauv' piti Man Loulou. La pauv' piti! Mieux li mouri!"

"You ready to go to sleep, Manzelle Titite?"
"No, not ready to sleep; I'm thinking. Ah, the poor baby, Man Loulou. The poor baby! Better she dies!"

Thus ends this tragic tale.[22]

Afro-French writer Madame Helen d'Aquin Allain published a book in France which contains five verses of the same Creole song used by Chopin, "Lisette quitté la plaine" in French and Creole. This book is notable because it is the first use in print of Creole by an Afro-French woman. Allain was a well-respected member of late-nineteenth-century Parisian society.[23]

The next Afro-French writer to use Creole was Alice Dunbar-Nelson. Many of Dunbar-Nelson's short stories have Creole/Cajun themes but are nevertheless written entirely in English. The turn-of-the-century "Natalie" makes use of French, but only sparingly, and another story with the theme similarly uses a few French words for spice. But in the sketch "The Praline Woman," published in *The Goodness of St. Rocque* (1899), Dunbar-Nelson employs a mixture of English and French to portray this colorful French Quarter merchant. The vignette is composed of bits of conversation as the praline seller presumably talks to her various customers in a dialect combining French and broken English.

22. Kate Chopin, *A Night in Acadie* (Chicago: Way and Williams, 1897), 199; Kate Chopin, *Bayou Folk* (1894; reprint, Ridgewood, N.J.: Gregg Press, 1967), 185, 281, 288, 290; Judith R. Berzon, *Neither White nor Black: The Mulatto Character in American Fiction* (New York: New York University Press, 1978), 102.

23. Madame Frederick Allain, *Souvenirs d'Amérique et de France, par une créole* (Paris: Perisse Frères, 1882).

"Pralines, pralines. Ah, ma'amzelle, you buy? S'il vous plaît, ma'amzelle, ces pralines, dey be fine, ver' fresh."
  "Mais non, maman, you are not sure?"
  "Sho', chile, ma bébé, ma petite, she put dese up hisself. He's hans'
so small, ma'amzelle, lak you's, mais brune."

Dunbar-Nelson includes a verse of one song, which is also in French:

Tu l'aime ces trois jours,
Tu l'aime ces trois jours,
Ma coeur à toi,
Ma coeur à toi,
Tu l'aime ces trois jours!

It seems that rather than writing entirely in Creole, Dunbar-Nelson preferred to merely hint at the language in her portrait of the candy seller.
Nevertheless, it is doubtful that such a merchant would not speak Creole,
especially considering that the clipped English words verify a speech that
is clearly French/Creole and not American English. The explanation is
likely that since the degradation of the Creole language had already taken
place, fledgling writer Dunbar-Nelson took care not to stereotype her
characters with what was considered a badge of ignorance.[24]

  After the fin de siècle, another woman writer, white novelist Helen
Pitkin Schertz, treated the Creole theme profusely in *An Angel by Brevet*,
a work that contains five Creole songs complete with words and music,
in arrangements for voice and piano. Set in the 1890s, this novel explores
the relationship of Voodoo to the lives of white Creoles. It is curious that
one of the main characters, Madame Euchariste d'Aquin de Marigny, is
described as having "mellow brown" skin and her granddaughter, the
protagonist Angelique, as having "a paler brown in her firm young skin
than in her grandmother's." Be that as it may, the story revolves around
Angelique, who is lured first into Voodoo and then away from it by
Christianity. One of the former servants of the household is convinced
that Madame de Marigny is responsible for the disappearance of her
daughter. Zebra confronts Madame with this accusation after the family
and friends have just finished their Sunday dinner. The youngest male
member of the family is angered by this accusation and kicks at Zebra

24. Gloria T. Hull, ed., *The Works of Alice Dunbar-Nelson* (New York: Oxford
University Press, 1988), 1:175, 178.

and calls her names: "Polisonne [rascal]. Vielle gribouille [dauber]." Zebra lashes back with a curse to the boy in English, "Boy, you'll never make a man!" and then another to the entire group in Creole, "Mo souhaite que malédictions layé possédé vous!" Angelique seeks the aid of the house servant, Victorine, in removing the curse. This involves the girl in meetings with Voodoos and even in participation in a Voodoo ritual. In the end, Angelique turns instead to Christian prayer and gives up her interest in Voodoo.[25]

Pitkin Schertz's treatment of the Creole characters is worth examining. Though not written in Creole, the following examples show the degree of stereotyping of characters through language use. Madame de Marigny is ailing from the curse, as Victorine is speaking with another servant:

> "Is dey got dat ooman Esebe nussin' dat chile, Tetess?" she asked. "She fool. She de kin' to give a chile footbat' ef he leg cut off! Me, ah don' see how Momzelle Titine kin stan' dem servant. Dere's Joseph. Ah nev' wants to work wid a Joseph. All de Joseph boys is mischeevous and de Joseph men is scolds."

When one of the Joseph men comes to Victorine's kitchen with a message, he grabs scraps of food from the shelf and says, "I prays dat some day de bayou will turn to one big san'wich and de Basin to whiskey." Further revealing is Victorine's response to Joseph: "Nigger was bawn on Good Friday w'en Gawd waz daid."

Along with this systematic stripping of dignity, the work of the novel seems to be a relegation of Afro-French people to the lowest rung on the social ladder, that of childlike, irresponsible, hopeless creatures who were meant to serve others. The Creole language is used by the servants and by Angelique, while the white Creoles speak French. Each chapter opens with a Creole proverb, such as "Dans la Louisiane yé trouvé bon calas, des huîtres, tchoupique, et bomboula" ("In Louisiana one finds good rice cakes, oysters, mud fish, and the bamboula dance"), which Pitkin Schertz is careful to call "Creole Negroisms." Despite its overt faults, the novel, which also includes some curious Voodoo chants in Creole, is a good source for the language in use.[26]

25. Helen Pitkin Schertz, *An Angel by Brevet* (Philadelphia: J. B. Lippincott, 1904), 13, 14, 45, 46.
26. Ibid., 11, 342, 343.

Others around this time did the important work of collecting and publishing the Creole songs. William Francis Allen, Charles Pickard Ware, and Lucy McKim Garrison's 1867 *Slave Songs of the United States* contains seven Creole songs with musical notation of the vocal line. Two years before that publication, the words to several songs were printed in Coleman's *Guide to New Orleans*. Clara Gottschalk Peterson, the composer's sister, compiled a number of songs with piano accompaniment in *Creole Songs from New Orleans* (1902). Nina Monroe included twelve Creole arrangements in her 1921 *Bayou Ballads*. In the same year, Maude Cuney-Hare's *Creole Folk Songs* contained six more tunes. And the words to several songs are found in Castellanos's *New Orleans As It Was* (1905), and in the 1919 volume of the *Louisiana Historical Quarterly*. These are also included in Dorothy Scarborough's *On the Trail of Negro Folk Songs* (1925). The words and some melodies also appeared in New Orleans newspapers, specifically the *Item-Tribune Magazine* and the *Times-Picayune*, between 1925 and 1927.[27]

Another use of the Creole language in literature is found in the poetry of a local writer, Margaret Dashiell, in her collection *Spanish Moss and English Myrtle*. Similar to Dunbar-Nelson, Dashiell used the French Quarter fixture of the praline seller as a subject for one of her poems. This vendor is described in English as a "picture" of the old South:

> Her plaid tignon is gay of hue,
> Starched her gown of calico blue;
> Rustling like silk her apron white,
> For brush and pencil a delight.

Unlike with Dunbar-Nelson, however, we find definite use of Creole in the last line of this poem, which closes:

> Pleasant her greeting:—"Bonne, c'est ça!"
> Bon jou' Madame, comment—ça va?
> Et po vous, M'sieur, Voici, masse-pain!
> Quen' Tante li fait, c'est assez, hein?
>
> These are good!
> Good day Madam, how are you?

---

27. William Francis Allen, Charles Pickard Ware, and Lucy McKim Garrison, *Slave Songs of the United States* (New York: A. Simpson, 1867), 109–13.

And for you, Mister, here, corn bread!
When Aunty makes it, that's enough, huh?

Also included in this little volume are the "Mammy" poems "Mammy Speaks," "Mammy Grown Old," "Everybody's Mammy," and "A Little Lad to Mammy." It is obvious that these sentimental verses speak of a longing for the "good ole days befo the wah," when "Mammy" was a more functional part of the social structure. One of the poems ends:

Whatever would we children do,
Oh, Mammy, dearest, but for you?

The second part of the book contains verses written in American Black dialect, portraying bits of slave life as happy times for stupid people:

Tis a yeah sence we done lay him
In dat grave-yahd ground—
An Marse John ain' took no foolin—
His niggers stood 'rown!

Shumate mek a mighty rustlin'!
Somefin' movin', I 'low.
Gawd, Marse John, I ain't got nuffin'!
Rooster, I draps yo' now!

The interminable shadow of stereotypes continued in the 1920s. We move from Chopin's Jim Crow character "Neg Creole" and tragic "yella gal" "Zoraide," to the mammies and coons of Pitkin Schertz and Dashiell, to variations on the theme of the tragic mulatto in Edward L. Tinker's *Toucoutou* and John Matheus's *Ti Yette*.[28]

Toucoutou, Tinker's novel based on the Beaumont song, was published in 1928. In his brief introduction, Tinker repeats the white-Creole apology in his definition of Creole:

The mistake current among certain misinformed people that Creole denotes a person of mixed white and negro blood is due possibly to the fact that they can confuse the noun Creole with the adjective Creole. It

28. Margaret Dashiell, *Spanish Moss and English Myrtle* (Boston: Stratford, 1920), 7, 8, 29, 43.

has been customary over a period of years to apply the adjective Creole to anything produced in Louisiana; so there are Creole carrots, Creole mules, Creole eggs, and in the same way, Creole negroes to differentiate them from the "bossals" as the negros imported from Africa were called. But when the noun Creole is used, it can mean only one thing and that is a pure white person born of European parents in Spanish or French colonies.

Later in the novel Tinker gives his opinion of the Creole language. " 'Pardon, Michie,' she spoke in the bastard French of the uneducated negros . . ." Moreover, his actual use of the language is stereotypical and confined to descriptions of Voodoo scenes, Creole lullabies, street vendor cries, the Calinda dance, and of course, Beaumont's song at the end of the novel. Tinker's "negro Creoles" speak mainly a mixture of Black American dialect and Creole words, as in Claircine's advice to her daughter who thinks that old Claircine is merely her nurse or guardian:

> Listen good, Toucoutou, she said, we don't want no lagniappe bébé
> 'round here, don't know he Papa name. You ack like one balayeuse.
> What will he think of you, kissin' lak' that the first time you see him?
> Where you think you belong? Over in those "Mahogany Hall" with
> those putains? Remember you w'ite, an' I got yo certificate of bapteme
> to prove it. You can marry in the Cathedral by a priest, you don't have
> to be placée like any yaller solopé.

At the end of the novel, Tinker includes a short glossary of Creole and other local terms with the English definitions. His attitude toward the people and the language seems inconsistent with his apparent interest in studying and writing about them. Besides his novel, he published two books, *Lafcadio Hearn's American Days*, which contains Hearn's research on the Creole language, and *Les écrits de langue française en Louisiane au XIXe siècle*, which includes summaries and bibliographies of many authors who used Creole, a bibliography of French newspapers and periodicals of Louisiana, and three articles on aspects of the Creole language and the people who use it.[29]

African American Renaissance writer John Matheus was professor of Romance Languages at West Virginia Collegiate Institute from 1922 to

29. Tinker, *Toucoutou*, 8, 23–4, 28–9, 45, 68, 92, 101–2, 116, 127, 132, 149, 277.

1929. Matheus's prize-winning prose appeared in *Opportunity* and *The Crisis* magazines, and in Locke's *The New Negro*. In the 1929 collection *Plays and Pageants from the Life of the Negro*, edited by Harlem Renaissance playwright William Richardson, we find Matheus's one-act "Ti Yette." This play is set in New Orleans in 1855 and involves a "Creole Quadroon" and his sister Ti Yette. Racine, a wharf worker and free man of color, is an admirer of Toussaint L'Ouverture and hates all whites, his father as well, for the injustices inflicted on him. He tells his sister at the beginning of the play:

> Ah, Ti Yette (bitterly) You speak like the baby you are. Free? Free? Ha! Ha! (he laughs derisively) When they pass laws that I must have a white guardian to represent me, speak for me in their courts, when I must not meet together with my fellow citizens, when I dare not assemble with other free men of color upon pain of convict labor! Free? I cannot leave this city of my birth to follow the Mississippi to its source without the bond of some white man, of some sacre Américain with the blood of his blood upon his hands, or some gentle-man of France, whom I loathe. God, if like Dessalines . . .

Racine then admonishes his sister for wishing to change her Creole name from Ti Yette to Henriette. "Henriette? Are you ashamed, too, of your mother's tongue, that you must forsake it for our father's Paris French, or discard it for these pigs's English?" His sister, who has been singing a Creole song, denies this and sings another Creole song to emphasize her point. We see her real attitude, however, when her brother leaves. She soliloquizes, "All this palaver about these conjuring Negroes. I hate them all. They are holding me down. I wish I had never been born. One drop of their blood and I must be black forever. This skin is as fair as the whitest woman's and my brother talks of marrying me to an African King. Is he crazy?" Ti Yette is in love with a white man who, in order to marry her, is willing to pay a judge to declare her white and is also willing to pay her brother who is "too dark" to "go away where no one knows you." Racine accuses his sister of plotting to be white and stabs her to death, a scene that takes place on Mardi Gras night.

This is indeed an embodiment of the tragic mulatto, but the employment of Creole is confined to the five bits of Creole songs (one sung by Ti Yette as she dies) and such occasional French expressions as "M'sieu" and "Mon Dieu." The language is not debased here, but the gross stereo-typing of the mulatto is evident. The plot echoes the minstrel-show tra-dition of obligatory death at the end for such figures.[30]

Two years later, another play was published using the Creole lan-guage, this one being written in entirely in Creole, with English transla-tion appended. If "Ti Yette" smacks of the minstrel tradition, Marguerite Wogan's *Can-Can Kisinières* follows that genre to the letter, including performances in blackface. As the author tells us in the notes to the first scene, *Can-Can Kisinières*, or *Cooks Gossip*, is a contrived one-act comedy set in 1878: "This little playlet is written in real negro dialect [notice the word *Creole* is not used], such as it was still spoken 50 or 60 years ago. Most of the funny proverbs or expressions have really been said by some of our old cooks or mammies." Victoria and Celestine are the two cooks. Celestine's white folks are rich; Victoria's are poor. They both are mem-bers of the "Society of the Ladies of Purity." They meet on the street to complain about their employers and to gossip. Both are shown to be stu-pid, as in the following:

> Celestine: Que qualité saussisson to acheté? Mo moune yé jis mangé saussisson de Lyon!
> Victoria: Mo pa connin quel qualité ça yé. . . . Lion, ou chat tigre. . . . Mo jus pran pou quarti, assé pou mété dan de chou!
> Celestine: Moin, mo gaignin canard! Mo Madame li pélé ça canard domestique!
> Victoria: Eh! ben rapélé vou . . . Jisqua Canard qui gaignin domes-tique!
>
> Celestine: What kind sausage you brought? My people joss eat Lyon sausage!
> Victoria: Me, I donno what kind it is—Lion or tiger sausage! I got joss enough to put in my cabbage!
> Celestine: I got duck for dey dinner. My Madam she calls dem: Do-mestic ducks!
> Victoria: Well I declai!—Even ducks got to have "domestiques!"[31]

---

30. Joseph Boris, ed., *Who's Who in Colored America* (New York: W. W. in C. A. Corp., 1927), 139; Willis Richardson, ed., *Plays and Pageants from the Life of the Negro* (Washington, D.C.: Associated Publishers, 1929), 81–2, 86–8, 102.

31. Marguerite B. Wogan, *Can-Can Kisinières* (New Orleans: Rogers, 1931), 5, 10, 11.

Scene two opens as Celestine comes home to her daughter whose child is sick. The black male's role is defined as useless. Babet, the daughter, calls Freddy a "lazy nigger" and he is described as "coming slowly—dressed in rags—a cigarette in the corner of his mouth." Babet sends him to the drugstore for medicine for the child but he asks her for the money; he has none even though he worked that day. He also demands money for beer. The scene ends with Celestine singing a Creole song—"Mam'zelle Zizi." In scene three, the two cooks are preparing for a wedding of one of their friends who is to be married on the Sunday before Mardi Gras. Victoria describes in English what they plan to do for Mardi Gras: "We all gone to mask—me, I's gone to get a costume like an Indian and all de rest gone to be dressed like devils . . . and at night we's all gone to go to de 'Black Crow' Ball." In the wedding scene, Celestine, who was too ill to go to the church, hears a Creole song from her window, indicating that the wedding party is returning. They all come into Celestine's house, still singing; the bride and groom are toasted, and Babet sings a Creole song, followed by general laughter and another song—"Toucoutou." The bride says, "Ernesse got to work for me—cause me, I likes nice dresses—and I wants plenty money—and plenty little niggers!" This leads to a chorus of another Creole song, "Mo Lemmé Toi." Finally Lolotte, a "barefoot girl of twelve," announces that dinner is ready at Nannaine's house and everyone leaves singing and dancing to still another Creole song, "Tan Patate la Tchutte." This "musical" has most of the classic characters of the minstrel shows: mammies, coons, and various pickaninnies, all laughing and singing and dancing. Both the language and the Afro-French people are being lampooned. The devastating stereotypes remind us that the language belongs to "niggers" and has nothing to do with intelligent, "pure-white" Creoles.[32]

Despite the savage depiction of the Creole language and songs in Wogan's play, there seems to have been an attempt to teach some of the songs in the state's public schools. In 1936, the music textbook used in Louisiana schools, *The Music Hour*, contained eight of the Creole folk songs as well as Abbé Rouquette's Creole song "Zozo Mokéur." These are described as "special Louisiana songs in the Negro-French dialect, still spoken by Negro laborers in many parts of Louisiana." It was also during the 1930s that Camille Nickerson, the Creole musician and col-

32. Ibid., 15, 17, 23, 31, 33.

lector of these songs, toured the schools to introduce them to school children.[33]

In the 1930s, 1940s, and 1950s, several white writers addressed the subject of the Creole language and people. Among these were Lyle Saxon, Robert Tallant, and Hewitt L. Ballowe. In *Lafitte the Pirate*, Saxon includes the words to the song "Mam'zelle Zizi," but nothing else in Creole. His novel *Children of Strangers* is "based on the story of the Melrose Plantation and the nearby Cane River community." Even though this story of interracial love deals with people who were historically Creole speakers, there is very little use of the language. Saxon lists four classes of people on Cane River: the storekeepers or prosperous whites, the storekeepers' clerks or white trash, the mulattoes, and the blacks. The white characters speak French, or so we are told, and the mulattoes speak "sometimes in the Cane River patois, sometimes in English." Black characters use exaggerated southern speech reminiscent of Joel Chandler Harris: " 'How come yo' sass a 'ooman two times as ole as yo'?' she snorted. Then, when she had eased her heavy body down from step to step: 'It's dese heah shutmouth, lazy, stay-at-home mens yo' got ter watch!' "[34]

Here again we have an example of an Afro-French speaker without an English accent, so that the black character is differentiated from other speakers of English. Saxon thus continues the general stereotyping. He and Robert Tallant worked on the Federal Writers' Project of the WPA to produce *Gumbo Ya-Ya* in 1945. This "book of living folklore of Louisiana" has a chapter called "The Creoles." In it we are given once again the standard white apology for *Creole*. "No true Creole ever had colored blood. This erroneous belief, still common among Americans in other sections of the country, is probably due to the Creoles' own habit of calling their slaves 'Creole slaves' and after simply 'Creole.' Too, there are proud light-colored families in New Orleans today who are known as Creole among themselves. But Creoles were always pure white. Any

33. Osborne McConathy et al., eds., *The Music Hour* (New York: Silver Burdette, 1936), foreword; Mrs. Florence Borders, interview by author, November 16, 1988.
34. Lyle Saxon, *Lafitte the Pirate* (New York: Century, 1930), 53; Lyle Saxon, *Children of Strangers* (Covington, La.: Mockingbird, 1937), frontispiece, 25, 76, 119.

trace of café au lait in a family was reason for complete ostracism." Yet a few paragraphs beneath this exclusive definition we are given the words to a song in Creole as sung by Creole boys who ran behind Americans in the streets to taunt them in the nineteenth century:

'Mericain Coquin
Billé en naquin
Voleur de pain
Chez Michie D'Aquin

American scamp
Dressed in nankeen
Stole bread
At Mr. D'Aquin

Were these Creole boys white? Maybe. Some examples of the language are provided in the form of proverbs. "Chacun sait ce qui bouille dans se chaudière" (Each one knows what boils in his own pot) and "On lavé son linge sal in famille" (Wash your dirty linen in your own family). This is the same type of French used by Armand Lanusse and the other writers of *Les Cenelles* in 1845. In the chapter on the songs, Saxon and Tallant give the words to twenty-two Creole melodies, accompanied by the comment, "The Creole songs—since the Creole inhabited no other part of the United States—are perhaps the most typical of all, exhibiting peculiarly exotic departures from the Anglo-Saxonism of practically all other American folk music." One may well ask, is this the music of the pure whites who were declared to be the only true Creoles in the previous chapter? The editors obviously forgot throughout this chapter on songs to add the appendage "Negro" to the word *Creole*.[35]

Voodoo in New Orleans, Robert Tallant's book published in 1946, contains a few Creole words as well as some of the Voodoo chants. Tallant's fascination with Voodoo continued, and in 1956 he published a novel based on the life of Marie Laveau, *The Voodoo Queen*. Again, the use of the language is confined to Voodoo chants and a few other words for flavor.

Another white writer, Hewitt L. Ballowe, published *Creole Folk Tales: Stories of the Marsh Country* in 1948. The language used in these stories

35. Lyle Saxon, Robert Tallant, and Edward Dreyer, *Gumbo YaYa* (New York: Bonanza, 1945), preface; 139, 143, 427–8.

points up an interesting connection between the Cajuns and the Creoles. The author identifies the people in his stories as Creoles from the Delta or Marsh country of Louisiana, but for the most part the language used is Cajun. Ballowe does not identify his characters as either white or black Creoles. He explains their belief in Voodoo as follows:

> When the Acadians were ruthlessly torn from their homes by the English, herded upon ships without regard to family units, and scattered to the four winds, the most pathetic were those set ashore upon the black islands of the Caribbean. After indescribable hardships their pitiful odyssey ended when they made their way in wretched groups, with a sort of homing instinct, as did the more fortunate, to Louisiana. These last refugees were saturated with belief in jungle magic, the efficacy of charms, and incidentally brought leprosy with them. . . . They reverted to the charms and fetishes of the cult, often wearing them upon the same tape around their necks with their scapulas and medals. Even today they practice bits of a modified ritual.

If the author meant for them to be descendants of the Acadians, why did he call them Creole and their stories Creole French? The Louisiana French words used are for the most part words used by both Creoles and Cajuns, for example, "gros bougres" (big men), "foutre" (damn), "faussée couche" (miscarriage), "nonc" (uncle), "tant pis" (so much the worse) and the like. These stories are written in English with a sprinkling of Louisiana French words on almost every page. There is also a reference in one story to "sauter le balai" or jumping the broom, a slave marriage ceremony. "We make one of the marsh people, 'sauter le balai,' before the grave of a good man to have him for our witness." There is also a description of one of the characters as "the Fabre—coarse hair, thick lips, the pointed ears that stand from the head." Who are these mysterious people? Probably a mixture of Haitian Creoles, Louisiana Creoles, and Acadians. The reference to blacks is unmistakable.[36]

In 1950, in his biography of Jelly Roll Morton, *Mister Jelly Roll*, Alan Lomax included in the list of Morton's songs two Creole songs, "C'eté N'aut Can-Can" and "Mo Pas L'aimez ça." The former was also recorded by Kid Ory (CL 835, Columbia Records in 1950). In this biography we also find the words to a Creole ballad, "La Misère," a song about

36. Hewitt L. Barlowe, *Creole Folk Tales: Stories of the Marsh Country* (Baton Rouge: Louisiana State University Press, 1948), x–xi, xvii, 1, 15, 27, 32, 164.

the Depression composed by Ulysses Picou, brother of Alphonse Picou, composer of the jazz standard "High Society."[37]

In the 1960s there appears to have been only a single mention of the language by one writer, as well as a single work including Creole songs, a collection of Louisiana French songs. Also, in Charles Haywood's 1966 *Folk Songs of the World* there is the Louisiana Creole "En Avant, Grenadiers," which was sung by Creole soldiers in the Battle of New Orleans in 1812. African American writer Ernest Gaines, a Louisiana native, published his novel set in the bayou country, *Catherine Carmier*, in 1964, but even though the protagonist is Creole, there is nothing more than a reference to the language being used by a Cajun character.[38]

Irene Whitfield's 1939 collection, *Louisiana French Folk Songs*, contains twenty-four Creole songs, words, and melody lines, and an excellent bibliography on the Creole music. Two other song collections appeared in the 1970s, both by Jeane and Robert Gilmore and edited for classroom use: *Chantez, la Louisiane* (1970) and *Chantez Encore* (1977). Even in this late decade, the Gilmores felt the need to define the language and the people as "the dialect spoken by African descendants, and hence the term Creole is misleading." This statement is footnoted with a reference to William A. Read's book *Louisiana French*, which reads, "The Creoles of Louisiana are generally defined as the white descendants of the French and Spanish settlers of the Colonial Period." Despite this confusion of terms, six Creole songs are found in *Chantez, la Louisiane* and five in *Chantez Encore*.[39]

Thus far in the twentieth century, the Creole language has been with few exceptions a device to create and fortify negative stereotypes and racist thinking. Further, it would seem that the definition of *Creole* has been distorted to continue the myth of those white Creoles who needed to hide their familial ties to free people of color and to slaves in order to escape the long arm of American segregation laws begun in the late nine-

37. Alan Lomax, *Mister Jelly Roll: The Fortunes of Jelly Roll Morton, New Orleans Creole and "Inventor of Jazz"* (Berkeley: University of California Press, 1973), 73–4.

38. Ernest Gaines, *Catherine Carmier* (New York: Atheneum, 1964), 156.

39. Irene Therese Whitfield, *Louisiana French Folk Songs* (Baton Rouge: Louisiana State University Press, 1939); Jeanne and Robert Gilmore, *Chantez, La Louisiane!* (Lafayette, La.: Acadiana Music, 1970), v, xvii; Jeanne and Robert Gilmore, *Chantez Encore* (Lafayette, La.: Acadiana Music, 1977).

teenth century. It was not until the publication of Anne Rice's *The Feast of All Saints* in 1979 that both the term and the people were restored to that degree of dignity demonstrated in Cable's nineteenth-century work. Although Rice correctly cites French as the language of these *gens de couleur*, her novel, set in "La Belle Epoque" before the Civil War, contains verses of the Creole song, "Mulâtraisse Courri dans Bal." Also in this work, Rice gives a revealing and realistic elegy to the *gens de couleur*. Tante Josette is speaking to her nephew:

> We are a doomed people, Marcel. . . . There is no equality. And there never will be. Our only hope is to hold onto our land here, to buy and cultivate more land so that we can keep our community as a world apart. Because the white Anglo-Saxon heart is so hardened against us that there's no hope for our descendants as the Anglo-Saxon takes over, as he supplants the French and the Spanish families around us who understood us and respected us. No, there is only one hope and that is for our descendants to pass when they can into the white race. And with each one who passes, we are diminished, our world, our class dies. That's what we are, Marcel, a dying people, if we are a people at all, flowers of the French and Spanish and the African, and the Americans have put their boot in our face.

Of course, descendants of these people are alive today; some, having discarded most of the negatives associated with such a caste system, are proudly African Americans; others are white, and others simply call themselves Creole.[40]

The beginning of the 1980s saw a renaissance of the use of the Creole language in original literature, owing mainly to the efforts of three Afro-French writers, Deborah Clifton-Hils, Ulysses Ricard, and myself. Deborah Clifton-Hils is a Creole poet, linguist, and cultural conservationist who works with Franco-American, Native American, and minority communities on a variety of concerns ranging from language planning to prisons to leadership development. Her special interest is the problems faced by traditional people. Her poetry was first published in *Cris sur le bayou* (1980), which contains "Joie et Misère," "Soleil et Nauges," "Blackie Frugé," "Ein de les aventures de Cocodrie et Tchoupoule," "Plaint: La Veuve de le Clos d'huile," and "Teinsbon." The subjects run

40. Anne Rice, *The Feast of All Saints* (New York: Fawcett Crest, 1981), 92, 528.

the gamut of human emotions, from fragile feelings of love to explosive anger. Clifton-Hils sometimes mixes her Creole with English, to add emphasis and to give the flavor of a bilingual speaker:

Blackie Frugé:
Hey Blackie, mo neg! ti gain pou d'être ein de ces
Dirty Red Frenchmen
I can tell by you marché
I can tell by you parlér
I can tell by you dirty Red lafidje
Et ein aut' chose, Blackie,
Nous—aut' don't serve no green-eyed
White-assed, sauvage Red Frenchman niggers icit . . .
pas dans honkey-tonk, oh no!

Clifton-Hils's poetry is robust and political. In "Ein de les aventures de Cocodrie et Tchoupoule," she pits the Creole speaker and promoter (Cocodrie) against the Louisiana speaker and promoter of French (Tchoupoule). *Tchoupoule* is derived from the way French speakers form their lips when speaking French, as in *tchou* (ass) and *poule* (chicken). The poem speaks out against the debasement of the Creole language and Creole-related projects by those who support the use of French in Louisiana for racist reasons. Clifton-Hils is also the author of an unpublished manuscript that will eventually be a welcome addition to the body of Creole literature; its title is *Le Bal aux Sacatras: Chants du Magnifique Pie Coundja (The Black Indians' Ball: Chants from the Magnificent Medicine Mound).* During the early 1980s, Clifton-Hils wrote a column on Creole for *Le F.A.R.O.G. Forum,* a bilingual journal published by the Franco-American Center at the University of Maine. Among her concerns are racial and ethnic prejudice, linguistic prejudice, problems of the Native Americans, and the relationship between Black Creoles and Native Americans. Both her prose and her poetry make use of the Creole language.[41]

   Ulysses Ricard Jr. was a New Orleans Creole philologist, poet, historian, and printer. He completed his undergraduate studies at Lake Forest College and the Instituto Internacional in Madrid, Spain. While a gradu-

41. Jean Arceneaux, ed., *Cris sur le bayou* (Montreal: Les Editions Intermède, 1980), 68; Ulysses Ricard Jr., interview by author, November 18, 1988.

ate student at Louisiana State University in Baton Rouge, he taught
Spanish and the first course in Cajun French to be offered on the university level in Louisiana. He also wrote the course textbook, which included a chapter on Louisiana Creole. He delivered papers on the Creole
French spoken in Pointe Coupée Parish in south central Louisiana, published a newsletter in Creole (*Souvenirs*, 1980), and was a consultant and
assistant archivist at the Amistad Research Center in New Orleans until
his death in 1993. His vital work in progress was a dictionary of the Creole language. Two of his poems in Creole, "L'Amant-Fantome" and
"L'Amant-Fantome II," were published in *Acadie Tropicale* in 1981. As
does Clifton-Hils's work, these poems correct the myth promoted by
critics who have held that Creole is not capable of expressing abstract
thought:

> Oh, fantome moquenne,
> Cofaire to pas laisse moin tranquille?
> Est-ce que to laimé vinir
> Chauffer moin dans mo reves-yé
> jisse pour fraidir moin
> Avec la realité?

> Oh, my own phantom,
> Why do you not leave me alone?
> Is it that you like to come
> To warn me in my dreams
> Just to chill me
> With reality?

The sparse lightness of the Creole words gives the poem a breathlike
feeling, a whisper quality that creates an atmosphere of surreal melancholy.[42]

It was largely through the efforts of the multitalented Ricard that the
publication of my *Gombo People* (1981) was made possible. This first anthology of poetry in Creole by a Creole writer was edited and printed by
Ricard, who also added the introductory prose in Creole, the glossary,
and the linguistic notes. The book parallels the previous century's *Les*

---

42. Mathé Allain and Barry Ancelet, eds., *Acadie Tropicale: Poésie de Louisiane*
(Lafayette: Center for Louisiana Studies, 1983), 39.

Cenelles in that it is a total Creole production printed by a Creole pub-lisher (Leo Hall, of the oldest Creole press in New Orleans), with art work by New Orleans Creole artist Diane Derusé. Rather than attempt-ing to assess my own work, let me simply say that *Gombo People* is an at-tempt to reclaim the full dignity of the Creole language and people. The poems seek to show the humanity of the Creole and claim a place for his language use. Among the pieces that aim to do this are "Neuf Rites de la Vie Creole," which focuses on Creole customs and rituals, and "Envie," which attempts to rebut the myth that all Creoles wish to be white:

Yé dit nous que
Nous oulé "passe à blanc."
Mo dit, "Non."
Nous pas oulé "passer" pour personne.
Tracas c'est avec queques blanc.
Yé oulé "passe à Dieu."

They tell us
We want to pass for white.
I say, "No."
We don't want to pass for anybody.
The trouble is with some whites.
They want to "pass" for God.

The poem is a plea to be recognized and accepted as a group without imposed labeling. Some of my other projects include *Des Gardénias et Roses: Les Chansons Créoles* (1985), a language supplementary text in five languages; *Maw-Maw's Creole ABC Book* (1984), a children's picture book; and *Sérénade Créole*, a cassette tape of original songs in French, Spanish, Haitian Creole, Louisiana Creole, and English. I am currently at work on a one-act play written in Creole and a new CD of the Creole folk songs.[43]

Also in the contemporary period, white author Lee Davis Willoughby published the historical novel *The Creoles* in 1982. This romantic tale

43. Sybil Kein, *Gombo People: Poésie Créole de la Nouvelle-Orléans* (New Orleans: Gosserand Press, 1981), 53.

only skims the surface of the history but includes two Creole songs, "Dansé Calinda" and "Po' la Belle Layotte," as well as a few Creole words throughout. Another work of the 1980s is a collection of novellas, *The Mayor of New Orleans* (1987), by New Orleans Creole Fatima Shaik. To flavor "Before Echo," one of the three novellas set in the modern period, Shaik makes use of a verse of the Creole song "Fait Dodo Minette," and several Creole words and expressions. In December 1988 a new journal of Louisiana literature appeared: *Chicory*, edited by Mrs. Florence Borders, former senior archivist at the Amistad Research Center. The premier issue of *Chicory* contains two poems in Creole by Deborah Clifton-Hils and a Creole folktale edited by Ulysses Ricard.[44]

The 1990s saw the publication of two books of poetry using the Creole language. In my volume *An American South* (Michigan State University Press, 1996) I employ quotations from the folklore and bits of Creole in various English poems, and also include entire poems in Creole with English translations appended. An example of the latter is "La lumière":

> Quand la lune est au visage plein,
> Mo va posé un poème
> sur so sein
> De sorte que
> Quand la lune té parti
> To sera capable souffler mes paroles
> Et connais que mo té là.
>
> When the moon is full
> I will place a poem
> On your bosom
> So that
> When the moon is gone
> You will breathe my words
> And know that I was there.

The book also contains a glossary of local terms, which includes many Creole words.[45]

---

44. Lee Davis Willoughby, *The Creoles* (New York: Dell, 1982), 102, 258; Fatima Shaik, *The Mayor of New Orleans: Just Talking Jazz* (Berkeley, Calif.: Creative Arts Book Company, 1987), 102.

45. Sybil Kein, *An American South* (East Lansing: Michigan State University Press, 1996), 63.

In 1997 *All Saints*, by Brenda Marie Osbey, was published by Louisiana State University Press. In the long poem "The Business of Pursuit: San Malo's Prayer," Osbey uses Creole to express the thoughts of St. Malo. She chose to do so because she was writing about a historical character who lived in the Spanish period and she wanted to impart "a feel for the language of the period, the sound of the period." The poem is also based on the Creole folksong about St. Malo. In the following sampling of Osbey's Creole, a few words are French and one is Spanish, but Osbey nevertheless considers the quote as a whole to be Creole. It is Osbey's own English translation that follows.

o señor
m'sieu
je vous connais en fin
et avec chacun des blanc je fais tué
en fin je gout ta sangue nègre
en fin mo mo trouve capab' di'
c'est mo, congo
c'est mo vous voyé à la rue de la rive
congo congo

Oh, Milord,
Milord
finally I know you
and with each white I kill
at last I can taste your black blood
at last I can say
it's me, congo
it's me you've seen on the river road
congo congo[46]

Until the 1980s, the use and portrayal of Creole in literature was chameleonic at best. Now, as we begin the next century, it seems that this language—the only "foreign" language to be developed in the United States—is, at least, in the hands of capable Creole writers. The tongue once used to degrade and dismiss a people now shows evidence of a re-

46. Brenda Marie Osbey, interview by author, January 13, 1998; Brenda Marie Osbey, *All Saints* (Baton Rouge: Louisiana State University Press, 1997), 112–3.

birth. From almost two hundred years of abuse in literature and *malgré* the concerted efforts of those who would crush it and its people, Louisiana Creole appears to be on the threshold of acceptance as a unique contribution from the Louisiana Francophone culture and a creative tool worthy of serious literature and serious scholarship.

II

Legacy

7

Marie Laveau

The Voodoo Queen Repossessed

BARBARA ROSENDALE DUGGAL

The past twenty years have yielded an enormous body of work aimed at recovering sources that give rise to a reconception of the role women have played in religious life. The task of discerning the total participation of women in the major "literary religions"—those religions whose foundations or practices are set down in written texts—is an arduous one. As June O'Connor puts it, "Rereading the traditions means re-examining materials and traditions with an eye attuned to women's presence and absence, women's words and women's silence, recognition given and denied women." Feminist scholars have vigorously challenged the male bias both in the study of religious texts and inherent within those texts. In an article surveying the expansion of research in the area of women and religion, O'Connor asks, "How might we read between and behind the lines of androcentric religious texts in order to reconstruct the experience of women who become a part of these traditions?"[1]

Feminist theologian Carol P. Christ discusses another bias: the reluctance of Western academicians to include in the core of religious study the myth and ritual celebrated within nonliterary traditions. Though the existence of nonliterary religions is acknowledged, most scholars are committed primarily to the interpretation of texts. Christ ar-

1. June O'Connor, "Feminist Research in Religion," *Studies in Gender and Culture* 4 (1989): 102.

gues for the expansion of our notions of history to include the study of traditions that have left no written records. If we accept the bias that text offers the only reliable evidence for historical analysis, we diminish the importance of all that came before the invention of writing. The preference for text over ritual, Christ claims, reveals a limitation inherent in Western conceptions of the nature of religion. "More is at stake here than simple inherited prejudice toward the study of texts. Ritual embodies in a fuller way than text, the nonrational, the physical side of religion."[2]

The field of folkloristics is founded on the study of nonliterary traditions and the lives of individuals who serve as informants of them. Folkloristics has valued—even relied on—the contributions of female informants to the collection and the analysis of data meant to reveal and comment on the things of daily and traditional significance to diverse groups of people. Nevertheless, the Western aversion to the physical side of religion, as well as the male bias toward the exclusion of women within religious traditions in general, has no doubt contributed to the limited documentation and slanted analysis of traditional material in folklore studies as well. Folklorists have a unique opportunity to dig through the vast archives compiled by their predecessors on every facet of social life and attempt the kind of re-viewing being done in other fields. When discrimination takes root, more often than not the crux is that Group A is dehumanized into the Other by Group B's assumptions about its members' *expressive behaviors:* how they worship, what they eat, who they love, what they wear or fail to wear, how they use and manage violence, how they deal with sexuality in daily and religious life, and what makes them laugh, cry and tremble with fear. No discipline is as capable of revealing essential insights into the expressive behaviors of human beings as folklore studies; and through its comparative, multicultural approach, it holds perhaps the greatest potential to expose and correct the very real consequences of bias. No one is without biases, of course, so that the ironic danger of a specious unseating of one set of biases for another should always be borne in mind. Perhaps all we can do is even the playing field by giving every bias an equal hearing.

2. Carol P. Christ, "Toward a Paradigm Shift in the Academy and in Religious Studies," in *The Impact of Feminist Research on the Academy*, ed. Christie Farnhamed (Bloomington: Indiana University Press, 1987), 71.

With these concerns in mind, I would like to reexamine a popular folkloric figure, nineteenth-century New Orleans Voodoo queen Marie Laveau, one who has been regarded not only through the biases already mentioned, but also those of race, class, and culture. The present essay is the result of a preliminary inquiry into the subject. Many of the issues discussed here will be fleshed out and tested only through extensive fieldwork and the review of primary source materials. Though the findings of a fieldwork excursion conducted in September 1992 are not fully reflected here, I found ample justification for continued research. Particularly, I discovered the power of Marie Laveau's legacy beyond the contemporary commercialization of her name. I heard a far less sensational, more respectful tone in the voices of those who speak of her today than that which is represented in official documents, and this in spite of the fact that most who regard her today owe much of their knowledge about her legend to those very sources.

This discovery of the power of Laveau's name makes for an interesting opportunity to explore what separates those who actually live a worldview from those who merely report on it. Historian Robert Tallant offers us the words of one New Orleanian who remembered seeing Laveau when he was young:

> It was her all right. . . . She came walkin' into Congo Square wit' her head up in the air like a queen. Her skirts swished when she walked and everybody step back to let her pass. All the people—white and colored—start sayin' that's the most powerful woman there is. They say, "There goes Marie Laveau!" and, me, I was little and I got kind of scared. You know they used to scare little children then by tellin' 'em they was gonna give 'em to Marie Laveau. Now let me tell you this. She was a great person. I don't care what nobody says.[3]

In her field study *Mules and Men*, Zora Neale Hurston observes, "New Orleans is now and has ever been the hoodoo capital of America. Great names in rites that vie with those of Hayti . . . keep alive the powers of Africa." Certainly the most celebrated name to be connected with

3. Robert Tallant, *Voodoo in New Orleans* (New York: Macmillan, 1946), 56–7. I will use the spelling *Voodoo* throughout my own commentary, as it is the one most frequently used in writings about New Orleans, but direct quotes will, of course, reflect the preferences of their authors.

New Orleans Voodoo (as, Hurston notes, it is pronounced by whites) is that of Marie Laveau.[4]

"Marie Laveau was the last great American witch." So begins the introduction to Tallant's *Voodoo Queen*, a work of fiction based on his research into the legends associated with the woman whose tomb in New Orleans' St. Louis Cemetery No. 1 still attracts the faithful and curious alike more than a century after her death. He continues, "Yet her art bore no more resemblance to that of the New England witches . . . than Boston resembles New Orleans. . . . Hers was jungle-born, African in origin, for she was the queen of the voodoos, and by far the most important voodooienne ever to reign on this continent." Tallant's rendering of Marie Laveau in both his novel and the now classic study *Voodoo in New Orleans* bears the touch of one not only possessed with an interest in folkloric documentation but also smitten by the witch's multiple alleged charms and contradictions. Images of the hapless detective in the old film *Laura*

4. Zora Neale Hurston, *Mules and Men* (New York: Negro Universities Press, 1969), 229. Charles Frye, former director of the Center for African and African American Studies at Southern University at New Orleans, writes that Hurston "can be recommended especially because of her accessibility and the primary nature of her work: she does not cite any other scholars. She also does not attempt an analysis, leaving the materials to speak for themselves." Charles Frye, "The African South: A Critique of Puckett's *Folk Beliefs in the Southern Negro*" (paper presented at the 1992 Popular Culture Association and the American Culture Association Meeting, Louisville, Ky., March 18–22, 1992), 13. Hurston is an accomplished folklorist, and her work is often cited by scholars.

It should be noted, however, that there is a general consensus that the distinctions between Voodoo and Hoodoo can be more precisely defined than a mere confusion of pronunciation. According to Frye, "Voodoo, or vodu, as practiced in Haiti and New Orleans (and New York City, etc.) . . . has priestesses and priests. It has fixed meeting places of consistent design which include a central column, vévé ground-signs, and an altar. It has standard prayers, songs, drum-patterns, and dances. And . . . has as its object spirit-possession. . . . The voodoo congregation seeks communion with the goddesses and gods of Yorubaland and Dahomey personified in the images of the Catholic Saints. When certain members of the congregation are possessed or 'ridden' by these *loas* or deities, other members use the possessed's temporary mediumship to address the gods directly: to offer petitions, seek divine advice, speak to dead relatives, and so on. . . . Hoodoo is not an organized religion; and it lacks the semi-public nature of voodoo. Hoodoo is usually practiced in secret by a single individual. It has as its object . . . the capturing, protecting, or releasing of the spirit of another person." Frye, "African South," 16a.

come to mind as Tallant freely admits "Marie Laveau has fascinated me
for most of my life." His descriptions of her are both visual and visceral;
he says she was "a mixture of Negro, Indian and white bloods . . . described as a tall, statuesque woman with curling black hair, 'good' features, dark skin that had a distinctly reddish cast, and fierce black eyes."
The witch's influence is said to have reached from boudoir to bench and
pulpit; according to Tallant, it was she "who popularized voodoo. The
meetings held at Bayou St. John . . . were regularly attended by hordes
of people, some of them of high social strata. Much of this was due to
her own personality, to her magnetism as a woman. Apparently no one
who saw her once ever forgot her. It is this about her that has interested
me most."[5]

But it is *this* about Robert Tallant that interests *me* most. His analysis
of the Marie Laveau phenomenon is ultimately romantic, even sentimental. Throughout his work, he reveals not just the bias of white romantici-
zation of black culture, but also that of man's dismissal of woman's
capacity for religious leadership. He implies that Laveau's influence
stemmed not from strength of character or spiritual commitment, but
from physical beauty, a gambler's cunning, and sexual magnetism, "for
from that came her real power, without a doubt." Tallant spent years im-
mersed in the study of New Orleans Voodoo, and his writings—which

5. Robert Tallant, *The Voodoo Queen* (Gretna, La.: Pelican, 1983), 1, 3, 4, 6; Tallant, *Voodoo in New Orleans*, 52–3. The ritual petitions performed at Laveau's tomb
involve some variation of making an "X" with a piece of red brick chalk, placing
one's hand over it, rubbing one's foot three times in "goofer dust" (soil or marble
dust at the grave), dropping silver coins (no pennies) into a cup provided, and making a wish. The tomb is the site of expensive guided tours; the cemetery is located
in what is now considered to be a very dangerous part of the city, and New Orleans
residents repeatedly warn visitors not to go there alone. The question whether
Marie Laveau is, or ever was, actually buried there arises often in conversation,
however.
    The 1944 film *Laura*, directed by Otto Preminger, is based on the Vera Caspary
novel of the same name. A detective, played by Dana Andrews, is brought in to
investigate the death of a woman, played by Gene Tierney, whose beautiful portrait dominates the alleged murder scene. His objectivity and effectiveness is called
into question as it becomes increasingly obvious that he has become excessively
fascinated with the stories told about the woman and has even fallen in love with
the image projected by the painting.

display an odd mixture of sympathy and scorn—are characterized by a sincerity that does little to mask the author's final dismissal of Voodoo as a cult of the superstitious and ignorant.[6]

Lyle Saxon, member of the Louisiana Writers' Project and co-author of the classic collection of New Orleans folklore *Gumbo Ya-Ya*, wrote in the foreword to *Voodoo in New Orleans* that "much nonsense has been written . . . [but] it seems to me that here is a truthful and definitive picture." Hurston, disagreeing, responded directly to the claim in a scathing review of the book: "*Voodoo in New Orleans* in no way tends to abate the nuisance." Tallant has, however, remained the most frequently cited authority on the subject, even though passages such as those appearing in his introduction to *Voodoo Queen* expose him as a privileged Christian white man caught in a web of attraction/repulsion, held, like generations of white men before him, by the exotic allure of the woman of color. And, one might argue, any woman of power.[7] With this in mind, we can proceed to use the facts to construct a more accurate picture of Marie Laveau.

New Orleans provided fertile ground for the growth of African-based religions in the New World. It took thirteen years for the slave rebellion in French colonial St. Domingue to succeed as a revolution, which established the black Republic of Haiti. During that time, French Creoles, free people of color, and slaves fled the carnage in significant numbers along with the white planter class. Migration has been traced to Cuba, Jamaica, Brazil, and many parts of the United States, but New Orleans became the site of the largest concentration of these emigres in North America, owing, at least in part, to the laws and attitudes regarding free

6. Tallant, *Voodoo Queen*, 6. In spite of the criticism Tallant receives here, it is clear the debt we owe him. A microfilm edition of the Robert Tallant Collection housed at the Amistad Research Center of Tulane University in New Orleans reflects the exhaustive fieldwork he conducted. The Collection contains, in addition to published works, a vast catalogue of unpublished materials. Again, I wish to emphasize the benefit we might earn by taking a new look at excellent collections such as these with a greater sensitivity to gender, class, and racial matters than is reasonable to expect from our predecessors.

7. Lyle Saxon, foreword to Tallant, *Voodoo in New Orleans*; Zora Neale Hurston, "Review of *Voodoo in New Orleans* by Robert Tallant," *Journal of American Folklore* 60 (1947): 438.

blacks, which were considerably more lenient than in any other slave state. Also, as a former French colony, Louisiana had absorbed much of the Gallic culture that many of St. Domingue's free people of color embraced as their own.[8]

As Tallant notes, Voodoo, which these people brought to their new home, "seems to have been a matriarch almost from its first days in Louisiana." Any inquiry into the subject, therefore, requires a significant focus on the participation of women in the religion. Most of the available literature, especially the personal accounts of journalists and other eyewitnesses, seems obsessively interested in the sexual aspects of both the rites and the practitioners of New Orleans Voodoo. In light of Hurston's comment in her review of *Voodoo in New Orleans* that Tallant "defines the functions of Hoodoo as a mere stimulation to sex," it is interesting to speculate whether Voodoo would have invited as much interest or met with as much tolerance had the dominant culture perceived its leaders to have been black men instead of black women. As it was, however, the New Orleans Voodoo matriarch who most successfully negotiated a bridge between her world and the white world was Marie Laveau. When Tallant asked an elderly black woman whether she had heard of Marie Laveau, he received this response: "Sure I heard of her. I don't know if she was good or bad; folks says both ways. But I know this: she was a *powerful* woman." Laveau is said to have traveled the streets of New Orleans as though she owned them, counseled the socially elite of both sexes, won every case she took to court, influenced city policy, borne fifteen children, grown rich, and died in bed (though legends hold she was reborn young again to reign as queen some twenty years more), all as a woman of color in the ante- and postbellum South. In the nineteenth century, a time when women of all races and classes endured legally as well as socially sanctioned sexual oppression, this is remarkable.[9]

So thoroughly shrouded in legend, Marie Laveau may be an impossible subject for a reliable biography. Hurston's inquiries about Laveau, published in her chapter on Hoodoo in *Mules and Men*, turned up multiple versions of the Voodoo queen's history: "Now I was in New Orleans and I asked. They told me Algiers, the part of New Orleans that is across

8. Alfred N. Hunt, *Haiti's Influence on Antebellum America* (Baton Rouge: Louisiana State University Press, 1987), 4.
9. Tallant, *Voodoo in New Orleans*, 21, 47; Hurston, "Review," 437.

the river to the west. . . . I found women reading cards and doing mail order business in names and insinuations of well known factors of conjure. Nothing worth putting on paper. But they all claimed some knowledge and link with Marie Leveau [*sic*]. From so much of hearing the name I asked everywhere for this Leveau and everybody told me differently."

According to Tallant in *Voodoo in New Orleans*, the earliest available legal document records a marriage to Jacques Paris on August 4, 1819, when Marie is either twenty-three or twenty-five. Allegedly quoting from the files of St. Louis Cathedral, the marriage contract identifies Marie as the illegitimate daughter of Charles Laveau, a wealthy white planter, and Marguerite Darcantel, a mulatto who was also part Indian. Although legal interracial marriages were extremely rare in Louisiana before 1870, "the desire of white men for sexual relations with Negro women was so great that special institutions grew up to satisfy it," in particular the institution of the quadroon balls and the *plaçage* unions resulting from them. Highly romanticized by writers of the period, the balls were attended by white men and beautiful young Creole girls escorted by their mothers for the straightforward purpose of pairing them up in *plaçage* arrangements. *Plaçage* was a common practice in Haiti and the British West Indies whereby a union was carefully negotiated, albeit lacking legal and religious sanctions. Though most of these unions dissolved upon the marriage of the white man to a woman of his own race and class, a financial settlement was usually arranged and the well-being of any children was seen to. Tallant identifies Marie Laveau as one of those children, and in his novel *The Voodoo Queen*, Marie and Jacques are given a house to live in by her father as part of the dowry.[10]

10. Hurston, *Mules and Men*, 239; John W. Blassingame, *Black New Orleans* (Chicago: University of Chicago Press, 1973), 17; Tallant, *Voodoo in New Orleans*, 53. It is generally accepted that there was a Marie Laveau I and a Marie Laveau II (mother and daughter), and speculation exists regarding a third, who may have appropriated the name to capitalize on the reputation. Hurston claims the first came directly from the Congo (Hurston, "Hoodoo in America," *Journal of American Folklore* 44 [1931]: 336). What remains unresolved and controversial is the question of which Marie Laveau certain deeds and accomplishments should be attributed to. Various legends hold that one was more powerful than the other, that one was good, the other an exploiter, and so on. Such a breakdown is grist for another mill; the purpose of the present essay is rather to question the assumptions on which Euro-American perceptions of the figure have been based.

Elsewhere in the present volume, Violet Harrington Bryan discusses the tradition of the quadroon balls in detail.

A marriage document recently uncovered by researchers challenges Tallant's authority on this point. Dated August 4, 1819, this license certifies the marriage of Santiago Paris to Maria Labeau, who is identified as the daughter of Carlos Labeau and Margarita D'arcantel. Setting aside the discrepancies in first names and spelling, the most significant distinction is that on the Notarial Record of this marriage, the parents of both Paris and Labeau are listed as Free People of Color.*

The authenticity of either document is yet to be verified. But if Marie Laveau was truly the issue of free people of color and was not "part white" as Tallant and most other versions of her story maintain, then clearly the white population appears to have been as eager to claim "some knowledge and link" with her as were the conjure women of Algiers. Contemporary stories are told in New Orleans recounting how free people of color had to steal Laveau's body away from whites who initially buried her in a white-only cemetery.

Whether he was called Jacques or Santiago, Marie's young husband seems to disappear from her life shortly after their marriage, though his death is not recorded until some years later. In the novel, a period of hard times is centered on a miscarriage and the loss of the home given to Marie by her father, by then deceased. Be this truth or fiction, we do know that Marie began a career as a professional hairdresser to support herself. Other women who, a century later and in various circumstances, accept leadership roles within Voodoo also refer to periods of hardship before answering the spiritual call; some great crisis is often experienced before the commitment is made to devote their lives to the service of spirits. Crisis or not, women appear to have occupied the most important leadership roles in Voodoo in Laveau's time, judging by the fact that at least several other strong women are also noted in the literature as spiritual leaders of nineteenth-century New Orleans Voodoo. In a study of the role of women as contemporary Vodou leaders, Karen McCarthy

*Editor's note: Many thanks to New Orleans researcher Barbara Trevigne for sharing the marriage certificate of Santiago Paris and Marie Laveau, and to Greg Osborn, archivist of the Louisiana Collection of the New Orleans Public Library, for providing information about this same marriage from the Notarial Archives of New Orleans, which shows both of Marie Laveau's parents to be free people of color. For further information on Laveau's relatives, see Barbara Trevigne, "Prominent People and Places," in *Gumbo People*, ed. Sybil Kein (New Orleans: Margaret Media, 1999), 184–5.—S.K.

Brown observes, "My impression is . . . that almost always women of this type—those who have both freedom and responsibility in large measures—are the successful Vodou priestesses." As a free woman of color earning her way in the world, Laveau epitomizes the profile. Michael Ventura, a Los Angeles–based newspaper columnist and critic of popular culture, offers the following characterization: "Marie Laveau was what we once would have called a witch and now might call a shaman. In Haiti she would have been called a mambo and in New Orleans she was a queen." Whatever label she eventually merited, the hairdresser Laveau—known as the Widow Paris—came to be much in demand by the ladies of Creole high society, and this work is generally thought to have served as the foundation of her career as a Voodooienne. One of the sources of her influence seems to have been the vast catalogue of secrets and family skeletons she maintained, and the network of servants and slaves she developed to collect information and do her bidding within the homes of the rich and powerful.[11]

Around this time Laveau began working with a root doctor known as Bayou John, or Doctor John. By all accounts, Doctor John cut an impressive figure himself. Descriptions have him dressed in elaborate Spanish costumes, bearing the tattooed marks of Senegalese royalty on his face. Tallant ventured that Laveau spent a period of apprenticeship with Doctor John, since "people say she learned a lot of tricks from old John Bayou." But however or by whom she was initiated, Marie Laveau was the reigning queen of the Voodoos by about 1830. Another historian had this to say: "In Haiti she would have been considered a mediocre priestess, but here she was a remarkable person, who gave the people what they wanted; she mixed up Voodooism with Christianity, which was in itself a great accomplishment, for it was what no sincere Voodoo priest or priestess of Haiti could have done—or would have done, for that matter. But it was the work of a very clever person. . . . To some she was a saint, to others, the devil incarnate." Much has been made over whether to attribute the "mixing up" of Catholicism and Voodoo to Laveau and Doctor

11. Karen McCarthy Brown, "Women's Leadership in Haitian Vodou," in *Weaving the Visions: New Patterns in Feminist Spirituality*, ed. Judith Plaskow and Carol P. Christ (San Francisco: Harper & Row, 1987), 156–201, 226; Luisah Teish, *Jambalaya: The Natural Women's Book of Personal Charms and Practical Rituals* (San Francisco: Harper & Row, 1985), 34; Michael Ventura, *Shadow Dancing in the U.S.A.* (New York: St. Martin's, 1985), 125.

John; the passage above, from one of the most judgmental works available on Laveau, even suggests that this is a practice unheard of in Haiti. But the practice of conflating the traditional gods of West Africa with the divine hierarchy of Catholicism is the structural essence of Voodoo, and was already common in Haiti, Cuba, and Brazil. Dr. John and especially Laveau are celebrated not for instituting the blend but for having publicized, popularized, and, some say, codified the practice in New Orleans.[12]

Luisah Teish is a priestess of Oshun in the Yoruba-based Lucumi tradition, the variety of Afro-Caribbean religion having its origins with the Yorubas of southern Nigeria and developed in Cuba. Born and raised in New Orleans, Teish, like the women of Algiers discussed by Hurston, claims "some knowledge and link" with Laveau. "Mam'zelle" is one of the three "Mothers" mentioned in the dedication of Teish's book *Jambalaya*, a title that compares Voodoo to the spicy dish in which many ingredients are cooked together. "It blends the practices of three continents into one tradition. It contains African ancestor reverence, Native American earth worship, and European Christian occultism." To Teish, Mam'zelle is spiritual mother as well as historical or legendary figure, and the stories she tells differ in detail from what is documented by more "official" sources. Efforts at deconstructing the Laveau mystery are irrelevant to her. Teish views the historical Laveau as "an adept social and cultural engineer" responsible for "standardizing the rituals and materials of the craft." Laveau's social influence was so great, according to Teish, that even the Catholic Church started cooperating with her. Teish claims that by 1863, known Voodoo practitioners were receiving the Catholic sacraments at St. Louis Cathedral in the Vieux Carré.[13]

Christian religious imagery and ritual practices within Voodoo, de-

12. Tallant, *Voodoo in New Orleans*, 36; Raymond J. Martinez, *Mysterious Marie Laveau* (New Orleans: Hope Publications, 1956), 3.

13. Teish, *Jambalaya*, x, 179. Objections to the use of books such as Teish's charge an unscholarly approach to the material. When Teish does rely on research, however, she draws from most of the same sources as do recognized scholars. As is the case for many others associated with the women's spirituality movement, Teish has no affiliation with a major academic institution, and is producing work herself for which she might have been merely an informant in times past. The trend to credit key informants as coresearchers and coauthors is, of course, commendable and just. But how threatening is it to the academy when the former subjects of scholarly scrutiny begin speaking in their own voices, rejecting its interpretive filter altogether?

veloped out of the imposition of French colonial Catholicism onto the slave population, remained a vital part of religious expression for free people of color outside the Caribbean. During Laveau's lifetime, such people, many of whom hailed directly from St. Domingue, constituted a significant portion of the New Orleans population. Though slave owners on the island of St. Domingue were compelled by law to baptize their slaves (moral justification for the slave trade rested on the conversion of pagans), generally no subsequent religious instruction was provided. Though it is commonly held that slaves were forced to practice Catholicism in lieu of their own religion, few planters would even allow priests on their land, fearing the exposure of brutalities. Metraux cites Vaissier: "the owners of Saint-Domingue . . . far from being concerned at seeing their Negroes live without religion, were, on the contrary, delighted, for in Catholic religion they saw nothing but the teaching of an equality which would be dangerous to put in the minds of slaves."[14]

What Laveau did do was to make certain aspects of Voodoo public, available, and even attractive to an audience of outsiders. Whether Laveau was conscious of, as Metraux puts it, "the revolutionary implications of the tenets of the Gospel" is speculative. But efforts toward a recognized identification with the dominant culture's official religion and her own might well have established a measure of social legitimization for her people without abandoning an ideology that nurtured a struggle for equality. Nowhere in the work of the Euro-Americans reporting on the deeds and accomplishments of Marie Laveau are they imagined, within a specific historical context, to have been motivated by the concerns of a community for which she was an acknowledged leader. As a woman of color closely related through heritage and practice to the traditions Laveau preserved, Teish offers, "let the record show that Luisah Teish finds Mam'zelle Marie Laveau to be neither saint nor demon but . . . a woman who responded appropriately to the demands of her time with the resources available to her."[15]

14. Alfred Metraux, *Voodoo in Haiti*, trans. Hugo Charteris (New York: Schocken Books, 1972), 33. In 1797, the city's population totaled 8,056, of which 1,335 were free Negroes, and 2,773 were slaves. The St. Domingue influence only increased following the conclusion of the revolution in 1804. By 1809, Governor Claiborne reported 5,754 refugees had entered Louisiana territory, including 2,060 free Negroes and 2,113 arriving as slaves (Hunt, *Haiti's Influence*, 46).

15. Metraux, *Voodoo in Haiti*, 33; Teish, *Jambalaya*, 169.

To return to Tallant on Voodooism as a matriarchy, he continues, "Mama was the entire show. The only men of importance were the witch doctors. . . . Women seem, too, to have made up at least eighty per cent of the cultists, and it was always the female of the white race who entered the sect. When white men were present it was usually because they sought handsome yellow girls rather than for reason of any belief in the Zombi." Three questions are thus raised: What meaning might the Zombi hold for the practitioners of New Orleans Voodoo? *Was* New Orleans Voodoo a matriarchy? And why might white women have been participants while white men were merely lascivious spectators?[16]

Among the many different conceptions of what a zombie might be in Haiti or popular American culture, the Zombi of New Orleans Voodoo was a great serpent "who was placed in a box and used as a major conduit for transmitting the energy that leads to possession by the spirit." The underlying principal of serpent worship is described in Melville Herskovits's *Dahomey: An Ancient West African Kingdom* as "a living quality expressed in all things that are flexible, sinuous, and moist." This quality, epitomized by the serpent figure "Da" is what makes any creature a living, moving organism rather than an inert mass. The role Da plays in a person's life concerns "collective and personal fortune." But this favor is fickle and shifting; it is envisioned as "wealth, prestige, and all those other things desired by a human being [which] are prone to slip away if not watched. . . . It is Da, then, who brings fortune and who takes it away, and that is why Da must be watched and placated so assiduously." In Dahomey, however, it is the responsibility of those in power to honor the Da, and the agents in control of Dahomean life, Herskovits claims, are men. Their responsibility is great, because all those who depend on the ritual leader will share in the fortune brought on by his vigilance or lack of it. This is no benevolent spirit; Herskovits quotes a Dahomean as saying, "One is never done with being anxious about placating him, for he does not forgive readily."[17]

Considering the validity of the claim that Voodoo was matriarchical, it is difficult to gauge the influence Doctor John and men like him may have had, for Marie and the Voodoo queens before her so monopolized

16. Tallant, *Voodoo in New Orleans*, 21.

17. Teish, *Jambalaya*, 181; Melville J. Herskovits, *Dahomey: An Ancient West African Kingdom* (Evanston, Ill.: Northwestern University Press, 1967), 2: 251, 255.

the attention of those recording Voodoo activities. There are stories of rivalries between Laveau and her immediate predecessor and also of threats to Laveau's throne during her lengthy reign. Martinez characterized the battle between Marie Laveau and Marie Saloppe as having "precipitated a terrible battle for supremacy, nearly as bad as the War of the Spanish Succession." Tallant describes the process by which rival queens were disposed of with only slightly less sensation. He claims that conflicts encompassed threats, gris-gris (magic charms) held responsible for deaths, decisions to flee the area, and "pure brute force when [a queen] met them on the street and beat them soundly until she extracted a promise from them that they would abdicate their thrones or serve under her as part of sub-queens."[18] (Interestingly, accounts of this nature seem to appear only in works by men; a good catfight, apparently, is rarely without appeal.) If the claim that Voodoo was a matriarchy is accurate, then it was the queens who held the awesome responsibility of leading the people in their Zombi serpent worship.

If the serpent who became the center of concern in the New Orleans Voodoo carried the same general meaning as it does in Dahomey, the seriousness of this responsibility is clear. The welfare of an entire community of worshipers would have been staked on the success of the person or persons in charge of placating the Da. Thus if there were in fact "terrible battles for supremacy"over the Voodoo throne, these may have had justification beyond simple vanity and lust for power. Obviously, the social structures dictating Dahomean spiritual protocol were no longer in place. Exactly why women began to assume ritual leadership roles would require analysis of the social and economic havoc wreaked by over four hundred years of West African diaspora. Speaking of the role of women in Haitian Vodou, Brown notes, "slavery broke the African family. Drought, corruption, and poverty broke the patriarchal extended family that reconstituted itself after Haiti's slave revolution. From the wreckage, women's previously muted voices began to emerge."[19] If women continued to find themselves in the position of being responsible for many dependents, there should be little wonder why the serpent remained a crucial spiritual focus.

But *was* New Orleans Voodoo a matriarchy? The evidence more re-

---

18. Martinez, *Mysterious Marie Laveau,*14; Tallant, *Voodoo in New Orleans,* 56.
19. Brown, "Women's Leadership," 254–5.

alistically suggests that the social arrangement might have consisted of new forms of a tradition of complementary male-female roles. Stories indicate that men served important ritual functions and that root doctors like Doctor John worked closely with the reigning queens.

One assumption underlying a discussion of Voodoo as a matriarchy is that the situation was necessarily an either/or arrangement—that either women were dominant or they were subjugated. Social scientists have overturned the thesis, however, that male slaves were mere puppets to a dominant female head of household. Deborah Gray White's research shows that slave women were "schooled in self-reliance and self-sufficiency. However the 'self' was more likely the female slave collective than the individual slave woman," and never precluded male-female cooperation. White reviews anthropological findings of African societies in which, similar to female slave society, women are not isolated from each other, but cooperate in the performance of tasks, forming groups and associations. Women have control within their world, ranking and ordering themselves amongst other women, not men.[20] Intrasexual cooperation might have been interpreted by the Euro-American as total independence from the opposite sex, which necessarily means dominance of one over the other within the either/or paradigm. It is possible the observers of New Orleans Voodoo bore just such a bias, unable to envision a negotiation of power between the sexes as an accepted and pragmatic response to the conditions of a harsh reality. To Euro-Americans of Marie Laveau's time, the characterization of New Orleans Voodoo as a matriarchy would hardly have stood as a positive example of the creative potential of womanhood. Rather, it might have framed yet another

20. Deborah Gray White, "Female Slaves: Sex Roles and Status in the Antebellum Plantation South," in *Unequal Sisters: A Multi-Cultural Reader in U.S. Women's History*, ed. Ellen Carol DuBois and Vicki L. Ruiz (New York: Routledge, 1989), 26, 27. White has analyzed the sex roles and status of female slaves in the antebellum plantation South, offering additional perspectives on the effects of slavery on the African family. Her arguments offer a balance to the matriarchal-slave-family thesis of sociologist E. Franklin Frazier and reach the conclusion that the belief in the prevalence of matrifocal slave households was a misconception. (Frazier blamed slavery for the self-sufficiency of the black woman and for her lack of subordination to masculine authority.) White, "Female Slaves," 22. In response to White's work, historians reappraised antebellum source material and concluded that, based on divisions of labor, the dominant role in slave society was in fact played by men.

abomination in the eyes of God, further extending the gulf between an Us and a Them.

Of the attention given to the participation of significant numbers of white women in the Voodoo ceremonies, Teish comments, "If we . . . look at this matter through the 'eyes of woman,' the mystery becomes common sense. In the 1800s upper-class women lived under a peculiar oppression (the curse of the pedestal); working-class white women were oppressed by indentured servitude (the curse of the totem pole); and Black women were oppressed by slavery (the curse of the chattel)." Teish's point is that the shared sense of sexual oppression might have been enough to put them in "psychic sympathy" with one another, leading to a common spiritual goal. Perhaps even more compelling is Teish's reminder of women's lack of access to abortion, and that white women of all classes sought herbal abortifacients from root women. Her claim that "Voudou is a science of the oppressed" is underscored by Brown's discussion of Haitian Vodou. "Haitian Vodou is not a religion of the empowered and the privileged." Haitians live with "an open-eyed acceptance of finitude . . . one reason the Vodou spirits have emerged as whole, three-dimensional characters. The oppressed are the most practiced analysts of human character and behavior, and Haitian traditional religion is the repository for wisdom accumulated by a people who have lived through slavery, hunger, disease, repression, corruption, and violence— all in excess."[21]

If we accept this as a premise, it is easy to see why there might have been limited appeal among the white male ruling class for the spiritual substance of this religion. There is little acknowledgment of any spiritual element in the religion in the work of men writing either at the time or at later times in popular accounts generally accepted as authoritative, such as Tallant's. What does appeal to these writers is the "excess":

21. Teish, *Jambalaya*, 170, 171; Karen McCarthy Brown, *Mama Lola: A Vodou Priestess in Brooklyn* (Berkeley: University of California Press, 1991), 98. The barriers of race, class, and culture to an idealized notion of "spiritual sisterhood" are acknowledged by Teish elsewhere (*Jambalaya*, 255–7). Feminist theory has been correctly challenged from within the discipline for its white, middle-class bias which has preferred to base its construction on the commonality of women's experience rather than the profound differences among women. Patricia Zavella, "The Problematic Relationship of Feminism and Chicana Studies," *Studies in Gender and Culture* 4 (1989): 32.

On an altar was the ornamented box containing Vodu, the Zombi, the holy serpent, and one by one the black people approached the bars set into one side of the box, swearing devotion, pledging secrecy, requesting favors. They took oaths to die or to kill, if necessary, for their god.

This over, the king touched the box with his hand, then seized the hand of the queen with his other hand. Both of them—Mama and Papa—began shaking and writhing. Papa picked Mama up and stood her on top of the box containing the snake. Her jerking became more violent. She flung her arms toward the black night sky, and her head rolled on her shoulders as if her neck were broken. A scream ripped from her throat.

Now invocations, curses and sacred words poured from her lips. She was possessed. The god had accepted her as an oracle, and the words she spoke came not from herself but from the snake within the box upon which she stood trembling and jerking.

Papa began the chant: "Eh! Eh! Bomba hen hen!"

The people became infected with the *power*. In a moment they were all possessed. Papa took the hand of the nearest devotee, who in turn took the hand of the person nearest him, and the current of *power* spread like electricity. The chant rose and fell in great crashing waves of sound, as steady and as rhythmic as the tom-toms. [Tallant's emphasis.]

Papa presented Mama with the bowl of warm blood from the sacrificed kid. She drank and handed it to each of the people as they whirled past. Her own lips drank the last drops.

The dance grew faster now. They spun and gyrated and leaped high into the air. They fell to their hands and knees, imitating the postures of animals, some chewing at the grass, shaking their posteriors violently. They bit and clawed at each other. Their scanty garments fell upon the hot earth, still panting and gyrating. Some fell unconscious and were dragged away, into the deep darkness of the trees that edged the clearing.[22]

This is Tallant's composite, representative rendering of the personal accounts he collected over the years. In most of the eyewitness reports there is as much or more emphasis on the physical attributes of the participants and the orgiastic nature of the finales, and virtually no acknowledgment of a religious form of possession taking place. Most accounts are described through a lens of fear, awe, and disgust, but certainly aroused widespread interest. It is hard to imagine a spectacle more alien

22. Tallant, *Voodoo in New Orleans*, 7–8.

to nineteenth- or even twentieth-century Western notions of proper Christian moral conduct, in which religious ethics and behaviors are safely located within text. Christian ritual behavior, historically officiated by men, is prescribed and ordered.

Carol Christ offers an analysis of the reluctance of students of Western religions to examine the kind of ritual common within nonliterary traditions. "Ritual puts us in the presence of body and blood, milk and honey and wine, song and dance, sexuality and ecstasy. Underlying the preference for texts in religious studies lies the fear of the nonrational and the physical, the fear of chaos." Tallant unabashedly exhibits such fear elsewhere in the same work: "While the wild chanting, the rhythmic movement of hands and feet, the barbarous dance, and the fiery incantations were at their height, it was difficult to believe that we were in a civilized city of an enlightened republic . . . it was so wild and bizarre that one might easily imagine he was in Africa *or in hell*." (Emphasis mine.)[23]

Though Christ argues specifically for feminist inquiry into the history of pre-Christian European goddess traditions, parallels can be drawn to the white-male-centered study of Voodoo. She notes that the field of religious studies is heavily influenced by Biblical notions of God, and that goddesses (and possibly, by extension, women) are presented as "abominations." "It is hard to shake the mindset that has encouraged us to think of goddesses in relation to terms such as 'idolatry,' 'fertility fetish,' 'nature religion,' 'orgiastic,' 'bloodthirsty,' 'cult prostitution.'" In an effort to deconstruct what Christ terms the Western ethos of objectivity, she encourages scholars to "transcend the philosophical tradition which tells us that divinity, humanity, and nature are three completely distinct categories." Such categorical divisions "reflect man's continuing attempt to ally himself with a principle, a transcendent and rational deity, that will enable him to escape finitude and mortality, which he then consigns to the realm of nature."[24]

How these ideas might be applied to the study of Voodoo is suggested by the work of Michael Ventura, who offers an interpretation of what he perceives to be the difference between the Western and African "metaphysic":

> Africans don't conceive of the other world—the world of the spirit, the divine—as existing above this one, or below it, or even alongside it. . . .

23. Christ, "Toward a Paradigm Shift," 71; Tallant, *Voodoo in New Orleans*, 30.
24. Christ, "Toward a Paradigm Shift," 71, 73.

For the African, the human world and the spirit world *intersect*. Their sign for this is the cross, but it has nothing to do with the Christianist cross, which impales a man in helpless agony upon the intersection. That is the way the West feels. In Africa, the cross is of two roads intersecting to flow into each other, to nourish each other. The earthly and the spirit worlds meet at right angles, and everything that is most important happens at the spot where they meet, which is neither solely of one world nor of the other.

This meeting of one's god *within* the body, especially a woman's body, would seemingly have been a horrifyingly exquisite thing for the voyeuristically inclined Christian white man to witness. He must have been ideologically incapable of viewing sexuality within any legitimate religious construct, much less as possessing a positive "cosmic power of transformation." But dismissive as he might have been about the sincerely religious nature of the activities he was allowed to witness, witness he did, it appears, at every opportunity. One chief source were the Sunday afternoon gatherings in Congo Square, presided over by Marie Laveau; while many believed these to be Voodoo rituals, they were in fact no more than pleasure dances held for the amusement of slaves and the white people who came to watch.[25]

More important ceremonies were held on Lake Pontchartrain and Bayou St. John every year on St. John's Eve, June 23. One of the innovations Laveau introduced was to invite the press, public, and police to her "secret" meetings out by the lake. Throughout the nineteenth century, periodic campaigns were waged resulting in bans on the right of people of color to congregate, but by the 1850s, newspaper articles and editorials were defending Voodoo ritual gatherings and questioning the right of police to interfere in them. In spite of the public nature of the June gatherings, Tallant offers numerous accounts suggesting that the most important religious rituals were entirely secret. One of these describes an event around 1825, just before Marie Laveau is thought to have become powerful. After having witnessed the ritual as a teenager, the writer described the experience years later:

> The chorus of Dante's hell had entered into the mad shouts of Africa.
> . . . Up sprang a magnificent specimen of human flesh—Ajona, a lithe,

25. Ventura, *Shadow Dancing*, 109–10; Christ, "Toward a Paradigm Shift," 71; Hurston, *Mules and Men*, 201; Tallant, *Voodoo in New Orleans*, 18.

tall black woman, with a body waving and undulating like Zozo's snake—a perfect Semiramis from the jungles of Africa. Confining herself to a spot not more than two feet in space, she began to sway on one and the other side. Gradually the undulating motion was imparted to her body from ankles to the hips. Then she tore the white handkerchief from her forehead. This was a signal, for the whole assembly sprang forward and entered the dance. . . . Under the passion of the hour, the women tore off their garments, and entirely nude, went on dancing, but wriggling like snakes.[26]

It is nowhere indicated that Marie Laveau did anything to lessen the intensity of these ceremonies, so it might be safe to assume that those attending later rites witnessed much the same thing presided over by the new queen. Interesting to remember at this point is that Marie bore fifteen children during the height of her reign. It thus seems probable that she performed some of her ceremonial tasks while in some stage of pregnancy. Imagine, if you will, a pair of nineteenth-century Western eyes beholding a rite such as the one described above performed by a woman seven or eight months pregnant. As Teish points out, in French *Laveau* means "the calf." The immediate associations are with Hathor and Isis of Egypt, and any of the earlier cow and moon goddesses of fertility. "Hathor, the goddess of fertility, was also the female principal."[27] Hathor was the patroness of women and marriage and the goddess of love, mirth, social pleasures, and beauty, but she also gave nourishment to the souls of the departed. If the responsibility of the queen is to summon the Da, the creative principle expressed in all living things, who better than one so capable, both symbolically and perhaps literally, of carrying life itself?

Whether *Laveau* was a self-appointed name, as Teish asserts, or the name taken from her white planter father is unknowable and, for the purpose of this analysis, irrelevant. It is the name by which she was primarily

26. Tallant, *Voodoo in New Orleans*, 28, 46, 56, 61, 66; Hurston, *Mules and Men*, 201–2. Zozo is identified by the observer as a well-known and elderly vendor of herbs, and as the ritual snake handler in the ceremony (Tallant, *Voodoo in New Orleans*, 45).

27. *Funk and Wagnall's Standard Dictionary of Folklore, Mythology, and Legend*, one-volume edition (1972), s.v. "Hathor."

identified among those who sought to document her life and deeds. What confusion might these images have evoked, however unconsciously, to the Western mind? Marie the Calf—the fertile virgin. The name alone embodies the full range of possibilities inherent in the feminine principle that the major Western religious traditions have reduced to simpler oppositions. Marie's reputation reflects these perceived contradictions, holding her to be not only an evil temptress and sorcerer, but also a saintly nurse during yellow fever epidemics and a ministering angel bringing last solace to condemned prisoners.

Marie Laveau's achievements become all the more significant when viewed against such a background. She embodied what the established power structure feared most and understood least, maintained a spiritual order and, within a precarious social and cultural context, manipulated it to her own and her people's benefit. And she did not merely escape retribution for this outrage, she prospered.

Audre Lorde reminds us that "the very word erotic comes from the Greek word *eros*, the personification of love in all its aspects—born of Chaos, and personifying creative power and harmony." Within the modern Western paradigm the threat to reason is the nonrational, the enemy of order, chaos. This dualistic intellectual and spiritual energy is configured by an either/or model of experience, rather than the *both/and* model of inclusiveness. To the Western mind, both/and introduces unarticulable chaos. But while the mind cannot fathom chaos, the body can experience it. Chaos charges the body, and this physical charge is often synonymous with the erotic experience. If, using Lorde's definition, the child of chaos becomes the creative power of the erotic, how truly dangerous the personification of creative power as an erotically charged spiritual force must appear to a rational, ordered, moral concept of the universe.[28]

Marie Laveau's power is evidenced by the persistence of her name and legend in American folklore. That she was feared is indisputable. In spite of her name's being etched on her supposed tombstone, numerous stories deny her death. She is thought to have wriggled out of her skin and been reborn young to continue her work.

28. Audre Lorde, *Sister Outsider* (Trumansburg, N.Y.: Crossing Press, 1984), 55. I wish to thank Vimal K. Duggal for helping me articulate the ideas in this paragraph.

Upon Octavio Paz's first trip to India, in 1951, he recorded his im-
pressions of Bombay. "I sat at the foot of a huge tree . . . and tried to
make an inventory of all I had seen, heard, smelled, and felt: dizziness,
horror, stupor, astonishment, joy, enthusiasm, nausea, inescapable attraction. What had attracted me? It was difficult to say: *Human kind cannot bear so much reality.* Yes, the excess of reality had become an unreality,
but that unreality had turned suddenly into a balcony from which I
peered into—what? Into that which is beyond and still has no name."
Marie Laveau embodies the kind of human ambivalence and social ambiguity considered alarming and morally suspect by the West. One can
hardly fault the Western sensibility for being so terrified of and attracted
to this relentless yet compelling reality. Pressing beyond the limits of the
linear and sequential model, the experience requires the connective tis-
sue of a living mythology mediating between the *was* and *will be* and ending in an acceptance of the *is* of existence. What constructs of the
Western intellect inhibit the bodily expression of the spiritual drive to
connect? What are the consequences of such inhibition? Lorde's answer
to the latter is that "the fear of our desires keeps them suspect and indis-
criminately powerful, for to suppress any truth is to give it strength beyond endurance."[29]

Images of the film *Laura* come to mind again: generations of white
culture captivated by the portrait of a beautiful, powerful, inaccessible
woman—saint or devil, fact or fantasy. It is not difficult to understand
how Marie Laveau came to embody the use and manifestation of different ways of being which have appeared exotic, provocative, even mythic
to the dominant culture, which was, and still is, both drawn to and repulsed by them.

29. Octavio Paz, *In Light of India*, trans. Eliot Weinberger (New York: Harcourt
Brace, 1995), 12; Christ, "Toward a Paradigm Shift," 60; Lorde, *Sister Outsider*, 57.
In Stanley Diamond's essay entitled "Job and the Trickster," he discusses the Book
of Job and Plato's *Republic* as partly capable of explicating the root of Western ethics. As Plato and Job insist on the obliteration of injustice in the world, they stand
in denial of human ambivalence and social ambiguity. Paul Radin, *The Trickster: A
Study in American Indian Mythology* (New York: Schocken Books, 1972), xiii.

8

New Orleans Creole Expatriates in France

Romance and Reality

Michel Fabre

In the nineteenth century, France was often claimed by New Orleans Creoles of color as a spiritual home to which they felt they belonged culturally. The sons and daughters of the New Orleans French-speaking elite typically studied in institutions like the Sainte-Barbe Academy or the Couvent School, which provided primary education in the French style. After graduation, many colored youngsters from among this group were sent by their wealthy parents to pursue their education in France, just as many white Creoles attended Louis-le-Grand college at mid-century. Among the colored, mathematician Basile Crocker, poet Pierre Dalcour, and military officer Francis Dumas were educated in Paris, physicians Oscar Guimbillote and Louis Roudanez obtained their medical degrees there, and Edmond Dédé, Lucien Lambert, and Eugene Victor (Victor-Eugène) Macarty were admitted to the Conservatoire de musique. The latter spent a couple of years studying voice, music, and composition in the city, where educator Louisa Lamotte later resided. The graphic arts followed a similar pattern. Jules Lion studied lithography and became interested in daguerreotype in Paris. And Eugene Warburg found France a more hospitable environment for pursuing his craft of marble sculpture. Born a slave and emancipated as an infant by his father, a German Jew, Warburg received his formal training in New Orleans from French sculptor Philippe Garbeille, who did busts of important people. In 1849, he shared a workshop with his thirteen-year-old brother Daniel, whom he taught to be a stonecutter. Warburg received commissions from St. Louis Cathedral and produced several statues, including "Ganymede," which was ecstatically praised by the New Orleans *Bee* on December 13, 1850, but economic rivalry and lack of opportunity in the city incited him to leave for Europe in November 1852. He rented a studio in Montparnasse and began studying at the Ecole des Beaux-Arts under Françoise Jouffroy. Warburg worked there for four years, and several of his works were accepted by the 1855 Salon de Paris.[1]

Educator Michel Séligny, half-brother of poet Camille Thierry, also studied in France before founding the Sainte-Barbe Academy in New Orleans. Later, he fell in love with a white married woman, and, because of his liaison, was cast out not only by the New Orleans colored high society, but by his family as well. Eventually he and his lover took refuge in Paris, where he died ten years later. One can even speak of a few dynasties among the emigrants: Richard Lucien Lambert, who had grown up playing piano in the pit of Théâtre d'Orléans, enjoying a friendly rivalry with Louis Moreau Gottschalk, went to Paris, where he made a career for some years. His son Lucien Léon was born there in 1858. Taught by Théodore Dubois and Jules Massenet, Lucien Léon left with his family for Rio de Janeiro in the 1860s but seems to have returned a decade

1. Lester Sullivan, "Composers of Color of Nineteenth Century New Orleans: The History Behind the Music," *Black Music Research Journal* 8 (1988): 11–41. Among white Creoles, Charles-Cyprien Turpin and Alfred Mercier studied at Louis-le-Grand, the latter returning to Paris for medical studies and earning a diploma. Jean-Charles Faget received his degree in medicine at Louis-le-Grand in 1844 and Dr. J. M. Durel studied in Paris until 1853. Charles Gayarré, already well known in Louisiana's political and literary life, lived in Paris for rest, research, and writing from 1835 to 1843. Amédée-Théodore Louis published a work in Paris in 1841. Father Adrien Rouquette and his physician brother Dominique-Armand also stayed in Paris in midcentury. The earliest example found of a mixed-blood sent to Paris by his father was from 1739 (Jacques Coustillon); scores more studied in France over the years.

I am indebted to the National Humanities Center for a spring 1997 fellowship that allowed me to update research for this essay. I thank Professors Frans Amelinckx, Joseph Logsdon, John J. Perret, and Charles Edwards O'Neill, S. J., for their kind help in New Orleans.

later, since his "Prométhée enchaîné" won the Concours Rossini in 1855. On December 8, 1911, "La Roussalka," a rural ballet pantomime by Hughes Lestour and A. de Dubor, with music by Lambert, opened at the Paris Opera. Lucien's half-brother, Sidney, a brilliant pianist, likewise went to Paris to pursue his career in the mid-1870s after living in Portugal.[2]

These are only a few cases among the many free people of color who sojourned in France in order to acquire academic degrees and skills when laws barred them from U.S. colleges, or to enjoy the benefits of a social climate largely free from racial discrimination. Temporary or lasting, their expatriation expressed their dissatisfaction with the prejudices that limited their aspirations and cut them off from the American cultural mainstream. But their expatriation was also strongly encouraged by white relatives (often French fathers) and by the favorable attitudes of New Orleans Creoles. Examples abound of influential whites' granting patronage to colored Creoles who wished to pursue careers abroad. One was Eugene Victor Macarty, who was allowed to attend music classes at the Conservatoire in Paris in 1840 even though he was over maximum age, because diplomat Pierre Soulé (who had been his family's lawyer) intervened with the French ambassador to the United States to have him admitted. This kind of support was by no means exceptional; in fact, it was customary for most New Orleans Creoles to sail to France with such recommendations.

Out of a score of distinguished free Creoles of color who established themselves in France, four outstanding figures are the subject of the present essay: engineer Norbert Rillieux, poet Camille Thierry, dramatist Victor Séjour, and composer Edmond Dédé, all of whom died expatriate. Considered in chronological sequence, these men stand as revealing instances of the successes and hardships that colored New Orleanians experienced on French soil. Their careers abroad have not yet been sufficiently documented, but comparing them will bring out common features which may help establish a paradigm for explaining their destinies.

2. Much information on the Lamberts was provided by Professor Lawrence Gushee. For a detailed treatment of their careers, as well as those of other composers, especially Dédé and Gottschalk, see Lester Sullivan's essay in this volume.

BACKGROUND

The political contexts of the four young men's departures from Louisiana were generally the sàme. New Orleans *gens de couleur* studied and even expatriated themselves in France as early as the 1740s, but they resorted to emigration in sizable numbers only after 1840, when measures aiming at containing their progress locally were enforced. Antebellum outmigration peaked when state laws and city regulations became more stringent and public attitudes more hostile toward free blacks. Victor Séjour (born 1817) moved to Paris as early as 1834; he was followed by Norbert Rillieux (born 1806) who studied there in 1830 and returned to settle indefinitely in 1854. Camille Thierry (born 1814) left his native land only in 1855, his departure for educational purposes having been planned in the forties but postponed because of his father's death. Edmond Dédé (born 1827) sailed to France in 1857 after a brief migration to Mexico. In addition to the political situations they were escaping, the four also had the common characteristic of direct French ancestry: two had French fathers and two were the grandsons of Frenchmen. Aided by their families who saw to their education, they were able to begin careers in New Orleans before exiling themselves to France.

Norbert Rillieux was the son of French engineer Vincent Rillieux and quadroon Constance Vivant, possibly M. Rillieux's slave but more likely a free woman. By 1822–23, Rillieux *père* had cotton presses and warehouses on Poydras and Tchoupitoulas Streets. In 1830, he sent Norbert to study at the Ecole Centrale in Paris, to specialize in evaporating engineering; young Rillieux was appointed instructor in applied mechanics at age twenty-four. He published a series of papers on steam-engine work and apparently developed the theory of the multiple-effect evaporator at that time. He tried without success to interest French machinery manufacturers in his invention. He went back home and struggled for thirteen years before being allowed to test the world's first triple-effect evaporator in a Louisiana refinery. When he did, success was immediate and the Rillieux apparatus was installed in several factories in the state in 1846. From then on, Rillieux worked as a much-sought-after consultant for plantations, with an office on Peters Street. He obtained a United States patent on the multiple-action vacuum refining pan, which operated by the placing of condensation coils in the vacuum chamber, thus enabling the vapor produced in the first stage of refining to be used as the heat source of the second, and so on; it yielded more granulated sugar than the open kettle and greatly reduced costs. This helped Louisiana sugar growers and practically saved the Cuban sugar industry.[3]

Camille Thierry's father had come to New Orleans from Bordeaux to make a fortune, and did business on Ursulines Street from the '40s until 1857 as a wholesale liquor dealer and distiller. He fell in love with an octoroon who already had a son, Michel Séligny, and who bore two boys to Thierry. He could well afford to provide his children with fine educations, but he died just as Camille was about to leave and study in France. Thus the young man started a career in business although he was more attracted to poetry. After he published his first poem, his brother Jacques, who had taken over their father's business, joked: "My brother puts spirit in his verse, I put spirits in barrels." Camille seems to have exiled himself to escape discrimination. "A few drops of black blood

3. Louis Haber, *Black Pioneers of Science and Invention* (New York: Harcourt, 1970), 13–23; George Peterkin Meade, "A Negro Scientist of Slavery Days," *Scientific Monthly* 62 (1946), 316–24; Edgar Allen Poppin, *Biographical History of Blacks in America Since 1928* (New York: McRay, 1971), 395–6; Eugene Winslow, *Great Negroes, Past and Present* (Chicago: American, 1969), 49–50, 62. Rillieux's own article on sugar is reprinted in *Louisiana Studies* 12 (1973): 425–36; also, a facsimile of his U.S. Patent Office record for the sugar-evaporating process is reproduced in Milton Harris et al., eds., *The Black Book* (New York: Random House, 1974), 112–3.

Historian R. L. Desdunes wrote erroneously that Rillieux was appointed head of the Ecole Centrale. See Rodolphe Lucien Desdunes, *Our People and Our History*, trans. Sister Dorothea Olga McCants (Baton Rouge: Louisiana State University Press, 1973), 74–5. Desdunes believed that Rillieux suffered from racial antagonism; his remark that the inventor "was made to feel the sting of humiliation and prejudice because of his race" may refer to the fact that, when working as a consultant on plantations, Rillieux was provided with a special house and slave servants, but not entertained in the white owner's house. Desdunes also claims that when singing Rillieux's praises after his death, the New Orleans papers never referred to him as a black man. Yet in 1894 sugar planter John Dymond, who operated one of Rillieux's original systems in his Belair sugarhouse, got the race correct when paying him tribute. See "Norbert Rillieux," in *The Louisiana State Planter and Sugar Manufacturer* 13 (1894): 276.

In January 1846 Rillieux ran an ad in *L'Abeille de la Nouvelle-Orléans* for "Chaudières à vide" of different capacities, with prices ranging from $1,700 to $3,100 ($1,800 to $4,300 installed), capable of bringing to boiling point from six to thirty bushels of sugar in twenty-four hours; the ad announced that a vacuum sugar pan could be observed on the plantation of Widow Vertoin in Jefferson Parish.

closed the high society circles to him," and he suffered from this in spite of the friendship of some prominent Frenchmen such as Dr. Alfred Testut. He sent Testut a poem, "Remerciements," in which he alluded to the death of his father and the demise of his own dreams:

> Lui dormant . . . adieu le collège
> Qu'il avait tant rêvé pour moi;
> Adieu la France qui protège
> Les enfants placès sous sa loi!
> Lui dormant, j'allai dans l'orgie.

> With him dead . . . farewell to college
> of which he had dreamed for me;
> farewell to France that protects
> the children placed under her laws.
> With him dead, I went into orgies.

Thierry seems to have had enough quirks in his temperament and bad luck in his life to make him a typical Romantic individualist. But he was talented. He published "Idées" in *L'Album littéraire* and, when Armand Lanusse put together his anthology, *Les Cenelles*, he selected fourteen poems by Thierry—more than by anyone else, evidence that the latter was considered a superior poet.[4]

Victor Séjour's father, Louis Séjour Marcou, was born not in France but at Saint-Marc, St. Domingue, the son of a white Frenchman and a free woman of color. At age twenty-two, in 1809, Marcou reached New Orleans via Cuba as a fugitive of the Haitian revolution and started working there as a tailor, none too successfully. He settled with Héloïse Ferrand, the daughter of a free man of color who may have been related to the actress Minette Ferrand. Their two sons, Victor and Ruojes, were legitimized in May 1826 when the couple married, shortly before a daughter was born to them. Louis ran a dry-goods store belonging to his wife, bought a building on Bourbon Street in 1831, and acquired real estate

---

4. Edward Larocque Tinker, *Les Ecrits de langue française en Louisiane au 19e siècle: Essai biographique et bibliographique* (Paris: Honoré Champion, 1932), 467. In the Bordeaux parish registers and archives, there seems to be no Thierry after 1744. It is probable that the ancestors of Camille Thierry—the name is a typical *langue d'oil* patronym—were natives of northern France. "Remerciements" was included in Alfred Testut's *Fleurs d'été* (New Orleans, 1851), 193.

and a dozen slaves in the 1830s. It was he who persuaded his younger son to seek fortune in France, probably as early as 1834. While Ruojes was investing in New Orleans real estate, Victor was gaining entry into Paris literary circles, after having made his literary debut before leaving the place of his birth. A member of the Société des Artisans at age seventeen, Séjour read his first poetic effort to its members on the occasion of the association's anniversary. It was reportedly a satire against the rival Société d'Economie, formed by Creoles and tending toward exclusiveness. Séjour's father before him had chosen the Société des Artisans, whose meetings offered its members a sounding board for literary expression as well as business considerations. In Paris, Victor would become more explicit in exposing the consequences of the other society's racial bar in a short story, "Le Mulâtre," published in 1837 in *La Revue des Colonies*, which was edited by racially committed French West Indian Cyrille Bissette.[5]

Séjour, Thierry, and especially Rillieux were all light-skinned with virtually no Negroid characteristics. Not so Edmond Dédé, who had an almost black complexion and distinctly African features. Dédé was born into a family of free people of color. Bazile Dédé and his wife Jeanne Marie Dupré had arrived from St. Domingue, probably by way of Cuba, in 1809. Bazile was the *chef de musique* of a band in the local militia unit and served as his son's first teacher, to be followed in that capacity by one Ludovico Gabici. Edmond Dédé later described himself as a composer and "second generation professional musician." In 1848, he moved to Mexico, as did a few other New Orleans *gens de couleur libre*, in reaction to the escalating problems in race relations. Illness drove him back home in 1851. The following year, his melody "Mon pauvre coeur" became the first piece of sheet music published by a New Orleans Creole of color. He supplemented his earnings with a day job as a cigar maker, a profession pursued by a number of other local musicians. By 1857, he had saved enough money to book his passage to Europe.[6]

CAREERS OF THE FOUR IN FRANCE

After making much money by speculating and then losing it during the 1837 crisis, Norbert Rillieux returned to live in France in 1854. R. L.

5. *L'Album littéraire*, August 15, 1843, 137.
6. The bibliographical data for Dédé's "Mon pauvre coeur"appears in the appendix to Sullivan's essay in this volume.

Desdunes suggests that this was because he faced discrimination, but his lack of success with projects for draining the city was owing to the intrigues of engineer Edmund Forstall, a personal adversary of Rillieux's father who prevented the municipality of New Orleans from adopting the son's plans. His problems with patents all occurred in Europe, with race discrimination not a factor. According to Horsin-Déon, a close associate of the inventor in Paris, a German employee of the Philadelphia firm that constructed the apparatus pilfered the drawings and took them to a factory in Magdeburg, Germany. From these plans, a multiple-effect evaporator was installed in 1852 in a beet sugar factory in northern France, but it was poorly made and became known as "triste effet" (sad effect) instead of "triple effet." The device was subsequently updated and marketed all over Europe, but Rillieux's priority was not recognized. In 1881, he was still active at age seventy-five and applied to patent a system for heating juice with vapors in a multiple-effect evaporator, which was adapted throughout Europe for making soap, glue, and especially beet sugar. In collaboration with engineer Horsin-Déon, a cane sugarhouse was constructed in Egypt on his system, incorporating all the refinements which created greater fuel savings.

Victor Séjour was an admirer of Napoleon, whom he praised in his writings as soon as he arrived in France, out of conviction and/or to win the favors of Emperor Napoléon III, whose private secretary, Jean-François Mocquard, later coauthored a couple of plays with him. Séjour's career in theater was enviable, especially considering that the best-known white Louisiana dramatist, Placide Canonge, had only one play accepted by the Théâtre Français. Séjour's *Diegarias* opened at that theater in July 1844; the following year, *La chute de Séjean*, another five-act drama in verse, was performed, and his version of *Richard III* enjoyed a longer run than the previous play in 1852. By then Séjour had established contacts with his French literary peers, having befriended dramatists Emile Augier, Jules Janin, and Alexandre Dumas père, and actresses Lia and Rachel Félix. His *L'argent du diable* (1854) and *Les noces vénitiennes* (1855) were quite successful. Dedicated to Alexandre Dumas, *Le fils de la nuit* (1856) played to full houses until the end of the year. In May 1857, the imperial couple attended the eighth night of *André Gérard*, a tear-jerking drama in which the great actor Frédérick Lemaître made his second comeback. *Le martyre du coeur* (1858), coauthored with Jules Brésil, was followed in 1859 by *Les grands vassaux* and *La tireuse de cartes*, written in collaboration with Mocquard. In 1860, *Compère Guillery*, *Les aventuriers*—a cape and sword drama—and *Les massacres de la Syrie*, to the glory of Napoléon, ran with success. The patriotic play, *Les volontaires de 1814* (which, incidentally, does not deal with the Battle of New Orleans) opened in April 1862, followed in 1864 by *Les fils de Charles Quint* and *Le Marquis Caporal*. Written in collaboration with Théodore Barrière, *Les enfants de la louve*, a serious historical drama, ran for a full month the following year. *La Madonne des roses* enjoyed nearly a season of warm applause in 1868–69. But Séjour failed to keep abreast of new trends, and his *Henri de Lorraine*, a historical drama in five acts, was panned by the critics in 1870.

In March 1872 Séjour began *Le Comte de Haag*, a novel published in serial form in the Bonapartist daily *L'Ordre*, but ill health prevented him from completing it. In the piece's preface, Séjour argued vehemently against a proposal to transfer the besieged capital of France (overwhelmed by the Prussian army) to a safer city, on the basis that safety was less important than the symbolical portentousness of Paris. Séjour had initially shown little interest in French politics, although many utterances in his plays were excised because the imperial censors deemed them too liberal or anticatholic. Séjour later became a member of a committee entrusted with honoring abolitionist *député* Isambart, and at age fifty-three gallantly volunteered to fight for France during the Prussian invasion of 1870. On the whole, he enjoyed adequate critical and popular success as a playwright, while box-office returns varied from one year to the next. He was known among Parisian dramatists more for his technical innovations, including grandiose settings and automated props, than for his able but not-very-original writing.[7]

Compared to Séjour's professionalism, Camille Thierry remained an amateur poet, although he possessed more talent than his half-brother, educator Michel Séligny, a prolific writer who also spent much time in France. In 1855, ready to establish himself in his adopted country, Thierry entrusted the brokerage firm Laffite, Dufilho & Company with

7. Most of the biographical information I gathered on Séjour has been updated by Charles Edwards O'Neill, *Victor Séjour, Parisian Playwright of French Louisiana* (Lafayette: Center for Louisiana Studies, University of Southwestern Louisiana, 1996). See also John Perret, "Victor Séjour, Black French Playwright from Louisiana," *French Review*, December 1983, 187–93. Séjour's only piece with a racial theme, "Le mulâtre," is reprinted in *Revue de la Louisiane*, winter 1972, 62–75.

his fortune. In Paris he mixed with literary circles and spent freely, but he sought retirement in Bordeaux, where Dédé was living, to complete *Les vagabondes: Poésies américaines.* The volume, issued jointly in 1874 by Lemerre in Paris and De Laporte in Bordeaux, included many previously published pieces and did not receive much notice outside of a group of friends and fellow New Orleanians.

Edmond Dédé's early French career was nearly as brilliant as Séjour's. Admitted as an auditor to the Paris Conservatoire in 1857, Dédé studied under Jacques Fromental Halévy and Jean-Delphin Alard. He was called to Bordeaux and offered an appointment as *second chef de ballet,* and went on to serve as *répétiteur de ballet* at the prestigious Grand Théâtre in the early 1860s. In 1865, Dédé worked for the Alcazar music hall in Bordeaux, and in 1869 he directed the grand orchestra at Arcachon, a sea resort nearby. From 1870 to 1872, he directed the Concerts Delta in Bordeaux, and experienced financial difficulties which he described as a consequence of the war. In April 1872 he was appointed director of the orchestra at the Alcazar, and authored every programme presented by the group that year. After the Delta concerts were terminated in 1872, Dédé moved to Marseilles, where he lived until 1876. On August 17, 1875, he could write to his professional organization, the Société des compositeurs et auteurs de musique, "I am one of the most productive and the most performed authors in the provinces." Indeed, his dances and divertissements were being performed in several music halls in Bordeaux and Paris. By June 1880, Dédé and his orchestra were at their post every night for concerts and operettas at the Folies Bordelaises. The critic who reviewed the season for *L'Artiste* noted that a total of forty-six operettas and vaudevilles had been created in 1883–84, twice as many as during the previous year, the orchestra led by Dédé always being equal to its reputation.[8]

The prolific Dédé arranged orchestrations of well-known themes like "The Barber of Sevilla," composed ballet music ("Les Faux Mandarins," "La Sensitive," "Le Palmier—an overture"), and in 1862 wrote a series of short "divertissements" and "danses" that were performed as

8. Dédé to Société des compositeurs et auteurs de musique, SCAM Archives, Paris; "L'orchestre, sous la direction de M. Edmond Dédé, contribue au succès de l'ensemble," *L'Artiste* 52 (1884): 4. Transcripts of the SCAM documents were secured with the kind help of Dr. Florence Martin.

interludes when he staged the opera *Hernani* in Bordeaux, where all his music produced between 1865 and 1881 was published. He wrote numerous light pieces, including the music for such operettas as "La Musique aux Lanternes," "Chik-Kang-Fo," and "Une Femme qui bégaie." The titles of these music-hall pieces reflect the fashion of the period: they suit the words, which are sentimental, popular, exotic; some refer to classical Greece, such as "Inéa," "Une Aventure de Télémaque"; some are comic, like the "Le Roi des boudinés" or satirical like "La Femme au vitriol" or "Femme de glace." Dédé remained at the Folies Bordelaises as bandleader probably until 1889. Yet Paris provided better opportunities than the provinces, and some of his pieces, among them "Le Chef de musique," were performed at the Gaîté-Montparnasse beginning about 1889, and by late 1891, the aging composer was living in the city.

A notable feature of the expatriates was their readiness to adopt French customs and, in most cases, to live with French companions. Rumors have propagated images of the New Orleans mulattoes as womanizers, possibly based on the notorious love life of Alexandre Dumas or on the assumption that a mixed-breed should have married "one of his kind." It was only natural, however, that they should take French companions, owing not only to the lack of colored Creole women in France but also to the fact that having a French-born wife was the best way to become integrated into the culture.

Rillieux's father had kept close connections with his family and lived a long time in France, so that in Paris Norbert was considered a Frenchman, not an American. He married a respectable young lady, Emily Cuckow, and for a time pursued as an avocation his interest in Egyptology, doing research on hieroglyphics while earning his living as an engineer. Rillieux associated with academics, savants, and the like. In spite of his success, however, he lost his patent in Europe because experts were unwilling or unable to recognize the anteriority (that is, the earlier date) of his invention. This lack of acceptance affected him greatly. The couple were living on rue de la Sorbonne when he died, brokenhearted, on October 8, 1894. He was buried in Père Lachaise cemetery.

Séjour had not one, but three, French companions. As early as the fall of 1839, he was living with Catherine Chambille in Saint-Mandé, on the eastern edge of the capital. She was nearly his age (twenty-two) when she gave birth to a son, Louis-Victor, in May 1840. In spite of Charles

E. O'Neill's tireless research, the rest of their story remains to be discovered. Séjour acknowledged his son a week after his birth, and there is no doubt that he was a staid companion and a responsible father. Seventeen years later, twenty-six-year-old Désirée Armande (family name unknown) gave birth to Séjour's second son, Denis Armand, at Boulogne-sur-Mer. Whether he was officially recognized or not, Denis was buried in the Marcou-Séjour family plot at Père Lachaise when, still a bachelor and an office worker, he died in 1885 at twenty-eight.

On February 18, 1858, Séjour's new common-law wife, Etiennette Octavie Dupin, gave birth to his third son, Henri Léonard. The young man was a second lieutenant in the 82nd Infantry when he died at twenty-nine, and he too was buried with his father. Although his liaison with the mother of his second son was short-lived, for reasons unknown, Séjour's life in France does not betoken philandering but a search for respectability quite in keeping with the moral and religious contents of his plays. There is also evidence that Séjour was a dutiful son. His mother came to sojourn in Paris around 1848 and stayed nearly a decade, until November 1856. Séjour's parents returned to Paris in 1863, where his father died in mid-May the following year, and Héloïse lived in Victor's apartment on Boulevard de Prince Eugène until her death in 1868.

Edmond Dédé, too, rapidly assimilated French life and culture and his correspondence with the Société des compositeurs et auteurs de musique reveals his sophisticated use of the niceties of the French past subjunctive. His private life followed the accepted run: in June 1864, he married a French woman seven years his junior. The wedding was mentioned with special emphasis in such black-interest newspapers as the *New Orleans Tribune* and the New York *National Antislavery Standard:*

> The "Quasimodo" of Mr. Edmond Dédé was enthusiastically received. Mr. E. D. is a black man, as black as one can be, who dragged from his country by the stubbornness of prejudice, went to France, and is now leader of orchestra in one of the Bordeaux theaters. We may add, by way of information, that our black friend contracted matrimony, in legitimate bonds, before the Mayor of the Imperial City, with a young lady of accomplishment, belonging to one of the best families, and, of course, of Caucasian blood.[9]

9. *New Orleans Tribune*, May 11, 1865. On June 18, 1864, Edmond Dédé married the twenty-nine-year-old daughter of Antoine Leflat and deceased Catherine

In fact, the wedding did not take place in Paris and Sylvie Anne Leflat was the daughter of a seamstress (deceased) and a landscape gardener (working in Cuba at the time). The couple's son, Eugène Arcade, in turn became a composer; in the spring of 1884, he had "a very successful comical song performed by M. Castel" in Bordeaux.[10]

The expatriates generally maintained a continuing relationship with New Orleans, whether they revisited it or not. The post-emancipation colored press readily dwelt, often in inflated terms, on the success of the French careers of the Creoles of color, while a few white newspapers were not unwilling to mention such items as reports of Séjour's plays.[11] His *Richard III* was printed by A. Gaux et L. Dutuit (1853) as an offering of the *Semaine Littéraire de la Nouvelle-Orléans* after the play was staged in the Crescent City on May 1, 1853.[12]

Dédé enjoyed greater notoriety than Séjour at home because his musical offerings were more often performed here. For instance, "Le Palmier—an overture" was part of a programme by colored musicians in New

---

Claverie. Anne was born in Toulouse, where her parents were living. An addendum (registered with dues paid on October 26, 1863) to her birth certificate states that her parents legalized their common-law union in Toulouse a few years after her birth. Anne and Edmond had separate residences before their wedding, and no trace of their son, Eugène, is found among the "enfants naturels" registered in Bordeaux from 1864 to 1870. Two of Dédé's witnesses were established music teachers. Archives de la Mairie de Bordeaux, Etat Civil, Mariages, 1864, 2e Section, no. 255.

10. See *L'Artiste*, 35. "M. Castel a créé ces jours derniers une chansonette comique fort réussie, due au jeune talent d'Eugène Dédé, fils du sympathique chef d'orchestre que tous les dilettantes bordelais connaissent et apprécient comme il le mérite." ("Recently, M. Castel premiered with a very successful comic song composed by the talented youngster, Eugène Dédé, the son of the congenial director whom all music lovers in Bordeaux know and appreciate as he deserves to be.")

11. See "Paul de Saint-Victor analyse *Les Mystères du Temple*," *La Renaissance Louisianaise*, September 21, 1862; Michel Séligny, "Correspondance de Paris sur les représentations du *Fils de la nuit* de Victor Séjour," *Le Courrier de la Louisiane*, September 5, 1856; Paul de Saint-Victor, "Review of *Le Marquis Caporal*," *Le Courrier de la Louisiane*, November 27, 1864, 8–9.

12. This information was provided by Professor C. I. Silin, but no playbill has been found of the 1853 New Orleans production. *L'argent du diable* (March 1854) was staged in New Orleans on Easter Sunday 1857. Séjour's "Propos interrompus" appeared in *Le Meschacébé* on April 20, 1872.

Orleans in August 1865, following "Quasimodo" in May. In 1893, Dédé returned to the United States to visit relatives. The steamer on which he was sailing was wrecked at sea and he was taken to Galveston, Texas, where he remained for two months and was acclaimed in concerts. Back in New Orleans, he received a royal welcome: he was made an honorary member of the Société des Jeunes Amis and gave recitals everywhere in town. The critic of *L'Abeille* heard him play "Il Trovatore" without a score and drew attention to the fine music and genuine talent of the composer.[13]

Rillieux's relationship to his birthplace seems to have been more problematic: according to Desdunes, prejudice continued to hinder his reputation in the United States, and after his death, "his color was never mentioned to deprive Creoles of his glory."[14] White Americans may have begrudged him public recognition, or ignored his color, but the acclaim

13. Desdunes, *Our People and Our History*, 86. Dédé introduced two new songs, "Si j'étais lui," published locally by A. E. Blackmar, and "Patriotisme" in January 1894. According to Maude Cuney-Hare, *Negro Musicians and Their Music* (Washington, D.C.: Associated Publishers, 1936), 238, the following program was given by the violinist in this country in 1894:

'Salle des Amis de l'Espérance'
Rue Trémé, entre Dumaine et St. Philippe
Grande soirée artistique pour les adieux, et au bénéfice du Professor Edmond Dédé donnée sous le patronage du Club Amis de l'Espérance avec le concours des amateurs et des artistes du Club Ida, et des distingués professeurs de la ville.
Dimanche 21 Janvier 1894.
1. Concerto de violon, Op. 64 Mendelssohn
accompagné par Mme. Serge
'Rigoletto' de Verdi. D. Alard
par Mlle. Lucie Barès et le Professeur E. Dédé.
2. 'Trovatore'—Verdi—Fantaisie pour violon, exécuté par Ed. Dédé, accompagnement de quatuor par Mme. Nickerson, Mauret, E. Colin et P. Dominguez.
'Si j'étais lui' (nocturne)
poésie de M. V. E. Rillieux, musique de Ed. Dédé
chanté par M. H. Beaurepaire
L'orchestre sous la direction du Prof. Nickerson
Le piano sera tenu par Mme. Serge et M. Basile Barès, professeurs.
14. Desdunes, *Our People and Our History*, 74.

his invention enjoyed in Louisiana was immediate and widespread when in 1846 it revolutionized the refining of sugar.

The final years of the four men differed greatly. Séjour's death came at the end of a steady decline in health, when he lacked the ability to renew himself as a writer and faced financial problems. He was living on Boulevard Magenta with one of his sons when tuberculosis brought his life to a close. He barely had time to acknowledge his parenthood of Victor-Henri before he was taken to the Maison Municipale de Santé on Boulevard Saint-Denis; the Société des auteurs et compositeurs paid the hospital bill since he was without funds. After his death on September 20, 1874, the funeral was dignified and well attended, with several leading French actors and fellow writers paying tribute to his talent in the ceremony at the Père Lachaise cemetery.

Camille Thierry's end in Bordeaux was bleak. During a trip to New Orleans in 1874, he arranged to receive a monthly allowance of fifty dollars from the firm of Sidney Thézan, who now managed his estate. Shortly after his return to Bordeaux, however, he got the news that the colored broker had gone bankrupt and shot himself. Ruined and beset with grief, Thierry died on April 16, 1875. He must have been living alone in his rented room at 11 rue Buffon, since his death was reported by Jean-Marie Dedieu, his landlord and a grocer specializing in colonial goods, and a neighboring baker. But Thierry was far from forgotten in his home city, and the Louisiana press continued to reprint several of his poems for years. In *Portraits Littéraires*, Dr. Charles Testut wrote:

> C'est un nom que nous avons toujours vu paraître avec plaisir dans les colonnes des journaux de cette ville. Rien de plus frais, de plus doux, que les vers de ce poète-amateur. Nous disons amateur parce que M. Camille Thierry ne fait des vers qu'à de rares intervalles, au grand regret de ceux qui aiment le sentiment et les douces passions. . . . Les muses ardentes et échevelées n'ont pas parlé à son âme, n'ont pas été du goût de son coeur.

> This is a name which we have always found with pleasure in the columns of this city's newspapers. Nothing fresher and softer than the verse of this "amateur" of poetry. We say "amateur" because M. Camille Thierry writes verse at rare occasions, much to the regret of those who are fond of sweet feelings and passion. . . . The fiery, disheveled muses do not touch his soul nor suit his heart's desire.

Later, Edward Tinker considered that "Thierry's later poems are full of the bitterness characteristic of colored writers in those days." Yet he felt that "original and eccentric, Thierry needed a stabilizing influence."[15]

Edmond Dédé returned to Paris forever after his visit to New Orleans and a concert tour in 1893 that stretched as far north as Chicago. He was living modestly in the 14th arrondissement, reportedly still working on "Le Sultan d'Ispahan," an opera in four acts, when he fell ill and died at age seventy-three. He was buried at the Bagneux cemetery January 7, 1901.[16]

Much research remains to be done on the French careers of Creoles of color in the nineteenth century. But the present project of documenting the lives of a handful of New Orleans expatriates offers evidence against the stereotype—generated in part by the flamboyant eccentricities of Alexandre Dumas—of colored artists living like profligate, lighthearted romantics. Rather, like most members of their class and caste, they behaved as staid, hardworking, responsible citizens imbued with middle-class values. They strove, with varying success, to maintain their families and earn comfortable livings as well as to build lasting reputations. They certainly enjoyed greater social freedom and professional opportunities

15. Charles Testut, *Portraits Littéraires*, 160–1; Tinker, *Les écrits de langue française*, 467. No trace has been found of Thierry's being buried in the Bordeaux cemetery. "Camille Thierry . . . quitta son pays natal pour aller s'établir à Bordeaux en 1855, laissant ses affaires entre les mains d'un mandataire infidèle qui lui fit perdre la plus grande partie de son patrimoine. Revenu à la Nouvelle-Orléans en 1874, il fit avec son chargé d'affaires un arrangement en vertu duquel ce dernier devait lui faire passer en France, mensuellement, la modique somme de cinquante piastres. Peu de temps après il s'embarqua de nouveau pour le France. A peine y était il depuis quelques mois qu'il reçut la nouvelle que son débiteur, pour se libérer vis-à-vis de lui, s'était brûlé la cervelle. Thierry, sans ressources, accablé de chagrins, mourut à Bordeaux au mois d'avril 1875." (Thierry left his native country to settle in Bordeaux in 1855, leaving his business in the hands of a disloyal trustee who caused him to lose the greater part of his estate. Back in New Orleans in 1874, he arranged for his new representative to send him a modest $50 allowance each month. Shortly after, he sailed for France again. He had been there a few months only, when the news came that his debtor had blown his brains out to discharge his debt toward him. Resourceless, grief-ridden, Thierry died in Bordeaux in April 1855.) Alfred Mercier, *Compte-Rendus de L'Athénée Louisianais*, January 1878, 135.

16. The year 1903, often found in biographical notices and printed sources, is definitely inaccurate.

in a country where they were largely exonerated from the burden of racial prejudice, and they fared well and felt at home in France. But they often found it difficult to carve out a territory for themselves, because competition was tough, because they lacked the supportive familial, social, and professional network of Creole New Orleans, and because their French culture was somehow too provincial for them to become part of the Paris elite.

Alice Ruth Moore (Dunbar-Nelson) ca. 1900.
Courtesy Amistad Research Center, Tulane University

COMMENCEMENT

❖ 1892. ❖

CHORUS—"Fair Morning on the Harbor"..........*Vogrich*.

❖ PRAYER. ❖

VIOLIN SOLO—"The Pirate".............. ....*Singelee*.
Julia E. Lewis.

ESSAY—Nature's Keys................ ....Valena C. McArthur.

ESSAY—The Influence of Woman .. ..Marie F. Demas.

ESSAY—The Meaning of Life ....Alice R. Moore.

DUET—Unfinished Symphony......................*Schubert*.
Mary B. Walker, Beatrice Rochon.

ORATION—The Colored Race in America..John M. Pittman.

ESSAY—The World's Levers..... ....Julia E. Lewis.

ESSAY—The Influence of the Crusades.....Hattie V. Feger.

TRIO—Kernwood Waltzes..........................*Russell*.
Cornet—Adolph Segura. Violin—Anita Rochon.
Piano—Mary B. Walker.

ESSAY—The Mission of Discontent........Thekla Crawford.

ESSAY—Heirs of the Ages................. Mary B. Walker.

PRESENTATION OF DIPLOMAS.

PART SONG—"The Bridal of the Birds"...........*Richards*

BENEDICTION.

☞ It is particularly requested that no presents
be made to the class during the exercises.

Hopkins' Printing Office, 22 Commercial Place, N. O.

Straight University commencement program, 1892; the essayists, including
the future Alice Dunbar-Nelson, took on large subjects.

Courtesy Amistad Research Center, Tulane University

Edmond Dédé, Creole violinist, conductor, and composer. *Courtesy Amistad Research Center, Tulane University*

Creole composer and pianist Basile Barès. This photograph was taken in 1867 in Paris, where Barès was performing at the World's Fair. Barès copyrighted his first piece of sheet music, "The Footsoldiers of Louisiana"—the only copyright ever held by a slave in the United States.

Courtesy Xavier University Archives, New Orleans

Historian Rodolphe L. Desdunes, who wrote *Nos hommes
et notre histoire* in "homage to
the Creole population, in re-
membrance of the great men it
has produced and the good
things it has accomplished."
Courtesy Sybil Kein

Thomy Lafon, Creole mer-
chant and philanthropist, aided
the Couvent School for Creole
children, among many other
causes. He died in 1893.
*Courtesy Amistad Research Center,
Tulane University*

The Sisters of the Holy Family religious order was founded by a wealthy Creole, Henriette Delille, in 1842. The nuns here are pictured in 1915 in the courtyard of the old Quadroon Ballroom. This building, which the order owned, housed the girls' school that the nuns operated, St. Mary's Academy.

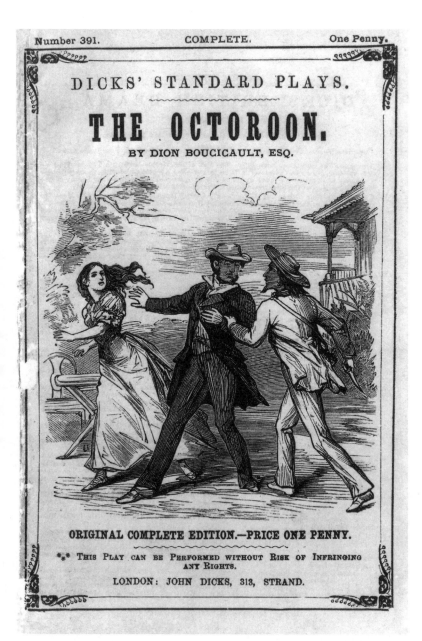

Title page, 1859 edition of Boucicault's *The Octoroon*. Oddly, the female character Zoe—who is the octoroon—is shown as white, while the two white male characters are darker.

Courtesy Victoria and Albert Museum, London

Portrait said to be that of Marie Laveau, although this identification, like many other things about the famed Voodoo priestess, is by no means certain.

Courtesy Louisiana State Museum, New Orleans

The Edwin O. Moss barbershop, photographed by Arthur P. Bedou in 1913. Owned and operated by Creole men, the shop served white patrons.

Courtesy Xavier University Archives, New Orleans

An unidentified Creole wedding party in New Orleans in the early 1920s. This Bedou photograph shows a typical middle-class wedding pose. Notice that the bride has no jewelry; it was customary for brides to wear little or no jewelry except perhaps tiny earrings, preferably heirlooms.

Courtesy Xavier University Archives, New Orleans

Arthur P. Bedou in a self-portrait. Bedou was the official photographer for Xavier University, Fisk University, the Tuskegee Institute, and for Booker T. Washington. Called the "Itinerant Photographer," he photographed the rites of passage of many Creoles in Louisiana. His studio was at Bienville and Prieur Streets in New Orleans.

Courtesy Xavier University Archives, New Orleans

Collage of Creole business establishments and a Masonic hall in New Orleans ca. 1920s.

Odette and Naomi Dubuclet, great-granddaughters of Antoine Dubuclet, who was Louisiana state treasurer during Reconstruction.

Courtesy Amistad Research Center, Tulane University

9

Visible Means of Support

Businesses, Professions, and Trades of
Free People of Color

MARY GEHMAN

Strolling down Chartres and Royal Streets in New Orleans in the 1830s
one passed dozens of elegant shops and offices with proprietors named
LaCroix, Dumas, Colvis, Foucher, Legoaster, and Forneret, all proper
French surnames, all wealthy businessmen of the ethnic group known as
les gens de couleur libre. Impeccably dressed, well-educated, and speaking
the best French, the owners of these shops would, in some cases, have
been difficult to distinguish from their white French Creole counterparts. In official records and censuses where people of color were always
to be designated as such, these entrepreneurs sometimes have no letters
behind their names to indicate race. Presumably they were powerful
enough in the Creole business community to be considered white. Customers of all classes and nationalities paid slight attention to the proprietor's racial composition; what mattered was that the best leather shoes,
the finest cigars, the most carefully tailored suits, and the latest millinery
were to be found in these shops.

While a common perception about free blacks in antebellum New
Orleans is that they were a small and fairly nameless group sandwiched
between the vast numbers of African slaves and the elite French Creole
rulers, the opposite was true. A close look into court and property
records as well as city directories of those years reveals an astonishingly

large and varied free black populace skilled and employed in dozens of trades and professions. It is hard to imagine New Orleans of the early 1800s without its massive work force of free people of color. Often employed in the same jobs as slaves with whom they worked side by side, they gained much of their knowledge either as or from members of that group, since records indicate a wide range of labor skills brought by bondsmen from their native Africa. Free people of color, however, had access to ownership of real estate and could enter into business contracts, lease or rent out their property, and trade on the open market. These privileges that distinguished the free men from slaves greatly affected their professional lives.

The 1850 New Orleans census lists 1,792 free people of color in fifty-four different occupations, including 355 carpenters, 325 masons, 156 cigar makers, 92 shoemakers, 61 clerks, 52 mechanics, 43 coopers, 41 barbers, 39 carmen, and 28 painters. Only 279, or about 9.9 percent, of free blacks were listed in the census as unskilled laborers. There were also blacksmiths, butchers, cooks, cabinetmakers, upholsterers, overseers, and stewards, and Loren Schweninger notes that 642 free blacks in this census owned real estate. Among the free women of color are listed 189 seamstresses, 21 dressmakers or *modistes*, and 10 hairdressers. Although occupations such as washerwoman, street vendor, and domestic were too humble to count in the census, many women—both free black and poor white immigrant—worked in such jobs to support their families. The 1850 figures are interpreted in greater detail by Robert Reinders.[1]

Trades, skills, and businesses were often handed down from parent to child going back generations into slavery. African and Creole slaves freed from the late 1700s into the early nineteenth century had usually learned trades from their slave ancestors. They had been selected in Africa for their knowledge of iron or woodworking, agriculture, food preparation, and nursing because they were better able to adapt to the tropical climate and primitive living conditions of the Louisiana swamps than were the skilled workers brought from France. Gwendolyn Midlo Hall's *Africans*

1. Loren Schweninger, "Antebellum Free Persons of Color in Postbellum Louisiana," *Louisiana History* 30 (1989): 362; Robert Reinders, "The Free Negro in the New Orleans Economy, 1850–1860," *Louisiana History* 6 (1965): 275–7.

in Colonial Louisiana explains the Louisiana slave concession in West Africa and the procurement of specifically skilled workers who were selected to be slaves. In addition, hundreds of slaves and free people of
color from St. Domingue (today Haiti) migrated to New Orleans at the
dawn of the nineteenth century, bringing with them tools and knowledge
that swelled the reputation of the black tradesman and artisan in the city
and outlying areas.

Unlike slaves in other parts of the South, those in colonial Louisiana
were encouraged to hire themselves out on municipal projects such as
digging canals, building forts and levees, and constructing government
buildings. A typical case translated in the *Louisiana Historical Quarterly* is
the lease of seven Delery slaves in 1747 to Sr. Dubois "for 930 livres pay-
able every six months."[2]

Kimberly Hanger has studied and interpreted court and church records of the Spanish period in Louisiana (1762–1802), uncovering a variety of living arrangements and occupations of slaves and free people of
color during that era. The large majority of free people of African descent, Hanger found, lived in female-headed families, raising the assumption that those females were often employed and supporting their
children. Many women had their own garden plots where they cultivated
fruit and vegetables which they sold either in the legitimate open-air
markets around the city or in their own ad hoc African market operating
just outside the ramparts in Place des Nègres, later called Congo Square.
Jerah Johnson's comprehensive history of Congo Square indicates a
century-long market and performance area that began in the 1740s and
remained active well into American rule.[3]

With commissions paid slaves by their masters for labor-for-hire,
augmented by unreported income from surreptitious sales, a slave could
eventually petition the government for his or her value to be assessed and
then pay the master that sum in order to be manumitted. The *Louisiana*

2. Gwendolyn Midlo Hall, *Africans in Colonial Louisiana: The Development of
Afro-Creole Culture in the Eighteenth Century* (Baton Rouge: Louisiana State University Press, 1992), 28–55; "Index to Spanish Judicial Records," *Louisiana Historical Quarterly* 18 (1935): 162.

3. Kimberly Hanger, "Household and Community Structure Among the Free
Population of Spanish New Orleans, 1778," *Louisiana History* 30 (1989): 70–1;
Jerah Johnson, "New Orleans' Congo Square: An Urban Setting for Early Afro-
American Culture Formation," *Louisiana History* 32 (1991): 117–57.

Historical Quarterly of the 1930s translates court proceedings of a number of slaves who did so. Some even mutilated themselves prior to assessment so that their value as skilled laborers would be lowered and they could more easily afford the price of their own freedom. Hanger, again studying the Spanish Period, reports that one-quarter of these purchases of freedom by slaves were contested by masters, but the court usually ruled in favor of the slave.[4]

Apprenticeships were available to the most promising young slaves who served along with young free men of color under a Creole master craftsman. The demographics of early census figures show that such apprentices sometimes lived in their masters' homes for the duration of their contracts. According to Daniel Usner, by 1726 black apprentices were replacing white coopers in New Orleans and in some of the ironworking trades as well. Slave children from their earliest years ran errands, delivered messages, waited on tables, and helped their parents do laundry, groom horses, and prepare and vend cakes and fruits. There was little place in the slave experience for idle or unskilled hands. Once freed, former slaves continued jobs they had learned from childhood. Employers preferred to hire freedmen because, as Marcus Christian points out in "The Negro in Louisiana," with them there was no liability to a master whose slave might be injured on the job.[5]

If work was slow in New Orleans, free blacks could sometimes hire on at the docks, ship out on steamboats and oceangoing vessels, or migrate north or west to try their luck in frontier areas. From the mid-1700s they were also employed as police and soldiers to patrol the city, round up runaway slaves, or fight with whites against indigenous tribes or slave uprisings. Christian notes how W. C. C. Claiborne, the first American governor after the Louisiana Purchase, and his cabinet were taken aback by the number of well-educated, middle-class free blacks in New Orleans, many of whom wore military uniforms and were seen marching fully armed in the streets.[6]

4. Kimberly Hanger, "Avenues to Freedom Open to New Orleans' Black Population, 1769–1779," *Louisiana History* 31 (1990): 244.

5. Daniel H. Usner Jr., "From African Captivity to American Slavery: The Introduction of Black Laborers to Colonial Louisiana," *Louisiana History* 20 (1979): 31; Marcus B. Christian, "The Negro in Louisiana," chapters 6 and 8, Marcus B. Christian Collection, Archives and Manuscripts Department, Earl K. Long Library, University of New Orleans.

6. Christian, "Negro in Louisiana."

Emigration was an option for the skilled professionals among the
free people of color. Once they had learned a trade, their expertise was
welcome in places like Haiti, Mexico, or the Indian territories, and hundreds left Louisiana to establish themselves in these foreign lands in the
first half of the nineteenth century. I have found documents, for example,
in the city archives of Tampico, Mexico, that list among heads of households in 1858 dozens of émigrés of color from New Orleans, with trades
given as shoemaker, baker, carpenter, mason, trader, tailor, and militia-
man. Typical was Eugenio Pabageau, a forty-three-year-old tailor, and
his forty-year-old wife, Carolina Paron, both from New Orleans. They
had seven children ranging in ages from one year to nineteen, all born in
Tampico, indicating the couple had been there since at least 1839. Carolina's brother Guillermo Paron, age forty-one and also a tailor, lived with
them. Completing the household were Eugenio's mother Luisia Pabageau, sixty, of New Orleans and three young Mexicans, Rafael Castillo,
sixteen, Nestor Cardenas, fourteen, and Genaro Geree, thirteen, all of
whom are listed as tailors and presumably were apprentices of Eugenio
and his brother-in-law Guillermo.

Access to property and businesses for free people of color in Louisiana
frequently came from their mothers and grandmothers who were *placées*,
or concubines (the contemporary legal term for free women of color
under the protection and financial support of white men). If the father
was a generous sort, the children of such unions stood to inherit property
and substantial sums of money and investments from their mothers. If
their fathers remained lifelong bachelors, as happened in a surprisingly
large number of cases, the children of color were the only immediate
blood relatives recognized in their fathers' wills. Although the law stated
that such families, because of their illegitimacy, could inherit no more
than one-tenth of the father's estate, and that even that tenth was subject
to loss if legitimate heirs sued to acquire it, ways were apparently found
in quite a few cases to circumvent the courts and transfer money and
property to influential men's families of color. Judith K. Schafer gives a
number of examples of this system, which she discovered in wills and
state supreme court records of the antebellum period.[7] The number of

7. Judith K. Schafer, " 'Open and Notorious Concubinage': The Emancipation
of Slave Mistresses by Will and the Supreme Court of Antebellum Louisiana,"
Louisiana History 28 (1987): 165–82.

free women of color who owned property acquired through liaisons with white men is not certain. Once given a house and investments, these women had to be savvy in the ways of business and law in order to hold on to what they had been given, improve it, and pass it on to their children. There is also no doubt that other free women, through hard work and frugality, were able to purchase property on their own. Boys whose mothers received the favors of white men were often educated in Paris or in northern American universities. If they chose to return to their native city despite the limitations of their racial status, they stood to make handsome fortunes by investing and developing their family's holdings. Girls were sometimes also educated and able to run their own businesses and manage property. In a compilation of names and occupations from antebellum city directories and early property records chronicled in the Vieux Carré Survey (a 1960s project of Tulane University School of Architecture), the following names and professions appear. (Many are also mentioned by writers like Donald Everett, James Haskins, and Loren Schweninger.)[8]

Tailors Etienne Cordeviolle and François LaCroix, who oversaw a large clothier business established in 1817 in New Orleans and were also wealthy real-estate developers, are examples of the heirs to the *plaçage* system. They acquired valuable properties through their mothers, respectively Maria del Rosario of Guinea and Elizabeth Norwood, both free women of color who had lengthy liaisons with their sons' white fathers, the Italian Estevan Cordeviola and the French Paul LaCroix. The 1853 city directory contains a large advertisement for LaCroix's tailor business at 23 St. Charles Avenue, which featured "French cloth, fancy casimere . . . and clothing made in Paris by fashionable tailors." LaCroix's brother Julien Adolphe LaCroix operated a grocery store at 506 Frenchman Street during the same period and left an estate worth $130,000 in 1868. Cordeviolle and LaCroix were so successful at New Orleans real estate speculation in the 1830s through the 1850s that whole city blocks passed through their hands.

Contemporaries of Cordeviolle and LaCroix were Julien Colvis

---

8. See Donald E. Everett, "Free Persons of Color in Colonial Louisiana," *Louisiana History* 7 (1966): 21–50; James Haskins, *The Creoles of Color in New Orleans* (New York: Thomas Y. Crowell, 1975); and Loren Schweninger, "A Negro Sojourner in Antebellum New Orleans," *Louisiana History* 20 (1979): 305–14.

(sometimes spelled Clovis) and Joseph Dumas, also tailors and real estate speculators, who descended from families formed by French army officers and mulatto women in St. Domingue. From their mothers they inherited real estate in both New Orleans and France. By the 1840s Colvis & Dumas tailors at 124 Chartres Street was well established, so that the partners could divide their time between interests in New Orleans and Paris. Dumas is believed to have been related to the French novelist Alexandre Dumas, who had a similar birthright in Paris. Colvis's son Joseph married Marguerite Dumas in 1869, thus joining the two families; the young couple lived as whites in France, along with the three Colvis daughters.

Philippe Aime and Erasme Legoaster operated another successful tailor business in the 1830s. Their mother may have been the free woman of color Adelaide Ferrand who descended from the Fornerets, a well-propertied family of color in early New Orleans. Erasme's marriage connected him with another well-to-do local family of color, that of Raimon Gaillard. The Legoaster brothers both had large estates. Philippe Aime Legoaster was noted as the wealthiest free man of color in New Orleans in 1850, when he reported $150,000 worth of taxable property to the census taker. Much of his property was in the Dryades Street area. Sister Aimee Legoaster owned much of the 800 block of Dauphine Street, which by 1924 had been donated to the Lafon Asylum for children of color.

Another influential family was the Merciers, who had the famous D. Mercier & Sons Emporium of Fashion and Fair Dealings in pre–Civil War New Orleans. Dominique Mercier, believed to be the natural son of French merchant Jean Baptiste Mercier, began with a shoe business at Dauphine and Bienville Streets in the mid-1800s and went on to become a wealthy planter. By the turn of the century his sons Joseph Anselme, Jean Leopold, and William J. Mercier were operating Mercier Realty and Investments. They owned large areas of Dauphine and Burgundy where those streets intersect with St. Louis and Bienville. A sister, Amelie Mercier, who passed for white, married Judge J. F. Canonge; their son Louis Placide Canonge was a journalist and professor who served in the Louisiana state legislature from 1884 to 1888.

Noel Carriere and Barthelemy Campanel were early real-estate moguls among the free people of color; both inherited parts of their white fathers' large estates. Carriere's father, Joseph Carriere, died in 1763, and by the time of Noel's death in 1835 he had amassed a fortune developing and speculating with family properties. Similarly, Campanel inherited nearly the whole 800 block of Dauphine Street in 1808 from his white father whose name he carried, Bartholome or Barthelemy Campanel. He parlayed those properties, plus others in the 900 block of Toulouse Street, into a large estate, which when he died in Paris in 1835 went to his son Soulange Campanel. A hardware store at 71 Old Levee Street in 1838 owned by a "B. Campanell" was probably his also.

Another speculator who followed these examples was Drausin or Drosin Barthelemy Macarty, who is credited with having bought $56,081 worth of real estate and sold $50,355 in properties in the decade 1849–1859. He was the son of propertied free woman of color Henriette Prieto, and married Anna Louise Courcelle, of another well-off free black family. Cecee Macarty, Drausin's sister, built an importing business that was worth $155,000 by the time of her death in 1845. She was also the largest slaveholder among the free people of color, listed as owning thirty-two slaves in 1850. Reportedly she had unlimited credit throughout Louisiana and did note discounting as a side business.

Free people of color owned plantations just as their white half-siblings did. Most of them also had large inventories of slaves to work their vast acreage. One of the earliest recorded planters of color is San Luis Lanuitte, who must have been an ambitious slave, for upon being freed in 1744 he bought a small plantation along Bayou Road outside New Orleans. He continued to work for his master as a business agent in France in 1767, indicating he was well-educated and deserving of great trust.

Antoine Dubuclet was named the wealthiest black planter in the United States in 1860, with a townhouse in New Orleans and a plantation in Iberville Parish valued at $206,400. He served as Louisiana state treasurer for eleven years during Reconstruction. In 1793 Jean Baptiste Roquiny or Rochon received from his white father, Louis Roquiny, a large tract of land at English Turn, which is today a suburb of the city. It was an original land grant from the governor, François-Louis Hector Carondelet, and Roquiny built a plantation there while maintaining a townhouse in the 700 block of Barracks Street. Martin Donato was another free black who had a large plantation in Plaquemine in the 1830s, and Jean Fleming, his contemporary and a wealthy planter of color, may have enlisted Donato's assistance in approaching the state legislature in

1838 for the right of free blacks who owned large estates to vote. They were turned down, but the mere fact that black planters in Louisiana had the clout to consider such a radical idea is noteworthy.

Other planters of color included Alexandre Aristide Mary (or Marie), whose white father left him a complete city block of property on Canal and Old Levee Streets in the 1850s. Mary was known for his wealth and philanthropy to other people of color, but his personal life unraveled after he lost a bid for governor during Reconstruction and left his unfaithful light-skinned common-law wife for New York, where in 1891 he committed suicide. The Durnfords, father Andrew and son Thomas, owned St. Rosalie Plantation in Plaquemines Parish from the 1820s through the Civil War and had property in New Orleans as well. David O. Whitten's book *Andrew Durnford: A Black Sugar Planter in Antebellum Louisiana* offers a rare look into the thoughts and life of a wealthy free man of color. The elder Durnford was the son of Thomas Durnford, an English friend of the famous white planter John McDonough, and Rosaline Mercier, a free woman of color. Andrew Durnford and McDonough were close friends for fifty years; McDonough was the godfather of Andrew's son Thomas McDonough Durnford and helped to put him through medical school in Pennsylvania.[9]

Among the elite of the free people of color were men whose professions or businesses brought them into close contact with whites. For example, Pierre A. D. Casenave, who was born in St. Domingue of free black parents and migrated to New Orleans, served as the clerk of the ice-importing business of one of the city's wealthiest men, Judah P. Touro, for whom Touro Hospital and Touro Synagogue are named. As the magnate's confidant, Casenave was one of the executors of the Touro estate in 1854 and received $10,000 as a beneficiary. In the mid-1850s Casenave was said to be worth approximately $40,000. He opened mortuary establishments on Toulouse Street in the old city and on Marais Street in the suburb of Tremé. Soon he became the director of some of the grandest funerals known in the city, most of them for whites. He is also credited by some writers as having introduced to New Orleans elaborate street parades for funerals. Descendants of the Casenave family continue to work as morticians in New Orleans today.

9. David O. Whitten, *Andrew Durnford: A Black Sugar Planter in Antebellum Louisiana* (Natchitoches, La.: Northwestern State University Press, 1981).

The lucrative business of cigar making was controlled by free men of color for many years. Lucien Mansion and his nephew Georges Alces owned large cigar factories in New Orleans during the mid-1800s; Alces is said to have employed as many as two hundred well-paid workers. Because there were close ties with St. Domingue and Cuba, the industry used local as well as foreign-grown tobaccos. In the 1850s D. Azereto, of the large family that Italian real estate developer Jean Baptiste Azereto had with free woman of color Eugenie Glesseau or Gresso, was a tobacconist with a large shop of tobacco products and pipes on Ursulines Street.

Builders also distinguished themselves in the community of free blacks. Families like the Dollioles, the Fouchés, and the Lamottes amassed fortunes as contractors and builders of much of the outer French Quarter and the *faubourgs*, or suburbs, Marigny and Tremé. They employed dozens of free black carpenters, masons, bricklayers, plasterers, woodworkers, and painters to construct complete buildings, from laying the foundations to putting on the finishing touches. Much of their work survives today. Two Dolliole brothers who were builders, Jean-François and Louis, migrated from France in the late 1700s and had families with free women of color in New Orleans. Joseph, Louis, Etienne, and Edmond Dolliole were the sons of Jean-François and Catherine. In 1816 on their father's death each son received $100. Louis Dolliole had two sons, Jean-Luis and Pierre Dolliole, with Genevieve. The cousins of color, Joseph and Jean-Luis Dolliole, followed in their fathers' profession as builders. Pierre was a carpenter. The families also did well speculating in real estate.

Louis Nelson Fouché (also spelled Foucher) was a mathematician and architect who put his skills to work building a number of houses in the Tremé section as it opened to development in the 1820s. He worked with Dutreil (or Dutre) Fouché, a relative who was also a ship broker. Myrtil Courcelle was another builder and speculator in Tremé. He was related to the French builder Achille Barthelemy Courcelle and left a large estate on his death in 1872. Other builders of note were Andre Martain Lamotte, who built much of Faubourg Marigny, George Jove (also spelled Hove or Hobe), J. Bauver, and B. Duncan McKennon.

Manufacturing was another career pursued by free people of color. Two mattress makers who made and sold beds and other furniture in the mid-

1800s were Thomas Atkins (or Adkins), with a warehouse at 212 Tchoupitoulas Street, and Joseph Belleville, whose shop was at 290 Dauphine. M. Francis was employed by Belleville as a mattress maker. A cooperage or barrel-making factory was operated in the 1830s by Jean and Henri Baptiste at 13 Toulouse Street.

Free blacks dominated the shoemaking and leatherworking trades of early New Orleans. They made leather harnesses, saddles, bags, and valises, while also turning out most of the shoes worn locally. Shoe stores were part of the large tailoring establishments of Cordeviolle and LaCroix, the Dumas Brothers, and the Legoasters. Manuel Bergel is listed as a clothier in the 1838 city directory, and Thomy Lafon, the renowned philanthropist for whom several institutions are named in New Orleans, owned a major shoe store operated by his sister Alphée Baudin. Sailmaker Arthur Esteves owned one of the largest sail companies in the region and in his retirement in the 1880s published a black newspaper, the *Crusader*. Watchmaker Joseph Forneret also made a fortune in real estate. There were dairies owned and operated by J. Hartwell in 1805 and Lewis Formonet in the 1850s, the latter in Carrollton; a brass foundry in the same period owned by Antonio Joseph, with one in the 1860s owned by Dominick Beman; and Joseph Plato's and Moses Briggs's stables, which rented out horses and carriages. Surely with so many surviving examples, the names of countless other entrepreneurs have been lost to history. Although few women were store owners, Josephine Nicholas, a free woman of color, appears in the 1838 city directory as having a clothing store at 84 Old Levee Street.

One type of establishment that women often did own and operate was grocery stores and market stands. The 1838 directory shows grocers J. L. Duminie (male) at 181 Girod Street and Caroline Duminy at 206 Philippa Street, but doesn't indicate if they were related. Elizabeth Fay or Foy had a grocery that year, as did A. C. Pellebon (female), Joseph Ravez, George Ridgeway, James St. Thomas, and Louis Desalle. Jane Williams operated a confectionery, while F. Pinear (male) had an oyster stand, Josh Mirac a fruit store, and Jean Bellonard a dry-goods store. By the 1850s some of these merchants of color had disappeared from the city directory, but others joined the ranks, such as Joseph Antoine with a vegetable stand in the Poydras Market, Jacob Green with a ham stall in the French Market, William Scott with a store for "coffee, fruits, etc.," and grocers

J. B. D. Bonseinneur, Alfred Braud, A. Cyprien (male), Marie Doliol, Louis Decoudreau, E. Dumas (female), Henry Fortin, Calice Fille (male), Edward Jones, William Mulford, Francis Nelson, and A. Toussaint (female).

Rose Nicaud, a free woman of color, is credited with being the first vendor of fresh coffee on the streets of the city. In the early 1800s she sold the steaming hot drink from a portable coffee pot near the church that is today St. Louis Cathedral. One customer is said to have praised her coffee as being "like the benediction that follows after a prayer." Within a few years, she had prospered enough to rent a stand in the French Market. Other free women of color followed her example of vending coffee in the streets. Agnes Miles, for example, is listed as having a permanent coffee stand in the Poydras Market in 1853.

Several free people of color operated eating houses in the 1830s, such as Elijah Gibson, John Henry, and Helene Toussaint. These were humble community kitchens, but the proprietors had to put up personal bonds of $1,000 each for permits to run them. Jane Dokes had a license for a cookshop in 1838. Restaurants, which were a step up in class from eating houses, were rarely owned by blacks. Only two free men of color, Andrew Brady in 1838 and Francis Brunetti in 1853, seem to have operated restaurants. A few men of color ran coffeehouses, such as Francis Carlon and J. Hurd in 1838, and there were even several who were licensed to operate grog shops that year: Durival Duminy, John François, V. Gonzales, Juin & Co., and C. Labatt. Some liquor was handled in the grog shops, and when regulations prohibiting blacks from selling alcoholic beverages tightened in the 1840s, these shops were probably closed or turned into coffeehouses. In any event, their proprietors' names had disappeared by the 1850s. To go along with the various eating and drinking establishments, travelers to New Orleans needed places to stay, and for this purpose free women of color were known for opening rooms of their homes for rent. Eventually such women were the proprietors of most of the better rooming houses and guesthouses in the Creole parts of the city.

Professions among free blacks were sometimes restricted by laws and lack of educational opportunities or political contacts, but a fairly impressive number of New Orleans free men of color did pursue careers that were almost unheard of for blacks in other parts of the country. Besides

the architect Fouché mentioned above, Joseph Abeilard was a quite respected member of that profession in antebellum Louisiana. The Bazaar
section of the French Market in New Orleans was his design. His brother
Jules was a talented artist and collaborated on some of Abeilard's contracts. Bysin Navarre and Louis Lucien Pessou were lithographers and
engravers with studios in the city in the 1840s and 1850s. There were
several physicians of color: Dr. James Derham in the 1780s, and Dr.
Oscar Guimbilotte, Dr. François Ruiz Alpuente, and Dr. John Chau-
mette in the early-to-mid-1800s. There were also a pharmacist, Albert
Bowman, a dentist, P. A. Snaër, and a number of free women of color
who worked as nurses and midwives, which required varying degrees of
formal education.

Coast traders M. Dangluse and F. Herbert operated out of New Orleans in the 1830s, when ship brokers Dutre Fouché and Joseph March-
and were active at their occupation. In the 1850s Victor Fitcher was a
river pilot, James Lynes an engineer and blacksmith, and Robert Rod-
gers, Murville Chevalle, and S. Goutier worked as clerks in downtown
offices. Beatrix Chenaux was the lone woman of color who worked as a
trader in the 1830s. Rodolphe Desdunes had the prestigious position of
weigher at the customshouse, Bazile Crocker taught fencing from his
salon at Exchange Place, and John Bradford had a hairdressing salon
nearby. Even the keeper of the cathedral in 1852 was a free black, Joseph
M. Cam.

Artists among the *gens de couleur libre* were generally sculptors and
marble engravers or ironworkers and wood millers, whose crafts provided much of the wrought iron for gates, fences, and balconies, the
wooden molding and balustrades that one still sees in New Orleans
today, or the sumptuous tombs for which the city's cemeteries are famous. The ironworkers shoed horses and also constructed wheels and
chassis for carriages, heavy iron cooking ware, and brackets, knobs, and
iron or brass fittings essential in lamps, shutters, doors, and gates.

In *Negro Ironworkers in Louisiana, 1718–1900*, Marcus Christian
chronicles the key role of blacksmiths, moulders, founders, and casters of
iron. The best-known blacksmith with his own foundry in New Orleans
in the post–Civil War years was A. J. Molière, a man of color who had a
shop at Broad and Esplanade Streets. His contemporary was blacksmith
Elisha Dillon, at Washington and Magnolia Streets. Robert Norbert Rillieux and Louis Charbonnet became machinists and inventors, but both

began as ironworkers in New Orleans. Rillieux, the son of Frenchman Vincent Rillieux and free woman of color Constance Vivant, revolutionized the sugar industry in Louisiana in the 1830s with his invention of several machines that made processing sugar faster and easier.[10]

Local marble sculptors who gained a widely respected clientele were Daniel and Eugene Warburg, sons of the wealthy German real estate speculator Daniel Warburg and his slave Marie Rose Blondeau, originally from Cuba. The elder Warburg freed Marie after their first son's birth in the 1820s. The brothers studied under French sculptor Philippe Garbeille in the city, and in 1849 set up a shop as marble cutters for statuary and tombs. Prior to the Civil War Eugene went to Europe with commissions in France and Belgium, and he died in Rome in 1859. His brother Daniel carried on the business at home, constructing many notable tombs, the most prominent being the elegant Holcomb Memorial in Metairie Cemetery.

A contemporary of the Warburgs was Prosper Florville Foy, son of French planter and sculptor René Prosper Foy and free woman of color Azelie Aubry. The younger Foy was sent to study art in France, and when his father retired from the marble yard in the late 1830s, he turned it over to his talented son, who, in collaboration with architect J. N. DePouilly, made some of the finest tombs in the city. Italian sculptor Achille Perelli was a close friend of Foy and made a bust of him in 1855.

The Civil War was obviously a turning point for many professional people of color. Those who were able and had the foresight to do so sold their property before the war and left the city to start over elsewhere. Others transferred their funds out of state into safer investments, while still others, through determination and shrewd handling of their resources, managed to ride out the storm. Many tradesmen and artisans worked throughout the war years or picked up their jobs soon after some semblance of order returned. The descendants of some of these free blacks continue to live well today, and a few even practice the same trades and keep the same shops as their great-grandparents. In general, however, the community of free people of color lost its identity and former

10. Marcus Christian, *Negro Ironworkers in Louisiana, 1718–1900* (Gretna, La.: Pelican, 1972). The life and career of Norbert Rillieux is examined in detail in Michel Fabre's essay in this volume.

means of support with the war (and, of course, the end of Reconstruction), and most families never recovered. Many had to content themselves with a greatly reduced standard of living arising from menial jobs and social isolation.

New Orleans today is a living monument to the labor and skills of the slaves and free people of color. Their imprint still shines in the buildings, tombs, and embellishments from Tremé to the Garden District. Although most of their work, such as the rolling of fine cigars, manufacturing of carriages, and tailoring of European suits, has passed into history, one occasionally finds an expert shoe repairman here or a butcher there with a Creole surname and the pride in his work that can only come from generations in the same family business.

10

The Origin of Louisiana Creole

FEHINTOLA MOSADOMI

Many linguists and ethnographers have discussed the three varieties of French that coexist in Louisiana: the Louisiana Creole (LC), the Cajun, and the Colonial French. According to William Read, only the first two varieties are considered "Louisiana French." Much controversy exists regarding all three, especially on the origin of Louisiana Creole. The goal of this article is to examine the grammar of this variety, with an eye to shedding some light on its origins. Before doing so, however, it is important to review the arguments and counterarguments on the origin of Louisiana Creole, while at the same time considering the history of the people who speak it.[1]

What is meant by the terms "Creole" and "Louisiana Creole"? Creole studies is a young field, and moreover there are racial biases regarding the origin of Louisiana Creole and its speakers. Accordingly, there have been quite a few different definitions of Louisiana Creole (LC) and Creole in general. According to Albert Valdman, the word *Creole* originates from *crioulo* or *criolo*, which entered the French language from the Spanish, which in turn probably derives from the past tense *crialdo* of the verb *criar* (from the Latin *creare*), which means "servants raised in the master's house." Valdman further claims that "Creole" implies the corrupted or rotten European language used by blacks, or by white Creoles in their dealings with blacks. In a restricted sense, the term denotes any child

---

1. William Read, *Louisiana French* (1931; reprint, Baton Rouge: Louisiana State University Press, 1963).

born in the colony to European parents, but to Valdman, "Creole" in a broader sense refers to two groups of people: blacks born in the American colonies, as opposed to those originating from Africa (Black Creoles versus Noir Bossals), and all people of mixed race (hybrids), as opposed to pure whites or pure blacks.[2]

Other researchers explain that Creole, or "nigger French," or "neg," is a language similar to the Haitian Creole in form and pronunciation. Hesseling defines "Creole" as "those languages which have arisen out of European languages in the mouths of Africans, Asians, Australians, or Americans (i.e., aboriginal Americans) in overseas provinces, and then later are also frequently spoken by Europeans or their descendants." L. Adam, cited by Valdman, suggests the linguistic inferiority of the black race in his definition, since he describes Creole as having been adapted phonetically and grammatically from French, English, and Spanish by a linguistically inferior group of speakers. Elodie Jourdain, also cited by Valdman, in reference to the physiological and psychological differences between whites and blacks, and in terms of what becomes of French, the great language of civilization, when it is expressed through the minds of blacks, affirms, "Nous nous bournerons à monter ce que devient une grande langue de civilisation telle que le français en passant par des cerveaux et des gosiers noirs." Beber-Gisler cites Jean Raspail's definition of Creole as a nonstandard French, and in agreement with the inferiority of the language, writes:

> La langue créole ne sortira jamais de l'enfance, qui marque à la fois son charme et ses limites. La simplification de ses mots, sa similigrammaire, en soulignent l'infantilisme. La simplification, les raccourcis, l'absence des genres et des nombres, la suppression des prépositions et des conjonctions sont le propre du créole . . . et sont le propre d'un enfant qui commence à parler. Quelqu'un qui dit "fini palé" pour "j'avais parlé," "tigoute" pour "un peu," "un zouézo" et "un zanimo" pour "un oiseau" et "un animal," "gadé" pour "regarder," "bitasion" pour "habitation," etc., créole ou pas créole, celui-là est bon pour le pédiatre.

Raspail, then, deems the Creole of the blacks inferior because of its simplification, its indicative grammar, its lack of gender and number, its shortened form, and its suppression of prepositions and conjunctions, all

2. Albert Valdman, *Le créole: Structure, statut et origine* (Paris: Editions Klincksieck, 1978).

of which are typical of creole languages as well as the language of a child just beginning to speak. Creole is thus believed to be a language that will never get beyond its childlike stage, because of these limitations.[3]

Other attempts at capturing the essence of Louisiana Creole include that of French linguist M. Harris, who describes it geographically, as a language spoken mainly by blacks but sometimes by whites in the plantations along the Mississippi between New Orleans and Pointe Coupée Parish and also in St. Martin Parish. Another French writer, Rousseve, adds to the picture: "This medium of communication, still a living language, was developed by the Negroes of Colonial Louisiana, and was fused from French, with traces of Spanish and African influence." For Read, it is almost taboo to describe Louisiana Creole as a "Creole dialect": "I have ventured, in spite of many misgivings, to group the dialect of the Creoles and that of the Acadians under the term *Louisiana-French.* I am debarred, unfortunately, from speaking to the former as the 'Creole dialect,' because this term is applied in Louisiana to the negro French patois." Valdman, on the contrary, considers Louisiana Creole as a Louisiana Creole dialect. He describes it as the Negro French or gumbo, imported from the Caribbean, specifically from Guadeloupe, Martinique, and St. Domingue. Read considers Louisiana Creole as a French patois (that is, an inferior dialect) consisting of a corrupt French vocabulary, some African words, and an essentially African syntax. He suggests that African borrowings into Louisiana Creole are rather few because the slaves were required to speak their masters' language, a phenomenon that results in the forgetting of their own, the substrate language.[4]

Louisiana Creole (LC), then, has been characterized by various descriptions and referred to by various terms, such as "patois" or "gumbo," in addition to the aforementioned "neg." The most accurate definition seems to be that of recent researcher Margaret Marshall, who argues that Creole is a variety of French that the slaves were exposed to, a vernacular

3. George S. Lane, "Notes on Louisiana Creole French II: The Negro French Dialect," *Language* 11 (1935), 5–16; Valdman, *Le créole,* 17; Dany Beber-Gisler, *La langue créole force jugulée* (Paris: Editions l'Harmattan, 1976), 110.

4. M. Harris, "Cofé 'pourquoi,' Un Africanisme parmi d'autres en créoles louisianais," *Revue de Louisiane* 2 (1973): 88; Margaret M. Marshall, "The Origins of Creole French in Louisiana," *Regional Dimensions* 8 (1990): 24; Read, *Louisiana French,* xxii, 118; Valdman, *Le créole,* 27, 30.

French characterized by regionalisms and reduced forms.[5] In spite of the fact that the perceptions of negative linguistic attributes are unwarranted, it is common knowledge that Louisiana Creole did develop in the course of years of contact between French colonists and African slaves. The question one should ask at this point is: "Where did the slaves come from, and what language(s) did they bring to Louisiana, in order for us to determine their linguistic influence(s) on Louisiana Creole?"

Read, Patrick Griolet, Marshall, and recent historian Gwendolyn Midlo Hall have traced the history of black Creoles in Louisiana to the period of the slave trade.[6] According to Griolet, the first shipment of 500 slaves of African origin was made in 1719, and the number of slaves gradually increased in the course of the eighteenth century. (In Hall's account, the table listing French slave ships that landed in Louisiana shows 450 arriving in 1719.) Griolet argues that in contrast to 1719's 500 Africans, the slaves who arrived much later were from the Caribbean. In 1809, a large number of Creoles from St. Domingue, who had taken refuge in Cuba after being expelled by the Spanish, were accepted by the United States even though in 1807 President Jefferson had banned all slave importation. These black francophones settled in New Orleans and along the plantations in the Mississippi region, and in St. Martinsville in the region of the Attakapas Prairie, where there was already a French-speaking population, the Acadians. John Holm believes that LC may have already stabilized by the early 1800s even though the Haitian Creole brought to Louisiana by the refugees left its mark.[7]

Because of the differing points of departure of African slaves, which included Senegal, Gambia, Sierra Leone, Liberia, Ghana, Togo, Dahomey (Republic of Benin), Nigeria, and Angola, researchers like Herskovits, Le Page du Pratz, and Lorenzo Don Turner all agree that the group

5. Margaret M. Marshall, "A Louisiana Speech Continuum," *Regional Dimensions* 5 (1987): 71–94.

6. See Read, *Louisiana French*; Patrick Griolet, *Cadjins et créoles en Louisiane: Histoire et survivance d'une francophone* (Paris: Payot, 1986); Marshall, "Origins of Creole French"; Gwendolyn Midlo Hall, *Africans in Colonial Louisiana: The Development of Afro-Creole Culture in the Eighteenth Century* (Baton Rouge: Louisiana State University Press, 1992).

7. Griolet, *Cadjins et créoles*, 70; John Holm, *Pidgins and Creoles* (New York: Cambridge University Press, 1988), 2: 388.

as a whole was linguistically diverse, with such substrate languages as, among others, Wolof, Malinke, Mandingo, Bambara, Foule, Mende, Vai, Twi, Fante, Gâ, Ewe, Fon, Yoruba, Bini, Hausa, Igbo, Ibibio, Efik, Congo, Umbundo, and Kimbundu. Hall methodically argues that two-thirds of the slaves that arrived in Louisiana were brought from Senegambia, "a site of the great medieval Ghana, Mali, and Songhai trade," a region homogeneous in culture and history, located between the rivers Senegal and Gambia. The slaves from this region spoke Serrer, Wolof, and Pulaar, which are closely related, and Malinke, spoken in the east by the Mande people. Hall supports with data the fact that Senegambia was the main source of slave trade between Africa and Louisiana in the eighteenth century. The Company of the Indies, a private organization licensed by the King of France, organized most slave-trade voyages between Senegal and Louisiana, and with such exclusive rights, the trading between the two points flourished. Even though the Company of the Indies had a trading post at Whydah (Juda) on the Gulf of Benin, there it had to compete with other European nations. Hall explains: "Between 1726 and 1731, almost all the slave trade voyages organized by the Company of the Indies went to Louisiana. Thirteen slave ships landed in Louisiana during those years; all but one of them left Senegambia. Over half the slaves brought to French Louisiana, 3,250 out of 5,987, arrived from Senegambia during this five-year period. The last ship, arriving in 1743, also came from Senegambia." It is therefore relevant, she concludes, "to look to Senegambia for the African roots of Louisiana's Afro-Creole culture." Only very few voyages came directly from Africa to Louisiana after 1743. According to Hall, during the Spanish rule in Louisiana, most of the newly arrived African slaves were supplied through reexport from Caribbean islands, including Curacao, St. Domingue, Martinique, and especially Jamaica and Cuba.[8]

8. Hall, *Africans in Colonial Louisiana*, 29, 34, Appendix A; Gwendolyn Midlo Hall, "African Women in French and Spanish Louisiana: Origins, Roles, Family, Work, Treatment," in *The Devil's Lane: Sex and Race in the Early South*, ed. Catherine Clinton and Michele Gillespie (New York: Oxford University Press, 1997), 248; Gwendolyn Midlo Hall, conversation with author, February 1998. Slaves were referred to as "captives" before their departure from the island of Gorée (Senegal) and Bissau (the coast of Upper Guinea) in West Africa. See Table 2, p. 60, of *Africans in Colonial Louisiana* for detailed information on French slave trading ships that landed in Louisiana from Senegambia. For a detailed treatment of Sene-

The question then becomes one of identifying specifically the slaves from Senegambia. The majority of those shipped to Louisiana in the 1720s, especially between 1727 and 1729, were Bambaras (mostly men) and Wolofs. The Bambara slaves were brought in large numbers from the upper Senegal and Niger area down to the coast of Senegal, and eventually constituted a large community who spoke the same language, stayed together (and even conspired with the Indians against the slave masters in 1731), thereby "playing a preponderant role in the formation of the Colony's Afro-Creole culture." Hall emphasizes, "There is little doubt that the Bambara brought to Louisiana were truly ethnic Bambara. They constituted a large community. Louisiana officials reported that four hundred Bambara slaves speaking the same language were involved in the conspiracy of 1731. There was a Bambara court interpreter in Louisiana. Slaves testifying in court identified their own nations." The Wolofs were referred to as "Senegal" by the French slave masters; an undetermined number were shipped to Louisiana in the 1720s. It is, however, important to note that Hall's 1992 study does not focus on the Wolofs as it does the Bambaras. In my meetings with her in January and February of 1998 (and as she also describes in her study of African women in colonial Louisiana), Hall stressed the importance of the Wolof women (in quantity and quality) as concubines of the French slave masters and their role in trade connections as well as in the language development of their children, especially since they came in relatively large numbers. Their tradition of long-standing ties with French men both in Africa and in Louisiana cannot be overemphasized. The Wolofs were the most conciliatory people toward the French, and part of this, according to Hall, spilled over to Louisiana. She elaborates, "It is women, especially mothers and surrogate mothers, who primarily mold the new generations. They most often speak, sing, and tell stories to impressionable infants and small children, passing on their verbal and body language, manners of expression and communication, feelings, perceptions and values. In no other colonial culture of the United States did African women play such a central role."[9]

---

gambia itself, see Philip D. Curtin, *Economic Change in Precolonial Africa: Senegambia in the Era of the Slave Trade*, 2 vols. (Madison: University of Wisconsin Press, 1975).

   9. Hall, *Africans in Colonial Louisiana*, 41–3; Hall, "African Women in French and Spanish Louisiana," 247–8.

The Bambaras and the Mandingas are described by Hall as the Mande peoples who claimed to have descended from the Mali empire established in the thirteenth century. The Mandingas protected their own people from slavery but did not extend that courtesy to the Bambaras, whom they sold into the institution. One obvious reason for this is the religious differences between the two groups; the Mandingas were practitioners of and strong believers in Islam, and the Bambaras practiced an African traditional religion. Therefore the shipment of the Bambara slaves was at its peak during the warfare between the groups, which also gave rise to the formation of the Segu empire. On yet another level, the Bambara slaves were preferred by the French slave traders, who considered them as "robust, good natured, intelligent," the "best men of all Africa for labor," loving, obedient, not revolting, not fleeing, not having cause for despair, "never refusing to work, provided their stomach is full," "brave, loyal, and skilled combatants." Regardless of the pattern of slave trade between Africa and Louisiana, the latter clearly preferred certain types of slaves. Also, the French slave masters deemed certain African nations unacceptable as sources for slaves, for various reasons.[10]

There is documented evidence of the arrival of a handful of African slaves in Louisiana in 1709, prior to the arrival in Louisiana in 1719 of the first two slave-trading ships (*Le Duc de Maine* and *L'Aurore*) in 1719 from the coast of west Africa. These early arrivals resulted from Bienville's bold ambition of slave smuggling that year. But their number was negligible; by 1712, only twelve blacks were documented as living in the whole of Louisiana.

Hall considers the coincidence in the creation of French Louisiana and the arrival of African slaves in the territory. Louisiana was founded in 1699 as a military post, but its population began to grow in earnest only with the founding of New Orleans in 1718; similarly, the first slave ships sailed from Africa in 1719. Between 1719 and 1731, sixteen ships arrived in Louisiana from the Senegal concession of the Company of the Indies. *Le Ruby* was the first slave ship to arrive in Louisiana from the Senegambia concession. During the same period, by 1721, six ships arrived from Juda (the Bight of Benin) and one, *La Néréide*, from Cabinda (Angola region). In 1723, slaves arrived in Louisiana from Gambia, Gorée, and Bissau. Only one more ship arrived, in 1743; thus most blacks

10. Hall, *Africans in Colonial Louisiana*, 42.

that came early to Louisiana were brought directly from Africa within the same decade. Reiterating that only a few blacks could have come from the French West Indies, Hall agrees with Marshall's hypothesis that the majority of the Louisiana slave population came directly from Africa rather than through Haiti. Based on demographic research and some Creole-like expressions uncovered by Le Page du Pratz and legal documents of 1773, "the earliest known records of such a language in Louisiana," Marshall (like Holm) believes that LC arose well before the arrival of slaves from St. Domingue.[11]

With Hall's data on the arrival of slaves from Africa, it seems fair to say that the formation of the Franco-Creole culture took place about the same time as the early contacts between the French masters and their African slaves. The precise date of complete formation of LC cannot be known, but Marshall argues, based on information retrieved from census data, judicial documents, and diaries, that blacks in Louisiana were speaking LC by about the middle of the eighteenth century. Writing in 1980, Maguire claimed that black Creoles then constituted about 35 percent of the population of St. Martin Parish.[12] Writing in 1992, Klingler suggested that the population of Creole speakers in Louisiana could be about 60,000 to 80,000, although there is no way to separate that number into white and black subgroups.

If LC is spoken mainly by blacks, and if many of these black Creoles are descendants of former slaves originating from Africa, one should not be surprised at the African linguistic features found in LC. But before examining the languages that influenced Louisiana Creole, we should consider the three ideological theories of the origin of Louisiana Creole proposed and expounded upon by linguists, historians, and ethnographers: that the language is of French origin, that it is a hybrid, and that it is of African origin.

In proposing the genesis of Louisiana Creole as French-based, George S. Lane writes, "The basis of the French Creole of Louisiana,

11. Ibid., Table 2; Marshall, "Origins of Creole French," 30, as cited in Thomas Klingler, "A Descriptive Study of the Creole Speech of Pointe Coupée Parish, Louisiana, with Focus on the Lexicon" (Ph.D. diss., Indiana University, 1992).
12. Robert Maguire, "Les Créoles Noirs," *Vie Française* 34 (1980): 22.

like that of the Antilles and the Mascarenes is French, not French and something else, no matter to what extent they may differ among themselves in the language wrought from the same base, and the English has had no influence upon the Creole of Louisiana except as it has worked first through the Standard French." Lane justifies his theory by giving examples of grammatical features in Louisiana Creole, such as the positioning of adjectives and the forms of indefinite pronouns, that pattern much like the Standard French. He gives as examples of the adjective positioning the following:

/ɛbɔ̃ lar ɔb/	"une bonne robe"
/dolo ʃo/	"eau chaude"
/ʃmiz-je blɔ̃/	"ces chemises sont blanches"

Indefinite pronouns /kekɛn/ and /kiʃɔ̃ʒ/ are similarly believed to derive from the French indefinite pronouns:

| /kekɛn | "quelqu'un" |
| /kiʃɔ̃ʒ/ | "quelque chose"[13] |

In making a similar claim, Alcée Fortier compares the equivalent of *La Chanson de Roland* in Creole to the Old French version of the Middle Ages and finds them similar:

Old French
Li quens Rollanz se jut desuz un pin,
Envers Espagne en ad turnet sun vis,
de plusurs choses a remembrer li prest;
de tantes terres cume li bers cunquist,

Creole dialect
Conte Roland assiste enba in pin,
côté l'Espagne li tournin so figuire,
li commencé pensé boucou Kochoge;
tou la terre yé li prenne comme inbrave,[14]

13. Lane, "Notes on Louisiana Creole French," 4, 13. See also Alcée Fortier, *Louisiana Studies: Literature, Customs and Dialects, History and Education* (New Orleans: F. F. Hansell, 1894).

14. Fortier, *Louisiana Studies*, 147.

Fortier also claims that adverbs of affirmation and negation have identical structures in both languages; however, he does not give examples.

Frenchman Harris quotes Jules Faine as having suggested the influence of African languages on Louisiana Creole to be small: "Nulle part en Amérique . . . on n'a pu observer une influence quelconque des langues africaines, en dehors de quelques vocables et certaines communes déficiences dans la pronunciation." He then presents the findings of Goodman, who held that the third-person plural pronoun of the French language influences the formation of the noun plural in Creole. Goodman also postulated that the plural morpheme indicator is in a position "post-posé," that is, after the noun, in Hollandese Creole, Spanish Creole, and French Creole. He offered the following examples:

Louisiana Creole
nomme-*yé* e femme-*yé*   "les hommes et les femmes"

Hollandese Creole
die boom *sende*   "les arbres" (i.e., sende = ils, elles)

Papiamento
e cas nam   "les maisons" (nam = d'origine incertaine = ils, elles)

Harris argues that the third-person plural could not have come from African language structures and goes on to say that the *yé* of Louisiana Creole derives from the French personal pronoun *eux* ("them") and that it is also used as a subject pronoun, as in the following example:

yé pas connain   "ils ne le connaissent pas"

Harris, however, does not explain how *yé* is derived from *eux*.[15]

Harris claims that the post-position of the particle *là* in Louisiana Creole is similar to the demonstrative particle in French. From this observation he infers that African languages have no influence with regard to this part of speech. He cites an example from Broussard:

Nomme-*là* et femme-*là* rivé hié
"l'homme et la femme . . . sont arrivés hier" ou "cet homme-là et cette femme-là . . ."

15. Harris, "Cofé 'pourquoi,' " 89, 90.

But the definite article is rarely used in Louisiana Creole, as Broussard demonstrates by this example, where my added Ø indicates absence of the definite article:

Le moustique perd son temps à piquer LE crocodile (français)
Ø maringuin perd so temps piquer Ø caiman (créole)[16]

Here it is worth noting that in some African languages there are no definite articles. Yoruba (one of the African languages spoken by slaves brought to Louisiana) has no definite articles, to wit:

1. Ø igi ré lulɛ
   Ø arbre tombé par terre
   l'arbre est tombé par terre
   "The tree fell down"
2. Ø ɔbá kú
   Ø roi mort
   le roi est mort
   "the king is dead"

The Yoruba examples just given, however, do not suggest that Yoruba is the major language that influenced LC. We will have to study the structure and other elements of the languages of other African peoples enslaved in Louisiana, especially the Bambaras and the Wolofs. Hall claims that the Bight of Benin cannot be a major source of the French slave trade to Louisiana and therefore the languages from that region could not have substantially influenced LC. But it is worth noting that Yoruba slaves from the Bight of Benin have been traced in large numbers to Pointe Coupée and St. Charles Parishes, where they arrived particularly during the Spanish rule. In a yet unpublished statistical study of the Yoruba slaves, Gwendolyn Hall reports that during the Spanish period (1770–1803) there were 239 slaves described as Nago (Yoruba) in Louisiana Creole documents. The ethnicity was recorded for 5.5 percent of all African slaves, and the Nago slaves were distributed among the Louisiana parishes as follows: Orleans 11.3 percent, St. Charles 22.2 percent, St. John the Baptist 10.9 percent, Ascension 8.4 percent, St. Martin 5.4 percent, Pointe Coupée 25 percent, and East Baton Rouge 5.4 percent. Two regions, St. Charles and St. John the Baptist, referred to as the German

16. Ibid., 91.

coast and found in the rural lower Mississippi valley, contained 33.1 percent of the Nagos. These regions developed variations of Louisiana Creole. Hall also reports that most Yoruba slaves were brought during the
1780s (23.1 percent), 1790s (31.3 percent), 1800s (19.1 percent), and
1810s (13.4 percent), while the Yoruba slaves who arrived at other times
totalled less than 10 percent. In our discussion, she noted that Yoruba
slaves certainly influenced the emergence of Voodoo in Louisiana "in its
almost unique, matriarchal form."[17]

While some commentators posit a single influence (i.e., Standard
French) on Louisiana Creole, others argue a double source. Harris, in his
quest for the language's origins, suggests a mixed influence of the African
languages and Standard French. For example, the interrogative *cofé*
("why," *pourquoi*) can be traced to the Standard French "*à quoi faire.*"
Cofé is also used in Canadian French, and "*quoi faire*" has also been used
in Louisiana Acadian, according to J. K. Ditchy, whom Harris cites.
Thus /kofer/ and /kwafer/ both seem to derive from "*quoi faire,*" with
"*quoi faire*" originating in French Provincial, entering into Canadian
French, and finally finding its way down to the Louisiana Creole of the
blacks. John Guilbeau, as well as Mayor and Pickens, confirm the use of /
kwafae/ as a characteristic element of black Creole. /kofer/ is also said to
be used by blacks along the Mississippi River in St. Charles, St. John the
Baptist, Pointe Coupee, St. Martin, Iberia, Lafourche, and Terrebonne
Parishes in Louisiana. As to the question why the Louisiana slaves used
cofé instead of "*quoi faire,*" and did not acquire the latter form at all, Harris suggests that *cofé* is a French-African hybrid; he explains that the *quoi
faire* of the dialectal French is similar to the interrogative found in the
African languages of the slaves: "L'emploi de 'quoi faire' dans le français
dialectal avec lequel certains noirs africains sont entrés en contact, sur
le sol louisianais, complémentait l'emploi dans certains de leurs langues
africaines d'une structure interrogative analogue de même sens que
'pourquoi.' "[18]

17. Gwendolyn Midlo Hall, "Louisiana Slave Database," in Gwendolyn Midlo
Hall, ed., *Databases for the Study of Afro-Louisiana History and Genealogy*, a compact
disc publication (Baton Rouge: Louisiana State University Press, 1999); Hall, conversations with author, February 1998 and August 1999.

18. Harris, "Cofé 'pourquoi,' " 94, 99.

For Harris, who agrees with Goodman that French is an important source of LC, Suzanne Sylvain's hypothesis for an African origin is an enormous exaggeration. Harris quotes Goodman:

> To what extent their contribution [c.-à-d. la contribution des Africains] to Creole was conditioned by their native African languages, and how large a role these have played in it, has been the subject of much speculation and dispute. A few have denied the experience of any influence in Creole. . . . In actuality, the linguistic diversity of the Africans is sufficient to account for their adoption of an overwhelming French vocabulary, while the widespread occurrence of certain structural features in their various languages is both necessary and sufficient to account for undeniably African structural features of Creole. . . . Certain other Creole structural features most likely represent a blend of African and French features. . . . It would be completely unwarranted to assume, however, that the grammatical or phonological structure of Creole is the identical replica of those of some African language or languages.[19]

In support of the linguistic fusion of French and African structures, Goodman, again quoted by Harris, explains why the inflection of verbal endings is abandoned in favor of preposed particles: "While all these French periphrastic expressions doubtless played the major role in the development of the Creole system of preposed tense and aspect particles, certain language[s] of West Africa, relevant in general to the formation of Creole grammatical structure, have very likely played an important reinforcing role. A clear-cut example of such a language with a system very like Creoleš is Mandingo, in which a set of preverbal particles fulfill much the same functions." Also cited by Harris, Guilbeau theorizes further that whenever two languages coexist there will always be a mutual influence; in reinforcement of this theory, he states, "What is apparent in many areas where the patois [c'est-à-dire le créole] co-existed with general Louisiana French is the result of absorption and mutual influence. Today, for instance, politicians who grew up in some of these areas frequently attract attention when campaigning in French communities where the patois is unknown. For while they address the people in a comprehensible Louisiana French, their speech is conspicuous because of certain characteristics or pronunciations or structures reminiscent of the patois."[20]

19. Ibid., 89.
20. Ibid., 92, 102.

A third hypothesis of the influence on Louisiana Creole is that of the African languages. Valdman argues that there is a striking similarity among the Creoles of the Caribbean and of the Indian Ocean, especially those of Haiti, the Lesser Antilles, Guyana, and Louisiana. Citing Whinom, Thompson, Stewart, and Taylor, Valdman states that all Creoles and Pidgins have a base in the European languages, but are eventually derived from an Afro-Portuguese pidgin found on the coast of West Africa in the sixteenth century. It is worth noting that the Portuguese were the first people to explore Sub-Saharan Africa, in the second half of the fifteenth century. While Valdman argues that there is a striking morphosyntactic resemblance between Creoles in general and the substrait languages of West Africa, he cautions against the ready assumption of a homogeneous Creole (even if the Creoles in America are influenced by West African languages, a hypothesis Valdman believes) because each Creole differs according to geographical region and social status of the speaker. Linguist Ingrid Neumann agrees with the differences in Creole based on these criteria.[21]

In regard to the question of African influence, the origin of the interrogative *pourquoi* ("why") mentioned earlier in this paper has been traced to two Kwa languages of the Niger-Congo language family: Yoruba and Igbo. The Yoruba *kini ʃe* ("why") and the Igbo *gini mere* ("why") illustrate that morphological and semantic structures of some West African languages are analogous to the dialectal French "*quoi faire.*" Harris goes on to show the similarity of the Igbo *gini mere* to the *wa mek* ("why") of the Jamaican (English) Creole. Cassidy and Le Page confirm this similarity between the I(g)bo and the Jamaican Creole. The interrogative "why" has also been traced by Lorenzo Dow Turner to Gullah, spoken along the southern coast of South Carolina, Georgia, and the neighboring islands by African Americans living there:

/mek una fa briŋ di bʌ kra/
"why did you bring the white man"
/mek una dɔ kʌm owa tʊ dIs said/
"why don't you come over to this side?"

21. Valdman, *Le créole*, 14; Ingrid Neumann-Holzschuh, *Le créole de Breaux Bridge, Louisiane: étude morphosyntaxique, textes, vocabulaire* (Hamburg: Helmut Buske Verlag, 1985), 2.

Considering the morphological, syntactic, and semantic similarities between LC and the substrate (African) languages he cites, Harris wonders whether there is a "possibility" or "probability" of the influence of African languages on the structure of Louisiana Creole.[22]

Faine underscores the importance of the influence of African language traits on Louisiana Creole by explaining, "Forcé d'apprendre la langue imposé par ses maîtres, il y mit cependant du sien, en y apportant son accent propre, cette douceur, ce rythme harmonieux, cette musicalité qui en sont la plus belle parure. De lui vient également ce 'ton signicatif,' point de départ des onomatopées si finement observées du creole et peut-être aussi, de son système de redoublement, usité par exemple dans le 'mandingue' et dont nous n'avons pu trouver de trace dans aucune des autres langues composantes."[23] What is important to Faine here is that despite the fact that the slaves were forced to learn the language imposed on them by their masters, they nevertheless brought in aspects of their own languages—the harmonious rhythm, the musicality, the tone, the softness, the onomatopoeia, and the system of reduplication such as those found in the Mandingo language, all of which have been observed in Louisiana Creole. The device of repetition can be found in the superlatives of Creole adjectives, which are formed by the repetition of the word. For example:

/loun bel, bel femme/
"une femme extrèmement jolie"
"a very, very beautiful woman"
/loun pitit, pitit tit bête/
"un animalcule infiniment petit"
"a very, very small animal"

Adverbs in Creole are similarly repeated in the following examples:

/li té bien bien malade/
"il était très gravement malade"
"he was seriously ill"

22. Cassidy and Le Page, *Dictionary of Jamaican English* (London, 1967); Harris, "Cofé 'pourquoi,' " 101.
23. Jules Faine, *Philologie créole* (Port au Prince: Imprimerie de l'Etat, 1936), 4.

Creole verbs can also be repeated:

/li marcher, l'marcher, l'marcher, jusque li river su tête loun gros
mourne/
"il a tant faut de marcher qu'il est arrivé sur le sommet d'une haute
montagne"

The same is true for pronouns:

/li-mine, mine/
"c'est bien lui-même"
"it is he himself"

The use of repetition or reduplication (the doubling of the initial syllable
or root to produce an inflected form) in African languages of the Kwa
group is widespread. In Yoruba, pronouns, verbs, adjectives, and adverbs
can be either repeated or reduplicated. An example is the following repeated pronoun:

/òuⁿ òuⁿ òuⁿ ʃá/[24]   "it's he/she always"

Some Yoruba fully reduplicated adverbs are from "pata" and "kia":

/kpátákpátá/   "completely"
/kíákíá/   "very quickly"

An example of a repeated verb:

/ó rìⁿ rìⁿ rìⁿ/   "s/he, it walked, walked, walked"

All of these repetitions are used for the purpose of emphasis or for intensity. Many studies have been done on reduplication in African languages;
what now needs to be undertaken is an examination of reduplication and
repetition in LC and a comparison of the findings to pertinent African
languages.

Creole proverbs are also said to have been influenced by African languages and cultures:

/fer couper fer/
"il faut du fer pour couper le fer"
"one needs an iron to cut an iron"
/tit cochon tit sang/
"à chacun ses moyens"
"to each his own"

24. The superscript *n* denotes a nasalized sound.

In order to judge the likelihood of this possibility, the grammatical structures of African proverbs should be examined and compared with those of LC proverbs. These proverbs, among many others cited by Faine, are also found in the Creoles of Jamaica, Guadeloupe, and Guyana.[25] Some of them mention African elements, such as tigers, elephants, and certain monkeys.

Haitian creolist Suzanne Sylvain argues that there is a tremendous syntactic influence of African languages on Haitian Creole: "Nous sommes en présence d'un français coulé dans le moule de la syntaxe africaine ou, comme on classe généralement le langues d'après leur parenté syntaxique, d'une langue ewe à vocabulaire français." Boudet also argues that the demonstrative and the definite article in African languages such as Ewe (E), Yoruba (Y), Ibo (I), Kpelle (K), and the Twi (T), as well as in the Haitian Creole (HC), are always placed after the noun. Some of her examples are:

E: afe—*a*
      house—that (det.)
      that house
Y: ile *yen*
      house—that
      that house
I: uno *afu*
      house that
      that house
K: pErE *ti*
      house that
      that house
T: abofra *yi*
      house that
      that house
HC: kay—*sa*—a
      house—that (det.)
      that house[26]

25. Faine, *Philologie créole*, 4–5.

26. Harris, "Café 'pourquoi,' " 89; Martha Boudet, "Identifying the Grammatical Base of the Caribbean Creoles: A Typological Approach," in *Historicity and Variation in Creole Studies*, ed. Arnold Highfield and Albert Valdman (Ann Arbor: Karioma, 1979), 109.

Concerning the post-position of the particle *là* as a demonstrative adjective, Harris proposes a single influence of the French language. It seems more accurate, however, to argue a double influence of both African and French. For instance, in Yoruba, the demonstrative adjective is also found after the noun. The following examples compare with those of Broussard:

1. LC: Liv'-*là*
   Y: lwe yẹn
   Y: lwe *yẹn* temi ni
      "lwe *yẹn* temi ni"
      "Ce livre là est à moi"
2. LC: Donne-li liv'-*là*
   Y: Fun un ni iwe *yẹn*
      "Donnez-lui ce livre"
3. LC: Femme-*là* 'vec qui to vini
   Y: Obinrin *yẹn* ti o ba wa
      "Obinrin *yẹn* ti o ba wa"
      "La femme avec qui tu es venu"

Mufwene expresses his concern regarding the question of African influence: "even though in a number of respects some Kwa languages such as Ewe and Yoruba do follow the creole pattern, the question of why features of only these Kwa languages have been selected over those of non-Kwa languages remain relevant here, making the need for an explanation of the principles regulating these selections rather imperative."[27] This concern is certainly warranted, and so is another, namely that we need to examine other African language families besides the Kwa that came in contact with French in Louisiana (such as the Mande, the West Atlantic, and the Bantu) in order to fully understand the principles operating in the formation of LC. The Mande, and Kwa languages, as well as French, certainly need to be researched.

Read as well as other researchers have traced Louisiana Creole lexical items to African origin. Such LC words include:

27. James F. Broussard, *Louisiana Creole* (London: Kennikat Press, 1972), 8; Salikoko S. Mufwene, "The Universalist and Substrate Hypotheses Complement One Another," in *Substrata vs. Universals in Creole Genesis*, ed. Muysken and Smith (Amsterdam: John Benjamin, 1986), 138.

congo "a snake, a dance, or a region in Central Africa"
gombo "a vegetable"
gris-gris "a protective place"

Others are *zombi*, *voodoo*, *jambalaya*, and the like. *Gris-gris* has been traced to Bambara. And *zinzin*, meaning "an amulet of support or power" in LC, is identical in both form and definition to its Bambara equivalent. According to Chaudenson, the 170 words identified by Sylvain as having originated from African languages into Haitian Creole constitute less than 5 percent of the total lexical items. Hall reports that a study is forthcoming by Michael Gomez that identifies *ounga* as a Mande word for "charm." All of these pioneering efforts need to be supplemented by further lexicographic and semantic studies before any conclusive arguments can be made.[28]

One of the problems surrounding the issue of the origin of the LC is the simplification of its grammar. According to Bloomfield, cited by Valdman, this simplification is a "defective imitation of the base language." Lane enumerates the characteristics of simplification: "the definite article attached to the noun, lack of definite article, pronoun reduction, one form of the verb, pronoun that replaces the noun or the person, the particle that replaces tense, and the reduction in verbs with more than two syllables." Alcée Fortier confirms this reduction of verbs among Creoles. While Chaudenson believes that Creoles are simplified composites in regard to the contact between African and European languages, no one has researched the similarities of simplification in African languages and in LC.[29]

Other theories, such as Mufwene's "African monogenetic hypothesis" [AMH] and "African geogenetic hypothesis" [AGH], have been proposed regarding the origin of creoles in general. These will not be discussed herein, since in fact LC should not be considered a homogeneous creole. Rather, we should direct our attention to dialect variations

28. Read, *Louisiana French*, 118; Hall, *Africans in Colonial Louisiana*, 163; Robert Chaudenson, "Créoles français de l'océan indien et langues africaines," in *Readings in Creole Studies*, ed. Ian F. Hancock (Ghent: E. Story Scientia, P.V.B.A., 1979), 217–37; Michael Gomez, *Exchanging Our Country Marks: The Transformation of African Identities in the Colonial Antebellum* (University of North Carolina Press, forthcoming).

29. Lane, "Notes on Louisiana Creole French," 8.

within LC, such as Pointe Coupée Creole, St. Martin Creole, St. Charles Creole, and New Orleans Creole, since the slaves came from different regions of Africa, spoke different languages, and settled in different parts of Louisiana at different times. LC could be considered a single entity only if there were no dialectal differences among all the Creoles spoken in Louisiana. While there are smaller dialectal differences in the French spoken by the slave masters who came from different regions of France, we can still talk of their base language as a homogeneous French. Nevertheless, it is feasible to use the term "Louisiana Creole" at the present time, since all varieties have not yet been studied. The controversy on the origin of Louisiana Creole, or of other Creoles for that matter, will continue for many more years.

The situation of LC will be rendered more tragic if LC disappears. According to Klingler,

> While it may no longer be discounted as mere wishful thinking to sug-gest that language varieties ranging along the continuum between CF and SF will continue to be used in Louisiana for a long time to come, it seems far less likely that LC will be spoken in any recognizable form beyond the next two or three decades. For many years LC remained largely unaffected by the renewed enthusiasm for French in Louisiana, and despite recent signs of interest among some African-American LC speakers in promoting an awareness of their cultural and linguistic heri-tage, no one so far has clearly advocated trying to maintain LC. Even if such a program were to be proposed, its chances of success would be small, indeed. Fluent speakers under the age of fifty are rare, and the language is not being passed on to younger generations.[30]

Apart from the possible danger of the disappearance of LC (if no ac-tion is taken soon), there is no published work or systematic, comprehen-sive analysis of the languages spoken by the slaves upon arrival in Louisiana for us to determine the linguistic influences on LC, a regret also voiced by Chaudenson. Similarly, we need to study the formative pe-riod of the "franco-créole" or the French Creole in order to establish the influences or parallelisms between them. Neither is there a study of LC lexicography by which we might verify the origin of some of the foreign words in Louisiana Creole, although such a study is supposedly under-

30. Klingler, *Descriptive Study*, 5.

way by Valdman et al. For a complete understanding of the origins of LC, the phonology, morphology, syntax, semantics, and discourse of all languages that came into contact with LC have to be researched. The feature "discourse" is included because language and culture are two inseparable entities. The need for comprehensive and in-depth linguistic studies of the discourses on voodoo, superstitions, the evocations of sorcerers, and the origin of legends such as those of Bouki-Lapin and Tit-Jean—all of which, according to Griolet, characterized the language of the slaves—is imperative. Another problem is that slaves on arrival in Louisiana were listed by names, not by the languages they spoke. Ideally we need to be able to identify the homelands of all the slaves in order to have a fairly accurate account of the languages they brought with them. It may be doubly difficult to identify the linguistic background of some of the slaves since some identified themselves on arrival by their European names. And sometimes there is no information on the number of slaves that embarked on some voyages.[31]

Not only is there a lack of complete information regarding the origin of Louisiana Creole, there is also a serious dearth of interest in the subject as a worthy object of study. Suppression of LC by the "super languages," as well as negative attitudes toward less commonly taught and less commonly spoken languages, may contribute further to the death of LC. Louisiana Creole is a dying language, and it is time to revive it through an in-depth study of the generation (gradually fading away) that currently speaks it.

31. Hall reports that Senegalese scholar Ibrahima Seck is currently at work on a comparative study of Wolof and LC versions of the folklores.

11

Louisiana Creole Food Culture

Afro-Caribbean Links

Sybil Kein

The old saying "Too many cooks spoil the pot" might, in reference to Creole cooking, be revised to "Many cooks spawn the pot." The historical links of food preference and methods of cooking for the dishes famous around the world as "Louisiana Creole cuisine" extend to all those countries that trace the pattern of the American slave trade route from West Africa to the Caribbean down to the northeastern coast of South America and finally back up to Louisiana. Once in the New World, these slaves not only grew the produce but were responsible for preparing and cooking dishes that fed slave owners and slaves for hundreds of years. The result of what these millions of cooks created from the cultural memory of cooking in Africa combined with the acculturated tastes and ingredients from indigenous peoples in the Caribbean, South America, and Louisiana was Creole cuisine.

The West African connection to Creole cuisine is apparent upon examination of the culinary habits of West African people. Mendes suggests that "West African cooking is a composite of the culinary methods used by the tribes of Senegal, Sierra Leone, Guinea, Gabon, the Ivory Coast, Liberia, Nigeria (particularly the Yoruba and Ibo), Dahomey, Togo, Cameroon, Angola and the Congo." Jessica B. Harris traces the early diet of West Africans from the Middle Ages before European contact via foreign voyagers in the later centuries. She summarizes her findings:

It all started in Africa. Scholars have researched old Arab manuscripts and discovered some of the foodstuffs that were eaten by West Africans during the European Middle Ages. Reports of Arab travelers reveal that the African diet was somewhat similar to that of today. Ibn-Faqih al-Hamadhani, the earliest known Arabic author to write about the foods of the West African peoples, emphasizes the role played by cultivated plants in the diets of people in the area that is now Mauritania and Mali. He mentions that they ate beans and a kind of millet known as dukhn. Other grains eaten by Africans during this period included some forms of sorghum, wheat, and rice. These grains were made into thick porridges, pancakes, fritters, bread, and various puddings served under a variety of sauces. Yams . . . were also a major part of the local diet. . . . Beans too formed a major part of West African diet before European arrival. As early as 901 A.D. there were mentions of kidney beans and black-eyed peas. Broad beans, chick peas, and lentils were also eaten. All manner of green leafy vegetables were consumed, as were onions and garlic. Other foodstuffs included turnips, cabbage, pumpkins and gourds, and even cucumbers. . . . During this period West Africans are known to have eaten watermelon, tamarind, ackee, plums, dates, figs, and pomegranates. Meats included beef, lamb, goat, camel, poultry, and varieties of game and fish.[1]

Although some foods brought to the New World by slaves were indigenous to Africa—such as okra, kidney beans, black-eyed peas, and watermelon—others were introduced to the African diet by European traders. From the mid-sixteenth to the end of the eighteenth century, the eating habits of Africa were transformed. The coconut tree arrived from South Asia sometime between 1520 and 1540, while sweet potatoes and maize came from America in the same century. The seventeenth century saw the arrival of cassava and pineapple, while the eighteenth brought guavas and peanuts. The Portuguese are responsible for the transplanting to Africa of those small hot chiles, as well as corn, cassava, and white potatoes. Other chile peppers and tomatoes were also transplanted from the New World.[2]

Although African American, Caribbean, and some South American food staples such as beans and rice, various greens, yams, and sweet potatoes

1. Helen Mendes, *The African Heritage Cookbook* (New York: Macmillan, 1971), 21; Jessica B. Harris, *Iron Pots and Wooden Spoons* (New York: Ballantine, 1991), xiii–xiv.

2. Harris, *Iron Pots*, xii–xiv.

form a direct link to African foodstuffs, the African link to Creole cuisine is perhaps strongest with regard to food preparation techniques and cooking methods. Mendes describes one such technique: "An important practice was to use the grating stone, which was approximately 20 inches tall, for pulverizing corn, beans, rice or cassava. By this means the cook obtained flour and meal for making cakes and breads. The most frequent practice, however, was the use of mortar and pestle for pounding dry peppers, seeds, nuts, fruits and vegetables. These foods were pounded into pastes and added to sauces, stews, cakes, or breads." Mrs. Florence Borders, former archivist of the Amistad Research Center of New Orleans, remembers the use of the mortar and pestle by her grandmother to grind rice for making Chaud Calas.[3]

This technique of making a paste to add to sauces is probably the origin of the Creole roux, the base for all gravies or sauces. When asked for many recipes, Creole cooks automatically answer: "First you make a roux." One of the meanings of the French *roux* is "brown sauce." According to Jules Faine, the Haitian Creole *roux* means "rouge," or red—but he adds, "Ainsi, les mulâtres sont dénommés: moune rouge." (Mulattos are designated: red people.) Father Jules Daigle's Cajun dictionary defines *roux* as "flour browned in fat and used for thickening gravies, gombos, courtbouillon, etc." Creole cooks not only brown the flour but they also brown onion, garlic, and other vegetable seasonings to add to gravies. Browning the vegetables in this manner releases their sugar content, thus caramelizing the vegetables and giving them a sweeter taste. Since many of the cooks during the period of slavery were mulatto women, all of these definitions come together; following the African tradition, Creole cooks served with many of their main dishes delicious sauces made with the roux technique.[4]

Another example of an African cooking method is barbecue. "Africans often roasted meats and served them with a sauce; . . . throughout the New World, barbecues are very popular only in those countries which have or have had a sizable number of black people." Creole fried

3. Mendes, *The African Heritage Cookbook*, 44; Florence Borders, interview by the author, May 13, 1993.

4. Girard, *Cassell's French Dictionary* (London: Cassell, 1981), s.v. "roux"; Jules Faine, ed., *Dictionnaire français-créole* (Ottawa: Les Editions Lemeac, 1974), 402; Father Jules O. Daigle, ed., *A Dictionary of the Cajun Language* (Ann Arbor: Edwards Brothers, 1984), s.v. "roux."

chicken is another dish that follows the African technique: "the cook prepared the poultry by dipping it in a batter and deep fat frying it. . . . [Also]
throughout West Africa, it was a favorite practice to serve chicken,
grilled or fried, with a sauce, over rice." A variety of Creole poultry
dishes follow this tradition of adding a sauce to the main dish and serving
it with rice, including such New Orleans dishes as cookbook entries
Chicken Fricassee and Stewed Chicken with Brown Gravy and Stewed
Chicken with Red Gravy (author's recipe). In the same category, a Caribbean cookbook boasts Chicken Colombo, Poulet à la Creole, Arroz con
pollo, Chicken in Almond Sauce, Chicken and Pigeon Peas, and Chicken
Oriental. From Brazil there is Frango ao Molho Pardo, chicken in brown
sauce. Each of these dishes begins with a roux.[5]

Another West African method of food preparation used by Creole
cooks is deep-fat frying of meats, fritters, and a variety of fish and shell-
fish dishes. This African technique is one of the reasons for the particular
flavor of the Creole fried cuisine. Africans cooked "by steaming, baking,
stewing, roasting, or frying. . . . Meats were roasted, stewed, or fried. Although fish was sometimes smoked or pickled, it was usually fried or
stewed. A variety of fish stews and fish gumbos were made. . . . Green
vegetables were steamed, stewed, or added to sauces. Yams and other tu-
bers were boiled, steamed, or roasted. Breads were made by steaming,
frying or baking the dough. All of these methods of food preparation and
cooking were . . . followed in varying degrees by Africans in the New
World."[6]

One characteristic of Creole dishes common to Africa, the Caribbean, South America, and Louisiana is the hot spicy peppers found in
sauces and often added to dishes after cooking. Whether it is the extremely hot "pilli-pilli" of West Africa, the burning hot "Bonda Mam'
Jacques" ("Mme Jacques' behind") used in Martinique and Guadeloupe,
the very hot chili jalapeño and habanero peppers of the Caribbean and

5. Mendes, *African Heritage Cookbook*, 39–40; Gwen McKee, *The Little New Or-
leans Cookbook* (Baton Rouge: Quail Ridge Press, 1991), 48; Nathaniel Burton and
Rudy Lombard, *Creole Feast: 15 Master Chefs of New Orleans Reveal Their Secrets*
(New York: Random House, 1978), 150; Christopher Idone, *Cooking Caribe* (New
York: Clarkston N. Potter, 1992), 85–93; Myra Waldo, *Seven Wonders of the Cook-
ing World* (New York: Dodd, Mead, 1971), 325.

6. Mendes, *African Heritage Cookbook*, 44–5.

South America, or the hot, hot cayenne pepper of Louisiana, this tongue-tingling spiciness is the signature of Creole food.[7]

Various African methods are used to prepare many Creole seafood dishes. Shrimp Creole from Louisiana, Pilau de Camarones from the Dominican Republic, Shrimp Curry from Trinidad, and many other stewed shrimp dishes are all served with a sauce over steamed rice. Similarly prepared crab dishes include Stuffed Crabs of Louisiana, Crabes Farcis from Martinique-Guadeloupe, and Crab Matoutou from the Caribbean. Creole cooks use the same steaming, sautéing, and baking methods to create a host of stuffed seafoods, such as stuffed oysters, stuffed crawfish, stuffed redfish, and stuffed flounder. Seafood gumbos employ a combination of the methods in a single dish: first you make a roux, then sauté the shrimp and set them aside, then add various stocks to form the sauce, then add crabs or crabmeat and oysters and simmer, adding the sautéed shrimp just before serving. Some Louisiana seafood gumbos are flavored with a Choctaw Indian spice called filé, which also functions as a thickening agent. A similar dish from the Dominican Republic is Monlondrones con Camarones, or okra with shrimp. "In much of West Africa 'gombo' means okra." Okra is used in gumbos for thickening the sauce. The West Indian soup called Callaloo is much like the Louisiana gumbos, and recipes for it can be found in Trinidad, Jamaica, Grenada, Haiti, Martinique, and Guadeloupe. Both Louisiana gumbos and West Indian Callaloos come in several varieties, from the seafood type to that made from various greens.[8]

In addition to seafood, Creole cooks prepare a variety of bean dishes. As in West Africa, the beans are boiled and a spicy sauce is made from or combined with the beans. Louisiana's own Creole red beans and rice is cooked that way with the addition of a salt meat or sausage for seasoning. Add coconut milk and the dish is known as Arroz con Frijoles in the Dominican Republic. Congris, a specialty of Cuba, is also a version of red beans and rice. In Haiti they are called "Pois Rouge en Sauce" or

7. Harris, *Iron Pots*, 58; Bea Sandler, *The African Cookbook* (New York: World, 1970), xiv; Idone, *Cooking Caribe*, 133.
8. Idone, *Cooking Caribe*, 104, 197; Burton and Lombard, *Creole Feast*, 95; Elizabeth Lambert Ortiz, *The Complete Book of Caribbean Cooking* (New York: M. Evans, 1973), 59, 113; Harris, *Iron Pots*, 79; Sandler, *The African Cookbook*, 187.

"Pois et Riz Colles." In Guadeloupe they are called "Pois et Riz." In each case the sauce is seasoned with a type of meat, usually ham or pork sausage or bacon, and peppers, garlic, onion, bay leaves, and butter, with a roux made from flour and onions.[9]

Jambalaya and Mirliton are other Louisiana Creole dishes with Afro-Caribbean links. Jambalaya is said by one author to be an African dish, based on her identification of the word as a combination of jamba (ham) and paella (rice), the main ingredients. The French word for ham, "jambon," also works here as well as the description of the Spanish dish "paella." The *American Heritage Dictionary* defines *paella* as "a saffron-flavored Spanish dish made with varying combinations of rice, vegetables, meat, chicken, and seafood," and says the word comes from the old French *paelle*. This definition of paella is a good description of Jambalaya, with the addition of ham and spices. The Louisiana recipe calls for ham, hot sausage, shrimp, rice, tomatoes, green peppers, onions, garlic, and other spices. The dish from Puerto Rico known as "Camarones Guisados" is close to Jambalaya in ingredients, calling for ham, salt pork, shrimp, rice, green peppers, tomatoes, onion, garlic, and other spices. Mirliton (or "milliton," as the word is pronounced in New Orleans) is another dish that has similar recipes in the Caribbean. Known by various names such as "chayote, . . . christophine, chocho, . . . mango squash, xuxu, and vegetable pear, this mild flavored squash is used in everything from soups to main dishes. In some parts of the Caribbean, it is served on its own as in Salade de Christophines, or stuffed into its own shell, as in Gratin de Christophines." In Louisiana it is fried, stuffed, pickled, or used in salads.[10]

Panné Meat is a Louisiana Creole dish that has a bit of mystery to it. The French word "panné" is a slang word meaning "hard up." Panné Meat is fried, breaded meat—usually veal, pork, or chicken—made by dipping seasoned meat into beaten eggs and then into seasoned bread crumbs. Then the meat is fried to a deep golden brown. Alternatively, the name may be a variation on *painée*, Creole for "breaded." Whatever the case, this is a well-honored Creole dish, especially in New Orleans.[11]

9. Ortiz, *Caribbean Cooking*, 274, 286, 300, 302; Mendes, *African Heritage Cookbook*, 38.

10. McKee, *Little New Orleans Cookbook*, 51; Ortiz, *Caribbean Cooking*, 94; Harris, *Iron Pots*, 6; Leon E. Soniat Jr., *La Bouche Créole* (Gretna, La.: Pelican, 1985), 251.

11. Girard, *Cassell's*, s.v. "panne."

Some Creole dessert foods with Afro-Caribbean links are the plantain, banana, and certain pastries. The plantain is native to all the Caribbean islands, and the fried ripe plantain is a favorite Louisiana dish. These fritters were also a popular West African dessert; "bananas were often sliced, dipped in batter and fried in palm oil to make mouthwatering fritters." One finds recipes for Fried Ripe Plantains or Stuffed Baked Plantains in the Caribbean and in South America. Another fritter or fried doughnut is the beignet, which is the main attraction at a popular New Orleans tourist spot, the Café du Monde. Beignets are deep-fried African style, sprinkled with powdered sugar, and served hot with café au lait. This Creole dessert is called Marinades in Haiti, Baigner in Dominica, and Beignets de Banane in Martinique. In West Africa both banana and pineapple fritters are served as well as "fufu," a fritter made of yam paste. A very old New Orleans Creole dessert is the "Calas Chaud," which shows up in the nineteenth century in the street cries of the black female merchants who peddled them in the Vieux Carré. The Calas is a delicious rice dessert or rice ball served hot with a sprinkling of powdered sugar. A Nigerian dessert which is made in a similar manner, but with fewer spices, is Rice Balls. The praline, a Creole candy made from sugar, cream, and pecans, was supposedly invented by the cook of one Marshall Dupleses-Preslin (1598–1675) and remains a popular sweet in New Orleans. It can also be found in other parts of the southern United States. A similar candy is "Tooloom," which is found in Puerto Rico, Martinique, Barbados, Haiti, and other parts of the West Indies. These are made from brown sugar, molasses, ginger, and coconut, which is the main ingredient. Toolooms are kin to the "dulce de coco" or coconut candy which is found in Africa on the island of Mozambique. It is interesting to note that with the making of cakes and candies, the African, West Indian, and Louisiana Creole cooks all hawked their wares with chants about the foods. "The market places of West Africa were enlivened by the voices of women calling out praises of the cakes they had baked for sale. . . . They also sold the candies they made out of sugar cane, which they peeled and boiled to extract the syrupy liquid. When the syrup was fairly thick, the cook added coconut or chopped fruit. Later, many of these women both slave and free earned a tidy sum of money selling pralines, as these candies were called in the streets of Brazil and the United

States." Mr. Preslin's cook referred to earlier seems to have been one of these Creole candy makers.[12]

Creole cookery has an amazing legacy from four continents. It is no wonder that Creole food is so popular around the world. The excellent use of indigenous spices and African cooking methods combined with talent for developing the new from the old make Creole food a valuable resource with deep roots in the African diaspora and an important element in defining Creole culture.

12. Idone, *Cooking Caribe*, 34, 35, 148; Laurens van der Post, et al., *African Cooking* (New York: Time-Life Books, 1970), 86, 122; Soniat, *La Bouche Créole*, 225–44; Harris, *Iron Pots*, 163–4; Mendes, *African Heritage Cookbook*, 43.

12

Light, Bright, Damn *Near* White

Race, the Politics of Genealogy, and the Strange Case of Susie Guillory

ANTHONY G. BARTHELEMY

Because most whites believed in white supremacy, their
attitudes had a profound effect on the way Negroes
viewed themselves. Since white skin was glorified, since
whites had all of the power and most of the wealth and
education, many Negroes accepted the concept of the
goodness, purity, and sanctity of whiteness and the
degradation of blackness. Consequently, many of them
tried and a number succeeded in passing for white.
Mulatto women sometimes spurned unions with blacks
and welcomed white males because they were flattered
by the attentions they received from the "superior" race.
—John Blassingame, *Black New Orleans*

What is metaphysics? A white mythology which
assembles and reflects Western culture: the white man
takes his own mythology (that is, Indo-European
mythology), his *logos*—that is, the *mythos* of his idiom, for
the universal form of that which it is still his inescapable
desire to call Reason.

What is white mythology? It is metaphysics which has
effaced in itself that fabulous scene which brought it into
being, and which yet remains, active and stirring,
inscribed in white ink, an invisible drawing covered over
in the palimpsest.
—Jacques Derrida, "White Mythology"

From 1970 to 1983, the state of Louisiana held the distinction of being the only state in the Union to have a legally mandated mathematical formula for determining the race of its citizens: "In signifying race, a person having one-thirty-second or less of Negro blood shall not be deemed, described, or designated by any public official in the State of Louisiana as 'colored,' a 'mulatto,' a 'black,' a 'negro,' a 'griffe,' an 'Afro-American,' a 'quadroon,' a 'mestizo,' a 'colored person,' or a 'person of color.' "[1]

This 1970 law was repealed because of the ignominy surrounding the case of Susie Guillory Phipps, who, in a Jane Doe case, sued the state in 1982 to have the racial classification on her birth certificate changed from "colored" to "white." Proclaiming herself to be "all white"—a needless redundancy, if not an impossibility, since what had been legislated was the "*not* negro"—Guillory, described in the *New Orleans Times-Picayune* as "a nervous, olive complexioned, neatly dressed woman," avowed: "I was raised as a white child. I went to a white school. I married white twice." Her suit made headlines around the country, as newspapers everywhere expressed delighted shock that in 1982 Louisiana proved itself still backward enough to have that one-thirty-second rule for determining the race of its citizens. The *New York Times* editorialized: "What is most offensive about the Louisiana law, and racial typing anywhere, is its extreme bias in favor of whites. If society must make a distinction, at least let it split the difference evenly: a person is white if 51 percent white, black if 51 percent black. And let us move as quickly as possible toward the day when any distinction is no longer useful." With suitable Mardi Gras flourish, the *Times-Picayune* commented, "Measuring in precise fractions the contribution of different races over generations—racial mixture is said to have entered Mrs. Phipps' ancestry in the late 1760s—is best left to the successors of those who counted angels dancing on the head of a pin." In the *Washington Post*, Dorothy Gilliam remarked, "Instead of tut-tutting Susie Phipps, those of us who have been fooling ourselves into thinking that something had changed fundamentally in America ought to be thankful for the reminder that it hasn't. This story is as old as the nation."[2]

1. Louisiana Revised Statutes, title 42, sec. 267.

2. Ed Anderson, "Parents Raised Her as a 'White Child,' Woman Tells Court," *New Orleans Times-Picayune*, September 14, 1982; Editorial, *New York Times*, September 26, 1982; Editorial, *New Orleans Times-Picayune*, September 23, 1982; Dorothy Gilliam, *Washington Post*, October 2, 1982.

All of the rhetoric in America's newspapers, however, could not possibly unravel the complicated web of Susie Guillory's case. Gilliam came
closest to appreciating its complexity in her comment that the story was
as old as the nation; indeed, this is a story even older than the nation, and
one that the very idea of "news" cannot properly comprehend or expli-
cate. That the story *was* news reveals the irony of its intrusion into the
American consciousness, since American culture at every level exhibits its
race consciousness. Even the drafting of the Constitution required discussions of race. Every modern presidential election since Mrs. Hoover
had Mrs. DePriest to tea has had a racial component, as did almost all
earlier elections that confronted problems with Native Americans, African Americans, or both. In *Playing in the Dark: Whiteness and the Literary
Imagination*, Toni Morrison maintains: "As for the culture, the imagina-
tive and historical terrain upon which early American writers journeyed
is in large measure shaped by the presence of the racial other. Statements
to the contrary, insisting on the meaninglessness of race to the American
identity, are themselves full of meaning. The world does not become
raceless or will not become unracialized by assertion. The act of enforcing racelessness in literary discourse is itself a racial act." Although Morrison is referring specifically to literary discourse, the truth of her
observation should be apparent to all who heard George Bush claim that
the Willie Horton theme of his 1988 campaign had nothing to do with
race. For many contemporary Americans, race remains the great unspo-
ken, but it has yet to become the unthought, the unfeared. Race still
shapes the American consciousness and the unconscious as well. Susie
Guillory's story, in spite of its local peculiarities, is America's story.[3]

II

> I ain't black. You can't put me black. I don't know what you'd call it.
> —*Victor Guillory*

3. Toni Morrison, *Playing in the Dark: Whiteness and the Literary Imagination*
(New York: Vintage Books, 1993), 46. On June 12, 1929, Mrs. Herbert Hoover
invited the wife of Chicago congressman Oscar DePriest (who served from 1929
to 1935) to tea at the White House. Mrs. Hoover had invited all congressional
wives to tea that summer. Mrs. DePriest attended the last tea with five other congressional wives who had agreed in advance to sip tea with the African American
guest. The uproar over the event was equal to that caused by Theodore Roosevelt's
dinner with Booker T. Washington in the White House, October 16, 1901.

The infamous Louisiana one-thirty-second law advances ten different terms to describe the condition of being nonwhite in Louisiana, from *black* to *quadroon* with several categories between. In 1910 the Louisiana Supreme Court went to great and ludicrous length to describe all the possibilities for descendants of Africans:

> We do not think there could be any serious denial of the fact that in Louisiana the words "mulatto," "quadroon," and "octoroon" are of as definite meaning as the word "man" or "child," and that, among educated people at least, they are as well and widely known. There is also the less widely known word "griff," which, in this state, has a definite meaning, indicating the issue of a negro and a mulatto. The person too black to be a mulatto and too pale in color to be a negro is a griff. The person too dark to be a white, and too bright to be a griff is a mulatto. The quadroon is distinctly whiter than the mulatto. Between these different shades, we do not believe there is much, if any, difficulty in distinguishing.[4]

The designations themselves reflect Louisiana's unique Latin history, a history that distinguishes the state from the rest of the slaveholding South as well as from the nation: "Louisiana is heir to both the rigid Anglo-American and the fluid Latin American patterns of race classification. Under Spanish and French rule in the eighteenth century, free mulattos held a distinct intermediate position between black slaves and the white population."[5] These distinctions occurred and were necessary in part because of the public acceptance of interracial sex and the open system of concubinage that existed in Louisiana at least until the antebellum period.[6] Joan M. Martin's pioneering work on *plaçage* documents the level of acceptance of these arrangements and their contractual nature.[7] Regardless of the legal nature of these interracial relationships,

4. Cited in Raymond T. Diamond and Robert J. Cottrol, "Codifying Caste: Louisiana's Racial Classification Scheme and the Fourteenth Amendment," *Loyola Law Review* 29 (1983): 280.

5. Ibid., 270. Munro Edmonson, an anthropologist from Tulane University, makes the same assertion; see Lionel Trillin, "American Chronicles: Black or White," *New Yorker*, April 14, 1986, 66.

6. See Paul F. Lachance, "The Formation of a Three-Caste Society: Evidence from Wills in Antebellum New Orleans," *Social Science History* 18 (1994): 211–42.

7. See John W. Blassingame, *Black New Orleans: 1860–1880* (Chicago: University of Chicago Press, 1973), 18–20.

records demonstrate their existence from the earliest days of the colonial period until the Civil War. The offspring of Africans born in the Louisiana colony and most especially the offspring of mixed European and African unions, along with the growing numbers of endogamously married free people of mixed race, helped create a distinctly different group of people who identified themselves as either "Creole" or *gens de couleur*.[8]

The complexity that surrounds the word *Creole* reflects the intricacies of social status and Creole identity, and of course, the inclusiveness of the term itself. Historians point out that most free people of color, *les gens de couleur libre*, were racially mixed. John Blassingame explains, "Social classes grew up around color primarily because a mulatto was generally a free man (77 percent of the free Negroes in 1860 were mulattoes) and a black man was almost always a slave (74 percent of the slaves in 1860 were black). In fact color was closely correlated with status: 80 percent of all blacks were slaves and 70 percent of all mulattoes were free

8. Although the meaning of the term "Creole" is still disputed, I use it here to mean people of French and/or Spanish and/or African ancestry in Louisiana, especially in and around New Orleans. Creoles of color need not be light-skinned but generally are thought to be; they need not be Catholic, but frequently are. Creoles did not use English as their primary language until English replaced French or Creole French as the dominant language in New Orleans. See the entry for "Creole" in the *Harvard Encyclopedia of American Ethnic Groups* (Cambridge, Mass.: Belknap Press of Harvard University, 1980). Also see Gwendolyn Midlo Hall, *Africans in Colonial Louisiana: The Development of Afro-Creole Culture in the Eighteenth Century* (Baton Rouge: Louisiana State University Press, 1992), 157–9; Arnold R. Hirsch and Joseph Logsdon, eds., *Creole New Orleans: Race and Americanization* (Baton Rouge: Louisiana State University Press, 1992), 60–1, 133–4, 170–83; Virginia R. Domínguez, *White by Definition: Social Classification in Creole Louisiana* (New Brunswick, N.J.: Rutgers University Press, 1986), 12–5, 93–4, 121–5.

Technically, *mulatto* means a person with one black and one white parent, although it is frequently used to describe light-skinned African Americans regardless of their parents' race. I personally prefer not to use the term because of its derivation from the Latin and Spanish words for "mule." The refusal of some to accept African Americans as Creoles reflects racist attitudes that constantly attempt to deny black people names that confer dignity upon them. Throughout this essay, *Creole* unmodified will be used to designate those people of African and European descent, or pure African descent who culturally identify themselves as Creole. When necessary for clarity, modifiers will be used. A "white Creole" is taken to be a person of French and/or Spanish descent born in the Louisiana colony.

men."⁹ Yet none of these categories had unbreachable boundaries. Some black men were free; some mulattoes, slaves. Some slaves were Creole, and after 1803 some freedmen were African American as opposed to Afro-French. Regardless of skin color, Creoles fused African and French culture, language, and customs to create an amalgamation that was uniquely New World and singularly New Orleanian. These Creoles took pride in their mixed culture, and some fetishized their European appearance.

But we must not mistake the fetishizing of whiteness outside of its particular context. Simply stated, people of mixed African-European descent gained privileges not allowed to people of pure African descent, free or slave. That some Creoles of the European phenotype reflected the white supremacist attitudes of those of unmixed European ancestry should surprise no one familiar with the psychological profile of those living under harsh oppressive conditions. The separation of the somewhat privileged from the unprivileged consequently did take place along a color line, with some Creoles drawing the line as rigidly as white society. According to Blassingame, the color line erected by Creoles found approval and encouragement from white Creoles and Anglo-Americans: "This separation was encouraged by the whites as a means of dividing the Negroes and making it easier to control them. . . . By law the light-skinned free Negro was barred from mingling with the dark-skinned slave, and he sometimes held slaves. The education, wealth, occupations, and refinement of mulattoes also acted as a barrier to their intercourse with the poorer, less-skilled, and less-educated blacks." This comment, however, reinforces the obvious, that separation was neither complete nor entirely voluntary, otherwise legislation would not have been necessary to compel it. "The strength of the family ties among Afro-Creoles, slave and free, black and mixed blood, was recognized by the syndic [police] of the Cabildo of New Orleans" writes Gwendolyn Midlo Hall of the city in the eighteenth century. These strong family ties among people of color, slave and free, existed from the colonial period in the eighteenth century through the antebellum American period in the nineteenth. During the era leading up to the Civil War, the Louisiana legislature

9. Blassingame, *Black New Orleans*, 21. It seems clear that Blassingame's use of *mulatto* includes all light-skinned and mixed-race people, and not only those who have one black and one white parent.

attempted, with mixed results, to curtail the privileges of free people of color and limit contact between them and their enslaved brethren.[10]

In spite of the familial and social contacts that did take place, however, the separation of people of African descent fostered by law, costume, and sometimes by color-prejudiced Creoles endured into the twentieth century. Creole Aline St. Julien documents this social division in her pamphlet "Colored Creole," as does Virginia R. Domínguez in her book *White by Definition*. Guillory herself unwittingly demonstrated the reality of this separation in her testimony before the court. Asked by her lawyer when she first thought she might not be considered white, Guillory replied:

> When I made my First Communion . . . I wondered what was wrong, but I didn't know. I was six years old, and we were in the church yard, and all of the little white children was [*sic*] in the front, and I was in the back, and then all of the little black people was [*sic*] in the back. Well, this black lady came and grabbed me by my arm and she pushed me. She shifted me. She put her little girl ahead of me . . . and my mother came and said, "You cannot move my child." . . . Well, I made my Confirmation there. . . . And it was the same way, always in the back of the white but ahead of the black.

Like her uncle Victor, Susie Guillory here expresses a common experience of Creoles of color, not white and not black but somewhere in between. But Guillory, like many others, chose to identify with her oppressors rather than fight them. She became obsessed not only with looking white but with being *named* white. She spent more than $40,000 to be so designated. She even rejected the opportunity to have "colored" removed from her birth certificate because she wanted more than not to be designated colored. She wanted to be certified white, in spite of the fact that the legislation designated only the "not colored," the "not mulatto," or the "not Negro." Guillory wanted the state that devised the system of racist oppression and degradation to verify that she was more than not one of the despised.[11]

10. Ibid., 21–2; Hall, *Africans in Colonial Louisiana*, 220.
11. Aline St. Julien, *Colored Creole: Color Conflict and Confusion in New Orleans* (New Orleans: Ahidiana Hobari, 1977); cited in Trillin, "American Chronicles," 74.

But the state offered no such validation. Like the Ethiopian of yore, Guillory could not wash herself white, and the state refused her ablution. In the process of verifying the legitimacy of Guillory's racial designation as "colored," however, the state dispelled one of the most enduring myths of American life: that the collective African American past and personal genealogy cannot be recovered because of the dearth of documentary evidence. In order to prove that Guillory was what she claimed not to be, the state introduced into the trial "two large cardboard boxes full of exhibits—dozens of pages of depositions" and a genealogy documenting Guillory's family back to 1762. The attorneys stunned Guillory and the public by revealing the names of her paternal great-great-great-great-grandparents. Much has been made of the state's ability to find Guillory's great-great-great-great-grandmother, an emancipated slave named Margarita, freed by her master, Guillory's great-great-great-great-grandfather Jean Gregoire Guillory. Yet there seems to have been little reaction—rather, almost total indifference—to the discovery of Jean Gregoire Guillory.[12]

By tracing Guillory's ancestors back to 1762 the state subverted the myth of the unrecoverable Creole and African American past and revealed how genealogy reflects America's and Louisiana's racist history. In fact, exploring Guillory's case reveals the interesting intersection of patriarchy, race, and gender. The absence of attention to Jean Gregoire Guillory illustrates how disinterested America is in white fathers and how interested it is in black—no matter how phenotypically white—sexuality. Good ol' boy Guillory got it on with his slave mistress and now *her* black blood has bubbled up to ruin the life of innocent Susie, a tragic mulatto romance metaleptically extending and duplicating itself into the twentieth century. Susie Guillory's case is the ultimate postemancipation reiteration of the child following the condition of the mother. Jean Gregoire finds absolution in his attempted manumission of Margarita, but the freed slave nevertheless returns from the grave to make her great-great-great-great-granddaughter "sick." "When I found out about the slave was last March," Guillory said, "and when Jack [Westholz] told me about this Margarita person I was so sick. I was so sick."[13]

12. Ibid., 65.
13. *New York Times*, September 30, 1982. Jack Westholz was chief of the New Orleans section of the General Counsel of the Louisiana Department of Health and Human Resources at the time of Guillory's suit.

What could possibly sicken Guillory upon learning of Margarita's existence? When Jean Gregoire died, Margarita had to pay his white children for herself and her children to secure their freedom, the white children actually owning their half-brothers and sisters. Was Susie Guillory proud of this behavior by her distant white relatives? Was she sickened by this? What were her feelings about the resourcefulness of Margarita the ex-slave who managed to challenge in court for her and her children's right to freedom? How ironic that Guillory emulates this "Margarita person" by challenging the state in order to repudiate Margarita's accomplishment. In the meantime, Jean Gregoire rests in peace, his memory undisturbed, his characteristically male behavior beyond reproach.

Unsurprisingly, Guillory, her lawyers, the state, and all the reports failed to recognize the gender issue in the case. Men, white men, had in the past and up to 1982 manipulated the racial classification system to their own advantage and economic gain. In 1808 the Louisiana Civil Code permitted the right to prove paternal descent only to children who were "free and white." Free illegitimate children of color could prove parental descent of a "father of colour only." Illegitimate children of slave mothers and white fathers had no right to prove paternal descent. Thus white men were absolved by law of any fiscal responsibility for their children. "For an illegitimate child to acquire any rights to inherit from his genitor, his genitor first has to acknowledge him as his child." Paternal acknowledgment makes an illegitimate child a "natural child" and enables him to inherit part of his father's estate. To deny illegitimate colored children the right to establish their white paternity, or to seek paternal acknowledgment, is to make it nearly impossible for them to inherit from him.[14]

Moreover, the state limited the rights of white men to acknowledge paternity freely, and it also severely restricted the amount of gifts and bequests that white men could make to their illegitimate children or their mistresses. Even into the twentieth century Louisiana restricted the methods by which white men could acknowledge their illegitimate children and the amount offspring or lovers could be given or bequeathed. Baptismal records from the Catholic Church reveal its complicity with the state in protecting white men by not identifying the fathers of illegitimate children in baptismal registries, in which for people of color the

14. Domínguez, *White by Definition*, 63.

routine was to record the name of the mother alone. The only pressure on the fathers came from social censure, and there seems not to have been enough of that to put an end to interracial sexual liaisons. Thus free of ecclesiastical censure and legal demand to claim responsibility for their children, white men enjoyed the kind of sexual license that moral commentators and politicians attribute to black men in the twentieth century.

Apparently great-great-great-great-granddad Guillory attempted to emancipate his mistress and children, but their price nevertheless enriched his estate and his legitimate heirs because the state refused to recognize Jean Gregoire's actions to emancipate. Wittingly or unwittingly, the father thus generously provided for his white children by leaving four black children as vendable chattel. Furthermore, Margarita, stigmatized both by her race and by the state for not being the wife of her children's father—the state would not permit or recognize such a marriage even had it been desired by the father—had to rely upon her own resources to protect herself in a legal system that had been designed to accommodate and reward the racist patriarchy that created it. Margarita's success at buying her and her children's freedom is nothing short of remarkable, especially in light of the disposition of nineteenth- and twentieth-century Louisiana court cases in which paternity and race were primary issues, cases not unlike the one that Margarita's great-great-great-great-granddaughter would file to repudiate the freedwoman's achievement.[15]

Yet the sexual license white Creoles enjoyed betrayed them and became the instrument to impugn their racial purity and their right to exercise the privileges of patriarchy in postbellum America. When the specter of black men voting and sharing political power in Reconstruction governments began to haunt white men in New Orleans, their cry for racial purity became more shrill. White Creoles who participated in *plaçage* or otherwise condoned miscegenation found themselves being accused of being less white, less pure than their puritan Anglo-American compatriots. White Creole anger at the victories of proponents of black citizenship and suffrage during Reconstruction turned to rage when George Washington Cable's *The Grandissimes* appeared in 1880. In the novel, Cable condemned white Creoles for their lax sexual morality in counte-

15. For an interesting discussion of Louisiana court cases that litigated paternity and bequests, see Domínguez, *White by Definition*, 62–89.

nancing sexual liaisons between white men and black women and for the
failure of these men to assume responsibility for the offspring of those
relationships. In 1890 the rage at Cable turned to hysteria when the author hinted broadly in *Encyclopedia Britannica* that white Creoles might
be less than pure white: "Their better class does not offer to the eye that
unpleasing evidence of gross admixture of race which distinguishes those
Latin-American communities around the borders of the adjacent seas;
and the name they have borrowed from those regions [Creole] does not
imply, *any more than it excludes*, a departure from a pure double line of
Latin descent" (emphasis added). Continuing, Cable wrote:

> The first settlers of New Orleans were such men as colonies in America
> were generally made of when planted by royal commercial enterprise,
> and such wives as could be gathered haphazard from the ranks of Indian
> allies, African slave cargoes, and the inmates of French houses of cor-
> rection. As time passed, gentler and often better blood was infused by
> the advent of the filles à la cassette, by victims of lettres-de-cachet by
> the cadets of noble families, holding land grants or military commis-
> sions, by Spanish officials glad to strengthen their influence in the col-
> ony through matrimonial alliances, and by royalists fleeing the terrors
> of the French Revolution.[16]

Threatened as they were by the tarbrush, white Creoles who had
previously found sexual alliances with nonwhites inconsequential now
discovered that their prerogatives literally denigrated them and their
families. The surest way to protect themselves from the insinuation of
taint was to cover their tracks, to deny their consanguinity with their
Creole brethren on the other side of the color line. Thus, in 1908, Louisiana made interracial concubinage a felony. White Creoles found it necessary to create the fantasy that Europeans and Africans, and their
descendants, lived absolutely apart, in a kind of apartheid state. And most
fantastic of all, white Creoles tried to convince themselves and everyone
else that all those people whom the French and Spanish called "mulatto"
or "octoroon" had been generated spontaneously and shared neither language, culture, or genes with the whites who fathered them and then legislated absolution for patriarchal indifference and irresponsibility. This

---

16. George Washington Cable, "New Orleans," *Encyclopedia Britannica*, 9th ed.
For interesting statistics on interracial relationships during this period, see Lachance, "Formation of a Three-Caste Society."

disavowal and hypocrisy reflected white Creoles' most primeval fear, that they would be made to share inferior status and debasement with those of their own blood whom they themselves so condemned. The white Creoles then faced a postbellum world more threatening than that faced by their Anglo-American counterparts who had cringed at the social changes brought on by Reconstruction: "In the midst of this convulsion, the creole was caught up not simply in a general southern explosion of antiblack fanaticism, but as well in a peculiar complication which once again set him apart. The American Louisianians, or indeed any other southerners anywhere, could hold to their intolerance secure in the generally acknowledged racial purity of their own group. But the creoles add to the common white man's rejection of the black this additional spur to hatred: they might be confused with blacks."[17]

The provisions that existed in Louisiana law to limit a child's right to knowledge of paternal descent, while originally designed for economic reasons, became more important in protecting white Creoles from the stigma of knowing their colored brothers, sisters, and collateral relatives. Ignorance became then a vital weapon in the white Creoles' hysterical quest for racial purity; they would henceforth pretend not to know their own and continue legally to absolve themselves of responsibility.

III

> How do I know? One of my ancestors may have jumped the fence.
> —*Warren G. Harding*

Susie Guillory's petition to the court, in effect, challenged the official ignorance of the state that had endorsed patriarchal indulgence and indifference. Of course, Guillory was not the first to petition the courts for a change of racial designation, but an examination of several important cases reveals a startling relationship between gender and legal redress.

17. Hirsch and Logsdon, *Creole New Orleans*, 173. In various periods, both colonial and American, all interracial sexual contacts including concubinage were illegal, although such laws were rarely enforced. Except briefly during Reconstruction from 1870 to 1894, interracial marriage was illegal in Louisiana from 1807 to 1972, when the United States Supreme Court declared statutes against interracial marriage unconstitutional. The Spanish administration that governed Louisiana from 1768 to 1803 generally prohibited interracial marriage but would grant dispensations.

Nothing demonstrates this relationship more clearly than the genesis of the famous 1970 Louisiana law that established the one-thirty-second standard. Prior to 1970, a citizen of Louisiana was designated black if s/he had "a traceable amount" of black blood. The traceable-amount standard prevailed throughout most of the South well into the twentieth century. Louisiana's 1970 law, it was thought, grew out of an attempt to liberalize the state's law to a "more reasonable" formula. Even though this "liberalization" made Louisiana's racial designation law more stringent than Hitler's Nuremberg law, the formula was certainly less rigid than the traceable-amount designation.[18] Inherent in all of these formulae, of course, is the fact that a person is tainted, made less human, by having the traceable amount of black blood. Even the word itself implies that the black blood has left its trace, has visibly marked the person—perhaps with the mark of Ham.

To remove this stigma from one who had no visible trace, however, proved to be the principal catalyst for revising the old statute. When a male, who like Susie Guillory believed himself to be white, was denied by the Division of Vital Records a birth certificate designating his son as white, this as-yet-unidentified man was able to rely upon the assistance of a known segregationist to have the law changed.[19] The father, it turned out, was approximately one-one-hundred-twenty-eighth (1/128) black; his son, who was denied a birth certificate designating him white, was approximately one-two-hundred-fifty-sixth, traceless traceable amounts. The lawyer attempted to have the law changed, and according to the *New York Times*, had to "hassle" because some legislators wanted to codify one-one-hundred-twenty-eighth, seven generations, as the law. He succeeded in reducing it to one-thirty-second, or five generations. That success permitted his client to obtain what was denied Guillory, the all-important "white" designation.[20]

Even if this story is not true, the myth of the law's genesis remains significant. A white man would not allow two other males whom he be-

18. The Nuremberg law declared anyone who was one-sixteenth Jewish to be officially a Jew.

19. My sources for this information are the *New York Times*, September 18, 1982, and the *New Yorker*, April 14, 1986, 70. I have spoken to several lawyers who all agree that the story as reported is accurate, but because of the sensitive nature of the case, written verification remains elusive.

20. Trillin, "American Chronicles," 70.

lieved to be white to suffer the racism and deprivation that he and his fellow racists perpetuate for nonwhites. "What I was trying to do was help a white person get a white birth certificate," the *New York Times* quotes the lawyer as saying. "Whatever you feel on the race question," he propounded, "it's a fact that white people don't want to be known as colored." Most important here was the desire to permit the son to follow the condition of the father. What in fact exists is at least three generations of paternal acknowledgment of sons. Significantly and ironically, however, the son inherits the reported trace from the father (the family name was one of the 250 French surnames that "race clerks" at the Vital Records had "flagged" for investigation of possible black ancestry), and the father feels he must act to erase or nullify that tragic one-two-hundred-fifty-sixth part. But father and son are ultimately spared the economic, political, and other direct consequences of their trace of blackness. If the case of Guillory is the ultimate reiteration of the child following the condition of the mother, the genesis of the 1970 law merely continues the South's good-ol'-boy tradition. The story, even if apocryphal, enshrines the belief that white men can shape the law to meet their own needs.[21]

In addition to revealing the power of white males, the subtext of this story points up the arbitrariness of racial classification in and out of Louisiana. At some point, behavior and culture substitute for race. A person enters a different cultural milieu and successfully reproduces that culture's behavioral dictates. How dark or light, how phenotypically European or African that person may be becomes irrelevant. This, of course, distinguishes Creoles from other African Americans, light or dark, because Creoles participated in and helped create a Eurocentric culture that assimilated African traditions. The melange equipped the Creole with the appropriate cultural behavior for assimilation by the European culture because his milieu had already been shaped by European culture and white Creole culture had been shaped by African culture. And the interchange did not stop even as Anglo-Americans and postbellum European immigrants attempted to impose a more rigid divide between the cultures. The lawyer who needed the traceable-amount law modified to one-thirty-second realized the significance of behavior and culture, for

21. *New York Times*, September 30, 1982. See Trillin, "American Chronicles," 70; Domínguez, *White by Definition*, 36–51.

had the client demonstrated behavior unacceptable to white culture his trace would have remained significant and visible. Race, therefore, embraces culture, and racism denies other cultures' validity. Efforts to classify phenotype reflect efforts to justify cultural domination. One sees this phenomenon carried to its horrific and sophistical conclusion in the efforts of various cultural groups to suppress one another regardless of racial similarities; thus Japanese and Koreans, Catholic and Protestant Celts, and Serbs and Croats willingly slaughter in the name of racial purity or dominance. In the case of Creoles, race allowed Anglo-Americans to subvert the cultural dominance of the Francophone inhabitants of Louisiana with the support and collusion of those who sacrificed their culture to be able to participate in the rising hegemony of Americanism.[22]

Dominance, then, shapes the history of racial classification and the Guillory story as well, for white male dominance created and promoted a patriarchal system in which men would not be held accountable for their actions. During slavery, moreover, infractions of the legal contract of marriage could in fact become enormously lucrative. That same patriarchy permitted Jean Gregoire Guillory the pleasure of a black mistress but left her with the burden of rescuing his children by her from those of his children who enjoyed the legal protection of marriage. Male dominance motivated the effort to find legal protection for a man and his son from the injustices of racial oppression. Several important twentieth-century legal cases amply demonstrate the power of racist patriarchy to sustain its power and maintain its privileges. As we shall see, in each case the source of the alarm is matrilineal, even in the one case where the mother is indisputably white.

In 1938 a civil court annulled the marriage of Cyril Sunseri to Verna Cassagne on the grounds that she was a person of color, and interracial marriages were illegal in the state of Louisiana at that time. Sunseri claimed that Cassagne's great-great-grandmother was colored. Cassagne maintained that the female ancestor was Indian, not Negro. On appeal, Cassagne prevailed because the judge found, in part, that all of the defendant's female ancestors had married white men from the time of the

22. Hirsch and Logsdon, *Creole New Orleans*, 96–7. See also Diamond and Cottrol, "Codifying Caste," and Hirsch and Logsdon, *Creole New Orleans*, 98, 173.

great-great-grandmother: "It is not disputed that Leander Ducre, the great-great-grandfather, Anatole Cousin the great-grandfather, and Joaquin J. Cusachs, the grandfather of Verna Cassagne, were white men. Nor is it disputed that Steve Cassagne, the father of Verna Cassagne, is a white man." Further, the court proclaimed, "Defendant's ancestors worshipped among the white Catholics in Lacombe. Her mother Stella Cusachs was christened apparently as a white child in the Catholic Church. . . . Stella Cusachs was married in New Orleans, on July 15, 1916, to Steve Cassagne, a white man. When about to be delivered of defendant, she went to Charity Hospital and was assigned to a white maternity ward, and on May 8, 1917, according to the certificate of the hospital, she gave birth to a white female child (the defendant)."[23]

Cassagne's forefathers and the legal marriage of the previous four generations saved her from reclassification and annulment. These documented white Creole men protected their daughter from falling victim to patriarchal privilege. The combined power of the fathers enforced their will on the white male who married their female descendant. The precedent of behavioral and cultural traditions sustained the judgment. What may on the surface look like a defeat of a white male in fact validates patriarchy and its triumph. Four generations of white men cannot be wrong. Guillory could produce only one white male in five generations, and he, in fact, certified her nonwhite status. The court in 1982 acted much as it did in 1938. Guillory with one white father follows the condition of the mother. No white men suffer here.

The mother again plays a vital role in providing the trace that dooms her offspring in the case of *Treadaway* v. *Louisiana State Board of Health* in 1952. Grant T. Treadaway sued to have the racial designation on his mother's death certificate changed from "colored" to "white." The state had relied on information provided by the brother of the plaintiff when it recorded the death in 1930. While the racial designation of the mother was the central issue of the case, the judge found it germane to include in the public record his doubts about the race of the plaintiff's patrilineal ancestors:

> There are in the record several other certificates showing the deaths of several other Treadaways who live in the area of Plaquemines Parish

23. *Sunseri* v. *Cassagne*, 191 La. 209, 185 So. 1 (1938), 211, 220.

ANTHONY G. BARTHELEMY

from which relator's [Treadaway's] father had migrated to St. Tammany
Parish, and in practically all of those the race of the various persons
named Treadaway was shown as colored. However, we are not concerned with the question of the race of relator's father, since on his
death certificate his name is shown as white, and no effort has been
made to change that entry.

It is interesting to note that though the race of relator's father is not
at issue, relator took pains to attempt to show that the Thomas Jefferson
Treadaway who was his father's father, and who had lived in Plaquemines
Parish for many years, was not the same Thomas Jefferson Treadaway
who had also lived in the same locality of Plaquemines Parish and who,
according to much evidence in the record was colored.

There is in the record considerable oral testimony of many witnesses
from the Parish of St. Tammany. Among the witnesses we find reputable
citizens whose testimony is that they were familiar with the mother and
the father of the relator and that they always considered them as white.
On the other hand, other reputable citizens testified that they were also
familiar with Daniel Treadaway and with his wife, Anna, and that they
always considered them as colored.[24]

For the judge the real issue was the absence of testifying fathers.
Verna Cassagne had had generations of white men to protect her from
the blemish of her foremothers' uncertain past. Treadaway, according to
the judge, struggled to silence all those colored Treadaways from claiming him. Treadaway left the court more sullied than he entered, for the
judge cast doubts on Treadaway's father and grandfather and all Treadaways from Plaquemines Parish. The patriarchal culture that the judge
was sworn to defend denies black men the right to defend their families
against the ruthless and arbitrary power of white men. Whether the
Treadaway males would want to support their descendant in his quest to
deny them cannot be known; nonetheless the state renders the fathers
impotent, reenacting the oppression that stripped black fathers of patriarchal prerogatives. And as the fathers are rendered powerless, the
mother becomes the site of the stain. Like poor women who were blamed
for the feminization of poverty even while Presidents Reagan and Bush
presided over the greatest upward redistribution of wealth in the coun-

24. *Treadaway v. Louisiana State Board of Health*, 61 So. 2nd (1952), 735, 738.

try's history, Treadaway's mother is made by the judge to bear the blame for blighting her son.

More bizarre than the Guillory case, *Robert Green* v. *City of New Orleans (Department of Public Health)* reveals just how inhumane the race laws of Louisiana really were. Robert Green attempted to have the racial designation of Jacqueline Ann Henley changed from white to colored in order to adopt her, since state law prohibited Green, an African American, from adopting a white child. Henley's white mother, Ruby Henley Preuc, terminally ill from a brain tumor, left her child with her sister, the child's maternal aunt, Mrs. Harold McBride. When Henley was twenty-one months old, two months *before* her mother's death, McBride sought to give up the child to the Department of Welfare because "[McBride] felt that it [Henley] was a Negro and she could no longer permit her to remain in her home, since the neighbors were beginning to comment about the medium brown color of the child's skin." Said the aunt of her niece: "She didn't fit in my family, she was too dark." The aunt confided to a welfare worker that "remarks were passed that the child possibly was a nigger." The neighbors' racist comments reflected their contempt for Preuc, who worked in a "Negro saloon" and who never revealed the name of the father.[25]

The court refused Green's petition in part because the evidence "left room for doubt" and because an anthropologist who testified that the child's father was not white also claimed that he could not determine if the child's father was Negro until the child was older. The court held: "The final cause of law is the welfare of society. The rule that misses this aim cannot permanently justify its existence." The welfare of society, the court determined, would be better served by waiting until the child "was more developed and mature." The court decided to allow the child to live without family in order not to make a mistake on racial designation. The welfare of society would be threatened by allowing Robert Green to adopt a white child or even to adopt a child who may not be white. Without white fathers present to attest to the child's "authenticity," the court acted *in loco parentis*. It could not possibly allow Robert Green the power to protect the child from the state's inhumane indifference. To allow that

25. *Robert Green* v. *City of New Orleans (Department of Public Health)*, Louisiana, 88 So. 2nd, 77–9.

would acknowledge the rights of a black man to be a father, which would be contrary to all of the traditions of the patriarchal state.[26]

In its opinion, the court observed: "We feel compelled to remark at the inception of this opinion that we were completely fascinated by the novel-like tenor of this record." Could the court be thinking of the 1948 novel *Raintree County*? Obviously the entire tradition of the tragic mulatto comes into play here, and it seems that the court wishes to continue the romance by creating its own tragic mulatto. Nor should we misconstrue the role of the mother in this drama. Left to die in the Home for Incurables, this white mother is as spotted as any black mother, for her behavior brought shame upon her and her kin. She openly socialized with blacks, apparently to such a degree as to allow the neighbors to speculate that the child's father was African American. The actions of McBride condemn her sister as McBride seeks to protect herself, Mr. McBride, and their home from the taint Preuc carried in. This child follows the condition of the mother, forced to suffer a life of indignity and indifference because of her racial ambiguity and her mother's sexual indiscretion if not crime.[27]

In the case of *Joseph Jules Schlumbrecht Jr.* v. *Louisiana State Board of Health* the inherent power of patriarchy can readily be perceived. In 1970 Schlumbrecht, a white male, wanted a copy of his daughter's birth cer-

26. Ibid., 81. The court relied heavily on the precedent of the *Sunseri* v. *Cassagne* case in reaching its decision. The anthropologist told the court: "There are three characteristics which are distinctly Negro in this child. One is the lip seam, the division between the integumental lip, the skin lip above here and the mucous lip, is clearly marked, the little ridge; and secondly, the distinctly small, delicate ears; and third, perhaps the most indicative of all, there are concentrations of pigments in diagnostic positions of the anatomy.

"While I could get these three characteristics occurring in an individual who had no Negro ancestry, it would be so rare—we have records of it—it would be so rare as not to be considered at all probable." Ibid., 79.

The dissenting judge wrote in his opinion: "We know that the father was not white or Caucasian because on that point the anthropologist . . . says he has no doubt at all. His only possible doubt was as to whether the race of the father might be something other than Negro, though as I will show hereafter, he found Negro characteristics and did not find any other characteristics." Ibid., 81.

27. Ibid., 78.

tificate, on which her racial classification was white, but the state withheld the certificate pending an investigation of the mother's racial heritage. Perhaps the mother's surname was one of those 250 suspicious French surnames flagged for possible black ancestry. The court found in favor of the plaintiff, writing:

> The defendant [the State Board of Health] does not contend that there is any trace of Negro or colored blood in the paternal line of Gwendolyn Ann [Schlumbrecht's daughter]. However, in the maternal line, we are confronted with numerous instances in which ancestors are designated as "white," "free persons of color," others as "mulattos," and still others as "colored." In some instances, children born of the same parents do not all have the same racial designation. These numerous inconsistencies suggest that the words "mulatto," "free persons of color" and "colored" were in at least some instances incorrectly used by the person or persons responsible for the racial entries made in the public records.[28]

While this case appears similar to the Green case, it more closely resembles the Treadaway and Sunseri cases. For the question remains, how does the court address ambiguities in racial designation? In the cases of Sunseri and Schlumbrecht, the court seems confused by the meaning of colored or mulatto, while in the case of Treadaway the court demonstrates no such confusion. Again, the appearance of white fathers dispels all confusion. Lexical difficulties exist only when the ambiguity reflects society's trouble with seeing colored when it wants to see white. How could a court of white men tell another white man that his marriage was legally void and his child was tarnished beyond hope? White fathers can rescue their children; unfortunately for Henley, the man who tried to claim her was black, and like Dred Scott he had no rights that any white man was required to respect. The Schlumbrecht case perhaps served as another catalyst for the 1970 one-thirty-second law. Could that one-hundred-twenty-eighth-part black man have feared that a court examination of his family tree would conclude with a declaration of confusion on his maternal line? Was he eager to spare himself, his father, his son, and perhaps even his mother that humiliation? His decision to go quietly

28. *Joseph Jules Schlumbrecht Jr.* v. *Louisiana State Board of Health*, 231 So. 2nd 730, 732.

through the legislative process left no public scrutiny of his claim to be white, but it laid the groundwork for the final legal overthrow of Louisiana's unique obsession with racial classification.

I V

> Individual racial designations are purely social and cultural perceptions, and the evidence conclusively proves those subjective perceptions were correctly recorded at the time appellants' birth certificates were issued. There is no proof in the record that Simea or Dominique Guillory preferred to be designated as white. They might well have been proud to be described as colored. Indeed, we have no evidence that during their lifetimes they objected to the racial designations in dispute in this case.
>
> —*Court of Appeals of Louisiana, Fourth Circuit*

The case of Susie Guillory represents the ultimate paradox of American racist culture, a recognition by African Americans of the subtext of all racial classification laws and a disdain by African Americans of those who seek to avoid the circumscription of hope and opportunity that results from being black in a racist society. Margarita and her son remind us of the condition of all peoples of color. In the patriarchal world of Louisiana, male and female must struggle to overcome the legal system of racial and gender oppression—had Henley been a boy, would the courts have confined him to the romance of the tragic mulatto? The fact that every Creole of mixed racial heritage testifies to the oppression of slavery, *plaçage*, legislative and judicial indifference, and intolerance must never be lost or forgotten. By denying Creole and African American fathers the right to defend their families, by making Creole mothers the victims of racist power, by creating the illusion that the mother bore the primary responsibility for her children's condition, white Creoles and the power of the state that served them indulged themselves in a fantasy that was self-perpetuating.

Creoles, however, discovered they had fathers enough among the strong and courageous men who raised their children in adversity and oppression. Creole women contributed their resourcefulness and pride to the effort. All the archives in New Orleans could shut their doors in conspiracy with the irresponsible men who fathered some of these mixed-race people, then forsook their parental duty. Creoles would con-

tinue to raise their children proud of their heritage, proud of mothers
and fathers whose names did appear on the records of birth and baptism.
Those who were not inoculated with that pride (like Treadaway), entered
the world of the *pasablanc*, turning their backs on their families. They repudiated their Margaritas, or their Thomas Jeffersons and Anna Treadaways, in essence saying: "I am changing sides and consorting with the
enemy." But the strong stuck by their families no matter how hard the
oppression. Obviously many did cross the line, as several of the cases I
have explored demonstrate. But many more stayed. The real history of
abandonment is the one that receives little or no attention. The wholesale desertion of mistresses, lovers, sons, and daughters by those protected by patriarchal privilege remains remarkably uninvestigated. The
politics of genealogy conspires to keep that record out of public view in
part as a result of the racist hysteria the very progenitors of the light-
skinned Creoles helped to create.

No amount of willful ignorance, irresponsibility, or hatred, however,
could destroy the culture that desire wrought. Consanguinity and intimacy fostered a culture that Creoles of African descent offered to and
shared with their white brethren. From the French the Afro-French
gleaned the ideological roots of the French Revolution, and France's celebrated *liberté, égalité, fraternité* were ideals cherished by Creoles of color.
The abolition of slavery by the French Revolution in 1794 and the con-
ferring of full civil and political rights to all peoples, including those of
color, within the jurisdiction of the Republic inspired all Louisiana Creoles of color regardless of their status or phenotype.[29] In the nineteenth
century the Afro-French Creoles saw in the image of France a promising
future that did not exist in Anglo-America. In fact, as France expanded
citizenship and its entitlements, Anglo-Americans circumscribed and
sought to further curtail what few privileges people of color, slave and free,
enjoyed in Louisiana. For Creoles of color, embracing France and
French culture did not necessarily indicate shame or disgust with blackness or African ancestry; it could simply reflect the hope that France genuinely intended to effect *liberté, égalité, fraternité*—the momentary
betrayal of those ideals by Napoleon notwithstanding. Their experience

29. Napoleon reinstated slavery throughout the empire in 1802. Slavery was
finally abolished by the Second Republic in 1848. In 1833 Britain abolished African
slavery throughout its empire.

since 1803 clearly demonstrated that in the United States all men were not created equal, and only some had a right to life, liberty, and the pursuit of happiness. In the realm of the symbolic, skin color mattered, language did not.

In a world of free-floating signifiers in which the language of brotherhood and equality could be repealed or rendered meaningless, Creoles of color already knowledgeable of the irresponsibility of white fathers constructed a culture that reflected their experience and their desires. Creoles assumed responsibility for themselves. White fathers continued to abdicate their responsibilities while indulging their pleasures. But most fathers of color stayed, passing on their names to their wives and their children. Margarita's son remained to pass on the Guillory name to his children. Guillory's father Dominique stayed to be buried next to his wife. To his credit, Jean Gregoire allowed his children to use his name. But all white Creoles were not so generous; some, like Jean Gregoire's white children, saw not kinship but chattel.

White Americans promised that hybridization, the mixing of black and white, would produce an impotent, if not a weak and sickly product—a mule, a mulatto, unable to reproduce. Creoles proved America wrong. They danced to their music with African rhythms and ate the food that had French delicacy and African hardiness. They created a culture that proclaimed their endurance and permanence. Much has been written about the bigotry of some Creoles, the fact that they were obsessed with being white, that they were as prejudiced as whites were, that they in fact would not celebrate being both. But the culture that they created, even when it mimicked whites, mocked them. This particular paradox defines being Creole. The celebration of being both, of creating a culture from what America has always believed, if not always said, was impossible. This splendid mixture of Africa and Europe defines Creole.

Guillory's gumbo must be a bland thing, without that wonderful African vegetable okra, or filé, the ground sassafras the indigenous people of Louisiana gave to the African arrivals. Rodolphe Lucien Desdunes wrote in 1911 the clearest statement of Creole ethnic pride and tolerance: "Some Creoles in our own day have fallen to such a point of moral weakness that they have disowned and rejected not only their fellow blacks but even their own kin. These same people, far from seeking deliverance, surrender to their weakness, without being able to determine the correct principles to follow or to fix up on any resolution, as though they wished to accustom themselves to absolute submission or to forget their individuality. They live in a moral depression that seems to represent the last degree of impotence."[30]

Guillory would do well to revisit these words, as would all who see the defining moment of Creole culture as the rejection of African ancestry. Creole identity rests on pride, not shame. Margarita would probably be sick to know that her descendant has not yet learned that truth.

30. Rodolphe Lucien Desdunes, *Our People and Our History*, trans. Sister Dorothea Olga McCants (Baton Rouge: Louisiana State University Press, 1973), 18.

13

Creole Poets on the Verge of a Nation

CAROLINE SENTER

In September of 1866 an editorial in the *Tribune de la Nouvelle-Orléans*, a newspaper published by Creoles of color in New Orleans, warned its readers to beware the volatile political climate of Reconstruction. "Never in the history of our dear but unfortunate country," the editorial read, "has there been a time whose events and vicissitudes called for greater care, watchfulness, and mutual counsel regarding our civil and political welfare, than the present." The newspaper reflected broad social concern. Indeed, it would be difficult to overstate the stakes of the time. Only two months before, several hundred people—Creoles, white Anglo-Americans, and recently freed black American citizens—gathered at the New Orleans statehouse to reconvene the suspended 1864 convention which had established equal rights and universal male suffrage. They were unarmed, but the violence of that day would come to be known as the Massacre of 1866. Police and armed whites, with the sanction of Mayor Monroe, arrived to prevent the assembly. General Baird of the United States Army, having been forewarned of this ad hoc white-supremacist militia, did nothing to stop it. When the group began its assault on the assembly, the conveners rushed into Mechanics' Hall for shelter but ended up trapped inside against the gunfire. One Creole of color was shot while offering a white flag of surrender; other people jumped from second floor windows. In the end, several dozen people were killed and many others wounded. The Massacre had national repercussions: Republicans won elections later that year, Congressional Reconstruction was instituted, and Mayor Monroe was removed from office by a newly appointed regional military commander. The Massacre of 1866 had a cultural impact as well; via poems published in the *Tribune*, it became part of a Creole literary tradition that for generations had linked literary arts to political and social concerns.[1]

In editorials, political news stories, fiction, and poetry published between 1865 and 1868, the *Tribune* sought to catalyze a nation devoted to racial equality and male suffrage. The several dozen poems published over the three-year period by various authors, including some published under pseudonym, inspired their readers' struggle for equal rights amid the tumultuous events of the time. The poems were remarkable for both literary and political reasons. The writers aggressively entered the contemporary debate over nation and race from the unique perspective their Creole experience afforded them: as *citoyens* under French rule, participants and/or supporters of the French Revolution, and descendants of and/or correspondents with Creoles of color in independent Haiti. The Creole poets employed radical literary traditions from the French and Haitian Revolutions to address the possibilities and circumstances of Reconstruction, using the medium of the newspaper to imagine with readers a nation of composite citizenry, an unprecedented United States. Their output was at once bold, brief, and inspired.

Printed in the *Tribune*'s front pages, the poems worked to create a vision of the nation based on the newly declared rights of all humans, against which the actual events could be judged. The poems constitute an overtly political manifestation of the Louisiana Creole literary consciousness. Elsewhere, historians Caryn Cossé Bell and Joseph Logsdon have documented the well-established tradition among the group of politicizing social and cultural practices such as literature and benevolent societies. French-derived organizations like Masonic lodges and spiritualist societies had aided Creoles of color in making "a bold and radical departure from the city's antebellum racial order." Similarly, the *Tribune* poets used the literary and political heritage of Romanticism to discuss

1. Editorial, *Tribune de la Nouvelle-Orléans*, September 4, 1866; W. E. B. DuBois, *Black Reconstruction in America, 1860–1880* (New York: Atheneum, 1985), 464, 466; Caryn Cossé Bell, "Revolution, Romanticism, and Reform: The Afro-Creole Protest Tradition in the Origins of Radical Republican Leadership, 1718–1868" (Ph.D. diss., Tulane University, 1993), 364.

Reconstruction. The poems are written in French and in the Romantic style, but their content focuses on current local and national events. Such a literary strategy had radical implications: Romanticism had allowed people to metaphorize and imagine the French Revolution. The political premises of Reconstruction were revolutionary, and *imagining* a nation of equality was necessary to carry people's spirits through the violence and disappointment that lay ahead. Invoking the dream of Reconstruction to remind, inspire, and shame readers, the *Tribune* poets created visionary works that affirmed or condemned the actual events reported in the surrounding news columns.[2]

Determined to bridge their group's past to the imagined American future, these writers specifically linked the dream of Reconstruction to Creole history. The poems constitute a unique literary subgenre: a mix of style, subject, and tone, they follow the French literary tradition but include Creole and American names, words, and events. Preferred historical figures were Abraham Lincoln, John Brown, Toussaint L'Ouverture, the French Revolution, and New Orleans Creoles. In the post–Civil War nation of multiracial citizenry, the Creole had an important place, and the myriad voices of the *Tribune* poets sang for all America to hear.

The use of the mass media to enlist citizens in a vision of a newborn nation fits precisely the model of "imagined communities" described by Benedict Anderson in his book of that title. Anderson's theory is that the newspaper creates a sense of community in two ways. First, the calendrical marking—"the most important element on it"—suggests to readers that all parts of the world, as they enter and exit the narrative of the news, are part of the same "homogeneous" inevitable march of progress. This would be especially important to readers of the *Tribune* as they learned of events that enabled or impeded Reconstruction's "progress." Second, the act of reading the newspaper unites readers in a "mass ceremony" no matter where they are, what time they read, or whatever their nationality, ethnicity, race, or language. They are all members of the modern nation. The *Tribune* hoped to use this aspect to unite all its readers—French or

2. Joseph Logsdon and Caryn Cossé Bell, "The Americanization of Black New Orleans," in *Creole New Orleans: Race and Americanization*, ed. Arnold R. Hirsch and Joseph Logsdon (Baton Rouge: Louisiana State University Press, 1992), 234.

English speaking, Creole or American, "white" or "black" or "mixed," etc.—in a nation devoted to principles of equality.[3]

The *Tribune*'s Creole publisher, Dr. Louis Charles Roudanez, and editor, Paul Trévigne, distinctly regarded the newspaper as an embodiment of and advocate for the imagined nation. They published an English-language edition as well as a French, hired a non-Creole black American and a Belgian socialist to the editorial board, and sent the paper to members of Congress. An 1866 editorial in the paper's French edition stated that the Creoles' "numerous connections with foreign nations, and the legal suppression of slavery, have opened Louisiana to the torrent of modern life and ideas." With its international news, multilingual reportage, and multiracial staff, the *Tribune* both chronicled and embodied this transition in the nation. Then-editor Jean-Charles Houzeau, a white Belgian, saw the *Tribune* as a "collective body, a representative" of Creole experience in the defining debates of the nation and wrote of this potential community: "Don't commercial relations, travel, newspapers, books . . . today link all regions, create a kind of unity? The result of this unity is to introduce a like spirit, a like character, into society at large." The newspaper aggressively inserted Creole identity into this national "spirit" or "character"; it urged Americans "to broaden their vision to areas beyond the English-speaking world"; for example, in the debate over universal suffrage, they pointed Americans to the French Constitution as a model under which "all Frenchmen without distinction of class or color [were made] equal before the law." The paper expressly linked contemporary political and cultural acts, with an inquiry in the editorial quoted above—"does this sound like the impossible dreams of poetry and fiction?"—urging readers to believe and to ensure that the ideals presented in the poetry were enacted in politics.[4]

It is important to think about this literature in terms of the context in which it was produced and the nation it sought to imagine, even though that nation never came into being. The *Tribune* was begun when the radi-

---

3. Benedict Anderson, *Imagined Communities* (London: Verso, 1991).

4. Editorial, *Tribune de la Nouvelle-Orléans*, September 4, 1866; Jean-Charles Houzeau, *My Passage at the New Orleans Tribune: A Memoir of the Civil War Era*, trans. Gerard F. Denault, ed. David C. Rankin (Baton Rouge: Louisiana State University Press, 1984), 91; Logsdon and Bell, "Americanization of Black New Orleans," 238.

cal Creole community, always politically and culturally active, and acutely aware of the precarious position they held in a society that rigidly divided rights and opportunities by race, saw in Reconstruction an opportunity in the United States that had not before existed. Historian C. Vann Woodward speaks of this brief but important opening in American society: "The era of stiff conformity and fanatical rigidity that was to come had not yet closed in and shut off all contact between the races. . . . There were still real choices to be made, and alternatives . . . were still available." The idea that people of color had rights was present in the atmosphere, and Creoles, having had political experience in the establishment of such rights in France and the French colony of Haiti, saw for the first time not only the possibility of establishing such rights in the United States, but also the possibility of getting America to listen to their voices.[5]

Creole cultural production and its reception in the United States have always been affected by the composite Creole identity. For example, Creole literature is known largely from the legacy of *Les Cenelles*, a poetry anthology edited and authored by Creoles of color and published in New Orleans in 1845. Most North American critics have compared these poems to the work of either the French Romantics or African Americans in the northern United States and have judged them unfavorably. In the 1978 Yale reissue of *Les Cenelles*, editors Gleason Latortue and Reginald Adams stated that, because legal restrictions prevented Creoles from addressing racial issues overtly, the poetry was "superficial and imitative since it lacks the subtext of revolution and liberty which existed in the works of the best of the French Romantics." (More recently, historian Caryn Cossé Bell has read the *Les Cenelles* poems against the articles and editorials written by the same authors in their newspaper *L'Union*, and considered the poems within the French Revolutionary cultural tradition practiced by Louisiana's Creoles of color, in a way that lends the poems considerable political weight.) Latortue and Adams continue with a description of Creoles in Anglo-American terms: "Trapped between races, between classes, and between cultures, the Louisiana Creoles could not or would not confront the problems and conflicts that blacks, no matter how elevated, experienced."[6]

5. C. Vann Woodward, *The Strange Career of Jim Crow* (New York: Oxford University Press, 1974), 44.

6. Armand Lanusse, *Les Cenelles* (1845; eds. Regine Latortue and Gleason Adams, New Haven, Conn.: Yale University Press, 1978), xiii, xiv.

This idea of Creoles as "trapped between" races, classes, and cultures indicates the difficulty of placing their literature in a genre that depends upon the fixity of such categories. Indeed, the definition of "Creole" precisely elides such fixity. The very existence of the group and its cultural production challenged the binary division that underlay American social, cultural, and—at that time—legal and political institutions. Creole historian Rodolphe Desdunes emphasized the group's characteristic mixture of race, nation, and culture; they were, he wrote, of "three classes . . . the children of the soil, those who came originally from Martinique, and those who immigrated from Sto. Domingo." Claiming that the racial mixture was only implied, Desdunes instead emphasizes a shared ethnicity: "resembling a people newly arrived together in a country, they formed one community, *alike in origin, language, and customs*" (my italics). Using this definition, we can see the Creoles' composite identity not as one "trapped between" categories, but one that draws from among many. The mixed identity produced a syncretic and mercurial culture, one whose overt expression could have only been possible during such a time of social transformation.[7]

The position of the Creole of color has been an issue in the relation between race and nation since the start of the Louisiana colony. As shown by historian Gwendolyn Midlo Hall, the frequent changing and inconsistent enforcing of colonial laws produced among free and freed blacks, mulattoes, and whites "an extremely fluid society where a socioracial hierarchy was ill defined and hard to enforce." The fluidity of this "socio-racial hierarchy" distinguished Louisiana from Anglo-America: after the Louisiana Purchase, according to Jerah Johnson, "the new American authorities . . . [viewed] New Orleans' free people of color as a peculiar and dangerous problem that had to be dealt with as soon as possible." In 1809 Governor Claiborne wrote that "we have at this time a much greater proportion of that kind of population than comports with our interests." The Haitian émigré community, to which Roudanez and Trévigne belonged, was of particular concern.[8]

7. Rodolphe Lucien Desdunes, *Our People and Our History*, trans. Sister Dorothea Olga McCants (Baton Rouge: Louisiana State University Press, 1973), 3.

8. Gwendolyn Midlo Hall, *Africans in Colonial Louisiana: The Development of Afro-Creole Culture in the Eighteenth Century* (Baton Rouge: Louisiana State University Press, 1992), 128; Jerah Johnson, "Colonial New Orleans: A Fragment of the Eighteenth Century French Ethos," in *Creole New Orleans*, ed. Hirsch and Logsdon, 56; Paul Lachance, "The 1809 Immigration of Saint-Domingue Refu-

The Creole position became increasingly volatile with the racial tension resulting from emancipation. Historian Charles Roussève wrote that Creoles of color recognized this time as "the beginning, in Louisiana, of a tendency to consider, as of the same status, both freemen and freedmen." The *Tribune* challenged these racial designations in an 1865 editorial that commanded its readers to "look at the color of the people of African descent, in the streets of New Orleans, and find a true Negro among the many thousands—if you can." Pained by these restraints and hesitant to see their culture subsumed in a nation increasingly defined as Anglo-American, many Creoles left the country for France, Haiti, or Mexico, often with assistance from other members of the community. An 1865 editorial in the *Tribune* objected to the constraint and contrasted it with their better standing under French rule: "We assert that the sons and grandsons of the colored men who were recognized French citizens, under the French rule, and whose rights were reserved in the treaty of cession—taken away from them since 1803—are not savages and uncivilized inhabitants of the wild swamps of Louisiana."[9]

In order to participate in reconstructing the nation, therefore, the Creole had to choose a racial designation in the binary system enforced by Protestant Anglo-America. Much has been written on how this issue split the Creole of color community. Evidently, the editors at the *Tribune* decided that this compromise was worth making in exchange for the establishment of constitutional equality, and in an 1866 editorial they relied on Creole memory of American discrimination to urge readers to protest it in the present: "Our . . . loyalty to the government which has from its foundation been untrue to us . . . should embolden us in speaking unreservedly to the Nation and demand boldly those rights and immunities guaranteed by all republican governments." The editors saw Reconstruction as the beginning of a new nation: philosophically, one based on human rights, and culturally, Anglo-American, and they were willing to negotiate with the latter in order to achieve the former. Leaders of the assimilationist group within the Creole community, they viewed assaults

gees to New Orleans: Reception, Integration, and Impact," in *The Road to Louisiana*, ed. Carl A. Brasseaux and Glenn R. Conrad (Lafayette: Center for Louisiana Studies, 1992), 259.

9. Charles B. Roussève, *The Negro in Louisiana* (New Orleans: Xavier University Press, 1937), 99; Editorial, *Tribune de la Nouvelle-Orléans*, May 23, 1865; DuBois, *Black Reconstruction*, 457.

on freed blacks as affecting their own position, and chose to side with free black Americans in a mixed-race coalition. An 1866 editorial declared, "our future is indissolubly bound up with that of the negro, and we have resolved . . . to rise or fall with them. We have no rights which we can reckon safe while the same are denied to the fieldhands on the sugar plantations."[10]

The strategic political use of race distinguished the *Tribune* writers as radical thinkers of the time. Throughout the nineteenth century the prevailing theories of race were biological. Race was not a position to be chosen for political purposes nor constructed in response to historical circumstance; it was a given, innate characteristic. Such "reasoning" served antebellum white supremacist arguments in favor of slavery and the inability of blacks to govern themselves. These arguments continued to be invoked in postbellum polemics regarding racial segregation. *Tribune* writers, acknowledging their past near-white privilege under French colonialism and making clear their political purpose in throwing their resources behind the newly freed blacks, were symbolically stating that race *is* a construct that had been used against them, and they were now going to use it to make the most of Reconstruction's promises.[11]

This bold move—extremely bold, given the dangers to life and freedom facing blacks in the years following the war—was another way in which the *Tribune* writers extended the Creole literary tradition. Creoles of color in Haiti, from whom some *Tribune* contributors were descended and with whom they still maintained ties, had chosen a similar path, as shown by Mike Nicholls in his important work on Haitian history. In the literary renaissance that followed the achievement of independence, the Haitian mulatto elite also sought to unify formerly divided groups of people of color. Much like the United States during Reconstruction, Haiti after its Revolution was faced with creating a new national identity that would incorporate black citizens and distinguish the new nation from that under the white rule of slavery and colonialism. Haitian writers

10. Virginia R. Domínguez, *White by Definition: Social Classification in Creole Louisiana* (New Brunswick, N.J.: Rutgers University Press, 1986), 136.
11. Brenda Gayle Plummer, *Haiti and the United States: The Psychological Moment* (Athens: University of Georgia Press, 1992), 27–34; Paul Gilroy, *The Black Atlantic* (Cambridge, Mass.: Harvard University Press, 1993), 56.

and political leaders used the term *noir*, or black, to create a racial unity that would supersede class and cultural barriers. Those barriers still existed, as they did in the United States, but were suppressed in favor of a unified national consciousness. Resurrecting this tradition in the context of Reconstruction, as they had that of the French Romantics, the Creoles of color writing in the *Tribune* constituted a major challenge to the United States' national identity. They were not only advising readers, including political leaders, to live up to their discourse on nation and race, they were questioning the very terms of that discourse.

A narrative of progress unified the poems, which took racial equality as its starting point and clocked current events as forward or backward movements along a linear time line. Because of their new sense of American unity with the modern world, in which equality had begun to be realized, the poets could now openly acknowledge acts of discrimination—unlike earlier Creole poets—and also expect their redress. For this purpose, poets looked to examples of liberty established in the French Revolution. One such poem, "La Liberté et L'Esclavage" ("Liberty and Slavery"), signed by Ad. Pecatier and published in August 1865, opens with figures from *La Marseillaise*, the French national anthem, and says that only these ideals may explain the defeat of slavery:

> Gloire! Patrie! Honneur! Independence!
> Qu'el noble cri! qu'il inspire le coeur!
> Luis seul écrase une indigne puissance,
> Et met en fuite un farouche oppresseur . . .

> Glory! Patriotism! Honor! Independence!
> What noble cry! how it inspires the heart!
> It alone crushes an unworthy power,
> and puts to flight a fierce oppressor . . .

In the ideal nation thus imagined, "unfortunate negroes" and "republicans" are joined as "brothers" in "liberty." The poet urges both free blacks and Creoles to keep these ideals in mind, while admonishing his readers to "Honor the cries of the oppressed / For the good of the nation." To the "negres infortunés," the former slaves, he said, "Rise up! Take courage! . . . Arm yourselves and cry out 'liberty'!" Do not judge yourselves by the standards of slavery, he advises. The poem goes on to urge freed people to carve out their own space vis-à-vis language in a Creole French tradition that precisely links words with deeds:

> De ton vainquere méprise le langage
> A ses désdains mesure ta fierté:
> Le déshonneur n'est pas dans l'esclavage.

> Scorn the language of your conqueror
> By his disdain measure your pride:
> Dishonor is not in having been a slave.

The ideal of universal justice is used here to explain the Creoles' choice to side with black Americans in a binary racial system at a time when this choice was considered and debated within the Creole community. The paper's editorials also employed Romantic imagery in repeating the imperative for, and indeed the inevitability of, revolutionary change: "The sun of liberty has risen upon us, with healing in his beams; all that is dead shall pass away; all that is living shall quicken into activity. In this general truth we have a high trust, and believe that revolutions never go backwards."[12]

The combination of French Romanticism and American Reconstruction served as a cultural bridge in which the ideal tracked the real. Of this deliberate strategy, Houzeau wrote, "In such a time of social transformation, it is always an advantage to stand firmly on principle. . . . It was necessary to invoke justice." In addition to promoting racial equality as their goal, the poets also wrote of events that they felt moved against that goal—against progress, as it were. "La Rebellion du Sud en Permanence" (The Permanent Rebellion of the South) conveyed this sense of history moving backwards when it was published under the pseudonym "Henry" on September 24, 1865, one month after "La Liberté et L'Esclavage." The poem's title worked as a headline, summarizing its theme, and its subtitle qualified it as a "response to a friend who asked

12. Ad. Pecatier, "La Liberté et L'Esclavage," *Tribune de la Nouvelle-Orléans*, August 13, 1865; Editorial, *Tribune de la Nouvelle-Orléans*, May 25, 1867. According to Marcus Christian, the poet's initials are an acronym for Adolphe Populus. Marcus B. Christian Collection, Archives and Manuscripts Department, Earl K. Long Library, University of New Orleans. All translations used in this paper are mine.

whether my muse was silent." Earlier that month, Democrats had won statewide elections, declared Louisiana a white state, thrown out the 1864 Constitution over the veto of the governor, and had installed as mayor of New Orleans John T. Monroe, mentioned above for his role in the Massacre of 1866 and a leader of the white supremacist group Southern Cross. The speaker of the poem questions whether the Romantic muse's "mission" of "love, peace and truth" will permit her to "curse the cowardly oppressors of all humanity?" Like the other Creole poets, the anonymous author repeated the ideals that justified slavery's defeat: "l'horrible domine" (slavery) was "condamné par le ciel, la raison, le devoir" (condemned by heaven, reason, and right). But against these ideals he or she measured the lingering lack of freedoms, including, interestingly, lack of freedom of the press:

> Quand le presse est vendue a l'or de l'esclavage
> Quand le spectre du Sud sans vergogne et sans peur
> Ajoute a ses forfaits l'universel outrage
> D'armer la barbarie au profit de l'erreur.

> When the press is sold to the gold of slavery
> When the shameless and fearless specter of the south
> Adds to its crimes the universal outrage
> Of arming barbarism for error's profit.[13]

At the end the speaker says the muse "anticipates a new fight" ("elle pressent bien plus d'un nouveau combat"), conveying the sense of foreboding that the events of that month had provoked.

> Quoiqu'on fasse, mon luthe ne peut vibrer de rage,
> Il prêche la concorde et la fraternité;
> Aux opprimés, il dit: frères, debout, courage,
> L'heure est près de sonner, sauvez la liberté!

> Whatever happens, my lute cannot vibrate with rage,
> It calls for peace and fraternity;
> To the oppressed, it says: brothers, arise and have courage,
> The hour is near, rescue liberty![14]

13. Houzeau, *My Passage*, 82; Henry [pseud.], "La Rebellion du Sud en Permenance," *Tribune de la Nouvelle-Orléans*, September 24, 1865; DuBois, *Black Reconstruction*, 454–5.
14. Henry, "La Rebellion du Sud en Permenance."

This author extends the Romantic ideal to include the fight of the "op-pressed," joining Creoles of color with freed slaves. At the same time, however, he or she writes that "*my* lute cannot vibrate with rage," and in the last two lines places the responsibility for achieving liberty fully on the freedmen: "brothers, arise . . . [you] rescue liberty!" This tension be-tween the ideal and the real suggests the extreme instability of meaning that existed in this volatile political climate, as the poem repeats the prin-ciples of racial equality but at the same time "anticipates a new fight"—the national retreat from those revolutionary goals and the resurgence of white supremacy as foreshadowed in the 1865 elections and 1866 mas-sacre.

Following the massacre the *Tribune* ceased publication for several months, but when it resumed, poets documented the assault and recalled it when writing of other events. In an 1867 poem, "Aux Conservateurs" (To the Conservatives), Joanni Questy speaks of the hypocrisy of equality in the context of conservative challenges to Reconstruction:

> Mes chers Conservateurs que le ciel vous conserve,
> Moi, qui vous aime en frere et que vous n'aimez pas,
> Je voudrais vous sauvez des sort qu'il vous reserve
> Si vous continuez d'inutiles combats.

> My dear Conservatives whom the heavens protect,
> I, who love you as brother and whom you love not,
> I would save you from the end that awaits you
> If you continue your futile fights.

Questy then associates the Conservative "fight" against equality with the Massacre as two events opposed to the progressive ideals of Reconstruc-tion. He warns alleged "Reconstructionists" against their alliance with former slaveholders, saying,

> Ils savent que leur cause est à jamais perdue
> Et que, pour châtiment de leur témerité,
> Tout chargés du remords de l'a defendue,
> Ils descendront honnis dans postérité.
> Et c'étaient de géants ces chefs esclavagistes!
> Ils avaient le génie et la puissance et l'or;

Et vous qui n'avez rien, Reconstructionnistes,
Vous voulez au Progres vous opposer encore! . . .
Pouvons nous oublier quelle main homicide
Tennait le revolver le Trente de Juilliet?

They know that their cause is forever lost
And in that, in punishment for their temerity,
Burdened with remorse for defending their cause,
They will descend with dishonor into posterity.
And these champions of slavery were giants!
They had genius and power and gold;
And you who have nothing, Reconstructionists,
You still want to oppose progress! . . .
Can we forget which murderous hand
Held the pistol on July 30th?

The poet associates the brutality of the July 30 massacre with the nation's political retreat from Reconstruction, foreshadowing the rigid racial repression to come. His outrage at the "Reconstructionists'" betrayal of "progress" shows the alliance forming between North and South, planters and alleged progressives, that would eventually exclude Creoles of color, not to mention freed blacks, from full participation in the new nation. Questy's juxtaposition and association of events distant in place and time embodies the turbulence of the era. The slippage between ideal and real, political label ("reconstructionist") and actual deed ("esclavagistes/slaveholders"), between racial marking and identity, shows the unsure position of the composite Creole in a time when national, cultural, and racial identities were becoming secured. Political defeat, personal betrayal, and social turbulence produced the instability of meaning evident in these poems.[15]

An 1867 poem by Camille Naudin (presumably a pseudonym) dramatically illustrates—in a narration of the 1866 massacre—the difficult position of the Creole of color during this period of national concern with racial delineation:

Viennent policemen et pompiers! C'est le calme?
Non, des horreurs du jour ils emportent la palme.

15. Joanni Questy, "Aux Conservateurs," *Tribune de la Nouvelle-Orléans*, March 14, 1867.

Police and firemen come! Is it calm?
No! to the horrors of the day they carry the palm!

Creole cultural mixture is evident in his diction, as French words surround the English "policemen." Racial mixture is evident in another line, which addresses the racial identity of a victim of the massacre, where the question of the Creole's color hangs in a life-threatening balance:

Est-il noir, celui-ci? Non, messieurs, il est blanc.

Is that one black? No, gentlemen, he is white.

The nation's post–Civil War obsession with racial marking placed the Creole of color in a position of life or death. Creole lives were threatened not only in isolated acts of mob terror in this early period of Reconstruction; such incidents also prefigured the "condition of open rebellion" that threatened the city's colored citizens in the 1860s and 1870s. The legal institutionalization of the segregation that Naudin addresses would later be challenged by the Creole of color organization *Comité des Citoyens*, in their staged protest of the "separate but equal" laws that resulted in the Supreme Court case *Plessy* v. *Ferguson*. The final couplet in Naudin's poem contrasts the triracial composition of the Creole community with the forthcoming white supremacy, as Creole leader Victor Lacroix is symbolically replaced by Confederate Jefferson Davis:

Mais je dirai toujours mulâtres, noirs, blancs
Victor Lacroix est mort. Jeff Davis est vivant.

But still I say mulattoes, blacks, whites
Victor Lacroix is dead. Jeff Davis lives.

This closing line is not simply an obituary for a slain Creole leader but is Naudin's symbolic interpretation of race in America. The North would sanction and assist a violent resurgence of Confederate sentiment; national reunion "necessitated political and legal separations that turned the 'Negro problem' over to the South." Race would be the binding thread of national reunion, and Creoles of color would once again have to choose, cross, or be placed on one side or another of the racial divide.[16]

16. Camille Naudin, "Ode aux Martyrs," *Tribune de la Nouvelle-Orléans*, July 30, 1867; Eric Sundquist, *To Wake the Nations* (Cambridge: Harvard University Press, 1993), 241.

The fixing of race in relation to the nation is evident in the literary history of another Naudin poem, "La Marseillaise Noire," which directly invokes the Creole's French and Haitian heritage. During secession, Confederate nationalists had published several southern versions of *The Marseillaise* in Confederate periodicals, as a rallying cry for southern nationhood. Indeed, the revolutionary song became so widely associated with the rebel cause that "a troupe of French actors visiting New York was jailed as southern sympathizers for singing [the original]." In 1867, the *Tribune* published Naudin's "La Marseillaise Noire." Naudin notes that the poem's inspiration is from a song in the play *Toussaint L'Ouverture* by the French Romantic writer Alphonse de Lamartine, but that "il n'y a que le titre qui ressemble a mon poème (only the title resembles my poem)." Naudin's modest disclaimer may be ironically, subtly, and threateningly false; it is also a reminder of the different situation of Lamartine's France, independent Haiti, and his own Louisiana.[17]

Such a public circulation of the name Toussaint L'Ouverture in 1845, when *Les Cenelles* was released, or when the antebellum restriction on racially "incitive" publications was in force, would have resulted in harsh consequences for the author. But the poet reminds readers of progress being made: Louisiana elections in the spring of 1867 resulted in a state legislature of forty-nine blacks and forty-nine whites that constructed a radical Reconstruction constitution. Naudin notes the changed times, intriguingly stating that the world is transforming at the very moment of writing (as well as reading).

> C'est l'heure solonnelle!
> Ou sur le vieux monde écroule
> Le despotisme qui changelle,
> Vient couronner la liberté.

> It is the solemn hour!
> Where over the old overthrown world
> A faltering despotism
> Comes to crown liberty.

---

17. Camille Naudin, "La Marseillaise Noire," *Tribune de la Nouvelle-Orléans*, June 17, 1867; Drew Gilpin Faust, *The Creation of Confederate Nationalism* (Baton Rouge: Louisiana State University Press, 1988), 11–3; Alphonse de Lamartine, *Toussaint L'Ouverture, Oeuvres Completes*, ed. Marius-François Guyard (Paris: Gallimard, 1963).

The poem's opening line speaks to "Fils Africains!" ("Sons of Africa!"), and aligns speaker and readers with freed slaves in the plural pronoun "nous" ("we"), saying

> Assez longtemps! le fouet infame
> de ses sillons nous a brisés.

> Long enough! has the infamous whip
> broken our backs.

The poem's title evokes Africa, Haiti, and France; its content speaks directly to contemporary events in the United States, illustrating the Creole's global context mentioned by editor Houzeau: "The cause that the 'Negro newspaper' was defending," he wrote, "was after all only one chapter in the great universal fight of the oppressed of all colors and nations." Naudin's recovery of *La Marseillaise* acknowledges the Confederacy's defeat in terms of universal, historical sanction and calls the recent black/white alliance "sainted":

> Que dans une sainte alliance
> Les noirs et les blancs confondus
> A la mort des anciens abus,
> Marchent tous plains de confiance. . . .

> That in a sainted alliance
> Blacks and Whites having condemned
> To death ancient abuse
> Walk full of confidence. . . .

And like others in this Creole tradition it celebrates equality:

> C'est l'intelligence et esprit
> Et non plus la peau qui fait l'homme.

> It is intelligence and soul
> And no longer the skin makes the man.[18]

Naudin additionally calls for *class* equality—a call that must have resonated with the postwar debate over plantation ownership and distribu-

---

18. DuBois, *Black Reconstruction*, 467–8; Houzeau, *My Passage*, 75.

tion: "à chaque travailleur / Le pain qu'il a gagné, qu'importe sa couleur" ("to each worker / The bread he has won, no matter his color"). These lines support the work of the Freedmen's Aid Association, advocated in *Tribune* editorials, in which freed slaves collectively bought plantations with assistance from Creoles of color. An editorial in the English edition on February 24, 1865, declared that "these associations of capital, furnished by small shares of freedmen who possess nothing more than their industry, good faith and courage, are destined not only to become powerful, but they will also enrich the state. They will inaugurate a new regime, and for the first time give a chance to field-laborers to obtain their rightful share in the sweats of their brows." The convention of 1867 may have given hope that this "new regime" would succeed, with laws passed to regulate labor and wages, ensure male suffrage, and provide integrated public education. Yet the poem's title makes clear the primacy of race in postwar national politics. The title *Southern Marseillaise* indicates a territorial nationalism whose white citizens' racial homogeneity is so mutually understood that it need not be acknowledged. It states "nation" but implies "race." *La Marseillaise Noire* states race and implies nation. The American circulation of *La Marseillaise* shows the bi-oppositional character of American racial politics.[19]

The *Tribune* poets practiced a Romantic Reconstruction, seeking to inspire specific citizens—readers—toward specific actions that would approach the ideals their poems invoked, or gain ascendancy over those that challenged them. As in *Aux Conservateurs*, they acknowledged the hypocrisy of abandoned ideals. But also, as in the anonymous 1865 poem *Le 13 Avril*, they urged that the equality of the ideals of *liberté, égalité, fraternité* be shared by all citizens. The poem's author lamented the death of Abraham Lincoln on that day, but transferred the power of the ideal of freedom from the fallen president to the former slaves:

Il n'est plus! Mais son nom appartient a l'histoire . . .
Ira, du Nord au Sud, apporte l'espérance
A celui qui, tombant de douleur, de souffrance,
Avait longtemps désésperé . . .

19. Editorial, *Tribune de la Nouvelle-Orléans*, February 24, 1865; DuBois, *Black Reconstruction*, 457–8.

He is no longer! But his name belongs to history . . .
From North to South it will carry hope
To he who, bent with sorrow and suffering,
Had long despaired . . .[20]

In addition to their desire to assert their composite identity, the Creole poets expressed a strong commitment to carrying out legislated racial equality in the racially binary United States. The author of *La Liberté et L'Esclavage* wrote that "Paris est là," and he reminded his readers that the dream of "le bonheur de la France" may be only that, a dream:

Vous, qui jaloux de la bonheur de la France,
Rêvez encore

You who are jealous of the fortune of France,
Are still dreaming

Not a poet "imitating" France, but one who employed his ethnic heritage to respond to his specific historical circumstances.

The *Tribune* poems enunciate the eclipse of Creole identity by that of the Protestant, English-speaking, white or black American. The combination of its adherence to civil equality and its insistence for recognition of Creole difference eventually cost the *Tribune* its life in an environment increasingly polarized around race. As racial and regional alliances formed after the war, the newspaper came under increasing attack from Creoles of color, African Americans, and white Creoles and Americans. Non-Creole African Americans in Louisiana aligned with northern, Protestant African Americans, and chose a clearly marked racial position encouraged by northern and southern whites.[21] Within this

20. Leila D——t [Adolphe Duhart], "Le 13 Avril," *Tribune de la Nouvelle-Orléans*, April 25, 1865.

21. Joseph Logsdon and Caryn Cossé Bell argue that the postwar split in the black community was begun by white Federals. Louisiana's Reconstruction general Banks was angered by the opposition among Creoles of color to Lincoln's plan for Reconstruction, which included only limited suffrage. In spite of the *Tribune*'s steady advocacy of rights for all freedmen, the Banks administration alleged that the Creoles were elitist. Banks found support from northern Protestant ministers who objected to the Creoles' Catholic culture and whose services many freed people, many Protestant rural immigrants to the city, needed. The 1866 massacre had also caused many people of color to retreat. The Banks administration established

context, the Creoles' French and Haitian traditions threatened white supremacy supported by an idea of racial separation and purity. Their history of black liberation and leadership challenged America's rigid racial
order by not only imagining but also demonstrating that another racial
order was viable and more profitable to blacks. Eventually losing its base
of support within a community pressured to assimilate, the paper ceased
publication in 1868. The poems show us that the rigid racial delineation
which enabled the subsequent subordination of black citizens under Jim
Crow was beginning to occur even at this early stage in Reconstruction.

For their brief output the *Tribune* poems also give us a vision of the nation with broader characteristics than we may be familiar with. That Creole difference did not secure a lasting place in the national identity is not
surprising today. It is hard to imagine the United States without the sub-
tle hegemony of Protestant morality, English-only impulses, and rigid
black/white opposition. The "opening" in society that C. Vann Woodward spoke of was small, and was closed with the defeat of Congressional
Reconstruction. Yet Creoles of color had resources and avenues to
power: social organizations, political offices, wealth, literacy. Our loss of
their voice cannot be attributed to their failure but rather to the demands
of their context. That context produced a national representation of race
as fixed and binary, not as a marker both produced and employed by institutions of power. The contrast between the nation imagined and the
nation enacted suggests the unwillingness of white Americans to concede
political, social, or cultural power to people of African descent at the very
moment when that power was being written into law.

---

the *Black Republican* newspaper under the auspices of black Protestant ministers.
Each of these strategies undermined the tenuous coalition the *Tribune* was building
and the more radical platform they were advocating.

14

"Lost Boundaries"

Racial Passing and Poverty in Segregated New Orleans[1]

ARTHÉ A. ANTHONY

On sunny summer Sunday afternoons in Harlem
when the air is one interminable ball game
and grandma cannot get her gospel hymns
from the Saints of God in Christ
on account of the Dodgers on the radio,
on sunny Sunday afternoons
when the kids look all new
and far too clean to stay that way,
and Harlem has its
washed-and-ironed-and-cleaned-best out,
the ones who've crossed the line
to live downtown
miss you,
Harlem of the bitter dream,
since their dream has
come true.
—Langston Hughes, 1951

1. A version of this paper, entitled "The Risks of Passing and the Stigma of Blackness: The Economics of Race and Racism in Segregated New Orleans," was presented at the joint meeting of the California and Rocky Mountain American Studies Associations at the University of Nevada, Reno, May 1, 1993. Special thanks to Barbara Bradshaw, Raúl Fernández, John Higginson, and Monique M. Taylor for their comments, Vivian Clecak for her interest, Jeannette Altimus for her generosity, Marcia McCall for her assistance as 1993 Ford Foundation Sum-

Racial passing is a well-known theme in pre–World War II African
American literature.[2] Adrian Piper's recent essay, "Passing for White,
Passing for Black," is an example of continued interest in the topic.[3] In
addition, "passing" is used in cultural studies as a metaphor for masking
the real—and most often marginalized—self.[4] This essay examines racial
passing, with an emphasis on the lives of black Creole women, in relation
to the economic impact of racial repression and segregation on black life

mer Research Fellow, and Gregory Osborn for his comments and research assistance. I am also indebted to Phenella Duplessis Perez for introducing me to the
phrase *they lost their boundaries*, in reference to individuals who assumed new identities and, as a result, lost their black families of origin. She also brought my attention to W. L. White's *Lost Boundaries* (New York: Harcourt, Brace, 1947); this was
also the title of a 1949 motion picture. Interview by author, Los Angeles, Calif.,
July 8, 1993.

2. Central texts include Charles W. Chesnutt, *The Marrow of Tradition* (1901);
James Weldon Johnson, *The Autobiography of an Ex-Colored Man* (1912); Jessie
Redmon Fauset, *Plum Bun: A Novel without a Moral* (1928); and Nella Larsen,
Passing (1929). Passing was also of interest, albeit for different reasons, to Euro-
pean American and European writers; see, for example, Joachim Warmbold, "If
Only She Didn't Have Negro Blood in Her Veins: The Concept of *Métissage* in
German Colonial Literature," *Journal of Black Studies* 23 (1992): 200–9; A. L.
Nielsen, "Mark Twain's *Pudd'nhead Wilson* and the Novel of the Tragic Mulatto,"
Greyfriar: Siena Studies in Literature 26 (1985): 14–30; Daniel Aaron, "The Inky
Curse: Miscegenation in the White American Literary Imagination," *Social Sci-
ence Information* 22 (1983): 169–90; and James Kinney, "The Rhetoric of Racism:
Thomas Dixon and the 'Damned Black Beast,' " *American Literary Realism* 15
(1982): 145–54.
3. Adrian Piper, "Passing for White, Passing for Black," *Transition* 58 (1992):
4–32. See also, for example, G. Reginald Daniels, "Passers and Pluralists: Subvert-
ing the Racial Divide," in *Racially Mixed People in America*, ed. Maria P. P. Root
(Newbury Park, Calif.: Sage, 1992); James F. Davis, *Who Is Black? One Nation's
Definition* (University Park: Pennsylvania State University Press, 1991); Paul R.
Spickard, *Mixed Blood: Intermarriage and Ethnic Identity in Twentieth-Century
America* (Madison: University of Wisconsin Press, 1989); and Virginia R. Domín-
guez, *White by Definition: Social Classification in Creole Louisiana* (New Brunswick,
N.J.: Rutgers University Press, 1986).
4. See, for example, Lauren Berlant, "National Brand/National Body: *Imitation
of Life*," in *Comparative American Identities*, ed. Hortense J. Spillers (New York:
Routledge, 1991), 110–40; and bell hooks, *Black Looks: Race and Representation*
(Boston: South End Press, 1992). Valerie Smith has applied the term to the subtext
of films in which black working-class characters attempt to transcend their class
background to "pass" for middle class (paper delivered at the Symposium on Criti-

in New Orleans.[5] My conclusions are drawn, in large part, from an analysis of thirty extensive oral history interviews that I conducted with eighteen women and twelve men born between 1885 and 1905, and living in downtown New Orleans in 1977.[6] Each of these men and women thought of him- or herself as "Creole," and participated in the familial and social networks of the city's black Creole community.[7]

Their occupations and education were representative of the choices available in New Orleans to their generation of Creoles of color. All of them worked, although the kind of work that they did changed during the life cycle; they were primarily cigar makers, seamstresses, skilled craftsmen in the building trades, postal carriers, printers, and school teachers. A few of them attended the city's private high schools and nor-

cal Issues in African-American Life and Thought, University of California, Irvine, October 27, 1992). Also of note is the popularity of the films *Paris Is Burning* and *The Crying Game*, pop singer RuPaul, and the comic persona of Dame Edna.

5. Twenty-seven of these interviews were taped and transcribed, and are in the author's possession. Additional interviews are as cited. The names of most of the interviewees have been changed. Note that throughout the essay the terms black Creole, Creole of color and Creole are used interchangeably unless otherwise indicated. "Creole" is the term used within this community, which does not mean that individuals do not also see themselves as Negro or black.

6. Sources on the value of oral history include Sherna Berger Gluck and Daphne Patai, eds., *Women's Words: The Feminist Practice of Oral History* (New York: Routledge, 1991) and Paul Thompson, *The Voice of the Past: Oral History* (Oxford: Oxford University Press, 1978).

7. There are differences between New Orleanian Creole-of-color identity and Creole identity in rural and small-town southern Louisiana. For a discussion of colored Creole identity in New Orleans, see, for example, Arthé A. Anthony, "The Negro Creole Community in New Orleans, 1880–1920s: An Oral History" (Ph.D. diss., University of California, Irvine, 1978); James H. Dormon refers to "prairie Creoles" in "Louisiana's 'Creoles of Color': Ethnicity, Marginality, and Identity," *Social Science Quarterly* 73 (1992): 615–26. The term *Creole* is also used by blacks outside of southern Louisiana, see for example, D. C. LaFoy, "A Historical Review of Three Gulf Coast Creole Communities," *Gulf Coast Historical Review* 3 (1988): 6–19 and William S. Coker, "Tom Moreno: A Pensacola Creole," *Florida Historical Quarterly* 67 (1989): 329–39. In addition, Carole Ione describes a South Carolinian black Creole family history in *Pride of Family: Four Generations of American Women of Color* (New York: Summit Books, 1991). For a discussion of white Creoles see, for example, Joseph G. Tregle Jr., "Creoles and Americans," in *Creole New Orleans: Race and Americanization* (Baton Rouge: Louisiana State University Press, 1992), 131–85.

mal schools, an accomplishment that has to be understood within the context of the limited availability of an education—private or public—for Negroes at the turn of the century.[8] Many others were forced to terminate their education, in more than one instance as early as the third grade, to begin working, whereas others finished apprenticeships.[9] Their personal lives were equally varied, as reflected in the extended, nuclear, and augmented households in which they lived and in their individual experiences with parenting, divorce, and remarriage, as well as widowhood and desertion. Most, but not all of them, were Catholics.[10] Despite their individual differences, as a group the Creoles of color I interviewed shared firsthand experiences with hard work and racial discrimination. The women—a group that has been overlooked in the historiography of New Orleans—experienced both racial and sexual discrimination.[11]

8. Donald E. DeVore and Joseph Logdson, *Crescent City Schools: Public Education in New Orleans, 1841–1991* (Lafayette: Center for Louisiana Studies, 1991), discuss the opening of Southern University's elementary and secondary departments in 1881 (94). They also note that after Southern left New Orleans and moved to Baton Rouge in 1913–1914, McDonough 35, the high school for Negroes, did not open until 1917. Of equal significance was the New Orleans school board's elimination of "the three bridge grades . . . between elementary and high school" in 1900 (189).

9. Straight University, established by the American Missionary Association in 1869, was the most important high school and normal school, and later college, for this generation. See Joe M. Richardson, "The American Missionary Association and Black Education in Louisiana, 1862–1878," in *Louisiana's Black Heritage* (New Orleans: Louisiana State Museum, 1979), 157–62. For a discussion of Straight, Leland, and New Orleans Universities—all established by Protestant organizations—see John W. Blassingame, *Black New Orleans, 1860–1880* (Chicago: University of Chicago Press, 1976), 124–30, and DeVore and Logsdon, *Crescent City Schools*. The other private schools that were important to this group of Creoles included St. Mary's Academy for Young Ladies of Color, established in 1880 by the Sisters of the Holy Family, and Medard Nelson's school. Small private schools of uneven quality that taught primarily Catholic cathechism in preparation for First Holy Communion were common.

10. Arthé A. Anthony, "Catholicism, Race, and New Orleanian Creole of Color Identity" (paper delivered at the American Anthropological Association annual conference, San Francisco, December 1992).

11. Discussions that emphasize the experiences of black female New Orleanians in the late nineteenth and twentieth centuries are rare. Examples include Violet Harrington Bryan's discussion of Alice Dunbar-Nelson in *The Myth of New Orleans in Literature: Dialogues of Race and Gender* (Knoxville: University of Tennessee

Each of the men and women whom I talked with offered insightful interpretations of the worlds in which they lived. They were all very familiar with the myriad practices of racial passing; although they were not all light-skinned, they all knew of individuals—often parents, spouses, or friends—who had passed. More important than examples of the intricate mechanics of passing were their observations about the reasons individuals did so. Lillian Gelbart Simonet, for example, born in 1904, identified a relationship between passing for white and poverty when she remarked:

> There are whole families of these people in New Orleans (who are not necessarily Creoles), who have just been absorbed and gone to various parts of the country and they're white. Sometimes you just can't blame them because they have had a hard time. Creole people, with all of the airs, had a hard time to get along [because] they [the young women] would not be domestics. Some were fortunate enough to get work at El Trelles, a cigar factory . . . and Wallace Marine had a cigar factory . . . they weren't prepared to do any kind of work that required any kind of education at all because half of them hadn't finished high school.[12]

The observations of Mrs. Simonet, a retired public school teacher, bring attention to the limited opportunities available to the majority of colored Creoles who were poor and—unlike herself—uneducated.

In the larger scheme of early twentieth century American race categorization, individuals were either black or white. Individual whites may have had their preferences for light-skinned or dark-skinned Negroes in, for instance, their employ.[13] But overall the ethnic and cultural nuances and phenotypical differences that were critical to the intraracial dynamics

Press, 1993), 62–78; Doris Dorcas Carter, "Refusing to Relinquish the Struggle: The Social Role of the Black Woman in Louisiana History," in *Louisiana's Black Heritage*, ed. Robert R. MacDonald, John R. Kemp, and Edward F. Haas (New Orleans: Louisiana State Museum, 1929), 163–89. Also worth noting is Vaughan B. Baker's critique of traditional historical methodology for its limited ability to examine the lives of women: "*Cherchez les Femmes:* Some Glimpses of Women in Early Eighteenth-Century Louisiana," *Journal of Louisiana History* 31 (1990): 21–37. The problems that he brings attention to are magnified exponentially when the complexities of not only gender but race and class are under consideration.

12. Lillian Gelbart Simonet, interview by author, New Orleans, February 14, 1977.

13. For example, advertisements in newspapers for the hiring of light-skinned girls continued to appear in the city's want ads into the 1960s.

of the black community were disregarded by whites in the segregated economy of New Orleans in the 1900s through the 1920s. Consequently, many colored Creoles were willing to accept the risks of passing for white rather than suffer within the boundaries of the deteriorating material and social conditions of living and working as colored.[14]

The instability of the colored Creoles' civil and economic status was not a new phenomenon despite their history of freedom and their colonial and antebellum privileges, often described as those of a third racial class. The historical basis of those privileges recently has been questioned by Thomas N. Ingersoll. He has concluded that between 1718 and 1812 planters used "the powers of the local, state, and federal governments against free blacks to degrade them and limit their numbers, [to ensure] the system of racial supremacy that allowed them to exploit blacks." Their social position eroded further between 1830 and the Civil War. As Loren Schweninger argues, however, a distinction has to be made between the changes in their civil status and their wealth because "during the 1840s and 1850s, the economic standing of the group remained strong."[15]

14. Passing for white was not a uniquely colored Creole phenomenon, as is made clear by the attention given to the topic in African American literature. Slave narratives, such as the story of William and Ellen Craft, also made references to this strategy. Racial passing has been discussed by historians and social scientists, e.g., Caroline Bond Day, *A Study of Some Negro-White Families* (1932; reprint, Westport, Conn.: Negro Universities Press, 1970); Ira Berlin, *Slaves without Masters: The Free Negro in the Antebellum South* (New York: Vintage Books, 1976), 160–4; and Blassingame, *Black New Orleans*, 201–2. For a more personal account, see Kathryn L. Morgan, *Children of Strangers: The Stories of a Black Family* (Philadelphia: Temple University Press, 1980), 25, 78–85.

15. Thomas N. Ingersoll, "Free Blacks in a Slave Society: New Orleans, 1718–1812," *William and Mary Quarterly* 48 (1991): 200; H. E. Sterkx, *The Free Negro in Ante-bellum Louisiana* (Rutherford, N.J.: Fairleigh Dickinson University Press, 1972), especially chapters 4 and 7, and Joseph Logsdon, "Americans and Creoles in New Orleans: The Origins of Black Citizenship in the United States," *Amerikastudien/American Studies (West Germany)* 34 (1989): 187–202; Loren Schweninger, "Antebellum Free Persons of Color in Postbellum Louisiana," *Louisiana History* 30 (1989): 358; Loren Schweninger, *Black Property Owners in the South, 1790–1915* (Urbana: University of Illinois Press, 1990), 112–21. For consideration of the Creoles of color as a third racial group, see Sterkx, *The Free Negro in Ante-bellum Louisiana*, 160–99; David C. Rankin, "The Politics of Caste: Free Colored Leadership in New Orleans during the Civil War," in *Louisiana's Black Heritage*,

If during the Civil War Louisiana's free people of color were anxious about their future, Schweninger makes it clear that they had every reason to be, since in the postbellum era their status, as evidenced by their property ownership, deteriorated. His study includes New Orleans black Creoles and demonstrates that they were no less affected by the changes brought by the war. For example, he notes that "a close study of Creoles of color in the Fourth, Fifth, and Sixth wards, the heart of the free mulatto community, reveals a marked decline." Only a few individuals survived the war with their wealth intact; moreover, a substantial percentage of those he studied, including the well-established skilled craftsmen, either "experienced losses" or "lost everything."[16]

The decades that followed Reconstruction have been described as the nadir of black life in the United States because of the increased racial violence, segregation, economic exploitation, and denial of citizenship rights that occurred. The colored Creole community of New Orleans was also affected by these circumscriptions. In response, black New Orleanians, including Creoles, utilized a variety of forms of social protest against the growing virulence of Jim Crow, including the courts, strikes, and interracial union collaboration.[17] A far less public strategy of resistance against the crises of racial repression was the practice of racial pass-

107–46; and Laura Foner, "The Free People of Color in Louisiana and St. Domingue: A Comparative Portrait of Two Three-Caste Slave Societies," *Journal of Social History* 3 (1970): 406–30. The more recent scholarship is represented by Gwendolyn Midlo Hall, *Africans in Colonial Louisiana: The Development of Afro-Creole Culture in the Eighteenth Century* (Baton Rouge: Louisiana State University Press, 1992); and Kimberly S. Hanger, "Avenues to Freedom Open to New Orleans' Black Population," *Louisiana History* 31 (1990): 237–64.

16. Schweninger, "Antebellum Free Persons of Color," 357, and *Black Property Owners*, 190–6. What we don't know is how many women and men chose to pass for white, and whether or not they remained in the area, in response to racial repression as well as economic losses. See Blassingame, *Black New Orleans*, 201–2. Stories abound regarding passing, including a version of Leander Perez's ancestry which asserts that his father was an Afro-Cuban whose birth records conveniently turned to ashes in a mysterious fire.

17. Eric Arnesen offers a concise overview of these events in *Waterfront Workers of New Orleans: Race, Class, and Politics, 1863–1923* (New York: Oxford University Press, 1991), 181–9. See also, for example, Otto H. Olsen, *The Thin Disguise: Turning Point in Negro History*, Plessy v. Ferguson (New York: A. I. M. S. by Humanities Press, 1967), and Charles A. Lofgren, *The Plessy Case: A Legal-Historical Interpretation* (New York: Oxford University Press, 1987).

ing. This was a well-known consequence of the economics of "race prejudice" as observed by Dr. William L. Bulkley when he addressed the National Negro Conference in 1909. He included racial passing as an indictment against race prejudice because it forced "across the line thousands of mixed-blood."[18]

"I wonder how the poor colored people got along."

The oral histories of black Creoles born at the turn of the century indicate that racial passing was a last-resort strategy employed by individuals in response to the pervasive racial repression that shaped occupational patterns in the early decades of the century. This group was born between 1885 and 1905, a period in which intertwined local and national events significantly curtailed the economic opportunities available to them as they matured. Their childhoods were shaped in part by white supremacy, as evidenced by the codification of segregation and the pervasiveness of racial violence. For example, the era was marked nationally by the 1896 U.S. Supreme Court decision *Plessy* v. *Ferguson* and locally by the "Robert Charles Riot" of 1900, as well as the labor-management conflicts that culminated in the city's strikes of the 1880s and 1890s. Concurrently, the Crescent City struggled to regain some of its antebellum economic prosperity against the backdrop of the depression of 1893–1897 and the panic of 1907.[19]

18. Dr. William L. Bulkley, "Race Prejudice as Viewed from an Economic Standpoint," in *The Voice of Black America*, vol. 2, ed. Philip S. Foner (New York: Capricorn Books, 1975), 64. Rodolphe L. Desdunes also refers to passing for white as a controversial strategy for enjoying "the rights and privileges accorded this standing." *Our People and Our History*, trans. Sister Dorothea Olga McCants (Baton Rouge: Louisiana State University Press, 1973), 62.

19. William H. Harris, *The Harder We Run: Black Workers since the Civil War* (New York: Oxford University Press, 1982). For a discussion of the male leaders of previous generations see, for example, Joseph Logsdon and Caryn Cossé Bell, "The Americanization of Black New Orleans 1850–1900," in *Creole New Orleans*, 201–61. For a discussion of the extremes of racial violence in Louisiana, see, for example, Gilles Vandal, "The Policy of Violence in Caddo Parish, 1865–1884," *Louisiana History* 32 (1991): 159–82; William Ivy Hair, *Carnival of Fury: Robert Charles and the New Orleans Race Riot of 1900* (Baton Rouge: Louisiana State University Press, 1976); and Joy J. Jackson, *New Orleans in the Gilded Age: Political and Urban Progress, 1880–1896* (Baton Rouge: Louisiana State University Press, 1969), 19–21, 226–31.

The city's attempts to diversify its economy included such changes as the growing importance of the "men's ready-to-wear clothing industry [which] became important by 1900, employing a large number of pieceworkers. . . . Another industry of significance was the manufacture of cigars and other tobacco products." Cigar making and the ready-to-wear clothing industry were major sources of jobs for Creoles of color, including Creole women. Negroes overall were marginal, however, as exploited workers in a segregated economy. Eugenia Lacarra, who not only worked as a cigar maker but was the daughter and granddaughter of cigar makers, recalled the impact of segregation on the ability of Negroes to make a living: "I stop to think sometimes, and I wonder how the poor colored people got along. You couldn't work in the department stores, the men couldn't drive a bus, you couldn't work for the telephone company, you couldn't work for the Public Service, so if you didn't do menial labor, or housework, or learn to be a cigar maker, or you weren't lucky enough to get an education to teach, well, you were in very bad luck because then these people had nothing to do. You see, they didn't give the poor colored people jobs."[20]

Specific occupations and job sites were defined by race. Colored cigar makers, for example, could work in the city at Marine's, a factory promoted by Mrs. Lacarra's father, but owned by two Jews. Those jobs, however short-lived, were welcomed because in the early decades of the century virtually all of the major cigar manufacturers—which were owned by whites—had "whites only" employment policies, or unsatisfactory segregated working conditions for Negroes. Consequently, according to Mrs. Lacarra, in order to find work some black Creoles passed for white while they worked as cigar makers at certain "whites only" companies, as well as in a number of other occupations throughout the city.[21]

Many of the black Creoles I spoke with also described more aggressive forms of resistance against the inequities of segregation. For in-

20. Jackson, *New Orleans in the Gilded Age*, 221–2; Eugenia Marine Lacarra, interview by the author, New Orleans, December 9, 1977. Construction on the new S. Hernsheim & Bros. cigar factory, at Magazine and Julia Streets, began in February 1882. *New Orleans Daily States*, February 14, 1882. The ownership of the company changed over the decades. For example, in 1900 the company was listed as a branch of the Havana-American Co., and in 1930 Hernsheim Cigar was located at 508 Iberville St. *Soards'* New Orleans City Directory, 1920–1942, Louisiana Division, New Orleans Public Library.
21. Lacarra, interview.

stance, Marguerite "Mag" Puryear (1902–1992) recalled that she and her older sister felt desperate when Marine's cigar factory closed in the early 1920s:

> We were desperate and we went to Hernsheim [a white-owned cigar manufacturing company]. Hernsheim gave us a job, but we weren't with the white girls, we were downstairs. We soon got tired of that. El Trelles was a new factory owned by Spanish people. . . . We felt that the girls working there were making good money so several of us decided to go there. We went there, and an old Spanish fella came out and he said that he didn't have colored girls. I told him that we could understand that but that we could make cigars as good as any of the girls that he did have—if he would give us a chance. He told us that he would consider it.

Mag and her sister were convincing, as she explained: "I shall always remember it was the day that . . . my niece was born [early 1920s]. . . . I got the letter telling me to come with the other two girls that had been with me. We went and got the job and it was paying so much more. So we went up and up [in promotions] and had the best jobs. And he put us with the white girls, and we sat even with the white girls. There was no segregation at Trelles."[22]

Male cigar makers had additional options such as trying their luck with one of the very small independent factories known as "buckeyes." Mrs. Lacarra described how they operated: "Different people had a little factory in their kitchen or they would make cigars out in a room somewhere, out in the back yard, or in the shade. They used to call them buckeyes, but they didn't pay too much. Most of the men who had those worked for themselves. They made their own and they sold them, but

22. Marguerite Puryear, interview by author, New Orleans, February 17, 1977. She recalled going to work at Trelles the same year her niece, who lives in Los Angeles, Calif., was born. According to her recollections, this dates the closure of Marine's as 1921. *Soards'*, however—a helpful but flawed source—has the Marine Cigar Inc. last listed in 1924. M. Trelles & Co., which moved several times in the early 1920s, is listed at 600 Tchoupitoulas St. in 1921–1924, and in 1925 at 701–715 S. Peters St., where it remained into the 1940s. *Soards'* and *Polk's* New Orleans City Directories, 1920–1942, Louisiana Division, New Orleans Public Library. Interviews with former cigar makers suggest that some black Creoles had passed while working for Hernsheim's, although it is also possible that at one point Hernsheim had a "whites only" employment policy.

those were little places." Some of the men, particularly the fathers and grandfathers of Mrs. Lacarra's generation, were forced to leave New Orleans to look for work in other American cities such as Tampa or Chicago, or outside of the country in Montreal, Canada, or Havana, Cuba. They had to leave, according to James M. Montoya Sr. (1891–1989), "to work when work was slack." He further explained that they traveled because "when there was no work here you went that far to survive."[23]

"He could see that she was a nigger."

Although economic reasons were a major motivation for passing, black Creoles confronted the inconsistencies and ironies of white Louisianians' relentless efforts at racial categorization, what Piper refers to as "the offensive and irrational instrument of racism," long before they looked for work. For instance, race affected such fundamental institutions of personal and public life as education and religion. Participation in the blessed sacraments was segregated, as Mr. Montoya recalled regarding passing for white when he made his First Communion:

> I made my First Communion when I was going to Straight when I was about thirteen or fourteen years old [in 1904 or 1905]. . . . I went to catechism at St. Louis Cathedral because my father didn't want me to go to Sacred Heart Church, which was a block or two from us, because he said there was too much discrimination there. I had an aunt living in St. Louis Cathedral's parish and I went there as [i.e., passed as] white. My father said that if I had to follow behind the white boys to make communion that I'd never make it. He wanted me to make First Communion like everybody else.[24]

23. Lacarra, interview; James M. Montoya Sr., interview by author, New Orleans, March 15, 1977. Mr. Montoya noted that his father had worked for Hernsheim's as well as in Tampa and Chicago. Mrs. Lacarra remembered that her father worked in Montreal, which is where her brother was born.
24. Piper, "Passing for White, Passing for Black," 30; Montoya, interview. Dolores Egger Labbé discusses the 1895 establishment of St. Katherine's as a "black" church despite the protests of many for whom it was designed; see *Jim Crow Comes to Church: The Establishment of Segregated Catholic Parishes in South Louisiana* (Lafayette: University of Southwestern Louisiana, 1971), 49–56. Although the church was intended for black parishioners, it was also attended by white nurses and doctors who worked at Charity Hospital (Lacarra, interview). Stephen J. Ochs examines the fitful history of black priests and the Church's views about race in

During my interview with Everette (1901–1980) and Alice Simon Chevalier (1905–1981), they recalled an experience at the uptown Mother of Perpetual Help Church which further exemplifies the pervasiveness and irrationality of racial classification. According to Alice: "We were standing up in the back [of the church]. The usher came and he took Everette in the front [white section] and left me standing in the back." Everette—in an effort to explain why they were separated—interjected that "he [the white usher] could see that she was a nigger, you understand." Much to their dismay, Everette was mistaken for white that evening, unlike his wife, whose facial features were more clearly Negroid. The recollection of the incident reminded Alice of numerous additional examples of mistaken racial identities, as well as planned decisions to cross over:

> We've had friends that have lived one life and died another. Not long ago [1970–1971], a friend of mine died. She and her husband worked as white, but they lived in a colored neighborhood. When she died she was laid out in a white funeral parlor. She always wanted to be white, and she looked white—she was fair and she had blue eyes. And her husband worked as white. When she died he laid her out in a white funeral parlor. Everette and I were the only niggers at the wake. That hasn't been any more than about six or seven years ago.[25]

My interview with the Chevaliers was also instructive regarding the dynamics of race, class, and gender and the world of work in New Orleans in the 1910s–1920s, the years in which my subjects grew to maturity. The Chevaliers' adolescence and young adulthood are examples of the many working-class Americans of their generation, because they "were poor and we had to work." Everette's father was a barber with a shop "at his house [on St. Ann Street] in the front room," and his mother "used to wash and iron for white people," an occupation well known to black women in this period. Therefore, it is not surprising that Everette went to work as a delivery boy at the St. Louis Drug Company in 1917 when he was sixteen. He was forced to work because his parents' collec-

---

25. Alice Simon and Everette Chevalier, interview by author, New Orleans, February 21, 1977. Part of the irony of their experience was that it was acceptable for a man who was believed to be white to be in the company of a colored woman.

tive wages in the service sector were inadequate to support the family. This was not unusual, as Alice Kessler-Harris has noted "the inability of families of unskilled [white] male workers to exist without several wage earners." Moreover, in addition to being "poor," Everette and his black contemporaries had to contend with the impact of racial discrimination on the types of jobs that were available. For instance, from the drug company he went to work lining barrels at a cooper shop where both white and colored were employed. When I asked him how his employers could determine his racial identity—given his light complexion—he replied, "When I went there I didn't go as white. When I got the job they asked me what I was." It is clear that when we talked he understood the profundity of that decision. Even as a young man, he knew he could have changed his racial identity for better work and better wages if he had passed for white. But he chose not to pass because of the importance of his family ties: "Because of my relations. I lived with my ma and them."[26]

Although Alice Simon Chevalier was unable to pass for white, her experiences illustrate the points made earlier by Mrs. Simonet about the economic conditions that those who did pass wanted to escape. For example, Alice was the youngest of seven children and one of six daughters born to Richard (1870–1908) and Anecia Paltron Simon (1871–1964). Alice's father, a cooper, died when she was three years old, in 1908. Consequently, in addition to the mother, who sewed piecework, everyone in the family went to work as soon as they were able. Alice began working in 1919 at age fourteen for $3.00 a week in the "mangle room," catching sheets and pillowcases to fold them when they came out of the "mangle," a pressing machine, of the Dixie Laundry on Tulane and Basin Streets. When asked about the amount of hours she worked a week, she replied: "for as long as they wanted." Her experiences with poverty and the fa-

26. Chevalier, interview; Gary Nash, et al., *The American People: Creating a Nation and a Society* (New York: Harper & Row, 1986), 699–705; Alice Kessler-Harris, *Women Have Always Worked: A Historical Overview* (Old Westbury, N.Y.: Feminist Press, 1981), 71; Melvyn Dubofsky, *Industrialism and the American Worker, 1865–1920* (Arlington Heights, Ill.: Harland Davidson, 1985), 27. The St. Louis Drug Company, according to *Soards'*, was at 841 N. Rampart St. in 1917. Chevalier's parents' work experiences, particularly the fact that his mother worked, are similar to those of other urban African American families in this period. See, for example, Mary White Ovington on "The Black Woman as Breadwinner," in *The Root of Bitterness*, ed. Nancy F. Cott (Boston: Northeastern University Press, 1986), 343–7, and Harris, *The Harder We Run*, 23–4, 36–7.

milial obligation to work are quite similar to those of white "working class daughters" discussed by Leslie Woodcock Tentler. Alice's low wages, however, are indicative of the limited choices for young colored girls. Tentler describes laundry workers in New York City as desperate married white women who averaged $6.16 per week in 1913, twice as much as what Alice remembered making six years later.[27]

Like many of the young, poor girls employed in cities in the late 1910s and early 1920s at places like the Dixie Laundry, Alice was not only underpaid but underage for employment. Therefore, when the inspectors "would come around to find if you were working under age," she recalled, "we used to go hide in the toilet." Next she worked for two or three years in the cigar factory promoted by Wallace C. Marine, Mrs. Lacarra's father, making $9.00 or $10.00 a week—what she thought was a fortune compared to her laundry wages. Over fifty years later she also remembered that the working conditions at Marine's were a significant improvement because "it wasn't as hot as the laundry." After she left Marine's she worked for close to twenty-five years at the Trelles cigar factory. At any point, particularly in her youth, Alice might have chosen to "cross over" for less arduous work and the possibilities of upward mobility if passing for white had been a viable option for her. She understood the decision of others to pass: "In those days if you were kind of fair you didn't want to be a nigger. That's a bad word to use, but that's the word they used in those days. You would go pass for white and try to get a job as white; you'd work as white. Now [1977] you don't have to do that."[28]

27. According to *Soards'*, Dixie Laundry was at 1126 Tulane Ave. in 1919. Alice Woodcock Tentler, *Wage-Earning Women: Industrial Work and Family Life in the United States, 1900–1930*, chapter 4 and 146–7. Regarding the hours Alice worked, a 1908 state regulation prohibited women from working more than a "10-hour day or 60-hour week . . . in any mill, factory, mine, packing house, manufacturing establishment, workshop, millinery, or dressmaking store or mercantile establishment." In 1930 these standards were reduced to a 9-hour day and a 54-hour week. Florence P. Smith, United States Department of Labor and Women's Bureau, *Chronological Development of Labor Legislation for Women in the United States*. Bulletin of the Women's Bureau, No. 66-II (Washington, D.C.: Government Printing Office, 1932), 46–7.

28. When she retired from M. Trelles & Co., she worked part-time in a school cafeteria. Her experience was representative of urban working-class African American women, and in contrast to the work histories of white working-class wives,

Alice Chevalier worked virtually all of her life although married black Creole women were not supposed to work at all. As Mrs. Justine Frank Marcard, who married at sixteen in 1920, put it: "The women were supposed to marry; men felt that a lady's place was in the house." Mrs. Macard recalled that she began working as a mere child—although it is important to note that she also described her childhood as "very happy." She left school after the third grade "because we were a very poor family; I used to go out and make little day's work for the people in my neighborhood—the white folks I'm talking about. When I was about fourteen I went and worked in a factory. . . . When I was about fifteen my husband began coming around my home with some of my brothers, and we met then. We had our courtship and I married when I was sixteen years old."[29]

Women like Justine Frank Marcard and Alice Simon Chevalier were forced to work as children and adolescents because of the deaths or inadequate wages of their fathers. And despite the turn-of-the-twentieth-century ideal of the middle class housewife, these women continued to work once they were married because of their husbands' insufficient wages. The ideal that married women didn't work was so widely believed, however, that many women (as well as many husbands) felt compelled to rationalize, and thereby diminish, the work that they did once they married. For example, when I asked Mrs. Marcard if she worked after her marriage, she replied, "I never worked after I got married." When I commented that a mutual friend had told me that she used to "write lottery," she elaborated: "I had a shop in my house. The people would come and they would play lottery [i.e., buy numbers] with me. I'd count up my sheets, tally it, and I'd get so much money and I'd have to turn in so much to the boss. I would take my amount out and I would bring the rest to the place where they had the drawing." Lottery sellers, praline and *calas* [a rice flour pastry] vendors, seamstresses, pieceworkers, and laundresses who worked at home are examples of the various forms of work that were available to poor colored women who were married. The

since only a minority of that group worked prior to World War II. See Tentler, *Wage-Earning Women*, chapter 6, and Harris, *The Harder We Run*, 22–4.

29. Justine Frank Marcard, interview by author, New Orleans, February 15, 1977.

women who worked for cash at home—"inside"—not only comple-
mented ideal notions of womanhood, but performed several jobs simultaneously: They were paid workers, housewives, and most often also
mothers.[30]

A significant number of the women I talked with, and virtually all of
their mothers, worked "inside." This was also true of the mothers and
wives of the men I interviewed. For example, when I asked Mr. Montoya
if his mother worked, he answered emphatically, "Never. She worked in
the home when the family got large. I am from a family of twelve . . .
when work [for my father] was scarce, my mother would sew. She would
also make *calas* and we [the children] would sell the *calas* in order to buy
bread to eat. That's the only work she did—in the house. She never went
outside one day to work." The twelve children and the difficulty his
father had finding work were only complicated by the fact that the father
was often sick with malaria. Consequently, the mother "did everything
to try and make money. She had a little store in the front room, and she
used to send us out with baskets of soap and needles, and things like that.
But she never worked outside." Mr. Montoya also proudly explained that
his wife "never" worked; however, he elaborated that she was a dress-
maker, "but she never worked outside, and my mother never worked
outside a day."[31]

As a result of the poverty of their families of origin, Creole boys were
also forced to begin working at an early age, as indicated by the experiences of James Montoya and Everette Chevalier. Their experiences were
representative of the hardships of many others of their generation. Mr.
Montoya (who was ten years older than Everette) began working as a

30. Marcard, interview. The Creole women's experiences, and those of their
mothers, were similar to those of other black women in that historically a larger
percentage of married black than married white women have worked. See, for example, Nancy Woloch, *Women and the American Experience* (New York: Knopf,
1984), 225–30.

According to Joy J. Jackson, the legal Louisiana Lottery was terminated on January 1, 1894, and continued to operate illegally via Honduras until 1907. *New Orleans in the Gilded Age*, 134–5. The experiences of my informants, however, suggest
that an illegal lottery lasted much longer than 1907.

For an interesting look at the African roots of pralines, *calas* pastries, and other
New Orleans cuisine, see Sybil Kein's essay in this volume.

31. Montoya, interview.

child as a street peddler. He formally went to work at about age fourteen because he was obligated, like Alice, Everette, and Justine, to help support the family. He remembered making $2.50 a week in about 1905, but he also recalled how difficult it was to make even that much money because it was hard to find a job in the city's Jim Crow economy. Therefore, he felt forced to work as white:

> The first [printing] shop I worked in was the only place where they hired Negroes at that time and I went there as a Negro. I got into an altercation with the foreman so I had to quit. . . . Then I turned around and I got a job as white boy . . . at one of the biggest [printing] companies in the city. I stayed with them for a few years. . . . It was against my grain to work as white. I didn't like to, and when I did it was because I had to—it was an economic necessity. I had gone to another place that hired Negroes but they offered me a salary that was the same thing that I had gotten for doing less.

"Passing," he explained, "was not easy, it was hard. You'd be around there and the whites would be talking about Negroes and you'd have to take it. Once I had been seen at night . . . and I was later asked what was I doing with all those niggers. I told them that it was none of their damn business who I was with. They never asked me that anymore, but I didn't like it."[32]

Although it is impossible to determine the frequency of passing, nor all of its often creative variations, the two most prevalent forms have been described as part-time, or discontinuous passing, e.g., passing for white at work, and continuous passing or "crossing over" the racial divide into a new life with a new racial identity.[33] That many members of their community passed full- or part-time was common knowledge among colored Creoles born at the turn of the twentieth century. But passing was not a frivolous matter because it was complicated by the tolerance one had to have for racism, as Mr. Montoya acknowledged, as well as the fear of discovery and betrayal, pressures that characterized maintaining a double life. In the early 1920s Mrs. Evelina Laserna, for exam-

32. Ibid.

33. Daniels, "Passers and Pluralists: Subverting the Racial Divide," in *Racially Mixed People in America*, 92–4, and Domínguez, *White by Definition*, 200–4. Some individuals also passed on very isolated occasions such as attending a movie, shopping, or sitting in the front of the screen on public transportation.

ple, enrolled for a short time in a commercial school for whites because
she thought she would learn more than at Guillaume's, the only commercial school for blacks in the city. She stopped attending the white school,
however, "because it made me nervous," she said. "I couldn't stand it especially because the girls wanted to visit and I just couldn't take that."[34]

One of Mrs. Laserna's contemporaries, Judith Wolf Aymard, attended Guillaume's commercial school in the early 1920s. Despite the
training, however, it was difficult to find a secretarial job as a colored
woman in 1923. Mrs. Aymard discovered that the city's black-owned
companies were not hiring; at the time, her guardian expressed concern
that she would lose her skills. Consequently, she was encouraged to seek
employment as white despite her disdain for doing so. Her guardian
helped her look for jobs advertised in the Sunday newspaper: "She had
cut some ads out of the paper and gave me my car fare, but I'd go anywhere but near the place. . . . I'd come back with some tale, that they had
somebody. She began to get suspicious because she knew that I never did
want to work on the 'outside.' " Clearly outwitted, Mrs. Aymard responded to an advertisement for young ladies to address envelopes. She
recalled going to the Maison Blanche building and being a part of a
group of applicants, all of whom were white—or so she assumed—except
herself, and being asked to give a sample of her writing. Much to her relief, she learned that the positions had been filled. "I was so happy that I
could go home and tell her that," she remembered. But before she could
leave, her name was called: " 'Now, who is Miss Judith Wolf?' I don't
know where the speech came from, but in a very faint voice I said, 'I am.'
When he asked that I remain I nearly died because the first thing I
thought he was going to ask me was 'why are you here?' I was scared unto
death, but he dismissed the others and put me to work." Foiled by her
excellent penmanship, Aymard was disheartened by what in her estima-
tion was a decidedly mixed fortune: she finally had a job, but it required
that she pass. Upon her return home that evening, though, she learned
that her fortune had quickly changed for the better. She recalled: "When
I got home the [black-owned] Louisiana Insurance Company had sent

34. Evelina Laserna, interview by author, New Orleans, March 2, 1977. According to Judith Wolf Aymard, the white school was located in the Pythian Temple building; tuition was $5 a month in the early 1920s. Judith Wolf Aymard,
interview by author, New Orleans, December 12, 1977.

for me—you talk about thanking the Lord." She was relieved to find employment in a black company because despite the lower wages, such a placement offered her the freedom to be herself; despite her appearance, she saw herself as a member of the black community.[35]

"Who would be the knave to disturb their peace?"

Piper's recent essay "Passing for White, Passing for Black" draws on her family's experiences with passing to analyze the meanings of racial categorization in the United States. She comments, "Although both of my parents had watched many of their relatives disappear permanently into the white community, passing for white was unthinkable within the branches of my father's and mother's families to which I belonged. That would have been a really, authentically shameful thing to do." By contrast, Dr. Bulkley, born a slave, interpreted racial passing as a consequence of "race prejudice." In his aforementioned 1909 address to the National Negro Conference, he identified passing as one of the five major economic consequences of race prejudice:

> In the fourth place, we do not get the full economic credit due to us, because of the loss of a host of mixed-bloods who cross the line. Even in the South this occasionally happens. Sometimes the whites know it and wink at it. . . . There is scarcely a [colored] man who could not tell of some friend or relative who has crossed the line North and South, now prominent in business, professors in institutions of learning, married into good society, and rearing families that have no dreams of the depths that their parents have escaped. We could tell the story, if we would—but who would be the knave to disturb their peace?

Although I have not focused on them, the stories of crossing the line are poignant because they are about individuals who were willing to "lose their boundaries"—evidence of the tragic legacy of slavery and the deep-seated nature of racism in our society.[36]

Most often the discussion of passing, full or part-time, focuses on members of the Negro middle class; it is rare that attention is paid to

35. Aymard, interview. In this context, "outside" is in reference to passing for white, i.e., posing as someone "outside of the race."

36. Piper, "Passing for White, Passing for Black," 10; Bulkley, "Race Prejudice as Viewed from an Economic Standpoint," 67.

members of the black working class. Perhaps this is because, much like the history of migration, the individuals who were most able to cross racial lines to assume a new identity also had the resources to do so, which included money and skills. The challenges of any type of passing were similar to the obstacles faced by black migrants prior to desegregation as well as to the even earlier experiences of runaway slaves. For example, it was probably much easier for men to find work, even if the disguise required underemployment, and to move outside or even within their hometown or region. A woman alone was hampered by the extremely limited options for making a living—even as white—as a respectable woman unless she had an education. The complexities when couples—which was not uncommon—and entire families tried to pass can only be imagined.[37]

Although the history of racial passing does not evoke the clear-cut ethical responses that we have to slavery, it is an important part of the larger story of racism and racial repression in this country. The frequency of passing is further evidence of the fraudulence of race as a meaningful construct for other than divisive exploitation. The experiences of the black Creole men and women I have focused on are examples of the extreme risks Negroes born at the turn of the century often felt forced to take to circumvent a poverty that was socially engineered by white supremacists who wanted to save the decently paying jobs for whites. To read the history of "passing" as a tragic mulatto story of self-hatred or as evidence of a devil-may-care, Caribbean-style multiracial identity in southern Louisiana is to misread the history of American race relations.[38]

37. For a discussion of the "great migration" of blacks in relation to migration theory, see Carol Marks, *Farewell—We're Good and Gone: The Great Black Migration* (Bloomington: Indiana University Press, 1989). I am familiar with many examples of wives and husbands who changed identities and remained in New Orleans, as well as cases of individuals who left Louisiana. For historical examples of passing, consider the experiences of Ellen Craft and her husband; she was disguised as an invalid white male while he posed as the invalid's colored servant. Arna Bontemps, comp., *Running a Thousand Miles for Freedom; or, The Escape of William and Ellen Craft from Slavery*, in *Great Slave Narratives* (Boston: Beacon Press, 1969). There is the better-known example of Harriet Jacobs, who felt compelled to hide in an attic for seven years because she could not bear to leave her children behind in order to run away. Linda Brent, *Incidents in the Life of a Slave Girl* (1861; reprint, New York: Harcourt Brace, Harvest/HBJ Book, 1973).

38. This does not mean to suggest that Creoles of another generation have not preferred to see themselves as other than black. But Creoles born at the turn of the

By way of conclusion, it seems appropriate to try to identify—or at least speculate about—the variables that might apply to those black Creoles born at the turn of the century who were able to pass but ultimately chose to be colored. Despite the deteriorating effect of the Civil War on the wealth of many of the black Creole elite, the community continued to pride itself on the integrity of their ethnic distinctiveness, which included a history of freedom and Catholicism. Their pride was reinforced by endogamous marriages and patterns of association reflected in the membership of unions and organizations such as benevolent societies. During the decades in which these men and women were young, many colored Creoles continued to benefit from their skills in such crafts as bricklaying and plastering. Many black Creoles were thus able to own their often modest homes, concentrated in the downtown ward, despite their working-class status. In addition, the city's residential segregation was less severe than was common in other southern cities. And in contrast to the overwhelming majority of blacks who were rural agricultural workers or recent arrivals in southern cities, black Creoles in New Orleans had experienced the relative anonymity of urban life for many generations. Taken together, the black Creole community had much to offer its members despite the racism, frequent poverty, and hard work; many blacks all over the country had far less. Perhaps it is for these reasons that this generation of Creoles were unlikely to participate in large numbers in the first "great migration" to the cities of the North.[39]

What is clear is that not all Negroes, including Creoles, who could pass for white did so. Perhaps Everette Chevalier's (1901–1980) explanation of why he did not take advantage of his appearance to pass for white is instructive; he explained that he did not pass "because of my relations. I lived with my ma and them." I think Uncle Everette, or *Paran* as we also called him, simply did not want to lose his most cherished bound-

century were born into a racially delineated world. For interpretations of Creole of color identity as flexible and multiracial, see Domínguez, *White by Definition*, and Daniels, "Passers and Pluralists," in *Racially Mixed People in America*. For a view of marginality as "the major determinant of the Creole ethnic experience," see Dormon, "Louisiana's 'Creoles of Color.' "

39. Arthé Anthony, "The Negro Creole Community in New Orleans, 1880–1920s"; Jerry Wilcox and Anthony V. Margavio, "Occupational Representation by Race, Ethnicity, and Residence in Turn-of-the-Century New Orleans," *Social Science Journal* 24 (1987): 1–16.

aries. Perhaps he understood, unlike James Weldon Johnson's 1912 anonymous narrator, that the real risk in crossing over was the possibility of regretting that he had "chosen the lesser part, that I have sold my birthright for a mess of pottage."[40]

Although a great deal is known about the politics, economics, and violence of segregation and discrimination, historians have documented painfully little about how daily life—or to paraphrase Mrs. Laserna, what people could and could not take—was shaped by race and racism for non-agricultural southern black workers.[41] Therefore, the experiences of Mr. and Mrs. Chevalier, Mrs. Lacarra, Mr. Montoya, Mrs. Puryear, and the others are significant because they augment, and therefore illuminate, our understanding of the impact of segregation on blacks in general, and on one ethnic community in particular. Moreover, to bring attention to the experiences of women who heretofore have been neglected is critical for an understanding of the dynamics of gender, as well as class, within New Orleans' colored Creole community.

40. Johnson, *The Autobiography of an Ex-Coloured Man* (1912; reprint, New York: Hill and Wang, American Century Series, 1960), 211. Arthur Flannigan-St. Aubin, an expert on Francophone literature, has pointed out that *paran* is an appropriate Creole spelling for the French *parrain*, meaning godfather. Everette acquired this name because he had been *paran* to many.

41. Experiences with segregation and the frequency of passing are stories well known in black families. During the writing of this essay, friends have shared with me countless anecdotes, e.g., of the aunt who worked in a Chicago department store in 1921, the cousin who worked as a librarian at Stanford University in the 1940s, and more recently the cousin who assumed an East Indian identity as she traveled from Indianapolis to Oakland in 1980.

15

Creole Culture in the Poetry of Sybil Kein

MARY L. MORTON

New Orleans has been built on a rich ethnic mix. Part of its cultural history consists of traditions shared among many groups, yet each group has its own particular history. Ironically, just when the leveling forces of the twentieth-century have threatened the diversity of Louisiana's cultural groups, Sybil Kein has perpetuated the Creole experience in her art. She affirms pride in her identity and the need to preserve the essence of the origins, struggles, and the life of the Louisiana Creole. The speakers in her poems weave the webs showing the past in the present, as they range from historical to contemporary.

The importance of Kein's poetry cannot be overestimated, not for the art alone, but for the artistic preservation of Creole history—creating voices of truth that deny the distortions, sentimentalized or not, of the "tragic mulatto" themes found in literature. Not since Alice Dunbar-Nelson's essay of 1916–1917, "People of Color in Louisiana," has there been such a vital depiction of Creole life, though the short-lived television show *Frank's Place* briefly gave the nation some cultural history of the New Orleans African Creole. In Louisiana, Dunbar-Nelson's "people of color" translates *"les gens de couleur libre,"* and though not all free people of color were Creole nor all Creoles free, the terms are often used synonymously because of the recurrent coincidence of the two. The opening poem found in Sybil Kein's collection *An American South*, "1724 La Nouvelle Orléans," celebrates and defines the New Orleans Creole.

Based on the historical wedding of Jean-Baptiste Raphael and Marie Gaspard recorded at St. Louis Cathedral, Kein's poetic account has the couple vowing to preserve their progeny's freedom: "Creoles. / Gens de couleur. / Libres" (3).

A major component of Creole cultural history is the French language in all its variations: Cajun, vernacular, Creole, gombo or patois, and *le bon français*. The careful distinctions are recorded in the literary history of the state and in Dorice Tentchoff's 1975 linguistic study found in *The Culture of Acadiana*, 1975. The variety of language spoken reflected complex social factors. Not only do the varieties of French delineate group association, but history and literature reflect the outsider status of the *Américain*, Texian, or whoever spoke no variety of French or who spoke some variety badly. The French Literature of Louisiana died until the publication of Kein's *Gombo People*, originally published in 1981. Here the original poems in the Gombo dialect were translated into English. One poem, dedicated to the Creole scholar Ulysses Ricard, credits him with helping to preserve *les cenelles*, the poems of nineteenth-century Creole poets, to "grow / once again, . . . / like your faithful Creole love" (26). Kein's poetry has not only aided a Creole renaissance, but one of celebrating French Louisiana.

Kein's ability with *le bon français*, along with her gombo-speaking personae, reflect her superb scholarship and living experience with the culture. She says, "The language was the language of my people, my ancestors, the language I love and admire. . . . I want to make sure the language is not forgotten or that the people who spoke it will not be forgotten."

In her poetry, while artfully incorporating linguistic history, Kein often makes jokes around the language, a way of ridiculing ignorant or snobbish people. Louisiana's most characteristic dish, enjoyed by all groups, a stew thickened with okra, gumbo or gombo, takes its name from the Bantu word for okra. Gombo also denotes Creoles and their language, the source for the title, *Gombo People*. In the introduction to that book, the scholar Ulysses S. Ricard Jr. describes his joy in Kein's using the Creole language as her medium; the art sanctioning the language and concomitantly celebrating and giving a voice to those whose voices have been lost.

The most specific linguistic metaphor of the collection is a humorous Creole rendition of "the melting pot" entitled "La Chaudrière pélé la gregue" (*Gombo People* 39–40). The title derives from an old proverb showing the irony of name calling when the pot calls the kettle black. A particular kind of white enameled drip coffee pot is called "la gregue," a Greek coffee pot, underscoring the rich ethnic mix described in the poem: "Nous tous descendants des Français, Espagnols, / Africains, Indiens, Acadiens, Haitiens / et tout z.autres Gombo People qui té vinir à / la Louisiane" (We are all descendants of the French, Spanish, Africans, Indians, Acadians, Haitians, and all the other people who came to Louisiana). Poetic compression does not allow the naming of all the others found in the ethnic mix. The Gumbo stew or dish is composed of contributions from all ethnic groups and is thus an ideal metaphor for the population, making logical the speaker's question, "Hé, Cajun, / et toi, Créole, / cofaire to pélé to même / blanc ou noir?" (Hey, Cajun, and you, Creole, why do you call yourself white or black?) Here we have the Louisiana equivalent of town and country dweller, combined with the practice of *passer à blanc*. In the most rigid construction, *Cajun* evolved to denote a descendant of those expelled from Nova Scotia in *le grand dérangement* of 1755. In popular parlance, however, *Cajun* denotes a culture signified by the usual markers of religion, entertainment, food, value systems and so on. In Louisiana, a Cajun is most often associated with rural areas and with a dialect different from the Creole or Gombo. In fact, differences exist in the Cajun dialect from the southwest prairie region to the wetlands. And though purists may insist the only Cajun is one descended from those involved in *le grand dérangement*, in fact Cajun culture cuts across all ethnic groups.

At any rate, Kein's speaker exhorts, "Mais mon ami, pas garrochez l'épice / Parce que li trop blanc ou trop noir. / Si vous fait ça, to sa pas gain Gombo / jamain plus, mas un ragout fondu salé-là / fait avec la chair niée de to l'ancestre-yé / to grandmère, to grandpère / . . . / to-même" (But my friend, do not throw away the spice because it is too light or too dark. Then you will not have gumbo, but a foul stew of your ancestors' and relatives' denied flesh—and of your own). The injunction contains a wry joke on gumbo-making—whether the roux is too light or too dark—but the universal truth of acceptance needs no translation.

Lighter humor based on fancied differences is found in Kein's "La Campagne et la Ville" (*Gombo People* 51–2). Tee-Ta claims to be Cajun, different from Tee-Teen, who is a Creole because she lives in New Orleans, though they both have the same papa. Tee-Teen laughingly concludes that " 'Cajun' and 'Créole,' we cousin, that's for true! / Cuz her 'French' folks is 'French'—same as mine!" Both are vivacious, but Tee-Teen claims to make the best gumbo and is disdainful of Tee-Ta's "passant à blanc." The poem has some biographical correlations in that Kein's great-grandfather Jean Boudreaux was a Cajun landowner and that it was once suggested to her to "pass," which she refused, of course. The mindless historical ethnic distinctions are deftly satirized in Kein's poetry. In her poem "Envy" the speaker notes that "We don't want to pass for anybody. / The trouble is with some whites. / They want to pass for God" (*Gombo People* 54).

But perhaps the most wonderful linguistic joke found in a poem on skin color is "Dans l'Hôpital" where a Creole answers what he can understand of some *Américain*'s questions. When the Creole says "aider," his name becomes Eddy. When he's asked his color, he replies, "Bleu" (the color of his broken leg). "Blue!? Impossible" "Non. C'est possible. Mo tombé et mo jambe vini bleu." "Probably Indian. O.K., Eddy?" The interview closes by the Creole with his broken leg taking his leave from such a fool: "Aidez to-même!" (*Gombo People* 55).

The versatility of Kein's poetry reflects her philosophy. Her linguistic jokes show the effectiveness of laughter in dealing with fools and sorrow. She also writes lyrics of love and time and healing in a spectrum of voices: Louisiana Creole, Haitian, Spanish, and English. First published in 1986, *Des Gardénias et Roses* has been incorporated into the 1999 publication of *Gombo People* (retitled *Gumbo People*). Found in the original collection, "Melody" contains the refrain: "Time pauses, time turns" to the "little flames" mending the broken heart (15). In addition to the healing quality of time is that of the Yoruban deity Erzuli. In the eponymous poem, "Angelique-Ezili" sings as she "glides towards the azure port, / past all sorrow, past the weeping-willow; / . . . walking on stepping-stones of green moss / . . . towards the sea. / . . . / Her bare feet on heated ground / make a whispering sound / which joins the soft wind, / . . . / She is carrying the moon, . . . / . . . she is singing, / to heal; to heal." The elemental presence of Erzuli haunts the deathsleep of the old pirates and comforts the living. She is an invincible life force, the epitome of woman, the giver of comfort and courage (35).

While the lyrics of *Des Gardénias* musically offer escape from sorrow and pain, the narratives found in *An American South* forthrightly convey the atrocities of slavery. "Mala" is the story of a woman crazed by her children having been sold away. The uneasy wife of her new owner, having tried both whipping and sending the consolation of "a buck," is relieved to be rid of her. But before delivery is made, an apocalyptic fire destroys all but the insane woman (30–1). "Swamp Legend" arises from the spectacle of a mother gone wild after her son was lynched (27). Kein also writes of women not crazed, but eternally, immeasurably sad, like "Zalli," otherwise known as Madame John, who must forswear her daughter and grandchildren to ensure them a better life than they would have if she acknowledged her child. Another poem is the voice of a slave suffering under an owner who is a free woman of color; yet another shows the long-suffering Sisters of the Holy Family, an order of Creole nuns. Kein also gives voice to a Caucasian woman who has a black lover. But Kein writes of her own immediate influences like her Tante Julia, whose words "Could kill you like razors!" and who "did not die" but only "lost [her] spirit to curse" (*Gombo People* 12). The family raconteuse was an undefeatable woman.

Kein's Voodoo women, in common with Erzuli, provide comfort. Kein has three poems to Marie Laveau, all showing Laveau 's power. In "Homage" Marie is "Isis of the south pouring comforting rain / to calm the terror of / the innocent betrayed" (*An American South* 48). The various incantations echo the rhythms of the Roman Catholic litanies to Mary. In the original *Gombo People* are two poems to Marie. In one Marie spits in the eye of the hurricane (38). In the other, "To the Widow Paris," Marie is appealed to, much as a saint would be, to give her people "mystery, hope, / Courage!" (34). Marie Laveau's legend is one with Kein's own family, for her Tante Julia relates that one of the Boudreaux children married one of Marie Laveau's children and lived in the Quarter near the Laveau house.

While Erzuli and Marie Laveau may provide comfort, New Orleans food, another mystery of the culture, is certain to do so. In addition to Kein's "La Chaudrière," previously discussed, are the details in "Nine Rituals": On St. Joseph's Day are the altars containing "black olives, honey candies, and big lucky beans" (*Gombo People* 62); Christmas, New Year's, Mardi Gras, and wakes all have their traditional ritual foods. (Kein incidentally has articles on New Orleans cookery , in addition to her poetic celebrations.)

But of these nine rites in the life of a Creole, four are sanctioned sacraments or practices of the universal Church: baptism, First Communion, marriage, sanctified burial. Added are some observances so common to south Louisiana that they have a sacramental force sanctioned by communities: St. Joseph's Day, All Saints, when graves are cleaned and decorated; Christmas and New Year's, of course; and finally, a wake, which is a subdued reunion of family and friends. Such regular, recurring rituals are the traditions of civilization and security, leading those growing up in it to an early and continuing awareness of all that is important in life. Each rite concludes with the participants returning to the house for "food and love and music everywhere"—or whatever variation is appropriate.

New Orleans music is another cultural item pervading Kein's poetry. She, an accomplished musician, celebrates New Orleans' musical heritage in poems to and about Bessie, Ma Rainey, and Billie Holliday, the quintessential ladies with the blues, along with other legendary figures in the "Blues" section of *Delta Dancer*. Kein herself is a violist, a graduate of Xavier of New Orleans and a former student of Clarence White. She has recorded Creole and New Orleans music. Her brothers, to whom she has also dedicated poems, are active in New Orleans music life. Kein does not limit her poetry to blue notes, sometimes giving us the joyful image of feminine movement in "Calinda" or "Merengue."

While certain poems by Sybil Kein are spoken by contemporary characters, many poems are the voices of historical archetypes, sometimes given voice for the first time, creating the Creole cultural milieu. Rhythms and images of femininity are manifest in poems from *Delta Dancer* (1984). An epigraph from Jean Toomer's poem: "The men, with vestiges of pomp, / Race memories of king and caravan, / High-priests, an ostrich, and a juju-man, / Go singing through the footpaths of the swamp" faces Kein's opening poem "Delta Dancer." Men "follow the trail" of this "Delta Dancer" who "holds ritual" "under full moons." The men then become spirit-men "who can only sleep / when she lights pale / blue candles . . . / and sinfully dances / alone." The Creole milieu is extended in another poem celebrating Colette as a forebear, a muse, who "will live in each golden / butterfly who touches opaline / roses to the end of time." Her "sensual wisdom" is imaged in lush tropical flowers.

Another "proud grandmother, sister" at whose bones the speaker "pick[s] and gouge[s]" is Marie Thérèze, or Coin-Coin, one of the most remarkable women in history. Although scholars quibble over particulars, the main story is that the woman, through incredible energy and hard work, established a successful plantation for her children in Natchitoches Parish along the Cane River. The area became a settlement for cultured, successful free people of color until the aftermath of the Civil War when their world fell victim to the economic woes ubiquitous to the South. For all that, Marie Thérèze and her descendants are a major example of the multiplicity of American experience.

Although Mardi Gras is not one of the "nine rites," it is a ritual tradition also celebrated in Kein's poetry, another time for food and love and music with family and friends. That is the tradition behind "The Black Indians" written in percussionist echoes, showing the idea behind the fantasy: "Black Choctaw's no slave." On the other hand, "Song for Mardi Gras" airs a plaintive *ubi sunt* motif. "Where are the Creole Belles and Beaux, / souvenirs of old New Orleans?" The theme entirely keeps the spirit of Mardi Gras, a celebration of life, a living out of fantasy, before the death symbolized by ashes of the next day. A yearly celebration, to "sing the old songs and start up the bands," ritualizes memory.

This questioning of history, the felt presence of the past, adds dimension to the celebration of the present. But sometimes in Kein's poetry the melancholy prevails. Time past is a place in "Lost Village" *(Des Gardénias et Roses);* that village is personified as a grotesque woman with bloody hair, soiled hands, dressed in rags. The speaker expresses her love and asks, if she returns for its sweet memories, what she will be given. Here are the poetics of the love of a past where it is no longer possible to be. When she left the village did not want her. It has become grotesque then through its own crime or through the ravages of men. Yet this lost past is "lovely." The speaker in "Dans le Vieux Carré," because of her sorrowing heart, offers to sell her memories so that she can forget. In this lament, the past is not something to return to, but to part with—if possible. This poem is collected in *An American South* as "The Old Vendor," though "Lost Village" is not. "The Old Vendor" fits in with vestigial memories of New Orleans history.

The poem expresses Sybil's feeling toward New Orleans. A professor at the University of Michigan at Flint, she lived in Michigan for years and has now returned to New Orleans. An accomplished musician, she was denied a seat with the New Orleans Symphony because of her color, being advised to "passe à blanc," which she refused to do. The hurt the Creoles have suffered is made concrete in the grotesquerie of that old, lost village. The history of the village is of course the history of the region. In the poem giving the title to her latest collection "An American South" the reader is lulled by the catalog of area beauty, to be shocked with the cruelty of "bloody hunks / of hair, flesh turned with earth to end with the question 'To live and die in Dixie?' "

The particular history of the New Orleans Creoles is one of repeatedly broken promises of enfranchisement, political betrayals, insults of all kinds to a group who contributed immeasurably to Louisiana. Increasingly, then, from 1864 through the leveling process of the twentieth century, the distinctive identity and culture of *les gens de couleur* has been threatened. In Ernest Gaines's first novel, *Catherine Carmier* (1964), Lillian wearies of her father's pride in being one of the *gens*. What difference, she thinks, who cares about that anymore? Lillian's question, however, could be answered that Sybil Kein does.

One of Kein's loveliest lyrics, "Soulangae," begins "There was a house by the river, / A house that sang with the rising / Of soft morning." The fairy-tale evocation beginning with the treatment of memory reminds one of Dylan Thomas's "Fern Hill." The human struggle is described in cosmic metaphors. Lush flowers bloom round the house, but inside "Uneasy ghosts weaved in and out / Of the thin, broken walls." "This was the house that sang, and tears were part of the singing." The mother's voice "swept aside cobwebs of spiteful / Poverty and arranged a glory of stars to cover / The cruelty of storms." The father "dug holes in the ground, in the sky, in the wind," he "kept the song in his eyes." "And it will be the children who will carry the secrets / Of the song to give to memory, to circle the need." In this poem Kein successfully uses the metaphor of the house for the heart, a universal figure embracing all our literary memory, but with the specifics of her own Louisiana Creole family. The parents are mythologized not only in daily heroics of raising a family, but in continuing palpable presences. To circle the need: the need not only to commemorate those heroics, but to expiate the memories by embodying them, to give them to others to share and admire. The circle is an ancient holy and perfect image and here sanctifies the human struggle to have food and love everywhere for its children, of whatever cultural group. Kein uses the metaphor of the house for the heart with both the house and the heart as havens for memories that not only shape each character's destiny, but are each character.

WORKS CITED

Bryan, Violet Harrington. "Evocations of Place and Culture in the Works of Four Contemporary Black Louisiana Writers: Brenda Osbey, Sybil Kein, Elizabeth Brown-Guillory, and Pinkie Gordon Lane." In *Louisiana Literature* (fall 1987).

Dunbar-Nelson, Alice. "People of Color in Louisiana," Part II. In *Journal of Negro History* (January 1917), 51–78.

Kein, Sybil. *An American South.* Lansing: Michigan State University Press, 1996.

———. *Delta Dancer.* Detroit: Lotus Press, 1984.

———. *Des Gardénias et Roses: Les Chansons des Creoles.* Detroit: Michigan Council for the Arts, 1986.

———. *Gombo People.* New Orleans: Leo J. Hall, 1981. Rev. ed., *Gumbo People.* New Orleans: Margaret Media, 1999.

———. Interview with Mary Morton, July 12, 1987.

Tentchoff, Dorice. "Cajun French and French Creole: Their Speakers and the Question of Identities." In *The Culture of Acadiana: Tradition and Change in South Louisiana,* edited by Steven L. Del Sesto and Jon L. Gibson. Lafayette: University of Southwestern Louisiana, 1975.

Contributors

Arthé A. Anthony, a Creole of Louisiana ancestry, is professor of American studies and director of the Irvine Leadership Scholars Program at Occidental College in Los Angeles. She holds a Ph.D. in comparative culture from the University of California, Irvine. Her current project is a biography of the New Orleans Creole photographer Florestine Perrault Collins.

Anthony Gerard Barthelemy is a Louisiana Creole and an associate professor of English at the University of Miami, Coral Gables, Florida. His published works include *Black Face, Maligned Race: The Representation of Blacks in English Drama from Shakespeare to Southern* (LSU Press, 1987). Professor Barthelemy holds a Ph.D. from Yale University.

Jennifer DeVere Brody, B.A., Vassar College, and Ph.D., University of Pennsylvania, currently teaches at George Washington University. She is an associate editor of *Callaloo* and has published such essays as "Effaced into Flesh: Black Women's Subjectivity" (*Genders*) and "The Return of Cleopatra Jones" (*Performing the Seventies*). Her book *Impossible Purities: Blackness, Femininity, and Victorian Culture,* from which the essay in this volume is excerpted, was published by Duke University Press in 1998.

Violet Harrington Bryan holds a Ph.D. from Harvard University and is currently an associate professor of English at Xavier University in New Orleans. She is researching the papers of Marcus Bruce Christian for a forthcoming book. A previous work, *The Myth of New Orleans in Literature: Dialogues of Race and Gender,* was published by the University of Tennessee Press in 1993. She has contributed articles to several books, including *Louisiana Women Writers* (LSU Press, 1993), and many journals.

Barbara Rosendale Duggal has been a production manager for the New York stage, an agent for jazz and blues artists, a schoolteacher, and an academic researcher. She holds an M.A. in folklore and mythology from UCLA. Writing interests include the examination of the role that myth, ritual, and gender issues play in popular culture. Ms. Duggal is currently at work on a novel for young adults.

Alice Ruth Moore Dunbar-Nelson (1875–1935) was a New Orleans Creole writer and journalist. Her creative works have recently been reprinted and critiqued by Gloria T. Hull and published in the Oxford University Press series of African American literature.

Michel Fabre is president of the Centre d'Etudes Afro-américaines in Paris and professor emeritus at the Université de la Sorbonne Nouvelle (Paris III). His latest books are *The French Critical Reception of African American Literature: From the Beginnings to 1970* (Greenwood Press, 1995), *Conversations with Chester Himes* (University Press of Mississippi, 1995), and *The Several Lives of Chester Himes* (University Press of Mississippi, 1997), all collaborative projects. He contributed "The Antebellum New Orleans Press and the Creoles of Color" to *Multilingual America*, edited by Werner Sollors (New York University Press, 1998).

Mary Gehman is the author of *Women in New Orleans: A History* (1988) and *The Free People of Color: An Introduction* (1994), published by Margaret Media Inc. Gehman holds a B.A. in journalism from Loyola University and an M.A. in English from the University of New Orleans. Besides lecturing and tour guiding, she currently teaches English at Delgado College in New Orleans. In the 1970s, she published *Distaff*, a women's monthly newspaper with a feminist perspective. Her articles and poetry have appeared in local periodicals.

Sybil Kein is a New Orleans Creole writer and musician. A one-hour tape recording of her poetry is housed in the National Archives, Library of Congress. In 1981 she published *Gumbo People*, a bilingual volume of poetry written in the Louisiana Creole language, the first contribution to American letters of original literature in that tongue. Recent works include *Delta Dancer* (Lotus Press, 1984), *Serenade Creole*, a cassette of original songs (1988), *An American South* (Michigan State University Press,

1996; reprinted as *Creole Journal*, Lotus Press, 1999), *Creole Ballads and Zydeco*, a CD and first recording of Creole folk songs (1996), *Maw-Maw's Creole Lullaby*, a multicultural CD for children (1997), and *Gumbo People* (Margaret Media, 1999). Kein holds a doctorate from the University of Michigan and is currently a distinguished professor of English emerita of that university. She is listed in *Black Women in America*, edited by Darlene Clark Hines, and in *Contemporary Authors*, published by Gale Research.

Joan M. Martin is a Creole from Louisiana and is on the faculty at Baker College in Flint, Michigan. She has lectured on the New Orleans Mardi Gras Indians and the customs and traditions of Louisiana Creoles. Her work-in-progress is a book on the origins and rituals of the Mardi Gras Indians. She holds a doctorate from the University of Michigan with a specialization in American ethnic literature.

Mary L. Morton has recently retired from Nicholls State University in Thibodaux, La., where she was Distinguished Service Professor for many years. Her doctorate is from Louisiana State University, and her publications include "How Language Works: Learning with Emily Dickinson" in *Approaches to Teaching the Poetry of Emily Dickinson;* "Anima and Animus in Flannery O'Connor's Female Characters" in *Southern Quarterly* (1985), and "Père Antoine and Père Dagobert" in *Louisiana Literature* (1984).

Fehintola Mosadomi is a linguist and poet. A former visiting assistant professor of French at Hampden-Sydney College, Virginia, she recently completed her Ph.D. at Tulane University in interdisciplinary linguistics with a minor in Francophone studies. She holds two master's degrees, one in languages and literature and the other in linguistics. A Dana-Dartmouth Fellow in 1990, Mosadomi has published poems in both French and English. Her interests include language and gender and Louisiana French, particularly Louisiana Creole.

Caroline Senter is a doctoral student in literature at the University of California, San Diego. She is a native of New Orleans, where she currently lives. Her publications have appeared in *Nation, Southern Exposure, Red Bass,* and other journals on American culture.

Lester Sullivan, a native of New Orleans, is university archivist and assistant librarian for special collections of Xavier University in New Orleans. He also teaches Louisiana and New Orleans history at Xavier, the University of New Orleans, and in the Jazzy Cabby program of the city of New Orleans. He was formerly a senior archivist at the Amistad Research Center.

Index

women and white men, 110, 260; and right to knowledge of paternal descent, 260, 263; and white fathers' acknowledgment of, 260–1

Chopin, Kate, 134–5, 139

Choppin, Jules, 130

Chretien, Frank D., 9–10n23

Christ, Carol P., 157–8, 174

Christian, Marcus, xviii, 42–56, 53n26, 72, 74, 76, 83, 85, 120, 211, 220

Cigar making, 217, 303–5, 303n20, 304n22, 308

Civil War, 31–4, 33–34nn84–5, 221, 301, 315

Claiborne, W. C. C., 18–23, 19n45, 168n14, 211, 281

Clifton-Hils, Deborah, 148–9, 151, 152

Code Noir. *See* Black Code

Colonial French language, 223

Colonial Louisiana. *See* French Louisiana; Spanish Louisiana

Colvis (Clovis) family, 213–4

Comité des Citoyens, 56, 289

Concubinage. See *Plaçage*

Congo Square, 26, 125, 175, 210

Constitutional Conventions, 35–6, 37, 37n98

Cook, John F., 29–30

Cordeviola, Estevan, 213

Cordeviolle, Etienne, 213, 218

Courcelle, Achille Barthelemy, 217

Courcelle, Anna Louise, 215

Courcelle, Myrtil, 217

Coustillon, Jacques, 180n1

Craft, William and Ellen, 300n14, 314n37

Creole: definitions of, xiii–xv, 7–9, 9n23, 58–9, 73, 113, 131, 132–3,

139–40, 144–5, 147, 223–4, 256–7, 256n8, 281. *See also* Creole women of color; Creoles of color

C.R.E.O.L.E. Inc., xvi

Creole Association of America, xvi

Creole Culture, xvi

Creole language: in literature, xix, 117–54, 317–24; definition of, xx, 223–6; origin of, xxi, 117–8, 223–43; African influences on, 118, 230–42; French influences on, 118, 230–3; in songs, 118–27, 138, 143–4, 145, 146–7, 148, 151, 152; earliest known written sample of, 119; of Black Indians, 124; of folklore, 126–30, 144, 145–6, 151, 152; white authors' use of, 126–35, 144–7, 151–2; negative associations with, 127–8, 131, 136–7, 147–8, 153–4; in proverbs, 129, 133, 145, 238–9; Afro- French authors' use of, 130–2, 135–6, 148–51; dictionary of, 150; current rebirth of, 153–4; and linguistic diversity of slaves from Africa, 226–30; statistics on speakers of, 230; danger of disappearance of, 242, 243; future research needs on, 242–3

Creole Preservation Society of America, xvi

Creole women of color: and interracial sexual relationships/*plaçage*, xviii, 22n53, 48–52, 57–70, 164, 212–3, 255–6, 261–2; and quadroon balls, xviii, 50–2, 65–8, 164; and racial "passing," xxii, 214, 295–316, 323; wealth and property of, 26, 68, 212–3, 214, 215; laws regulating, 47–8, 53–5, 62; as music composers,